CW00833139

The Life and Work of Adelaide Procter:
Poetry, Feminism and Fathers

To
Tricia Bickerton
with gratitude and affection

The Life and Work
of Adelaide Procter:
Poetry, Feminism and Fathers

Gill Gregory

Ashgate

Aldershot • Brookfield USA • Singapore • Sydney

© Gill Gregory, 1998

All rights reserved. No part of this publication may be reproduced, stored in a retrieval system or transmitted in any form or by any means, electronic, mechanical, photocopying, recording, or otherwise without the prior permission of the publisher.

Published by
Ashgate Publishing Limited
Gower House, Croft Road,
Aldershot, Hampshire GU11 3HR
Great Britain

Ashgate Publishing Company
Old Post Road,
Brookfield, Vermont 05036-9704
USA

The author has asserted her moral right under the Copyright, Designs and Patents Act, 1988, to be identified as the author of this work.

British Library Cataloguing-in-Publication Data
Gregory, Gill
    The life and work of Adelaide Procter: poetry, feminism and fathers. -
(The Nineteenth-century series)
    1. Procter, Adelaide   2. Women - Great Britain - Social conditions   3. Great Britain - Social conditions - 19th century
    I. Title
    821.8

Library of Congress Cataloging-in-Publication Data
Gregory, Gill
    The life and work of Adelaide Procter: poetry, feminism and fathers \ Gill Gregory.
    (The Nineteenth-century series)
    1. Procter, Adelaide Anne, 1825-1864.   2. Feminism and literature - England - History - 19th century.   3. Fathers and daughters - England - History - 19th century.   4. Women and literature - England - History - 19th century.   5. Women poets, English - 19th century - Biography.   6. Social problems in literature.   7. Homelessness in literature.   8. Poor in literature.   I. Procter, Adelaide Anne, 1825-1864.   II. Title   III. Series: Nineteenth century (Aldershot, England)
    PR5191.Z5G74 1998
    821'.8
    [B]—DC21   98-33797
                                                                            CIP

ISBN 1-84014-670-2

This book is printed on acid-free paper

Phototypeset by N²productions and printed in Great Britain by
MPG Books Ltd, Bodmin, Cornwall

Contents

All page and line numbers in brackets after quotations, unless otherwise attributed, refer to Adelaide Anne Procter, *Legends and Lyrics Together with a Chaplet of Verses*, Intro. Charles Dickens, Oxford University Press, 1914.

The Nineteenth Century
General Editors' Preface

The aim of this series is to reflect, develop and extend the great burgeoning of interest in the nineteenth century that has been an inevitable feature of recent decades, as that former epoch has come more sharply into focus as a locus for our understanding, not only of the past but of the contours of our modernity. Though it is dedicated principally to the publication of original monographs and symposia in literature, history, cultural analysis, and associated fields, there will be a salient role for reprints of significant texts from, or about, the period. Our overarching policy is to address the spectrum of nineteenth-century studies without exception, achieving the widest scope in chronology, approach and range of concern. This, we believe, distinguishes our project from comparable ones, and means, for example, that in the relevant areas of scholarship we both recognise and cut innovatively across such parameters as those suggested by the designations 'Romantic' and 'Victorian'. We welcome new ideas, while valuing tradition. It is hoped that the world which predates yet so forcibly predicts and engages our own will emerge in parts, as a whole, and in the lively currents of debate and change that are so manifest an aspect of its intellectual, artistic and social landscape.

Vincent Newey
Joanne Shattock

University of Leicester

List of Illustrations

Acknowledgements

With many thanks to Isobel Armstrong, Laura Marcus and Michael Slater at Birkbeck College for their inspiration, insight and support. I should also like to thank Mark Turner, Joanne Winning, Sally Kilmister, Deryn Rees-Jones, Caroline Levine and Caterina Albano for sharing their ideas and time. Many thanks, too, to Morena Capovilla and Diana Godden, the secretaries in the English Department at Birkbeck College, for their help and encouragement; to Philip Jenkins and Astrid Poll for translations; to Rachel Campbell and Chris Brandon-Jones for help with typing; and to Kate Perry at Girton College Library for her interest and help.

Especial thanks to my mother, sister and brother for their encouragement, belief and love. And in memory of my father who opened my eyes to thought and wonder.

The portrait of Adelaide Procter reproduced on the jacket and in Figure 2 is copyright The British Museum.

Extracts from Procter manuscripts and letters relating to the Procter family are reprinted by permission of the University of Iowa Libraries (Iowa City).

Permission to reprint the letter from Procter, 1855, Houghton mss, has been granted by the Master and Fellows of Trinity College Cambridge.

Extracts from the BL Add.MS 34625 are reprinted by permission of the British Library.

Letters from Procter contained in the Parkes Papers are reprinted by permission of The Mistress and Fellows, Girton College, Cambridge.

Introduction

Read chronologically Adelaide Procter's poetry tells a story. It is the story of a Victorian woman who slowly moved from the position of dutiful daughter and retiring, ladylike poetess to that of a woman who challenged mid-Victorian mores and conventions and championed the cause of single and homeless women.

Isobel Armstrong has recognised Adelaide Procter's importance as a poet in the mid-nineteenth century in the chapter 'A Music of Thine Own', *Victorian Poetry. Poetry, poetics and politics* (1993). She pays tribute to some of Procter's powerful lyrics and narrative poems and to the strength and poignancy of her poetic voice.

Armstrong also writes that Procter 'virtually typifies the woman poet's interests at this time'. Like many other women poets, Elizabeth Barrett Browning, Dora Greenwell and Christina Rossetti for example, Procter was concerned with poverty and homelessness and with the many areas in which women were oppressed and restricted. She was an active member of the Langham Place Circle group of campaigning women and served on the Committee of the Society for Promoting the Employment of Women. Procter was also involved with the Catholic Providence Row Hostel for Homeless Women and Children at Finsbury Square in East London, which continues its work to this day.

However, Procter was alone among contemporary women poets in capturing the public mood and her readers' hearts to the extent that she did. Many commentators have remarked on her enormous popularity and express the widely held belief that in her day she outsold most poets bar Tennyson. Her most famous poem, 'A Lost Chord', published in 1860, drew an emotional and enthusiastic response, especially when it was set to music by Arthur Sullivan.

What was it about Procter's poetry which held such an appeal for her audiences? Her campaigning women friends (Bessie Parkes, Barbara Bodichon, Jessie Boucherett) and *The English Woman's Journal* readership would have responded to her ironic and witty lyrics about the position of women ('A Woman's Question, 'A Woman's Answer', 'A Woman's Last

Word') and to narrative poems such as 'A Legend of Provence' which boldly and sympathetically draws attention to the position of the fallen woman. Her Catholic readers (Procter was a Roman Catholic convert) would have been inspired by the religious lyrics in 'A Chaplet of Verses' which was published to raise funds for the Providence Row Hostel.

However, I believe it is Procter's concern with the capacity for expression and the problems of articulation, her preoccupation with what lies unexpressed and dormant within ourselves, that accounts for her popularity. She writes of women who struggle for an articulate voice and defined place in the world. In her two most accomplished narrative poems, 'A Tomb in Ghent' and 'A Legend of Provence', the women depicted are anonymous and displaced and seek a space in which to find and consolidate a more substantial identity. Many of Procter's poems are concerned with listening and hearing, as though expressing an anxiety about whether her own poetic voice will be heard. Her Victorian admirers seem to have responded to her concern with expression and dispossession, her often anguished awareness of the transience and instability of identity in a world which was changing rapidly, especially for women.

Today Adelaide Procter's name is unknown to most readers, apart from those engaged in Victorian studies. This study of her life and poetry aims to re-establish her name and place as an important figure of the period and as a writer who produced poems of penetration, subtlety and great lyric power. It will also consider her strong poetic response to the various male authorities which shaped her whilst simultaneously she struggled to emerge from beneath their shadow.

Chapter 1

Adelaide Procter (1825-1864)

In his Introduction to Adelaide Procter's collected works, *Legends and Lyrics* (1866), Charles Dickens records that in the early hours of the morning on the 3rd February 1864 Adelaide Procter died after a long illness (p. 10).* She was only 38 and had been bedridden with tuberculosis for over a year; her close friend Bessie Parkes, a fellow campaigner on women's issues at *The English Woman's Journal*, records that she had fought 'a battle royal with the power of Death'.[1]

By the time of her death Procter had won an enormous amount of popularity and acclaim as a poet. Many commentators, including Coventry Patmore, Ferdinand Janku (the writer of a 1912 monograph on Procter) and Margaret Maison, have stated that demand for her poetry was greater than for any other English writer bar Tennyson.[2] Procter wrote religious, didactic and love lyrics and poems which are passionately concerned with homelessness, poverty and the fallen woman. She also wrote several fine narrative

---

*   All page and line numbers in brackets, unless otherwise attributed, refer to Adelaide Anne Procter, *Legends and Lyrics Together with a Chaplet of Verses*, Intro. Charles Dickens, Oxford University Press, 1914.

[1]   Bessie Rayner Belloc (née Parkes), *In a Walled Garden*, London: Ward and Downey Limited, 1895, p. 170. Bessie Parkes (1829-1925) was the daughter of Joseph Parkes, a radical lawyer and friend of J.S. Mill. Parkes co-edited the *English Woman's Journal* from 1858 with Matilda Hays. She later married Louis Belloc and they had two children, Hilaire Belloc and Marie Belloc-Lowndes.

[2]   *Bryan Waller Procter (Barry Cornwall). An Autobiographical Fragment and Biographical Notes With Personal Sketches of Contemporaries. Unpublished Lyrics, and Letters of Literary Friends*, [Ed. Coventry Patmore], London: George Bell and Sons, 1877. Patmore writes of the 'present demand' for Procter's poems 'being far in excess of that for the writings of any living poet, except Mr Tennyson' (p. 98).

Ferdinand Janku, *Adelaide Anne Procter. Ihr Leben Und Ihre Werke*, Wien und Liepzig: Wilhelm Braumuller, 1912, p. 9. Janku writes that her poems were, along with Tennyson's, the most widely read in the 1870s.

Margaret Maison, 'Queen Victoria's favourite poet', *The Listener*, 73, 1965, p. 636. Queen Victoria referred to Procter's poem 'The Angel of Death' in a letter to the Empress Augusta, wife of Wilhelm I of Germany, in 1872, 'I have just read a most beautiful poem by Ad. Procter which I am sending to you' (*Further Letters of Queen Victoria*, Ed. Hector Bolitho, London: Thornton Butterworth Ltd., 1938, p. 191).

poems about displacement, particularly that of the single woman.

Charles Dickens published many of Procter's poems in the journals *Household Words* and *All the Year Round* between 1853 and 1860 and her work was also published in *The English Woman's Journal*, *The Cornhill Magazine* and *Good Words* (see Appendix). Procter submitted her poems under the pseudonym Miss Berwick, and it was not until December of 1854 that Dickens, a friend of Procter's parents (the poet Bryan Procter and the salon hostess, Anne Skepper) discovered her true identity. In his Introduction to *Legends and Lyrics* (1866), which he wrote at the request of her parents, Dickens tells the story of her unmasking.[3] Up until Christmas 1854 all Dickens had known of 'Miss Berwick' was that she sent in her poems via a 'circulating library in the western district of London' and that she was a governess who seemed to be 'remarkably business-like, punctual, self-reliant, and reliable' (p. 1). Dickens continues:

> This went on until December, 1854, when the Christmas Number, entitled, The Seven Poor Travellers, was sent to press. Happening to be going to dine that day with an old and dear friend, distinguished in literature as BARRY CORNWALL, I took with me an early proof of that Number, and remarked, as I laid it on the drawing-room table, that it contained a very pretty poem, written by a certain Miss Berwick. Next day brought me the disclosure that I had spoken of the poem to the mother of its writer, in its writer's presence; that I had no such correspondent in existence as Miss Berwick; and that the name had been assumed by Barry Cornwall's eldest daughter, MISS ADELAIDE ANNE PROCTER.   (pp. 1-2)

According to Dickens, Procter was worried that he might print her poems even if he did not like them, 'for papa's sake, and not for their own', and that she preferred to take her chance 'fairly with the unknown volunteers' (p. 2).

Procter finally became Dickens's most published poet in *Household Words*, with 'about a sixth of the poems being attributable to her'.[4] Seventy-three poems were published in *Household Words* and seven in *All The Year*

---

      3   On 15th February 1865 Dickens wrote in reply to Mrs Procter's request, 'Of course I will do it, and of course I will do it for the love of you and Procter' (*The Letters of Charles Dickens*, Ed. Walter Dexter, 3 Vols, Bloomsbury: The Nonesuch Press, 1938, III, p. 415).

      4   *Household Words. A Weekly Journal. 1850-1859. Conducted by Charles Dickens.* Table of Contents. List of Contributors and Their Contributions based on the *Household Words* Office Book in the Morris L. Parrish Collection of Victorian Novelists. Princeton University Library. Compiled by Anne Lohrli, University of Toronto Press, 1973, p. 405.

Round (see Appendix). She was often the only poet who contributed to the Christmas number, and the narrative poems printed in these numbers are amongst Procter's most interesting and finely worked poems.

In 1858 Bell & Daldy published the 'First Series' of *Legends and Lyrics* and in 1861 the 'Second Series' which include most of the poems published in Dickens's journals.[5] The two Series were combined in the 1866 illustrated edition published after Procter's death, which included Dickens's Introduction.[6] Procter was a Roman Catholic convert and 'A Chaplet of Verses', a book of religious poetry, was published by Longman, Green, Longman & Roberts in 1862 for the benefit of a Catholic Night Refuge for Women and Children established at Providence Row in East London in 1860.[7] 'A Chaplet of Verses' was later included in editions of *Legends and Lyrics*.

Ferdinand Janku in *Ihr Leben Und Ihre Werke* (1912) states that by 1881 the First Series of *Legends and Lyrics* was into its 19th edition and the Second Series into its 14th edition.[8] An edition of the 'First Series', published by George Bell & Sons in 1903, numbers the sales at 137,000.[9] Procter's poetry was also published in Boston and in Germany where her work was much admired.[10]

The only poem remembered today is the emotionally charged and finely worked lyric 'A Lost Chord', which was set to music by Arthur Sullivan in 1877.[11] Bessie Parkes writes of the 'enthusiasm infused by this song. The vast audience of St James's Hall thrills as one man when it is given.'[12]

The immense popular appeal of Procter's poetry owed much to the invariably simple and direct language and strongly affective rhetoric. This

---

[5]   Adelaide Anne Procter, *Legends and Lyrics. A Book of Verses*, London: Bell and Daldy, 1858-1861, 2 vols.

[6]   Adelaide Anne Procter, *Legends and Lyrics*, Intro. Charles Dickens. Illustrated by W.T.C. Dobson, Samuel Palmer, John Tenniel, George H. Thomas, Lorenz Frohlich, W.H. Millais, G. Du Maurier, W.P. Burton, J.D. Watson, Charles Keene, J.M. Carrick, M.E. Edwards, T. Morten, London: Bell and Daldy, 1866.

[7]   Adelaide Anne Procter, *A Chaplet of Verses*, With an Illustration by Richard Doyle, London: Longman, Green, Longman, & Roberts, 1862.

[8]   Janku, op. cit., p. 106.

[9]   Adelaide Anne Procter, *Legends and Lyrics. A Book of Verses*, First Series, London: George Bell & Sons, 1903.

[10]   *The Poems of Adelaide A. Procter*, Boston: Fields, Osgood & Co., 1870. *The Poems of Adelaide ¡A. Procter*, Boston: Houghton, Mifflin and Company, 1881.

Adelheid Anna Procter, *Ausgewahlte Gedichte*, Ed. C. Schluter & H. Brinckmann, Koln und Neuss, 1867.

[11]   B.W. Findon, *Sir Arthur Sullivan. His Life and Music*, London: James Nisbet & Co., Limited, 1904, p. 211. Findon writes that '"The Lost Chord" was composed while Sullivan was watching by the bedside of his dying brother' (p. 151).

[12]   Belloc, op. cit., pp. 172-173.

simplicity, however, masks a complexity of thought and feeling which deserves reappraisal and further exploration. This study gives a detailed consideration of several key poems but it is also important to provide a vital introduction to a poet who is little known today. Her parents, Bryan Procter and Anne Skepper, warrant particular consideration. Her father, an important but now forgotten Keatsian poet, was a significant formative influence in Adelaide's life.

Adelaide Procter was born at 25 Bedford Square, London on the 30th October, 1825 (p. 3). The eldest child of six, she had two brothers and three sisters: Edward, Edythe, Montagu and Florence (twins) and Agnes.[13] Adelaide was the 'sweet beloved first-born' of Bryan Procter, who wrote under the pseudonym of Barry Cornwall, and Anne Skepper, the daughter of Anne Benson Skepper by her first marriage to a lawyer called Skepper.[14] Anne Benson Skepper had been widowed when young and married Basil Montagu, the son of the 4th Earl of Sandwich.

Bryan and Anne Procter lived with the Montagus at 25 Bedford Square. The Montagu establishment was described by Thomas Carlyle as a 'singular social and spiritual menagerie' combining the eccentricities of Basil Montagu, a barrister and devotee of Francis Bacon, and the queenliness of the presiding Anne Benson Skepper.[15]

During Adelaide Procter's lifetime Bryan Procter and his family moved from 25 Bedford Square to a 'little Gothic cottage' at 5 Grove End Road, St John's Wood opposite the artist Edwin Landseer's house in 1832; to 13 Upper Harley Street in 1843; and to 32 Weymouth Street in 1853.[16] At these various residences Anne Skepper was well known in her role as literary

---

[13] Montagu served in the British army in India and became a General. He was serving at the time of the Indian Mutiny (1857-1858) and made a dramatic escape from Delhi to Meerut. Bryan Procter wrote to James Fields, his Boston editor 'They were seven days and seven nights in the jungle, without money or meat' (James T. Fields, *Old Acquaintance. Barry Cornwall and Some of His Friends*, Boston: James R. Osgood and Company, 1876, p. 113).

[14] Barry Cornwall, 'To Adelaide', *English Songs and Other small Poems*, London: Chapman and Hall, 1851, p. 199. MS, 'To my Child written on her Birthday. Oct. 30th 1825', University of Iowa Libraries.

[15] *Reminiscences by Thomas Carlyle*, Ed. James Anthony Froude, 2 Vols, London: Longmans, Green, and Co., 1881, I, pp. 223-229. Basil Montagu campaigned with Sir Samuel Romilly for the abolition of the death penalty for numerous offences short of murder. (Belloc, op. cit., pp. 142-143) In 1808 and 1811 Romilly secured the passage of statutes removing the death penalty for a variety of offences.

[16] Richard Willard Armour, *Barry Cornwall. A Biography of Bryan Waller Procter. With A Selected Collection of Hitherto Unpublished Letters*, Boston: Meador Publishing Company, 1935, pp. 90-91, 104, 109.

salon hostess. Bessie Parkes writes in her collection of biographical sketches, *In a Walled Garden* (1895):

> everybody of any literary pretension whatever seemed to flow in and out of the house. The Kembles, the Macreadys, the Rossettis, the Dickens, the Thackerays, never seemed to be exactly visitors, but to belong to the place.[17]

Elizabeth Gaskell, in a letter to the painter Eliza Fox (1849) wrote that she was 'intoxicated with sparkling conversation heard tonight at Mrs Procter's'.[18]

Friends of the Procters described Adelaide as both a sickly and thriving member of this household. The actress Fanny Kemble wrote:

> That child looks like a poet's child, and a poet. It has something 'doomed' (what the Germans call *'fatal'*) in its appearance – such a preter-naturally thoughtful, mournful expression for a little child, such a marked brow over the heavy blue eyes, such a transparent skin, such pale-golden hair. John says the little creature is an elf-child.[19]

The 'fatal' look of Adelaide may have been primarily associated with an early awareness of death rather than with her status as a poet's child. Edward, her younger brother by three years, died from scarlet fever at the age of six in 1835 when she was nine, and her own health had been poor from an early age.[20] William Makepeace Thackeray, who was to become a good friend of Adelaide, wrote to Anne Carmichael-Smyth in a letter dated 16–20 December, 1839, when Adelaide was fourteen, that Bryan Procter's eldest child 'has the most frightful bleedings vomits basins of blood &c.' Thackeray adds that he 'wd. not mind in such a case calling Quin'. (Frederick Hervey Foster Quin was the first homeopathic physician to

---

[17] Belloc, op. cit., p. 162.
[18] *The Letters of Mrs Gaskell*, Ed. J.A.V. Chapple and Arthur Pollard, Manchester University Press, 1966, p. 77. Gaskell writes 'I keep smiling to myself and trying to remember things – all to no purpose, – the foam has faded from the Champagne.'
[19] Frances Ann Kemble, *Record of a Girlhood*, 3 Vols, London: Richard Bentley and Son, 1879, III, p. 176.
[20] *The Diaries of William Charles Macready 1833–1851*, Ed. William Toynbee, 2 Vols, London: Chapman and Hall, Ltd., 1912, I, p. 221. Macready writes 'Calling at Forster's, Procter came in, haggard, old and miserable with grief and care; he very soon told his story – nine of his family sick at once with the scarlet fever! – in one month 100 visits from a physician to his boy, his hope and delight, whom he had buried, only six years old, ten days since'.

practise in England).[21] In 1853 Adelaide, aged 27, spent a year in Italy with her aunt Emily de Viry to improve her 'very indifferent' health.[22]

In spite of the fact that, in Samuel Carter Hall's words, she may have 'anticipated removal in early life', Adelaide also possessed considerable vital energy and talents.[23] In his Introduction Dickens wrote that as a child she had 'displayed a remarkable memory, and great quickness of apprehension':

> When she was quite a young child, she learnt with facility several of the problems of Euclid. As she grew older, she acquired the French, Italian, and German languages; became a clever piano-forte player; and showed a true taste and sentiment in drawing. But, as soon as she had completely vanquished the difficulties of any one branch of study, it was her way to lose interest in it, and pass to another.   (p. 3)

Dickens adds that by the time Adelaide 'attained to womanhood' she had read 'an extraordinary number of books, and throughout her life she was always largely adding to the number' (p. 3). Procter's wide reading and facility with languages is evident in many of her narrative poems which are based on folk-tales collected from various countries.[24]

Bessie Parkes, before establishing a closer friendship with Adelaide, had written to a friend Mary Swainson in 1848 that she was:

> a strikingly clever and accomplished girl, but does not turn her talent to any definite object, which I think a great pity, as she has real genius and might become a good Artist or Authoress from all I hear.[25]

Parkes's words were prophetic. The rather feverish and unconsolidated activity described by Dickens made way for a commitment to writing poetry. Dickens wrote of Adelaide's 'love of poetry' in his 'Introduction':

> Her love of poetry was conspicuous at so early an age, that I have before me a tiny album made of small note-paper, into which her

[21] *The Letters and Private Papers of William Makepeace Thackeray*, Ed. Gordon N. Ray, 4 Vols, London: Oxford University Press, 1945, 1946, I, p. 400. Anne was married to Henry Carmichael-Smyth, an ensign of the Bengal Engineers.
[22] ibid., III, p. 230. Mrs Procter wrote to Thackeray on 8th March 1853 'Adelaide before you receive this will be in Turin – Her health is so very indifferent that she is going to try a complete change'.
[23] S.C. Hall, *A Book of Memories of Great Men and Women of the Age*, London: Virtue & Co., 1871, p. 416. Samuel Carter Hall was editor and sub-editor of the *New Monthly Magazine* in the 1830s.
[24] See Ferdinand Janku (op. cit.) for bibliography of folk-tales.
[25] MS BRP III, 17, Parkes papers, Girton College Library.

favourite passages were copied for her by her mother's hand before she herself could write. It looks as if she had carried it about, as another little girl might have carried a doll. (p. 3)

Mrs Steuart Erskine writes of her 'precocity' of talent which was evident at the age of twelve. She quotes Adelaide's poem 'On the Coronation of Queen Victoria' (28.6.1838). In this youthful paeon to the Queen, Adelaide applauds Victoria's youth and beauty:

> For so young and fair a Queen
> In old England ne'er was seen.[26]

Mrs Erskine also includes the poem 'To Fanny Elssler' written when Adelaide was fourteen. (Fanny Elssler (1810-1884) was an Austrian ballerina who had visited England in 1840). As in her poem to Victoria Adelaide admires her beauty which she describes as dreamlike but 'embodied'. The poem is more subtle than the earlier poem and its light touch combined with more robust imagery prefigure Adelaide's later poetry. The poem concludes:

> Like some dream or fancy
>   Floating once in air
> Thou comest down embodied
>   Beauty! bright and rare.[27]

'To Mrs Sartoris', an undated poem but probably written when Procter was in her early twenties, is also included by Mrs Erskine. Adelaide Sartoris (née Kemble) was Fanny Kemble's sister and a distinguished opera singer who finally settled with her husband in Rome. In this poem Adelaide welcomes 'The spirit of the southern land of song' to England.[28]

Included with Mrs Erskine's examples of Procter's juvenilia is the poem 'Ministering Angels' which was published in *Heath's Book of Beauty* (1843) edited by Marguerite Power, the Countess of Blessington and friend of Byron. This poem contrasts with the others in that it is primarily a religious poem and it is poignant in its plea for protection in a 'sad world'. The poem concludes:

---

[26] *Anna Jameson. Letters and Friendships (1812-1860)*, Ed. Mrs Steuart Erskine, London: T. Fisher Unwin Ltd., 1915, pp. 161-162.

[27] ibid., p. 183.

[28] ibid., p. 202.

> Leave me not lone to struggle with the world,
> Whilst here I roam,
> And at the end, with your bright wings unfurled,
> Oh! take me home![29]

'Ministering Angels' establishes the deeply religious tone of Procter's poetry which is predominant throughout her work. A consideration of her religion and her conversion to Catholicism is therefore fundamental to an understanding of Procter's poetics.

Adelaide Procter's Catholicism

An admiration for women's strength and beauty along with a fear of a precarious and 'perilous' life, which are expressed in the juvenilia, may have contributed to Procter's conversion to Roman Catholicism. The iconic figure of the Virgin Mary and the power with which she was associated, combined with the apparent strength of Roman Catholic conviction, may well have appealed to Procter's imagination. The date of Procter's conversion is given by Bessie Parkes as about 1849, when she was twenty four, and by Dickens, in his 'Introduction' to *Legends and Lyrics*, as around 1851 (p. 4).[30] As Anne Skepper had approved the 'Introduction' it seems likely that Dickens's date was the correct one.

Procter, like many others, was influenced by the Oxford or Tractarian Movement, which sought to restore the faith and authority of the Church Fathers. The movement had many followers as well as numerous detractors who deplored its catholicising tendency which had culminated in John Henry Newman's conversion to Roman Catholicism in 1845.

Bessie Parkes (who converted in 1864) suggests that Procter's conversion was also influenced by the Catholic marriage of her aunt, Emily de Viry, the only daughter of Basil Montagu and Anne Skepper and fifteen years younger than her half sister Anne. Emily married the Comte William de Viry, a Sardinian Count and nephew of Basil Montagu, and had left England for Turin in 1840 as the Comtesse de Viry. She subsequently became a devout Catholic.[31]

---

[29]   ibid., p. 292.
   Heath's Book of Beauty, Ed. The Countess of Blessington, London: Longman, Brown, Green, and Longmans, 1843, p. 38.
[30]   *The Month*, IV, 1866, p. 80.
[31]   Belloc, op. cit., pp. 154–156, 164.

Procter visited Italy between 1853 and 1854 to improve her health and Bessie Parkes writes that she stayed with Emily who was attached to the Court circle at Turin.[32] Bessie records Procter's glimpse of the Queen of Sardinia:

> At Aix-les-Bains is a large portrait *en pied* of the young Queen of Sardinia in her bridal dress. It looks at first sight, to be a purely conventional picture, but the eyes are of a haunting depth. They recall a word-picture of the Queen returning from Holy Communion, which Adelaide Procter gave. The wife of Victor Emmanuel was passing along one of the galleries of the Palace, her face 'shining as with an interior lamp,' when she was met by the young English girl, who never forgot the sight.[33]

Parkes describes Procter in her religious attitude as resembling that of a 'foreign rather than an English Catholic'. She writes:

> She looked like a Frenchwoman mounting the steps of the Madeleine, or a veiled Italian in St Peter's.[34]

According to Dickens, Procter had also 'entered with the greater ardour on the study of the Piedmontese dialect, and the observation of the habits and manners of the peasantry. In the former, she soon became proficient' (p. 4). The romantic foreignness of the Catholic religion along with an energetic desire to explore and learn the language of a foreign country may also have contributed to Adelaide's decision to convert. Several of her narrative poems are set in foreign locations, and in 'A Tomb in Ghent' and 'A Legend of Provence' the single woman's place within and in relation to the foreign church are central motifs (see Chapters 2 and 4).

The figure of Mary is also important for Procter in many of her poems, particularly in 'A Legend of Provence' where Mary appears as a miraculous vision. Many of the poems in 'A Chaplet of Verses' (1862) are paeons to Mary and in 'The Shrines of Mary' her presence is described as pervasive and catholic in that it is shown to extend beyond national and class boundaries. Mary's 'shrines' are depicted as ranging from that of 'a vast Cathedral' (p. 307, l. 33) to a poor Lady's Chapel:

---

[32] ibid., p. 164.
[33] ibid., p. 165.
[34] ibid.

> There are no rich gifts on the Altar
>   The shrine is humble and bare,
> Yet the poor and the sick and the tempted
>   Think their home and their heaven is there.
>
> And before that humble Altar
>   Where Our Lady of Sorrow stands,
> I knelt with a weary longing
>   And I laid a vow in her hands.
>   (p. 310, ll. 133-140)

The strength of Procter's conviction clearly impressed her sisters as either two or all three of them followed her example and coverted to Roman Catholicism. Coventry Patmore writes that two sisters converted, and Richard Armour states that 'each of Procter's daughters had followed her lead'.[35] Adelaide's sister Agnes became a nun with the Irish Sisters of Mercy.[36] Bessie Parkes refers to the 'great misery' suffered by Bryan Procter at the loss of 'close union' with his daughters, and in a letter to Anne Carmichael-Smyth (1853) Thackeray wonders if Procter's home is unhappy 'with a priest between him and his children'.[37] By contrast Coventry Patmore states that the conversions did not 'appear to have even ruffled the family peace and affection'.[38]

   Whatever the truth, Procter's conversion was a brave move at a time of virulent anti-Catholicism. The establishment of a Catholic hierarchy in England in 1850 had led to an upsurge of at times vicious hostility towards Catholics. Father Frederick Faber of the London Oratory and later the Brompton Oratory, who was much admired by Procter, wrote in 1850 to Mr Watts Russell:

> London is a frightful place for work . . . All over the walls you see, 'Down with the Oratorians,' 'Beware of the Oratorians,' 'Don't go to the Oratory,', 'Banishment to the Oratorians,' and in Leicester Square a triple placard of singular truthfulness, 'No Popery! Down with the Oratorians! No religion at all!' We are cursed in the streets: even gentlemen shout from their carriage windows at us.[39]

---

[35] Patmore, op. cit., pp. 98–99. Armour, op. cit., p. 110.

[36] Belloc, op. cit., p. 165.

[37] ibid., p. 162. Ray, op. cit., III, p. 198.

[38] Patmore, op. cit., p. 99.

[39] Rev. James F. Cassidy, *The Life of Father Faber*, London: Sands & Co. (Publishers) Ltd., 1946, p. 91.

Procter's conversion also aligned her with the most deprived sectors of the population. In her Introduction to 'A Chaplet of Verses', the book of poems published to raise funds for the Roman Catholic Providence Row hostel, Procter writes:

> In this country, as we all know, the very poorest and most destitute
> are in many cases Catholics ...   (p. 341)

Geoffrey Best writes that 'the dominant characteristics of British Roman Catholicism were that it was mainly working class and mainly Irish'.[40]

Procter wrote two poems which relate to Ireland, 'Millie's Expiation' and 'An Appeal', both of which were published in 'A Chaplet of Verses' in 1862 (pp. 316-327, 287-289). 'Millie's Expiation' is a Catholic priest's account of 'the fatal famine year' in Ireland (p. 316, l. 20) with the priest recounting the suffering of the Connaught peasantry. He observes that 'the rich were growing poorer, / The poor, poorer than before' (p. 320, ll. 143-144).

In the poem, 'An Appeal', Procter's rhetoric is angry and incisive. The poem's epigraph is 'The Irish Church Mission for Converting the Catholics', and the speaker appeals to 'cruel England' (p. 287, l. 1) to spare Ireland the enforced relinquishing of her faith. The speaker ironically permits the coloniser England, with its 'empire of the sea' (p. 287, l. 8), to continue to exploit the Irish peasant so long as she leaves them their faith:

> Take, if thou wilt, the earnings
>   Of the poor peasant's toil,
> Take all the scanty produce
>   That grows on Irish soil,
> To pay the alien preachers
>   Whom Ireland will not hear,
> To pay the scoffers at a Creed
>   Which Irish hearts hold dear:
> But leave them, cruel England,
>   The gift their God has given,
> Leave them their ancient worship,
>   Leave them their faith in Heaven.
>   (p. 288, ll. 17-28)

Procter's fundraising for the Providence Row Night Refuge would almost certainly have brought her into contact with immigrant Irish Catholics. She

---

[40] Geoffrey Best, *Mid-Victorian Britain 1851-75*, London: Fontana Press, 1979, p. 206.

writes that the refuge for homeless women and children was 'the first Catholic Refuge in England or Ireland, and still the only one in England' (p. 341).[41] It was established by Father Daniel Gilbert (Procter's confessor) in 1860 in a converted stable at the back of 14 Finsbury Square in East London, and was run by the Sisters of Mercy (pp. 341–342).[42] Protestants and Catholics alike were admitted, although 'character' was a condition of entry (p. 342). Procter's 'Preface' to 'A Chaplet of Verses' begins:

> A shelter through the bleak winter nights, leave to rest in some poor shed instead of wandering through the pitiless streets, is a boon we could hardly deny to a starving dog. And yet we have all known that in this country, in this town, many of our miserable fellow-creatures were pacing the streets through the long weary nights, without a roof to shelter them, without food to eat, with their poor rags soaked in rain, and only the bitter winds of Heaven for companions; women and children utterly forlorn and helpless, either wandering about all night, or crouching under a miserable archway, or, worst of all, seeking in death or sin the refuge denied them elsewhere. It is a marvel that we could sleep in peace in our warm comfortable homes with this horror at our very door.   (p. 341)

This language is compelling and 'A Chaplet of Verses' also has rhetorical power, exemplified in poems such as 'The Homeless Poor', 'Homeless' and 'A Beggar' (pp. 311–316, 338–339, 335–336). The following are some stanzas from 'The Homeless Poor':

> 'In that very street, at that same hour,
>   In the bitter air and drifting sleet,
> Crouching in a doorway was a mother,
>   With her children shuddering at her feet.
>
> 'She was silent – who would hear her pleading?
>   Men and beasts were housed – but she must stay
> Houseless in the great and pitiless city,
>   Till the dawning of the winter day.

[41] The Providence Row Night Refuge exists today as The Providence Row Housing Association, which runs several hostels from its offices at 50 Crispin St., E1. The Association is funded by the London Boroughs Grants Unit and is still assisted by the Sisters of Mercy. *Providence Row Annual Review 1993/1994*, London: Lansdowne Press, 1994.

[42] Belloc, op. cit., p. 175, note 1.

'Homeless – while her fellow-men are resting
Calm and blest: their very dogs are fed,
Warm and sheltered, and their sleeping children
Safely nestled in each little bed.
(p. 313, ll. 51–62)

The 'Chaplet' sold well and Procter wrote to Bessie Parkes in July, 1862 that the public were 'clamouring for more' and suggests that Longmans might get out a third edition.[43]

Procter's humane commitment to alleviating homelessness may have been influenced by her attendance at Queen's College at 66, Harley Street in 1850 (when the Procters lived down the road at No. 13).[44] The college had opened in 1848 and was founded by the Christian Socialist, F.D. Maurice.[45] Other teachers included Charles Kingsley, John Hullah (the composer and music teacher) and Henry Morley.[46] Patriots who had fled Europe after the failure of the Liberal Revolutions of 1848 taught languages and Procter's interest in foreign locations may have partly derived from her contact with these teachers.[47]

Rosalie Glynn Grylls writes that the school was run in accordance with liberal, humanist and deeply religious tenets in an atmosphere of relative freedom. She states that it was without 'the numerous and petty restrictions imposed in private schools at the time'.[48] The last verse of the College hymn emphasised the importance of love as opposed to fear:

---

[43]   MS VIII, 25, Parkes papers, Girton College Library.

Bessie Parkes writes that 'Monsignor Gilbert founded a bed in the Refuge called the "Adelaide Procter Bed", a permanent memento and reminder of prayer for her soul' (Belloc, op. cit., p. 176).

[44]   Jenny FitzGerald, Queen's College Archivist, has confirmed that Procter attended Queen's in 1850 and that she probably attended 'just for the lectures and did not bother about any qualifications'. Barbara Bodichon attended on the same basis. (See Queen's College register for dates of registration.) Queen's College is now at 43-49 Harley Street; the Principal is The Hon. Lady Goodhart.

[45]   Maurice gave an Inaugural Lecture on 29th March, 1848 at the Hanover Square Rooms. *Inaugural: Lecture. Queen's College: 1848*, London: The Saint George Series, Alexander Moring Limited, The De La More Press.

[46]   Rosalie Glynn Grylls, *Queen's College 1848-1948*, London: George Routledge & Sons, Ltd., 1948, Appendix I, p. 113.

[47]   ibid., p. 8.

[48]   ibid., p. 33.

> By the pattern Thou hast shown,
>   Wisely may we ask and hear;
> Humbly all the guidance own,
>   Ours in love and not in fear.[49]

In her poetry Procter expresses a humane and socially committed Christianity alongside a more conservative religious position advocating resignation to suffering, apparent in poems such as 'Friend Sorrow', 'Be Strong', 'A Crown of Sorrow' and 'Strive, Wait and Pray':

> STRIVE; yet I do not promise
>   The prize you dream of to-day
> Will not fade when you think to grasp it,
>   And melt in your hand away;
> But another and holier treasure,
>   You would now perchance disdain,
> Will come when your toil is over,
>   And pay you for all your pain.
>   (p. 79, ll. 1–8)

Procter's religious poetry is, however, most interesting when it explores the relationship between her religion and a woman's capacity for expressiveness. The narrative poem 'A Tomb in Ghent' is a compelling *tour de force* which subtly and beautifully explores the problematics of a woman's expression within the foreign cathedral of St Bavon's, Ghent (see Chapter 1).

Religion appears to have enabled Procter to express herself strongly both in her poetry and in expounding her ideas. When she talks about religion she paradoxically appears to be both bigoted and critically aware of the extreme positions she adopts. In both cases her expression is forceful. In an undated letter to Bessie Parkes from 10 Sussex Square, Brighton, where Procter was probably staying for her health, she berates Parkes for not demonstrating a total commitment to her Unitarian belief:

> I do not think there is any neutral ground in belief ... I don't think the fact of not throwing yourself heart and soul into Unitarianism is any satisfaction. I could more clearly understand a person who did ...

She concludes her letter with the words:

---

[49]   ibid., Appendix IX, p. 123.

I cannot help laughing when I reread this letter and see myself . . . mounting the chair of Theology and favouring you with a Lecture.[50]

In another undated letter to Bessie from 32 Weymouth Street, Procter asserts that she has 'no particular interest in education' except to free people 'from Protestant prejudices'. Later in the letter she asks Bessie:

Don't you think we are like two intelligent savages each speaking the language of their own tribe and making out their meaning by gesticulations . . .[51]

In both letters a bigoted and unqualified statement is followed by an expression of wry and self-parodying humour. What is notable is her capacity for passionate belief and prejudice, which co-exists with an ability to critically look at herself and the inadequacies of her expression.

The seriousness of Procter's religion is often matched by her ability to refer to it in a more lighthearted vein. In a letter dated 1855 to her friend Richard Monckton-Milnes (Baron Houghton), the philanthropist and politician, Procter enthusiastically recommends Father Faber's preaching at the Brompton Oratory:

The Church is so crowded it would be safe to get there in good time. The Oratory is in the Brompton Road, opposite a ? Public House called the Hare & Hounds and next door to the Protestant Parish Church. Pray do not mistake and go into either of these places of entertainment instead of the Oratory but if either let it be the Public House.[52]

At its best Procter's religion seems to have been catholic in the widest sense in that it was humane, socially committed and associated with pleasure and good humour as well as with rigorous self-denial.

---

50 MS VIII, 37/1, Parkes papers, Girton College Library.
51 ibid., 38/2.
52 MS, Houghton, Trinity College Library, Cambridge.
Frederick Faber was famous for the introduction of hymns written in English and his services attracted a huge congregation, Protestant and Catholic. 'These services became a focus of attraction for considerable crowds although at the time but few Catholics resided in the neighbourhood' (Cassidy, op. cit. p. 98).

'A Young Lady who has Dreams'

Procter's wholehearted commitment to Catholicism was not matched by a commitment to a love relationship. In her poetry she shows great reticence and hesitancy about entering into a closer relationship (sexual and marital). In poems such as 'A Love Token', 'Fidelis' and 'True or False' the women speakers suggest that love may be tokenistic, false and not truly valued, and that the 'promise' given may be withdrawn:

> You have taken back the promise
>   That you spoke so long ago;
> Taken back the heart you gave me –
>   I must even let it go.
> Where Love once has breathed, Pride dieth:
>   So I struggled, but in vain,
> First to keep the links together,
>   Then to piece the broken chain.
>   ('Fidelis', p. 113, ll. 1–8)

In the beautiful lyric 'Three Roses' (see Chapter 3) a woman who gives herself freely to a man is shown to die after giving full expression to her desire.

Caution and fear may have been fuelled to some degree by Procter's extensive and sophisticated reading. Jane Brookfield (a close friend of W.M. Thackeray) wrote in 1849 to Harry Hallam, Arthur Hallam's brother:

> I am deep in Quintus Fixlein at present. Lent me by Miss Procter, not Mrs (Mark me) but Miss Procter, with whom I find congeniality and an undercurrent which ought to be encouraged.[53]

It is a sign of Procter's early sophistication that she had read Jean Paul Richter's 'Life of Quintus Fixlein', translated by Thomas Carlyle and published in 1827.[54] 'Quintus Fixlein' is the story of an obsessional man who writes a biography which he divides between fifteen separate letter boxes marking each phase of his life. Quintus lives his life under the shadow of

---

[53] Charles and Frances Brookfield, *Mrs Brookfield and Her Circle*, 2 Vols, London: Sir Isaac Pitman and Sons, Ltd., 1905, II, p. 280. Jane Octavia Brookfield was the daughter of Sir Charles Elton whose sister was the wife of the historian, Henry Hallam. William Brookfield, Jane's husband was honorary chaplain to the queen.
[54] Jean Paul Friedrich Richter, 'Life of Quintus Fixlein Extracted from Fifteen Letter Boxes', *German Romance. Specimens of Its Chief Authors; With Biographical and Critical Notices*, Trans. Thomas Carlyle, 4 Vols, Edinburgh: William Tait, 1827, III.

impending death, as traditionally all Fixleins died at the age of thirty two. He marries Thiennette, a woman who has already attempted suicide, and their marriage (recorded in the ninth letter box) is notable for the couple's post-ceremonial stroll through a graveyard. Quintus walks over the graves and presses tulips deep into the earth whilst Thiennette is overcome on seeing her parents rise from the dead:

> The bride wept aloud; she saw the mouldering coffins of her parents open, and the two dead arise and look round for their daughter, who had stayed so long behind them, forsaken on the Earth.

Her shock is followed by a marital embrace 'at a father's grave' and Richter ironically blesses the couple with the words: 'let this day of joy be holily concluded'.[55]

Quintus's obsessional habits enable him to weather such shocks and Richter states that Quintus was in no danger of being eaten up by emotion like some couples he might name:

> Some wedded pairs eat each other's lips and hearts and love away by kisses; as in Rome, the statues of Christ (by Angelo) have lost their feet by the same process of kissing, and got leaden ones instead . . .[56]

Procter would surely have enormously enjoyed Richter's ironic humour and more seriously, as several of her poems suggest, she may have recognised the close association between sexuality and death – along with the consuming quality of passion. These emotions were perhaps channelled into her religious faith and her many other activities which, like Quintus's letter boxes, served to contain energies and desires. An awareness of her own ill health – a consumptive condition – and the anticipation of an early death may have exacerbated or even produced these fears.

However, at the age of twenty three Procter was also vital and capable of entering into a world of socialising and soirées, with her own home providing many gatherings. Jane Brookfield, in a letter to her husband William, writes of Procter's three month visit to a family in Dunse Castle (the family is not named):

> Adelaide is in a highly excited state about Dunse Castle and her three months' visit, 'making her feel so completely one of the family,' sitting

55 ibid., p. 250.
56 ibid., p. 278.

down twenty to dinner and breakfast every day as the mere family party, and guests frequently in addition.

I suppose she is in love with one of the sons, but she did not confide it to me. I thought the shooting sounded suspicious and 'we used to practise music often five hours a day. I, on the pianoforte and the sons' (as she always called them, clubbing them together) 'on the Violincello and Violin.' [57]

In 1851 Jane wrote to her husband that Procter and her sister Agnes had dressed 'in fancy costumes for a ball at Lady Talford's'.[58]

Procter seems to have enjoyed herself in men's company and they often took an interest in her. For example Thackeray, who was a very close friend of the Procters, in particular Anne Skepper, took a keen interest in Procter and there seems to have been affection on both sides. In a letter to William Brookfield dated October 1848 Thackeray writes of a visit to the Procters at their home at 13 Upper Harley Street:

Tother day I went to Harley Street and saw the most beautiful pair of embroidered slippers worked for a lady, at whose feet I & c – and I begin more and more to think Adelaide Procter an uncommonly nice dear good girl.[59]

And in a letter to Anne Skepper (1848?) Thackeray sends his compliments 'to a young lady who has dreams', although it is not clear to what kind of 'dreams' he is referring.[60]

Their friendship, however, temporarily cooled in 1849 when they quarrelled over the treatment of Emma Gaggiotti Richards. (Emma Gaggiotti Richards was a figure and portrait painter and in the 1850s her work was commissioned by Queen Victoria and Prince Albert. She painted a fine portrait of Adelaide Procter which is now stored at the National Portrait Gallery.[61]) The reason for Procter's quarrel with Thackeray is unknown, but it was in some way connected with a dispute between Emma and her

---

[57] Brookfield, op. cit., II, p. 304.
[58] ibid., II, p. 361. Sir Thomas Noon Talfourd (1795–1854) was a barrister, literary critic and Member of Parliament. He is best known for his Copyright Act (1842) which secured legal protection for authors' copyright.
[59] Ray, op. cit., II, p. 441.
[60] ibid., II, p. 492.
[61] Emma Gaggiotti Richards (1825–1912). Emma painted a self-portrait for Queen Victoria in 1853. The portrait shows a woman artist at work holding 'a palette and a mahlstick'. Another self-portrait was exhibited at the Royal Academy in 1851. (Deborah Cherry, *Painting Women. Victorian women artists*, London and New York: Routledge, 1993, pp. 83–84, 240, 102) See Figure 1, Portrait of Adelaide Procter.

Figure 1: Adelaide A. Procter, Painting by Emma Gaggiotti Richards

husband Richards. In April, 1849, Thackeray wrote to the Brookfields that Emma and her mother had fled to the Procters from the reported 'brutal language and outrages' of Richards. Thackeray adds that the mother-in-law had made Emma marry Richards and then 'declined leaving her daughter', and that he pitied Richards as their victim.[62] In the same month he wrote to Mrs Brookfield that 'Adelaide Procter would hardly shake hands with me because of my cowardly conduct in the R— affair'.[63] Two months later, early in June 1849, Thackeray wrote to Mrs Procter:

> Ten minutes reflection in the cab as it brought me home has convinced me that I was very wrong in showing any anger I might feel much more in saying that I would never shake hands with Adelaide as long as I lived. That is very absurd. I shall be very happy, whenever she is minded, to shake hands with Miss Procter. But I have made the attempt more than half a dozen times lately and it has been always met with so much reluctance on your daughter's part, that I am tired on mine of making any more efforts at showing my good will; and can afford no further advances when they are met with so very little cordiality.

Thackeray goes on to say that he knows he has offended both Adelaide and her mother in some way but does not know what his offence was. However, he adds 'I never intend to inquire'. Thackeray's pride and vanity seem to have been quite badly wounded by Procter's disapproval of his behaviour: 'A man of my age and I hope character has no right to the reception my friend's daughter has chosen to give me'.[64]

Her friendship was, though, important to him as by August of that year the quarrel seems to have been forgotten. It may be that Procter had climbed down as Thackeray was thanking her for a beautiful purse she had sent him which he refers to as a 'peace-offering' in a letter to William Brookfield.[65] It is a warm and affectionate letter which pays tribute to the Procters, 'the best friends I have ever had', who had supported him when he was 'a poor struggling fellow'. In thanks for the purse he writes:

---

[62]   Ray, op. cit., II, pp. 514–515.
[63]   *A Collection of Letters of W.M. Thackeray. 1847–1855*, Intro. Jane Brookfield, London: Smith, Elder & Co., 1887, p. 47.
[64]   Ray, op. cit., II, pp. 549–550.
[65]   ibid., p. 572.
W.M. Thackeray to William Brookfield, *A Collection of Letters. W.M. Thackeray*, p. 70.

I shall keep it and value it sincerely and hope that the donor for whom I had a regard ever since the time when my head was black and she wore a pinafore, and the owner of the purse will be good friends until we stop altogether.[66]

Thackeray continued to feel warmly towards Procter and on the 4th December 1858 wrote to his daughters Anne and Harriet:

Adelaide going to be married: it was time: she has lost her front tooth *my* tooth. but looks very much happier & comfortabler.[67]

There is no evidence as to who Adelaide Procter's fiancé was. Thackeray was, though, clearly pleased and along with Dickens, another paternal friend and admirer, was keen to see Adelaide married off (see Chapter 5).

One of Adelaide's admirers was the publisher George Smith (founder of the *Cornhill Magazine* in 1860, which was edited by Thackeray). In *George Smith. A Memoir with some pages of autobiography* (1902) Smith recounts the story of the lionising reception Thackeray gave for Charlotte Brontë in 1850. The Procters were among the guests and, according to Smith, 'Mrs Procter was accustomed to tell the story of that evening with much humour. It was, she always declared, "one of the dullest evenings she ever spent in her life"'.[68] Smith writes of Adelaide Procter:

One of Mr Thackeray's guests was Miss Adelaide Procter, and those who remember that lady's charming personality will not be surprised to learn that I was greatly attracted by her. During our drive home I was seated opposite to Miss Brontë, and I was startled by her leaning forward, putting her hands on my knees, and saying 'She would make you a very nice wife.' 'Whom do you mean?' I replied. 'Oh! you know whom I mean,' she said; and we relapsed into silence. Though I admired Miss Procter very much, it was not a case of love at first sight, as Miss Brontë supposed.[69]

There is no other mention of Procter in his Memoir so apparently a relationship did not develop.

---

[66] Ray, op cit., II, p. 572.

[67] ibid., IV, p. 122.

[68] *George Smith. A Memoir with Some Pages of Autobiography.* For Private Circulation, Ed. Mrs E. Smith, London, [1902], p. 98. George Smith was the founder of *The Dictionary of National Biography* in 1882.

[69] ibid., pp. 98–99.

Smith's reference to the fact that 'it was not a case of love at first sight' may have been an allusion to Procter's actual appearance. Bessie Parkes, writes of Adelaide's 'singular and interesting face':

> There was something of Dante in the contour of its thin lines, and the colouring was a pale, delicate brown, which harmonized with the darker hair, while the eyes were blue, less intense in hue than those of Shelley; and like his also was the exquisitely fine, fluffy hair, which when ruffled stood out in a halo round the brow.[70]

It is interesting that Parkes describes Procter by comparing her looks with the appearance of male writers, as though adding to Procter's credibility as a poet. Leigh Hunt, for whom Adelaide had illuminated a copy of his poem 'Abou Ben Adhem', wrote to Bryan Procter in June, 1857 of her 'interesting face'.[71] Elizabeth Barrett Browning commented to Anna Jameson in 1855 'How I like Adelaide's face! That's a face worth a drove of beauties!'.[72]

Three pictures of Procter appear in different editions of *Legends and Lyrics*. The portrait by Emma Gaggiotti Richards (undated) depicts a composed and sympathetic looking woman.[73] The entry in the *National Portrait Gallery. Early Victorian Portraits* (Richard Ormond) reads:

> Pale complexion, greenish eyes, brown hair. Dressed in black costume, trimmed with red, and with red tassels, wearing various gold rings.[74]

The other two pictures are an engraved portrait by C. H. Jeens which appears in the 1866 edition of *Legends and Lyrics* and an unattributed picture. They show respectively a striking and passionate looking woman

---

[70] Belloc, op. cit., p. 167.

[71] MS, James Leigh Hunt to B.W. Procter (22.6.1857), University of Iowa Libraries. In the poem 'Abou Ben Adhem and the Angel' Abou wakes to find an 'angel writing in a book of gold'. He asks if his name is inscribed as one of those who love God, to which the angel replies it is not. Abou asks that his name go down as one who 'loves his fellow-men' (Leigh Hunt, *Rimini and Other Poems*, Boston: William D. Ticknor & Company, 1844, p. 124). Leigh Hunt hung Adelaide Procter's illuminated copy of the poem above 'his writing-table' (Edmund Blunden, *Leigh Hunt. A Biography*, London: Cobden-Sanderson, 1930, p. 273).

[72] MS, English Poetry Collection, Wellesley College Library, Wellesley, MA.

[73] Adelaide Anne Procter, *Legends and Lyrics. A Book of Verses*, Intro. Charles Dickens, London: George Bell and Sons, 1882. Woodcut by C.D. Mitton (see Figure 1).

[74] The painting is presently out on loan. It is described as an Oil on Canvas 37 inches X 31 inches (Richard Ormond, *National Portrait Gallery. Early Victorian Portraits*, London: HMSO, 1973, I, p. 385).

Figure 2: Adelaide A. Procter, Engraved Portrait of Charles Henry Jeens, 1866
© The British Museum.

wearing a mantilla, and a pretty woman with a look of gentle humour.[75] In all three pictures Procter's face and expression are 'interesting' and compelling.

Despite the interest Procter attracted she remained single. F. Janku in his monograph of Procter writes of a broken engagement, possibly in 1856:

> We know that the poet fell deeply in love with a man and that suddenly this relationship ended after a couple of years when her fiance broke off the engagement.

Janku adds, 'but we do not know anything about who this person was or when exactly it happened'![76]

Whatever the truth of Procter's romantic involvements many of her narrative poems, such as 'A Legend of Bregenz', 'A Tomb in Ghent', 'A Legend of Provence' and 'The Story of the Faithful Soul', primarily depict and are concerned with single women. Many of her lyrics, even when expressing an attraction for entering into love and marriage, often convey a sense of deep ambivalence and a distrust of entering into a more committed relationship. This is seen particularly in the trio of poems 'A Woman's Question', 'A Woman's Answer' and 'A Woman's Last Word' (see Chapter 3). These three lyrics were published at a time when Procter had become involved with the work of *The English Woman's Journal* which was established in 1858, the same year as the publication of the 'First Series' of *Legends and Lyrics* and also the year in which Thackeray announced that Procter 'was to be married'. Procter's energies were clearly being channelled in many directions.

Adelaide Procter and *The English Woman's Journal*

In March 1858 *The English Woman's Journal* was launched as a limited liability company, with Bessie Parkes and Matilda Hays as its co-editors.[77] Parkes and Hays were close friends of Procter and she dedicated the 'First Series' of *Legends and Lyrics* to 'Matilda M. Hays'. On the 23rd January

---

75 Adelaide Anne Procter, *Legends and Lyrics* (1914). The painting is attributed to Charles Henry Jeens in the DNB entry on Adelaide Procter (see Figure 2). Adelaide Anne Procter, *Legends and Lyrics*, London: Bell and Daldy, 1868.

76 Janku, op. cit., p. 21.

77 Hester Burton, *Barbara Bodichon 1827–1891*, London: John Murray, 1949, p. 98. Barbara Leigh Smith Bodichon was one of the founders of *The English Woman's Journal* and contributed several articles.

1858 Procter wrote a poem titled 'To M.M.H.', which was later published in *Legends and Lyrics* under the title 'A Retrospect'.[78] It is a poem which expresses love for Hays, the novelist and translator of George Sand and a controversial figure on the Journal who dressed in men's clothes and had lived with the sculptor Harriet Hosmer in Rome earlier in the 1850s.[79]

It is not known whether Procter's poem is a lesbian love lyric but by dedicating it to 'M.M.H.' she was clearly identifying herself with a more radical way of thinking. 'A Retrospect' suggests that she wished to start a new chapter in her life in which her love for women would assume more prominence:

> From this fair point of present bliss,
>   Where we together stand,
> Let me look back once more, and trace
>   That long and desert land,
> Wherein till now was cast my lot, and I could live,
>   and thou wert not.
>   (p. 151, ll. 1-5)

This vision of a brighter and perhaps a pioneering future with Matilda may also be read as an anticipation of their future work together on the Journal.

The English Woman's Journal's offices, along with a Ladies Reading Room, were located at 19 Langham Place in London and the group of women became known as the Langham Place Circle.[80] The Journal was to run from 1858 to 1864 and David Doughan has numbered its sales at 'never more than about 500' but states that the readership was 'probably much greater'. Doughan argues that the Langham Place Circle became the 'theoretical and practical source of organised feminism'.[81]

The journal published articles on women's property rights, conditions in prisons and lunatic asylums and assisted emigration for women.[82] But its

---

[78]   MS BRP X 79, Parkes papers, Girton College Library.

[79]   *The Feminist Companion to Literature in English. Women Writers from the Middle Ages to the Present*, Ed. Virginia Blain, Patricia Clements, Isobel Grundy, London: B.T. Batsford Ltd., 1990, pp. 503-504.

[80]   Burton, op. cit., p. 108.

[81]   *Feminist Periodicals 1855-1984. An Annotated Critical Bibliography of British, Irish, Commonwealth and International Titles*, Ed. David Doughan, Denise Sanchez, Brighton: The Harvester Press, 1987, pp. 1-2.

[82]   For a selection of articles from *The English Woman's Journal* see *Barbara Leigh Smith Bodichon and the Langham Place Group*, Ed. Candida Ann Lacey, New York and London: Routledge & Kegan Paul, 1987.

primary concern was with women's employment. Jane Rendall has written that the Journal:

> moved beyond the purely philanthropic towards demands primarily rooted in the experiences of single women, for education and for employment . . .[83]

The 1851 Census had revealed that:

> 42 percent of the women between the ages of twenty and forty were unmarried and that two million out of Britain's six million women were self-supporting.[84]

It was the cause of single women in particular which the Journal espoused and they included the many middle-class women who often took on the work of the low-paid, but higher status, governess.[85]

In 1859 the Society for Promoting the Employment of Women, with the Earl of Shaftesbury as President, was established as an affiliate of the National Association for the Promotion of Social Science (established in 1857). Procter was a key member of the Committee on which sat Richard Monckton Milnes, Jessie Boucherett, Isa Craig, Matilda Hays and Bessie Parkes amongst others.[86] A training and job register was established, the register being open for:

> ladies who wish to become candidates for remunerative employment in charitable institutions, as nurses in hospitals, matrons in workhouses, teachers or superintendents in industrial schools, likewise for those who desire to obtain situations as secretaries, clerks, or book-keepers.[87]

---

[83] *Equal or Different. Women's Politics. 1800–1914*, Ed. Jane Rendall, Oxford: Basil Blackwell Ltd., 1987, p. 13.

[84] Mary Poovey, *Uneven Developments. The Ideological Work of Gender in Mid-Victorian England*, London: Virago Press Limited, 1989, p. 4.

[85] Papers and articles by Bessie Parkes were published in *The English Woman's Journal* with titles such as 'The Market for Educated Female Labour', 'What Can Educated Women Do? (I) and (II), (Vol. IV, 1859, 1860).

[86] Helen Blackburn, *Women's Suffrage. A Record of the Women's Suffrage Movement in the British Isles with Biographical Sketches of Miss Becker*, London: Williams & Norgate, 1902, p. 251.

[87] ibid., p. 250. This is an extract from a copy of a circular printed by the Langham Place Circle in 1860. It describes the work of 'The Ladies' Institute, 19 Langham Place, W.' (p. 248).

(Registers for governesses and domestic servants were already in operation). Classes in arithmetic, bookkeeping and law-copying were also opened.[88]

Jessie Boucherett in her obituary of Procter which was published in the Journal, writes that Procter's role was that of 'animating spirit' who, although not in the public role of Secretary, nevertheless exerted a powerful influence. (Emily Faithfull was the Secretary.) She writes:

> In almost every committee there is a leading person, an animating spirit, some one, in fact, who does more than a fair share of work and does it well, and thus gains influence over the rest; this was the part taken by Miss Procter ... she was continually in the office, sometimes helping in the regular work, sometimes devising new plans and studying how to put them in execution. In the autumn of 1859, she wrote a letter on the 'Women Watchmakers at Christchurch,' which will be found in the December number of the 'English Woman's Journal' for that year.[89]

Jessie Boucherett expresses surprise and gratitude at 'a poet of no small reputation' performing 'the drudgery of a clerk'.[90]

Despite the 'drudgery' Procter clearly enjoyed some of the work. Her article on women watchmakers at Christchurch, Dorset describes her visit to a factory in which a majority of women worked. In this piece Procter describes the fine and intricate process of chain making with poetic lyricism. Her diplomatic skills are also evident when she reassures her readers that she is keen not to provoke the 'opposition of working men' who may fear that their jobs are threatened by women coming into the trade. Instead she gives an example of women's work in a factory where their employment has apparently been happily accepted 'without opposition by men'. Her description of the chain making process is worth quoting:

> We saw thirty different processes gone through, beginning with the thick rusty iron wire, beaten and striped till it became a delicate steel ribbon; which ribbon was pierced with invisible holes; punched out into minute figures of eight – which we could only distinguish by

---

[88]   ibid., p. 252.

[89]   *The English Woman's Journal*, XIII, 1864, 17-21. Boucherett writes that in 1861 Procter 'took Miss Thackeray on a visit of inspection to some of the Institutions connected with the Society' (p. 19). This tour of inspection was the subject of an article, 'Toilers and Spinsters', by Anne Ritchie (née Thackeray) (*The Cornhill Magazine*, III, 1861, pp. 318-331).

[90]   ibid., p. 18.

means of a magnifying glass–; and then rivetted and polished till a beautiful jointed steel chain was produced; the finer ones being no thicker than a coarse silk thread.[91]

Procter was obviously impressed and gained aesthetic pleasure from watching this finely executed and laborious process.

Women workers were also employed as the compositors for the Victoria Press established by Emily Faithfull at Great Coram Street in March 1860.[92] In 1861 Procter edited *The Victoria Regia* which was printed by the Victoria Press, and as the publication had a royal seal of approval it was hoped that it would prove to be, in Emily Faithfull's words, 'a choice specimen of the skill attained by my compositors'.[93] *The Victoria Regia* certainly demonstrated the professionalism of its women printers. As a text, though, it lacks any thematic or structural coherence but includes some interesting contributions, for example Harriet Martineau's 'The Birth of a Free Nation' which recounts the history of Haiti, and Trollope's short story 'The Journey to Panama'. Other contributors were Tennyson, Aubrey de Vere, William Allingham, J.R. Lowell, Geraldine Jewsbury, W.M. Thackeray, Mary Howitt, Coventry Patmore, Isa Craig, Matthew Arnold, George Macdonald, Trollope, Richard Monckton Milnes, Barry Cornwall (Bryan Procter) and F.D. Maurice. Adelaide Procter contributed the religious lyric 'Links with Heaven'.

At this period Procter also attended the Portfolio Society, an informal group of mostly women writers and artists who met to discuss their work in the late 1850s and early 1860s. The group met at 5 Blandford Square, the London home of Barbara Leigh Smith (Bodichon) and they sometimes wrote and painted in response to set themes such as 'Separation', 'Refuge', 'Strife and Peace'. Procter's poetic output decreased considerably from 1860 as her health deteriorated, but some of the poems published during this period may well have resulted from discussions at the Portfolio.[94]

Procter's life was extremely busy at this time and Dickens wrote in his Introduction that her 'incessant occupation' had contributed to her early

[91] *The English Woman's Journal*, IV, 1859, pp. 278–279.

[92] See Eric Ratcliffe, *The Caxton of her Age. The Career and Family Background of Emily Faithfull (1835–95)*, Upton-Upon-Severn: Images Publishing (Malvern) Ltd., 1993.

[93] *The Victoria Regia: A Volume of Original Contributions in Poetry and Prose*, Ed. Adelaide A. Procter, London: Printed and Published by Emily Faithfull and Co., Victoria Press, (for the Employment of Women,) Great Coram Street, W.C., 1861, p. vii.

[94] Jan Marsh, *Christina Rossetti – a literary biography*, London: Jonathan Cape, 1994, pp. 274–275. See note 80 (Bodichon).

death (p. 9). Procter's persona as a campaigner for women was caricatured
by Dickens in a cameo of her which he had included in the frame narrative
of 'The Haunted House', the 1859 Christmas Number of *All the Year Round*.
Belinda Bates, the character Dickens describes, later tells a story which takes
the form of the narrative poem 'A Legend of Provence' Procter contributed
to this Christmas Number. His description reads:

> Belinda Bates, bosom friend of my sister, and a most intellectual,
> amiable, and delightful girl, got the Picture Room. She has a fine
> genius for poetry, combined with real business earnestness, and 'goes
> in' – to use an expression of Alfred's – for Woman's mission, Woman's
> rights, Woman's wrongs, and everything that is Woman's with a
> capital W, or is not and ought to be, or is and ought not to be. 'Most
> praiseworthy, my dear, and Heaven prosper you!' I whispered to her
> on the first night of my taking leave of her at the Picture Room door,
> 'but don't overdo it. And in respect of the great necessity there is, my
> darling, for more employments being within the reach of Woman than
> our civilisation has as yet assigned to her, don't fly at the unfortunate
> men, even those men who are at first sight in your way, as if they
> were the natural oppressors of your sex; for, trust me, Belinda, they
> do sometimes spend their wages among wives and daughters, sisters,
> mothers, aunts, and grandmothers; and the play is, really, not *all* Wolf
> and Red Riding-Hood, but has other parts in it.' However, I digress.[95]

This condescending caricature would no doubt have greatly irritated, even if
it amused Procter. What is especially interesting is the contrast this caricature makes with the poem Belinda / Procter narrates which is about a young
nun who is depicted as anonymous and, despite working in a convent, is
without any clearly defining role (see Chapter 4).

Procter's attitude towards *The English Woman's Journal*, one of her
workplaces, is unclear. In July, 1862, she wrote a letter to Bessie Parkes in
which she passionately defends Matilda Hays's position as editor, which was
threatened by Emily Faithfull's supporters lobbying for Emily to be
appointed in Hays's place. Adelaide writes that:

> anything which throws the EWJ into E. Faithfull's power, which
> giving it to Isa Craig does, is a positively wrong and wicked thing –

Having shown how involved she is in the internal politics of the Journal

95   *All The Year Round*, II, 1859, p. 7.

Procter then adds, 'though I don't see the Journal as the "moral engine" you do'.[96]

Jessie Boucherett, in her obituary of Procter, wrote of Adelaide's repudiation of the idea that 'poets ought to be excused the usual duties of life'. Boucherett writes:

> She would argue that if poetic genius really did unfit its owners for the practical business of life, then its possession was a misfortune, and poets ought to be classed with cripples and other helpless or deficient beings.[97]

This caustic and unsympathetic statement sits interestingly with Adelaide's comment on the 'moral engine'. It is as though a more punitive strain urges excessive involvement in the business of life which may prove to be 'drudgery', whilst there may be a desire to escape the demands of the 'moral engine' in which she was an important cog and to which she was clearly committed.

Procter was perhaps also attempting to escape from her own commanding didactic poetic voice which is heard in poems such as 'Now', 'Give' and 'Cleansing Fires':

> In the cruel fire of Sorrow
>   Cast thy heart, do not faint or wail;
> Let thy hand be firm and steady,
>   Do not let thy spirit quail:
> But wait till the trial is over,
>   And take thy heart again;
> For as gold is tried by fire,
>   So a heart must be tried by pain!
> ('Cleansing Fires', pp. 47–48, ll. 9–16)

Procter's narrative poems by contrast are often about anonymous women or children who lack a more potent voice and definition and it is the search for more definition, often in a foreign location, which is central to these poems. The poems provided Procter with a means of exploring her own more anonymous emotions and thoughts.

In concluding this résumé of Procter's sadly curtailed life it is interesting

---

96 MS BRP VIII, 24/1, Parkes papers, Girton College Library. I have not been able to discover why Procter was so vehemently opposed to Emily Faithful's challenge to the editorship.

97 *The English Woman's Journal*, XIII, 1864, p. 19.

to consider an article by Procter, published in *The English Woman's Journal*, which suggests that certain energies and exploratory drives were seeking expression in a place which was less cluttered by commitments and ties.

'In Search of Solitude'

In two letters to Bessie Parkes, one dated 17th February 1855 and the other undated, Procter's energy and humour are on display. In the first she writes that on walking back from Church she was waylaid by a 'fiend':

> On my way back a 'fiend in human form' perched on a high waggon throws with all his force an enormous cabbage – or bundle of cabbages, directly on to my head, knocking off my bonnet and stunning me to an extent I would not have believed so innocent a thing could do . . . The man has knocked me up completely if he did not quite knock me down.[98]

In the second letter Procter recounts an incident with a 'milk can' on returning from a visit to her sister Agnes in Chelsea:

> I have been to Chelsea to see Agnes, and got out of the omnibus at the Circus, and as I was walking home my braid on my gown hooked on to a milk can, and caught a little one and overturned it – one of the tiny ones that hang round, and I had to give the woman a shilling – and I doubt if the milk could be worth it. Perhaps it was cream.[99]

In these amusing and self-parodying accounts it is interesting that Procter presents herself as being bombarded. She describes herself as caught up in a 'Circus' in which Fuselian fiends, cabbages, milkcans and their offspring 'knock' her both up and down. Perhaps London, and the many activities in which she was involved, seemed at times like a giddying circus from which she sought escape.

In 1859 Procter did make an actual or metaphorical escape from her busy life. 'Adventures of Your Own Correspondents in Search of Solitude' appeared in *The English Woman's Journal* in two parts in the September and October 1859 editions. It is an account of an actual or fictional journey to the Lake District made by Procter, who narrates the account, and a woman friend called 'A'. 'A' may have been Anne Leigh Smith, Barbara Bodichon's

---

[98]   MS BRP VIII 3/1, Parkes papers, Girton College Library.
[99]   ibid. 58/1.

younger sister, or perhaps an imaginary alter ego if the account is fictional. The account begins:

> Your O.Cs. started, as you are aware, on an excursion of some weeks into the North; society had become burthensome to us; humanity distasteful; civilisation and its accompaniments unendurable. Shall I call ourselves female Timons, who fled away into the wilds of York-shire to enjoy at our ease the comfort of despising the world in general and our friends in particular? Hardly that; because Humanity, divested of any conventional fetters, had inexpressible attractions for us.[100]

Procter sets the ironic tone and the Wordsworthian 'solitude' and unfettered 'Humanity' which they apparently seek forever elude the two women. They travel by train, on foot, on horseback and in carts from one location to another and finally arrive at a place which seems to epitomise 'solitude' – the 'lovely, lonely Wastdale Head!' an envious friend writing from London romantically recalls.[101]

Tedium sets in as lack of contact (letters take a long time to arrive) and a monotonous diet of interminable eggs, bacon and stifling mountains proves too much for the friends. Their move is also triggered by a reading of Shakespeare's *Cymbeline* to while away the time. Procter refers to 'Imogen's patient fidelity' and 'Posthumous's very undeserved happiness', suggesting that she and 'A' may become 'posthumous' if they keep waiting for an unspecified something which may not be worth the wait. Procter also expresses a weariness with reading *Cymbeline* which like the 'eggs and bacon' does not give enough sustenance under the circumstances.[102]

An impatience with the weight of books the two carry around with them is expressed throughout the commentary. At the start of their journey, when boarding the train, Procter refers to the 'solid character' of their literature which the porters find 'remarkably heavy'. Amongst the texts 'A' has designated 'light reading' are *Buckle's History of Civilization*, Wordsworth's *The Excursion* and Browning's 'Paracelsus'![103] At one point in their journey a load of texts which have been stacked in their traveller's cart, fall out on to the road:

---

[100] *The English Woman's Journal*, IV, 1859, p. 35.

[101] ibid., p. 105.

[102] ibid., pp. 104–105.

[103] ibid., p. 36. Henry Thomas Buckle's *History of Civilization in England* was published in 1857. Buckle argues that human actions are 'governed by mental and physical laws' over which an individual has little control (Buckle, *History of Civilization in England*, 3 Vols, London: Longmans, Green and Co., 1869, I, p. 1).

one after another, they had dropped out at the back of the cart, and
no doubt, strewing the ground for the last few miles, would have
traced our progress much more accurately than Hop-o'-my-thumb's
many ineffectual devices.

Procter wonders if it is worth going back for the books, but when she
remembers that among them is her private 'pocket book' she decides that
they must be retrieved:

> 'They *must* be found,' I mentally ejaculated, and at that moment
> caught sight of the yellow cover of the last number of the
> 'Virginians'; farther on gleamed the green back of the 'King's Idylls';
> a 'Saturday Review' fluttered in the breeze; our 'Bradshaw' lay
> securely under a furze bush; Mrs Jameson's 'Sisters of Charity' were
> nestling under a tuft of fern; letters and pocket-book were all safe, and
> I ran back joyfully to A., who evidently wished they had not been
> discovered so soon, as her drawing was not half done.[104]

The friends' 'light' reading and scattered books provide a fascinating range
of texts, with a substantial representation of male nineteenth-century poets
whose 'Romantic' territory the women are metaphorically negotiating.
Alongside them W.M. Thackeray's recently published *The Virginians*
(1857–59), with its exploration of the virgin territory of the United States
and its struggle for independence, mirrors the explorations of the two women.
Texts about women also figure strongly – devoted, destructive, virginal and
fallen women are represented by Tennyson's *Idylls*, the first four of which
(*Enid, Vivien, Elaine* and *Guinevere*) were published in 1859, and Anna
Jameson's *Sisters of Charity* (reprinted in 1859). The *Saturday Review*,
which had mocked *The English Woman's Journal* for its campaigning, is
shown 'fluttering' ineffectually whilst the 'Sisters of Charity' are actively
nestling.[105] Only *Bradshaw* 'lay securely' – the railway time-table which will

---

[104] ibid., pp. 109–110.

[105] In an article entitled 'The English Woman's Journal' in *The Saturday Review*
(10.4.1858) the reviewer wrote of the journal's 'foppery' in campaigning for widening
women's employment opportunities. He adds that 'society wants no reorganization to
give more facilities than it does to several second-rate lady moralists and inferior
female manufacturers of magazines and journals' (*The Saturday Review of Politics,
Literature, Science, and Art*, V, 1858, pp. 369–370).

Sisters of Charity was a lecture given by Anna Jameson in 1855. Jameson
argues that although 'no friend to nunneries' she applauds the work of 'active
charitable Orders' and their work with fallen women in penitentiaries and houses of
refuge (Jameson, *Sisters of Charity and The Communion of Labour*, London:
Longman, Brown, Green, Longmans, and Roberts, 1859, pp. 34–39).

enable the texts and the women to travel back to London together at the right time.

Procter draws attention to the accumulated weight of her knowledge and to a wide range of formative and influential texts, whilst simultaneously expressing a desire to free herself of such epistemological bulk. Without this solidity, however, she may not be able to retrieve herself (in the form of the journal).

The friends, along with their weight of books, do eventually find solitude at a location between Crummock Water and Lowes Water. They find a site by a river for 'A''s morning picture which 'A' names the 'Secret Place' of Wordsworth's 'Lucy' poems. This 'secret place' may only be reached, though, by making a difficult and time-consuming journey:

> It can only be reached by wading ankle deep through the stream, and four times daily is that operation performed by our enterprising A., for two journies each way are needed to carry over easel, picture, canvas, umbrella, and colors; to say nothing of shoes and stockings.[106]

Despite the unromantic difficulties they encounter in negotiating this 'Romantic' landscape they do manage to bathe, read, paint and pose for six enjoyable weeks. Procter also finds time for a lyrical moment which contrasts dramatically with the rather relentlessly ironic tone of this commentary:

> Shade and trees and verdure we have in abundance, and yet by mounting a few yards behind our house, we see the two lakes outspread before us, and thither every evening does A. repair for the sunset lights which flood Lowes Water, and are cast back by the eastern clouds and the reddening hills that rise up one behind another far away to our right, always the same, and yet never alike, colors and shadows and vapours hourly changing their aspect.
>
> I do believe that the sea and the mountains appeal so much more strongly to our heart than any other form of scenery, just because they share our human power of changing their mood . . .[107]

Procter creates a sudden change of mood and our attention is drawn to the more lyrical poet who seems to have been left behind in these articles. The two lakes suggest the existence of two personas, the ironic and the lyrical – Adelaide and 'A'.

---

106 ibid., p. 112.
107 ibid., p. 113.

Finally, well-intentioned friends of friends arrive with visiting cards which Adelaide and 'A' take as their cue to leave:

> I rose. I brought down Bradshaw; we bewildered our brains for a short time over that enigma, then guessed at a train; and at this moment your O.Cs. trunks are packed. To that real solitude of London, not the chimerical solitude of the country, we are about to hasten in the first instance, and a civilly worded note is on its way to the Grange, affirming that 'our return to London will prevent our having the honor, etc.'
>
> A.A.P.[108]

Procter's account of her journey to the Lakes provides a metaphorical mapping of the terrain of her poetic imagination. Many of her narrative poems explore the desire to cut off from family and home, and the protagonists are depicted more in transition or on a threshold than settled, or even uncomfortably settled, inside a home.

Like many other nineteenth-century women poets Procter explores foreign locations in her narrative poems (which often figure in the work of Felicia Hemans, Letitia Landon and Elizabeth Barrett Browning). Isobel Armstrong has written that the movement to Italy in Victorian women's poetry is important in that the foreign country provides an 'emotional space *outside* the definitions and circumscriptions of the poet's specific culture and nationality'.[109] By exploring the Lake District in *In Search of Solitude* Procter enters into a location much closer to home, but 'foreign' to the extent that it is the poetic landscape of her male predecessors. Procter looks into what is both well known to her whilst also being 'foreign' territory and difficult to negotiate.

The women's journeyings are depicted as a series of rapid movements from one location to another, and when the friends do settle for six weeks their time spent is described fleetingly and in very little detail. The 'secret place' suggests a place of secret emotion. As in Elizabeth Barrett Browning's poems 'The Lost Bower' and 'The Romance of the Swan's Nest', Procter depicts this place as extremely vulnerable and of uncertain location.[110] It is for the most part concealed from the reader and protected by Procter's

---

[108] ibid., p. 114.
[109] Isobel Armstrong, *Victorian Poetry. Poetry, poetics and politics*, London and New York: Routledge, 1993, p. 324.
[110] Elizabeth Barrett Barrett, *Poems*, 2 Vols, London: Edward Moxon, 1844, II, pp. 100-122, 254-259.

ironic and defensive voice caricaturing the women's entry into the 'Romantic' bower.

There is a sense that Procter is closing the door on or to a 'bower' which may have been discovered, and that she is shutting herself both out and in. Similarly she opens, closes and indeed at one point throws away the books which have been such formative influences for her. The weight of her poetic inheritance, which is primarily male and has provided her with a poetic home, appears to be both welcomed and rejected.

The authority of male figures – John Keble, Robert Browning, Bryan Procter and Charles Dickens – is the primary focus of discussion in this study and in *In Search of Solitude* Procter literally enacts some of the problems which a woman poet faced in attempting to establish a place for herself.

Women poets sought to travel imaginatively in their search for a poetic voice, but their travels sometimes brought them face to face with a condition of loss and disillusionment. In Elizabeth Barrett Browning's *Aurora Leigh* Aurora faces the disappointments attached to locating a home in a foreign country. When she thinks of her dead father's house ('Without his presence!') in Italy she encounters 'The heaviest grave-stone on this burying earth'. It is a home which is imagined as a dead and obstructive weight, once it is denuded of the fantasy associated with its foreignness:

> 'Tis only good to be, or here or there,
> Because we had a dream on such a stone,
> Or this or that, – but, once being wholly waked,
> And come back to the stone without the dream,
> We trip upon't, – alas! and hurt ourselves;
> Or else it falls on us and grinds us flat,
> The heaviest grave-stone on this burying earth.[111]

The romance attached to the father and his 'foreignness' (the father is English but lived in Italy) is replaced by a sense of loss as well as an awareness of the burden that the father's past might present to the daughter.

It is the solid weight of poetic tradition, metaphorised by the Romantic landscape of her poetic fathers (a foreign place to the extent that it is the land of the fathers), which Procter avoids in *In Search of Solitude* through incessant movement and the metaphorical shedding of literary burdens. By avoiding the lyricism and beauty along with the weight of her inheritance, however, Procter comes close to shedding a more lyrical self altogether. She

---

[111] Elizabeth Barrett Browning, *Aurora Leigh*, London: Chapman and Hall, 1857 [1856], pp. 292-293.

searches for a Wordsworthian solitude without Wordsworth.

Two months after the publication of *In Search of Solitude* the narrative poem 'A Legend of Provence' was published. The legend is the tale of a young nun's exploratory movements away from and back to her home in a convent, a house of women. The dazzling lyricism of this poem clearly resulted from Procter's immersion within a 'Romantic' landscape and in her 'weighty' books earlier in the summer. The combination of the influence of male poetic predecessors with an emergent poetic voice which is challenging the authority of male poets (particularly that of her father) come together in this poem to powerful effect (see Chapter 4).

Procter's return 'home' to London and her many activities included a return to the women's home of *The English Woman's Journal* and to the topics which were the concern of many women poets, for example the fallen woman, homelessness and a woman's place and displacement. Procter's poetic voice developed from and was facilitated by her work with the Journal. However, it is a voice which expresses great anxiety about feeling secure within a 'home'. Her poetry is at its most resonant and expressive when she is articulating fears about finding a home anywhere. The most interesting poems express an unresolved ambivalence about any kind of locatedness, a state of being, in Elizabeth Barrett Browning's words, 'or here or there'.

The place where Procter first metaphorically found herself was of course her own home and as a poet's daughter that place is especially significant. It is therefore important to provide an introduction to both her parents – the 'home' being a place from which the protagonists in her poetry so often move away.

Fanny Kemble, the actress, wrote of the 'incomparable compound' which Procter's parents, Bryan Procter and Anne Skepper made:

> Their house was the resort of all the choice spirits of the London society of their day, her pungent epigrams and brilliant sallies making the most delightful contrast imaginable to the cordial kindness of his conversation and the affectionate tenderness of his manner; she was like a fresh lemon, – golden, fragrant, firm, and wholesome, – and he was like honey of Hymettus; they were an incomparable compound.[112]

Whether or not Anne Skepper and Bryan Procter did make such a perfect 'compound' they certainly made a very interesting combination which would no doubt have made an important and formative impact on their daughter.

---

[112] Kemble, op. cit., II, p. 277.

Anne Skepper (1799–1888)

Anne Skepper was the daughter of Anne Benson Skepper and Thomas Skepper, a lawyer who died when Anne was a child. Her mother had then met and married Basil Montagu, who had had two previous marriages and several children.[113] He was the son of the fourth Earl of Sandwich, John Montagu, whom Thomas Carlyle described as 'dissolute' and 'questionable'.[114] His mother was the Earl's mistress of seventeen years' standing, the singer Martha Ray who became involved with the clergyman James Hackman. Hackman's love had turned to obsession and in 1779 he killed Martha by shooting her in the head after an opera at Covent Garden.[115]

Basil Montagu and Anne Benson Skepper, along with his children and her daughter, lived at 25 Bedford Square where Adelaide was born in 1825. They had three children of their own, two sons and a daughter, Emily.[116] Thomas Carlyle, who had been a friend of the Montagus, came to disapprove of Montagu and his 'menagerie'. He describes Basil Montagu, a Chancery barrister, sarcastically as:

> hugely, *a sage*, too, busy all his days upon 'Bacon's Works', and continually preaching a superfinish morality about benevolence, munificence, health, peace, unfailing happiness. Much a bore to you by degrees, and considerably a humbug if you probed too strictly.[117]

In addition to the 'preaching' disliked by Carlyle, Montagu did in fact campaign successfully with Sir Samuel Romilly for the abolition of the death penalty for numerous offences short of murder, and also worked to secure changes in the copyright and bankruptcy laws.

Anne Benson Skepper, by contrast with her husband, is described by Carlyle as exemplary in her management of the 'miscellany of a household'. He describes her 'queenly beauty' and royal demeanour which distanced her from her 'subjects', and as possessing a voice with 'something of metallic in it, akin to that smile in her eyes'.[118]

Of all the family Carlyle most liked Anne Skepper who became a close

[113] Belloc, op. cit., pp. 148–149.
[114] Froude, op. cit., I, p. 224.
[115] N.A.M. Rodger, *The Insatiable Earl. A Life of John Montagu, Fourth Earl of Sandwich 1718–1792*, London: Harper Collins, 1993, pp. 122–124.
[116] Froude, op. cit., I, p. 226.
[117] ibid., I, p. 224.
[118] ibid., pp. 226–227.

friend of his wife, Jane Carlyle. He describes her as 'a brisk, witty, prettyish, sufficiently clear-eyed and sharp-tongued young lady' and admires her practicality and sense.[119] Bessie Parkes writes of her:

> She had a habit of going into the world, a habit of dressing fashion-
> ably, a habit of writing the neatest and most concise notes possible;
> but her consistent, steady kindness had assuredly some deep spiritual
> root, of which she never spoke. Like her mother, she never abdicated
> for a moment her great *tenue*, never kept her room, never lowered the
> scale of her dress, never lost her composure . . .[120]

Fanny Kemble also pays tribute to Anne Skepper's kindliness, but it is the 'sharp tongue' and 'wit' Carlyle mentions for which she is remembered primarily. Kemble refers to the 'power of sarcasm':

> that made the tongue she spoke in and the tongue she spoke with two
> of the most formidable weapons any woman was ever armed with . . .
> such was her severity of speech, not unfrequently exercised on those
> she appeared to like best, that Thackeray, Browning, and Kinglake,
> who were all her friendly intimates, sometimes designated her as 'Our
> Lady of Bitterness', and she is alluded to by that title in the opening
> chapter of 'Eothen'.[121]

In a letter to Washington Irving (5.7.1856) Dickens writes of a meeting he had had with Mrs Procter and Mrs Carlyle and refers to Mrs Procter as a 'brilliant discourser'.[122] Gordon Ray, W.M. Thackeray's biographer, wrote that Anne Skepper was 'a force in English intellectual life' in her role as literary salon hostess. Thackeray was a close friend who admired her intellect and wit and respected her as a literary critic.[123] On the publication of Charlotte Brontë's *Villete* in 1853, Anne Skepper had written to Thackeray that she thought it 'an excellently written book – but a very disagreeable one':

---

[119] ibid., p. 226.

[120] Belloc, op. cit., p. 163.

[121] Kemble, op. cit., I, p. 206. Alexander Kinglake, historian and traveller, referred to Anne Skepper as 'Our Lady of Bitterness' in his 'Preface' to *Eothen* (1844), an account of his travels in the east (Kinglake, *Eothen*, Intro. Barbara Kreiger, Vermont: The Marlboro Press, 1992, p. xix).

[122] *The Letters of Charles Dickens*, op. cit., II (1855 to 1870), p. 47.

[123] Gordon N. Ray, *Thackeray: The Uses of Adversity (1811–1846)*, London: Oxford University Press, 1955, pp. 291–292.

She turns every one 'The seamy side out' – So plain a person as Miss Brontë must see all things darkly – but the book is like a fine dutch picture the painting is as minute and as delicate.[124]

Thackeray replied, largely agreeing with her:

That's a plaguy book that Villete. How clever it is – and how I don't like the heroine.[125]

Anne Skepper in turn admired Thackeray's *Vanity Fair* (1847–1848) which he had dedicated to Bryan Procter, and Gordon Ray writes that Abraham Hayward relied heavily on some of Anne Skepper's views on the novel in his essay on 'Thackeray's Writings' published in the *Edinburgh Review* in January 1848.[126]

She was not, however, universally liked and respected. William Brookfield refers to her in a letter to Jane as the 'Proctrix' without 'one smallest sparklet of humour', although 'Witty' and 'well informed'.[127] Elizabeth Barrett Browning was extremely angry when she heard that Mrs Procter had been saying it was a pity Robert Browning 'had not seven or eight hours a day of occupation'. She wrote to Robert:

if Mr Procter had looked as simply to his art as an end, he would have done better things.

Browning, who was and continued to be a good friend of the Procters, replied:

Mrs Procter is very exactly the Mrs Procter I knew long ago. What she says is of course purely foolish. The world does seem incurably stupid on this, as on other points.[128]

---

[124] Ray, *The Letters and Private Papers of William Makepeace Thackeray*, III, p. 231.

[125] ibid., p. 252.

[126] ibid., II, p. 312. Mrs Procter expressed her views to Abraham Hayward in a letter dated 23rd July 1847, comparing aspects of Thackeray's writing with the work of Oliver Goldsmith and Laurence Sterne (p. 312).

[Abraham Hayward], 'Thackeray's Writings', *The Edinburgh Review*, 87, 1848, pp. 46–67.

[127] Brookfield, op. cit., I, p. 161.

[128] *Robert Browning and Elizabeth Barrett. The Courtship Correspondence 1845–1846*, Ed. Daniel Karlin, Oxford University Press, 1990, pp. 239–240.

Respectability and being seen to do the right thing were important to Anne Skepper. In a letter from a Miss Wynn to Jane Brookfield, Miss Wynn recounts Anne Skepper's humorous attitude towards the Protestant clergy. According to Miss Wynn she treated them as 'a machine for a certain purpose' who should pretend to pass the 'whole of Sunday in meditation' even if they didn't:

> as long as it was good acting for the Miss Procters, she cared not a pin, for the harm it was to do the Clergy to have that mass of untruth on their souls . . .[129]

From this very sketchy but at times compelling evidence the picture of a sharp but kind, intelligent but worldly, woman emerges. At the close of her long life she lived in Albert Hall Mansions where she still played the role of literary hostess to friends such as Browning, Henry James and Thomas Hardy (who dedicated *Under the Greenwood Tree* to her).[130]

There is little evidence relating to her relationship with Adelaide. According to Augustus Hare, when Anne Skepper was nearing death she had a serious disagreement with her daughter Agnes (who had become a nun) over the publication of her letters. Agnes had also wanted her mother to see a priest but Anne Skepper had refused. Hare writes that Agnes 'put the whole of the correspondence on the kitchen-fire' in retaliation.[131] Many of Adelaide Procter's letters may have gone up in smoke too.

Without more evidence it is not possible to do more than make some speculative comments on the extent to which Adelaide was her mother's daughter. Like her mother she shows a keen intelligence and strength of voice (apparent in some of her later lyrics) but she is less worldly, and her ironic humour, although sharp, is not as acerbic as Anne Skepper's wit. Procter's capacity for self-parody, as seen in the travel commentary and letters, counters the sense of 'bitterness' with which Anne Skepper was credited.

In relation to Procter's poetry the poetic reserve Procter employs (discussed in Chapter 2), along with the simplicity and tight control of her

---

[129] Brookfield, op. cit., II, pp. 452–453.

[130] *New Letters of Robert Browning*, Ed. William Clyde DeVane and Kenneth Leslie Knickerbocker, Yale University Press, 1950, note 2, p. 226.

Edmund Blunden writes of Mrs Procter's friendship with Thomas Hardy, to whom she 'sent . . . some of her famous candid letters (rejoicing over his works)' as well as making 'the best of his company' (Blunden, *Thomas Hardy*, London: Macmillan and Co., Limited, 1941, pp. 35–36).

[131] Augustus J.C. Hare, *The Story of My Life*, 6 Vols, London: George Allen, 1900, VI, pp. 462–463. Augustus Hare (1792–1834) was a pastor and writer.

writing may well have been influenced by the control exercised by her mother within the family. It may also be the case that the aristocratic eccentricity of Basil Montagu and the dramatic murder of his mistress Martha Ray contributed to a general anxiety that loose and uncontrolled expression be kept at bay.

As Procter was the daughter of the poet Bryan Procter there is obviously much more material to work with when it comes to her father. His work and ideas were important and instrumental in Adelaide Procter's development as both poet and philanthropist.

Bryan Procter (Barry Cornwall) (1787–1874)

Thomas Carlyle wrote of Bryan Procter:

> A decidedly rather pretty little fellow Procter, bodily and spiritually; manners prepossessing, slightly London-elegant, not unpleasant; clear judgment in him, though of narrow field; a sound honourable morality, and airy friendly ways; of slight neat figure, vigorous for his size; fine genially rugged little face, fine head; something curiously dreamy in the eyes of him, lids drooping at the *outer* ends into a cordially meditative and drooping expression; would break out suddenly now and then into opera attitude and a *La ci darem la mano* for a moment; had something of real fun, though in London style.[132]

Carlyle's description, although partly complimentary, presents Mr Procter as a diminutive, insubstantial and dreamy figure who lacks a more robust masculine frame and forcefulness. William Brookfield and Thackeray both joke in letters about Procter's sleepiness.[133] He is described by Bessie Parkes as a 'refined and somewhat silent man' whose 'interior life' was difficult to penetrate.[134] An exploration of Procter's poetry in fact reveals the presence of some strong and expressive thoughts and feelings which co-exist strangely with Procter's repeated disclaimer as to any desire to make an impression, or to express himself more forcefully either in his poetry or in his life.

Bryan Waller Procter was born in Leeds in 1787. His family had been small farmers for several generations, but his father had entered into business

---

[132] Froude, op. cit., I, pp. 233–234.

[133] Brookfield, op. cit., I, p. 161.
Ray, *The Letters and Private Papers of William Makepeace Thackeray*, II, p. 14.

[134] Belloc, op. cit., p. 158.

as a property owner and moved to London where he owned several properties which he let. Procter was educated at Harrow, along with his contemporaries Byron and Robert Peel, and at the age of seventeen he was articled to a solicitor in Calne, a small market town in Wiltshire.[135]

In 1807, aged twenty, Procter moved to London and in 1811 was admitted to Chancery as a solicitor, working as a conveyancer at 10 Brunswick Square.[136] He was called to the Bar in 1831. Although he was successful in his chosen profession Procter's career as a poet was equally important to him. In his *Autobiographical Fragment* (1877) edited by Coventry Patmore, Procter describes the law as being unconcerned with the affective life: 'It may refer to prosperity or misfortune, but does not deal intimately with the affections.'[137]

For Procter 'affections' were the matter of poetry. He was a fairly prolific poet and wrote under the pseudonym Barry Cornwall (a loose anagram of Bryan Waller Procter). Associated with the 'Cockney School' of poetry, he was a close friend of James Leigh Hunt who had been the subject of attacks by J.G. Lockhart in *Blackwood's Magazine* for his 'pretence, affectation, finery, and gaudiness'.[138] Procter was an admirer of Keats, whose 'Endymion' Lockhart had described as 'drivelling idiocy'.[139] In an obituary notice for Keats in *The London Magazine* (April 1821) Procter urges the public to 'cast aside every little and unworthy prejudice, and do justice to the high memory of a young but undoubted poet'.[140]

The London Magazine, edited by John Scott, supported writers such as Keats, Leigh Hunt, William Hazlitt and Procter himself, whose work the magazine published and reviewed. Procter's poetry was also published in albums such as *Heath's Book of Beauty*, edited by the Countess of Blessington, and in *The Literary Gazette*, edited by William Jerdan.[141] In addition Procter wrote numerous essays which were collected in *Essays and Tales in Prose* (1853). They include a memoir of Shakespeare, 'A Chapter on Portraits' (an essay promoting the portrait as opposed to the history

---

[135] Patmore, op. cit., Chapters I-III.

[136] Armour, op. cit., pp. 41-42.

[137] Patmore, op. cit., p. 28.

[138] [J.G. Lockhart], 'On the Cockney School of Poetry. No. I', *Blackwood's Edinburgh Magazine*, II, 1817, p. 39.

[139] [J.G. Lockhart], 'On the Cockney School of Poetry. No. IV', *Blackwood's Edinburgh Magazine*, III, 1818, p. 519.

[140] *The London Magazine*, III, 1821, p. 427.

[141] *The Literary Gazette* (1817-1862) published book reviews and long extracts from works reviewed. Contributors included George Crabbe, Mary Russell Mitford and Letitia Landon.

painting) and two essays on poetry, 'On English Poetry' and 'A Defence of Poetry', which argue for the importance of the imagination and for the status of poetry as the first of the fine arts.

Procter's published poetry and drama include *Dramatic Scenes, and other Poems* (1819); *A Sicilian Story, with Diego de Montilla, and Other Poems* (1820); *Marcian Colonna, an Italian Tale, with three Dramatic Scenes, and other Poems* (1820); *Mirandola* (1821) (a tragedy which had a successful run at Covent Garden Theatre with W.C. Macready in the lead role); *The Flood of Thessaly, the Girl of Provence and Other Poems* (1823); *English Songs* (1832) and *Dramatic Scenes with Other Poems* (1857).

Reviews of Procter's poetry in *The London Magazine*, *The Literary Gazette* and *The Edinburgh Review* (edited by Lord Francis Jeffrey, the Whig politician and Scottish judge) were generally favourable. However, the *Blackwoods* reviewer, almost certainly John Lockhart, moved from admiring and encouraging Procter's work to denigrating him as a 'Greekish Cockney'. Lockhart had praised *Dramatic Scenes and Other Poems* (1819) for their 'modesty', by contrast with the 'sottish self-sufficiency of the Cockney School' who, he adds, 'are desirous of investing Mr Cornwall with the insignia of their order'. He applauds Procter's 'exquisite tact' and 'original power', and his ability to depict 'the feelings of our daily human life through the soft light of imagination'.[142]

But Lockhart's review of *The Flood of Thessaly, The Girl of Provence and other Poems* (1823) was damning. He refers to it as a 'very dull volume' which lacks the vigour of a 'masculine intellect' and advises Procter to 'give up the trade'. Lockhart singles out 'The Flood of Thessaly', a reworking of the Pyrrha and Deucalion story, for its silliness in jumping on to the 'Cockney' bandwagon and wishing to be 'Greekish'. He attacks the narrative poem 'The Girl of Provence' as a tale of the 'drivelling of idiotcy' and refers to Procter's earlier poem 'Marcian Colonna' (1821) as 'totally uninteresting'.[143]

Although Procter's poetry is indeed often cluttered up with classical allusions and the language and plots are at times exaggerated to the point of absurdity, the simplicity and sympathetic tone of his depictions of emotional states often counter poetic excess. *The London Magazine* had praised *The Flood of Thessaly, The Girl of Provence, and Other Poems* as Procter's 'very best work by far' and certainly 'The Flood of Thessaly' and particu-

---

[142] [J.G. Lockhart?], 'Dramatic Scenes, and Other Poems, by Barry Cornwall', *Blackwood's Edinburgh Magazine*, V, 1819, pp. 310-316.
[143] [J.G. Lockhart], 'Remarks on Mr Barry Cornwall's New Poems', *Blackwood's Edinburgh Magazine*, XIII, 1823, pp. 532-541.

larly 'The Girl of Provence', are powerful depictions of emotions taken to their furthest limits.[144]

The sea figures in many of Procter's poems ('Marcian Colonna', 'Midsummer Madness', 'A Dream') as a place where extremes of emotion and madness may find some relief but where those emotions may also prove to be overwhelming. The deluge which vexes 'the air / To madness' in 'The Flood of Thessaly' metaphorically describes a flood of stormy emotion which engulfs human frailty. Procter describes this state poignantly:

> All perished then:- The last who lived was one
> Who clung to life because a frail child lay
> Upon her heart: weary, and gaunt, and worn,
> From point to point she sped . . .[145]

'The Girl of Provence', 'Marcian Colonna' and 'A Sicilian Story' (another rendering of the Boccaccian tale upon which Keats based 'The Eve of St Agnes') are notable for the immense sympathy Procter shows to the women protagonists and to Marcian, an exile and a lunatic (see Chapter 4). The protagonists are all driven or self-driven to insanity, and Procter depicts the state of madness with great sensitivity.[146]

In 'Marcian Colonna' the protagonist Marcian is depicted as maddened by the favouritism shown to his elder brother.[147] He is incarcerated by his father in a Franciscan 'convent prison' in the Appenines where he recovers some of his sanity and then returns to his family.[148] After his brother dies he elopes with his brother's widow Julia who has remarried and been widowed a second time. When Marcian discovers that Julia's second husband is alive he escapes to sea with Julia and they end up in a cave where Marcian poisons her when she tries to return to her husband. Throughout the tale Marcian moves in and out of a state of lunacy.

In an admiring review in *The Literary Gazette* ('the style is eminently sweet') the writer compares Marcian's disturbed emotional condition with

---

[144] *The London Magazine*, VII, 1823, pp. 460-462.

[145] Barry Cornwall, *The Flood of Thessaly, The Girl of Provence and Other Poems*, London: Henry Colburn and Co., 1823, pp. 29, 30.

[146] Procter was reflecting a contemporary change to a more sympathetic attitude towards insanity. The 'moral management' of lunatics was being advocated as an alternative to physical restraint. (See Michael Mason, 'Browning and the Dramatic Monologue', *Writers and Their Background. Robert Browning*, Ed. Isobel Armstrong, London: G. Bell & Sons, 1974, pp. 259-260.)

[147] *The Poetical Works of Milman, Bowles, Wilson and Barry Cornwall*, Paris: A. and W. Galignani, 1829, pp. 90-103.

[148] ibid., p. 92, V.

that of Hamlet.[149] It is an interesting comparison as it may be that Procter was himself identified with this Hamlet figure in that his poetry often indirectly expresses the confused desire to both articulate and escape from strong and painful emotions, either through travel and exile, or by recourse to madness. Emotions frequently remain unresolved.

Procter's dramatic works often take the form of 'Dramatic Scenes' and even his autobiography is presented as a 'fragment'.[150] It is as though he cannot quite commit himself to a more complete exploration of his protagonists or of himself, along with their and his emotional states. The sense of incompleteness in Procter's work may be linked to the view that he had not worked out a more defined view of the world. Donald Reiman has written that Bryan Procter's poems have 'no philosophic center, stated or implied' and that 'he had nothing specific to say to the world'.[151] Richard Armour also expresses this view: 'We look in vain for philosophic penetration.'[152]

Procter's poems do lack a binding philosophical viewpoint. He tells stories, often of lost or doomed love, which do not arrive at any philosophical conclusion. They do, however, often have a strong affective 'centre' which gives the poems some coherence and strength. His poetry might be considered feminine in that Procter seems less keen to make a forceful philosophical point than to describe difficult emotional states. He portrays himself in some of his writings as unconcerned about making his mark as a poet, and to that extent his apparent lack of ambition also aligns him with a more feminine position. In his 'Autobiographical Fragment' Procter writes of his schooldays at Harrow:

> Then I was without ambition, – a fatal defect, and one which (as some critics say) argues a corresponding defect of intellect . . . I always wrote for the mere pleasure of writing.[153]

Procter's lack of ambition may be linked to his expressed desire not to be identified as a man involved in politics. Patmore writes:

> It has been made a matter of complaint by some of his friends that it was difficult or impossible to get him to reveal his opinions upon

---

[149] *The Literary Gazette and Journal of Belles Lettres, Arts, Sciences, etc.,* 1820, pp. 369–371.

[150] Patmore, op. cit.

[151] Bryan Waller Procter, *A Sicilian Story and Mirandola,* Intro. Donald H. Reiman, New York and London: Garland Publishing, Inc., 1977, p. viii.

[152] Armour, op. cit., p. 179.

[153] Patmore, op. cit., pp. 23–24.

political, philosophical, and other matters, some of which lie at the
root of life and action.[154]

Richard Armour writes that Procter was 'only mildly a Whig', but married
Anne Skepper 'who was avowedly High Tory'.[155] Even when Procter does
express a view he does so unwillingly or apologetically. In a letter to John
Bowring, the first editor of the *Westminster Review*, he writes:

> I hate politics it is true – But in the case of Greece – and of Spain also
> – one is forced amongst one's antipathies – for the sake of our own
> private comfortable opinion.[156]

Procter is referring to the Greek War of Independence (1821–1829) and the
civil war being fought in Spain. In a letter to James Fields dated 1854 he
refers to the Czar's 'unscrupulous greediness' with reference to the Crimean
War, but adds 'what have I to do with politics, or you?'[157] Procter did,
however, adopt an anti-slavery position and wrote to Fields in 1861:

> If you were to stand up at once (and finally) against the slave-trade,
> your band of soldiers would have a more decided *principle* to fight
> for. But –

But again Procter undermines and apologises for expressing his opinion by
adding that he really knows 'little or nothing' and that he knows that in
Boston they 'are more abolitionist than in the more southern countries'.[158]

Procter's lack of ambition and unwillingness to express a political opinion
both contribute to his failure to make a more definite mark within his wide
circle of friends and contemporaries. In his own words he appears to have
settled for floating along 'on the happy stream of mediocrity' in which he
found himself.[159] Coventry Patmore writes that the extinction of Procter's
'literary ambition' coincided with his marriage to Anne Skepper in 1824.[160]
Richard Armour states that Procter realized that 'law work' was a better
guarantee 'of a regular income than a career of letters'.[161]

In 1832 Procter's *English Songs* were published. Along with *Dramatic*

---

[154] ibid., p. 103.
[155] Armour, op. cit., p. 26.
[156] MS, B.W. Procter to John Bowring (4.3.1824), University of Iowa Libraries.
[157] Fields, op. cit., p. 110.
[158] ibid., p. 115.
[159] Patmore, op. cit., p. 10.
[160] ibid., p. 57.
[161] Armour, op. cit., p. 82.

Scenes with Other Poems (1857) these were his final publications. In his 'Introduction' to *English Songs* Procter states that 'England is singularly barren of Song-writers' and that song has been neglected in favour of 'long compositions' which are often tedious and mere 'verbiage'.[162] Procter seems to be unconsciously expressing some frustration with his own fragmentary and inconclusive narrative poems.

English Songs include some interesting lyrics about fallen women and an extremely poignant reworking of Mignon's song from Goethe's *Wilhelm Meister's Apprenticeship*, 'Home (A Duet)' (see Chapter 4), but many of the lyrics are fairly unimpressive. They were, however, very popular. Richard Armour writes that acclaim for *English Songs* probably exceeded 'that of any other of his works'. Longfellow, amongst others, expressed his admiration to Procter:

> They are almost the only real songs in the language; that is, lyrics that have the pulsation of music in them.[163]

Many of the lyrics were set to music by Chevalier Neukomm (Sigismund Von Neukomm).[164] Longfellow particuarly admired the gentle lyric 'A Petition to Time' which is an expression of Procter's general philosophy insofar as he possessed one:

> Touch us gently, Time!
>   We've not proud nor soaring wings:
> *Our* ambition, *our* content
>   Lies in simple things.
> Humble voyagers are We,
> O'er Life's dim unsounded sea,
> Seeking only some calm clime:-
> Touch us *gently*, gentle Time![165]

Time would become precious to Procter. The date of the publication of *English Songs*, 1832, coincided with his appointment as one of the Metropolitan Commissioners of Lunacy. This office would occupy much of his time as it involved visiting asylums within the London area and drawing up an annual report for the Lord Chancellor. The post carried a stipend of £800

[162] Barry Cornwall, *English Songs and Other small Poems*, London: Edward Moxon, 1832, pp. v, ix–x.

[163] Armour, op. cit., p. 177. Patmore, op. cit., pp. 298-299.

[164] Sigismund Von Neukomm (1778-1858). Neukomm was a pupil of Haydn and composed songs and oratorios which achieved great popularity.

[165] Barry Cornwall, *English Songs and Other small Poems* (1832), p. 191.

per annum which was a comfortable income at this period.[166] Armour describes it as a 'political office' and writes that Procter 'was enough aligned with the Whigs that, with the return of their party to office, Lord Brougham could appoint him one of the Metropolitan Commissioners of Lunacy'.[167]

In 1845 Procter was appointed a permanent Commissioner, one of six, three legal and three medical, who were appointed to the Board under the Act for the Regulation of the Care and Treatment of Lunatics. As a legal commissioner he received an annual salary of £1500 which was a considerable income. His duties included visiting asylums throughout England to inspect them thoroughly and enquire 'whether any Patient is under Restraint, and why'.[168] In a letter to Macvey Napier (a Scottish lawyer and editor of the *Edinburgh Review* from 1829), dated 1844, Procter writes 'I have seen *all* the asylums in England and Wales'.[169]

In 1858 Procter wrote to John Forster giving some graphic descriptions of a Liverpool Workhouse infirmary:

> In the infirmiary appropriated to Idiots we saw, at the foot of one bed, a coffin – *in* the bed the poor dead patient, who had escaped from the world – happily. The Nurse covered the face at Wilkes's request. A poor nervous Epileptic was in the next bed – within a couple of feet of – the BODY! We then went through the ward for children – there were 100 of them (more) – some helpless and almost all deserted. In one large room there was a crowd – 60 or 70 – none of them above 3 years old. The more cheerful the little faces looked the more dismal it appeared. I cannot tell you how affecting I thought it.

Procter describes the 'Saturnalia' of Williamson Square, Liverpool which comprised 'Irish and English and Scotch vagabonds – sailors, dockmen etc. blackguards of all sorts – and *women* in crowds'.[170]

In the following year, 1859, Procter's series of poems called 'Trade Songs' appeared weekly between 30th April and 25th June in *All The Year Round* (Ed. C. Dickens). They had titles such as 'The Workhouse Nurse', 'The Blacksmith', 'Spinners and Weavers' and 'The Night Beggar'.[171]

---

[166] Armour, op. cit., pp. 95-96. This stipend was roughly equivalent to the salary of a Senior Clerk in the Civil Service (Best, op. cit., p. 107).

[167] ibid., p. 95.

[168] ibid., pp. 104-105.

[169] MS 34625, B.W. Procter to M. Napier (1844), British Library.

[170] Armour, op. cit., p. 261.

[171] *All The Year Round*, I, 1859.

Procter's work as a Commissioner had clearly provided him with material for his poems.

These songs are less rhetorically powerful than the poems of Thomas Hood, Procter's contemporary. There are, however, some interesting lyrics. For example 'Spinners and Weavers', is about exploited women who imagine the places their flax, along with the labour which has gone into spinning it, will end up:

> Twine the flax, oh, pretty flax,
> Thou shalt be hidden in wax;
> Thou shalt rise a blazing torch,
> Fit for lamp or palace porch;
> Thou shalt look on mighty things,
> Noble eyes, – perhaps a king's!
>> Draw the threads, twist the twine,
>> Whose bright labour equals mine?

The 'sister spinners' are described as looking like 'the Furies that they were within'.[172] Significantly it is a poem about exploited women, with whom Procter was nearly always sympathetic.

In some of the letters written whilst touring the circuits as a Commissioner Procter does express some weariness and distaste for his office. In 1844 he wrote to John Forster:

> I hear nothing – I see nothing, but tunnels and railroads – madmen and chambermaids . . . I am sick of travelling . . . the frightful number of children at Manchester – in the suburbs leading to Oldham – I saw and groaned at. They are like little locusts, come to eat away all the corn and food.[173]

He did, however, serve as a Commissioner for another seventeen years. In 1861, aged 74, Procter relinquished the office after thirty years' service and was replaced by John Forster. He was awarded a pension of £625 per annum.[174] Two to three years earlier Procter had been bequeathed a legacy of £6500 (a solatium) by John Kenyon, so the Procters still had a substantial income.[175]

Between 1832 and 1861 much of Procter's time was taken up with

[172] ibid., I (21.5.1859), p. 88.
[173] Armour, op. cit., pp. 224–225.
[174] ibid., p. 114.
[175] ibid., p. 111.

Commission work, but he found time to write *The Life of Edmund Kean* which was published in 1835.[176] This biography received poor reviews, with Blackwoods designating it the 'silliest book of the season'.[177] Richard Armour refers to it as 'a splenetic account'.[178] It is certainly a biography which focuses on the florid, debauched and profligate Kean and does not concern itself much with any finer points. Procter is, though, amused by Kean's exploits as well as being mildly 'splenetic'. The most interesting aspect of the biography is the discussion of Kean's playing of Shylock at Drury Lane in 1814 and more generally the maltreatment of Jews and their ignominious place in the history of 'heroism'.[179]

In 1866 Procter's final work, *Charles Lamb. A Memoir*, was published to much critical acclaim. Dickens wrote to Procter that he had read the biography with 'inexpressible pleasure and interest'.[180] In the biography Procter admires Lamb's modesty: 'He had no craving for popularity, nor even for fame.' Although Lamb was a Whig he 'seldom ventured upon the stormy sea of politics' Procter states.[181] He was clearly a kindred spirit.

The biography is notable for its account of Lamb's intermittently 'insane' sister, Mary Lamb. He provides a graphic account of Mary's horrific murder of her mother:

> Mary seized a 'case knife' . . . pursued a little girl (her apprentice) round the room; hurled about the dinner forks; and, finally, in a fit of uncontrollable frenzy, stabbed her mother to the heart.[182]

Procter refers to William Hazlitt's observation that, when sane, Mary was in fact the 'most rational and wisest woman whom he had ever known'.[183] Lamb himself was subject to bouts of lunacy and was once placed for six weeks in Hoxton Lunatic Asylum.[184] The brother and sister are described by Procter with affection and sympathy, and it as though writing this biography provided Procter with solace for what appears to be some considerable disturbance in his own mind.

---

176 [Barry Cornwall], *The Life of Edmund Kean*, 2 Vols, London: Edward Moxon, 1835.
177 *Blackwood's Edinburgh Magazine*, 38, 1835, p. 71.
178 Armour, op. cit., p. 70.
179 [Cornwall], *The Life of Edmund Kean*, pp. 46-50.
180 *The Letters of Charles Dickens*, op. cit., II, p. 265.
181 Barry Cornwall, *Charles Lamb. A Memoir*, London: Edward Moxon & Co., 1866, pp. 11, 16.
182 ibid., p. 29.
183 ibid., p. 126.
184 ibid., p. 28.

Procter was disturbed by his relationship to his own writing. Despite the fact that he described himself as being 'without ambition' several of his poems express an anxiety about not having achieved greater fame. In 'A Poet's Reply' the speaker addresses his critics:

> Jeer me no more. What would you have? Speak out!
> You bid me 'Dare!' Well, then, I *dare*? What more?

In reply to their fear that his work will 'lie i' the dark' he asks if there's not 'wide room for all?' He concludes that some day he will 'burst abroad; / And take a flight, as the wild eagles do'.[185]

Some reviewers of Procter's early work had anticipated that he might give up on or let slip his career and early success. John Wilson (?), in his admiring review of 'A Sicilian Story' in *Blackwood's*, urges Procter to 'write now that he is young and hopeful'.[186] In a 'Sonnet' published in September 1820 in *The London Magazine* the writer urges 'Barry Cornwall' to reveal himself as Bryan Procter. He writes:

> No longer then, as 'lowly substitute,
> Factor, or PROCTOR, for another's gains,'
> Suffer the admiring world to be deceived;
> Lest thou thyself, by self of fame bereaved.[187]

In a poem titled 'An Apology in Verse' Procter writes: 'Vain effort! I resign the pen', but in the poem, 'To a Poet, abandoning his Art' he writes 'Friend! desert not thou the Muse!'[188]

Procter was involved in a painful struggle relating to his writing. It is interesting that he chose the name 'Cornwall' as his pseudonym. The name is suggestive of a desire to explore his own creative limits whilst signalling that he may come up against a 'wall' or imaginary 'land's end' when it comes to writing. The poem 'A Sea-Shore Echo' poignantly expresses Procter's sense that his own voice might finally become an anonymous 'echo':

---

[185] *English Songs and Other small Poems* (1851), p. 254.

[186] [John Wilson (?)], 'A Sicilian Story, With Other Poems; by Barry Cornwall', *Blackwood's Edinburgh Magazine*, VI, 1820, p. 643.

[187] *The London Magazine*, II, 1820, p. 302.

[188] *Heath's Book of Beauty*, 1843, pp. 270-271. *English Songs and Other small Poems* (1851), pp. 30-31.

No power, no shrine, no gold hast thou:
So Fame, the harlot, leaves thee now,
    A frail, false friend!
And thus, like all things here below,
    Thy fortunes end![189]

Procter was clearly disturbed by his status as a 'minor' and perhaps in the future an anonymous poet.

Finally, he chose to remain in the shadows of the writers he advised and supported, in particular Robert Browning. Procter, John Forster and Thomas Noon Talfourd had helped prepare the first collected edition of Browning's works published in 1849, and had edited a second collected edition in 1863.[190] In a poem titled 'A Familiar Epistle to Robert Browning' written in 1839 Procter urges Browning to 'Freely sing!' and to 'Soar freely, like the eagle strong of wing!'. He describes himself as 'weak, and old' and imprisoned:

                by the long day's ceaseless toil,
        'Of wearisome law-winding, coil on coil.'
        Such toil fills up *my* life.[191]

Procter presents a sad but endearing figure who might have achieved the status of 'major' poet if he had spent more time on his writing as Elizabeth Barrett Browning had suggested.

He was, though, an extremely important formative influence on his daughter. The powerful affectivity of many of his poems and his exploration of disturbing emotional states, along with his sympathetic interest in women – particularly fallen women – and conditions of poverty, made a strong impact on Adelaide. His decision to devote most of his time to law and Commission work may also have impressed Adelaide with the importance of making a substantial contribution to social and philanthropic work.

Procter's complex relationship to his own writing and his lack of ambition, however, would have provided his daughter with a difficult model for her own writing. Several poems in *English Songs and Other small Poems* (1851) are addressed to his daughter. They include 'Golden-Tressed

---

[189] *The Poetical Works of Milman, Bowles, Wilson and Barry Cornwall*, pp. 176–177.

[190] *New Letters of Robert Browning*, p. 50, note 1. *Selections from the Poetical Works of Robert Browning*, Ed. J. Forster and B.W. Procter, London: Chapman & Hall, 1863.

[191] *English Songs and Other small Poems* (1851), pp. xxv–xxx.

Adelaide', 'To Adelaide' ('Child of my heart! My sweet, belov'd First-born!'), 'Love the Poet, Pretty One!' and 'To a Poetess'. The last two I am assuming are addressed to his daughter and these two poems taken together convey a very mixed message. In 'Love the Poet, Pretty One' the speaker urges his child to love the poet who will teach her 'how to reap / Music from the golden lyre'. He also reassures her that when the poet seems 'Dark and still, and cold as clay' he is only 'shadowed by his Dream!' which will 'pass away'.[192] In 'To a Poetess' the speaker asks the poetess:

> Dread'st thou lest thou should'st die unknown?
> Why fear? since all the strength of Fame
> And Death have this poor power alone,-
> To give thee an uncertain fame.[193]

Enthusiasm for poetry and the creative process are countered by a rather bleak foreshadowing of the possibility of future anonymity, which seems a depressing message to convey to an aspiring daughter.

In a general sense, though, Procter was an advocate of women's writing. On his birthday in 1856 he wrote to Browning expressing his admiration for Elizabeth Barrett Browning's *Aurora Leigh* which he describes as being 'alive with fine & brilliant thoughts'.[194] Procter also praised Charlotte Brontë's *Villette* which he describes as 'very clever, graphic, vigorous' and as '"man's meat". and not the whipped syllabub, which is *all* froth, without any jam at the bottom.'[195]

Interestingly Procter, along with his wife Anne Skepper, had been mistaken for Charlotte Brontë when they were identified by Charles Dilke of *The Athenaeum* as the co-authors of *Jane Eyre* (1848). Thackeray wrote to William Brookfield 'Old Dilke of the Athenaeum vows that Procter & his wife between them wrote Jane Eyre'. As *Jane Eyre* had been dedicated to Thackeray and *Vanity Fair* to Bryan Procter, Dilke assumed that the authors were reciprocating dedications.[196]

The 'lemon and honey' combination of Anne Skepper and Bryan Procter was interesting and impressive. As the daughter of parents who made a significant mark on the London literary landscape Procter, whilst benefiting from their interests and encouragement, would almost certainly have

---

[192] ibid., pp. 121-122.

[193] ibid., p. 207.

[194] MS, B.W. Procter to R. Browning (21.11.1856), University of Iowa Libraries.

[195] Fields, op. cit., p. 104.

[196] Ray, *The Letters and Private Papers of W.M. Thackeray*, II, p. 441.

encountered difficulties in finding her own voice and place as a poet –
difficulties which would have been exacerbated by her father's ambivalence
about writing and making a more forceful impression.

Adelaide Procter's response to and critique of a series of 'fathers' or
familiar authorities – religious, poetic and editorial – are the focus of this
study. Her negotiations with these authorities include an extremely interesting
reworking of her father's preoccupation with anonymity. Procter explores
the notion of anonymity and in the process her own poetic voice emerges as
strong and compelling (see Chapter 4). It was a voice which finally totally
eclipsed her father's and strongly appealed to mid to late nineteenth-century
readers.

Nineteenth-century Reviews

From the beginning of Procter's career as a poet she shows considerable
reserve in terms of promoting her work, and in this she may well have been
affected by her father's anxiety about his writing. She had created the fairly
elaborate persona of the shy, retiring Miss Berwick whom Dickens
uncovered in 1854. In a letter to Procter, expressing his great surprise at the
revelation, he refers to the cameo Procter provided for W.H. Wills, Dickens's
sub-editor. Miss Berwick was, according to Wills, a governess who was
'rather advanced in life'. She had 'taken to writing verses' as her feelings
had been 'desperately wounded'. She was 'unhappy' but 'keenly sensitive to
encouragement' and sometimes thought of never writing again.[197]

Although Procter clearly enjoyed the joke, the shyness of the 'Miss
Berwick' persona is significant. Procter's reason for submitting her poems
under a pseudonym – that she did not want them to be published on account
of her status as Bryan Procter's daughter – may have been compounded by a
fear that she might outstrip her father. Bessie Parkes writes of Procter:

> I think it caused her a feeling of shyness amounting to pain to have so
> far outstripped her poet-father in popular estimation. 'Papa is a poet. I
> only write verses.'[198]

Procter was also keen not to elevate the position of the poet when she
expressed the view, referred to by Jessie Boucherett, that poetry should not

---

[197] *The Letters of Charles Dickens*, Ed. Walter Dexter, Bloomsbury: The
Nonesuch Press, 1938, 3 Vols, II, pp. 608–609.

[198] Belloc, op. cit., p. 170.

'unfit' the poet for 'the practical business of life' (p. 39). The picture of Procter Dickens paints in his Introduction to *Legends and Lyrics* suggests that poetry was just one amongst many activities which claimed her attention. The epigraph to *Legends and Lyrics* reads:

> 'Our tokens of love are for the most part barbarous. Cold and lifeless, because they do not represent our life. The only gift is a portion of thyself. Therefore let the farmer give his corn; the miner, a gem; the sailor, coral and shells; the painter, his picture; and the poet, his poem.' – Emerson's Essays.
>
> A.A.P.
> May, 1858 [199]

This epigraph renders the poet important in that her poetry is described as a 'gift' which is integral to the person who gives it – the poem defines the poet – and the list does culminate with the 'poet'. But the epigraph also adds to the sense that Procter wished herself to be seen as a worker amongst other workers.

The figure of Procter, as a shy daughter who holds back within the shadow of her father, and as a worker who modestly labours alongside her fellow workers, is suggestive of the presence of a reticence and humility which may have undermined real ambition. Procter's apparently reserved position is interesting, though, when considered in the light of her immense popularity whereby she was not at all anonymous.

Unlike other nineteenth-century women poets, such as Felicia Hemans, Letitia Landon, Elizabeth Barrett Browning and Christina Rossetti, Procter does not overtly ponder the vexed question of the poet, particularly the woman poet and her accession to fame. Felicia Hemans in the poem 'Joan of Arc in Rheims' concludes the poem with a paeon to the 'home' Joan has forsaken for 'fame': 'too much of fame / Had shed its radiance on thy peasant name'. 'Fame' is nonetheless a central preoccupation for Hemans who writes about famous women in history and the wives of famous men.[200]

In Letitia Landon's 'The History of the Lyre' and Elizabeth Barrett Browning's *Aurora Leigh* the lonely position of the woman poet is considered. In 'The History of the Lyre' the male speaker observes the

[199] Adelaide Anne Procter, *Legends and Lyrics. A Book of Verses*, Intro. Charles Dickens, London: George Bell and Sons, 1882. The quotation is an extract from 'Gifts', 'Second Series' (1844), *The Essays of Ralph Waldo Emerson*, Intro. Edward F. O'Day, San Francisco: John Henry Nash, 1934, p. 212.

[200] *The Complete Works of Mrs Hemans*, Edited by Her Sister [Harriet Hughes], 2 Vols, New York: D. Appleton and Company, 1856, II, p. 120.

loneliness of Eulalie, a singer and poet. In her own words she has given up the possibility of 'the loveliness of home', which she might have created, to pursue her art.[201] Aurora in *Aurora Leigh* moves away from Romney and the 'garden' of love and it is only after ten years of pursuing the lonely but successful path of the woman poet that Aurora may be reconciled with Romney.[202] In Christina Rossetti's sonnet sequence 'Monna Innominata' (1880) an unnamed woman poet assumes the usually male role of sonneteer and draws attention to the 'poetic aptitude' of the unknown woman poet.[203]

For all these writers the position of the woman poet, even when unnamed, is a central preoccupation. By contrast, Procter is much more concerned with anonymous and often lower class women who have not successfully found a place or a role. When she does write about the poet in the narrative poem 'True Honours' a blind male poet, a writer of 'humble verses' loved by the poor but not achieving wider fame, is the central figure depicted (and the figure is suggestive of her father) (pp. 24–30).

Procter may not have discussed 'the poet' in her work because she was reserved about her writing and was not as bold as some of her contemporaries who wished to foreground the difficulties encountered by women poets. However, her poems may have appealed to her readers partly because they were not so much concerned with the specific position of the poetess as with the position of women generally. In her important and fine narrative poems, 'A Tomb in Ghent' and 'A Legend of Provence', Procter's exploration of anonymity is less concerned with accession to fame than with the emotions of the women protagonists which have not fully found expression.

B.W. Findon in his biography of Arthur Sullivan, who composed the music for Procter's poem 'A Lost Chord', writes that this poem 'has gone straight to the heart of a great nation'.[204] In *The Publishers' Circular* the writer describes Procter's poems as showing 'an intensity of feeling not often found in feminine verse'.[205] When the speaker unconsciously strikes the elusive chord ('I do not know what I was playing', p. 177, l. 5) in 'A Lost Chord' this intensity is felt:

---

[201] *The Poetical Works of L.E.L.*, London: Longman, Rees, Orme, Brown & Green, 1830 , p. 99.

[202] Elizabeth Barrett Browning, *Aurora Leigh*.

[203] Christina Rossetti, *Poems and Prose*, Ed. Jan Marsh, London: Everyman, 1994, pp. 229–237.

[204] Findon, op. cit., p. 150.

[205] *The Publishers' Circular*, 27, 16th February 1864, p. 90.

It flooded the crimson twilight
  Like the close of an Angel's Psalm,
And it lay on my fevered spirit
  With a touch of infinite calm.
                    (p. 177, ll. 9–12)

These tributes to the power and intensity of affective feeling expressed in Procter's poetry are interesting when read alongside the general response of her reviewers and friends, who mostly applaud her lightness of touch and gentle femininity rather than a more penetrating intensity of expression. Aubrey de Vere in his obituary poem, 'On a Catholic poetess', wrote:

She stooped o'er earth's poor brink, light as a breeze . . .[206]

Edwin Arnold, in 'Ilicet', an obituary poem published in *The Victoria Magazine*, wrote of 'her gentle, certain, spirit of ruth' and Procter's close friend, Matilda Hays, praises Adelaide for 'A pure life – purely run' in a memorial poem published in *The English Woman's Journal*.[207] Henry Fothergill Chorley of *The Athenaeum*, in his review of Procter's 'Second Series' of *Legends and Lyrics*, describes Procter's work as ranking 'among the most complete and gentlest poems which we owe to women.'[208] Bessie Parkes writes in the Catholic journal *The Month* in 1866 that 'unruly passion' seemed rarely 'to cross this gentle imagination'. She describes some of Procter's lyrics as being 'destined to float on the surface of English literature' like Wordsworth's 'picture of the maid who dwelt by the banks of Dove'.[209] In *English Poetesses* Eric Robertson describes Procter as being 'very unobtrusive as a literary personage'.[210]

Although apparently complimentary these descriptions create the sense that Procter's poetry is gentle rather than forceful and impressive. Even though Parkes compares Procter with Wordsworth it is his 'Lucy' with whom her poetry is identified. It is as though Procter's poetry merges with, rather than makes a more striking impression on, the literary landscape, or, 'light as a breeze', disappears.

---

[206] MS, BRP X, 84, Parkes papers, Girton College Library.

[207] *The Victoria Magazine*, II, 1864, p. 386. *The English Woman's Journal*, XIII, 1864, p. 109.

[208] [Henry Fothergill Chorley], 'Legends and Lyrics: A Book of Verses. By Adelaide Anne Procter. Second Volume (Bell & Daldy)', *The Athenaeum*, II, 1860, p. 907.

[209] *The Month*, IV, 1866, pp. 84, 87.

[210] Eric S. Robertson, *English Poetesses: A Series of Critical Biographies With Illustrative Extracts*, London: Cassell & Company Limited, 1883, p. 226.

In these descriptions Procter apparently conforms to John Keble's view of the poet as one who brings relief, 'soothing men's emotions and steadying the balance of their mind'. For Keble, good poetry is essentially devotional and the poet should not be concerned with originality or making an impression. He describes a 'becoming shrinking from publicity' enabled by the method and art of poetry which, like medicine, brings relief.[211] Procter is reviewed as a poet who does not disturb her readers. She is also represented as a writer whose expression is simple, direct and free of complexity. Bessie Parkes in the poem 'For Adelaide' writes:

> Who is the Poet? He who sings
> Of high, abstruse, and hidden things,
> Or rather he who with a liberal voice
> Does with the glad hearts of all earth rejoice?[212]

Similarly the reviewer in *The English Woman's Journal* contrasts Procter's 'distinct utterance' with the 'brain-weaving' and 'intellectual harlequinades' of the Spasmodic school of poetry.[213]

These reviews suggest that Procter was considered to be quintessentially a poet, but a poet who was not preoccupied with complexity and 'hidden things'. Henry Fothergill Chorley wrote that 'Without any startling originality, it is Miss Procter's own' and not attributable to her father, Wordsworth, Tennyson or the Brownings. He admires Procter's fine lyric 'A Doubting Heart' for its sweetness, and compares the lyric 'A Dream' with the work of the German Romantic poet Heinrich Heine.[214] In his review of the 'Second Series' of *Legends and Lyrics*, Fothergill Chorley quotes Procter's lyric 'Three Roses' and again compares Procter's poetry with that of Heine. He writes:

> Were what we offer next signed Heine, . . . we should have dozens of translations of it ere Valentine's Day comes.[215]

---

[211] *Keble's Lectures on Poetry, 1832–41*, Trans. Edward Kershaw Francis, 2 Vols, Oxford at the Clarendon Press, 1912, I, pp. 21–22.

[212] Bessie Rayner Parkes, *Poems*, London: John Chapman, 1855, pp. 26–27.

[213] *The English Woman's Journal*, I, 1858, p. 341. The Spasmodic School was the name given to a group of poets which included P.J. Bailey, J.W. Marston, S. Dobell and Alexander Smith. The poetry was notable for its obscurity and extravagant imagery.

[214] [Henry Fothergill Chorley], 'Legends and Lyrics: a Book of Verses. By Adelaide Procter. (Bell & Daldy)', *The Athenaeum*, I, 1858, p. 712.

[215] ibid., II, 1860, p. 907.

The poem 'Three Roses' (see Chapter 3) is in fact ironic, subtle and complex, as well as being intensely lyrical, as were many of Heine's lyrics. A woman who initiates a relationship with a gift of a rose to a man is shown to end up in the grave as a result of her initiative. The poem demonstrates both 'originality', in that a woman is shown to take the initiative in a love relationship, and a power of expression which is sexually rather than just sweetly suggestive:

> Just when the red June Roses blow
> She gave me one, – a year ago.
> A Rose whose crimson breath revealed
> The secret that its heart concealed,
> And whose half shy, half tender grace
> Blushed back upon the giver's face.
>   A year ago – a year ago –
>   To hope was not to know.
>   (p. 199, ll. 1–8)

Procter's use of symbolism to express emotion accords with J.S. Mill's view that poetry is the 'thoughts and words in which emotion spontaneously embodies itself'.[216] The body of the rose in the poem is depicted as robust and as potentially surviving its demise. A reviewer for the *Dublin University Magazine* in 1859 describes Procter as having 'the power of making the abstract concrete, which is the chief intellectual characteristic of the mind of woman'.[217] Inadvertently he draws attention to the intellectual strength of some of Procter's poetry.

The reviews of the two series of *Legends and Lyrics* in *The English Woman's Journal* come closest to recognising the real substance of Procter's poetry. The first describes Procter's poems as 'vigorous and healthy' and the reviewer of the 'Second Series' of *Legends and Lyrics* writes that Procter is gifted with 'a profound insight into the subtler portions of common humanity'.[218] The fine lyric 'Unexpressed' is quoted in the first review, providing an example of Procter's exploration of the difficulties of expression:

[216] John Stuart Mill, 'Thoughts on Poetry and its Varieties' (1833, revised 1859), *English Critical Essays (Nineteenth Century)*, Ed. Edmund D. Jones, London: Oxford University Press, 1916, p. 355.

[217] *Dublin University Magazine. A Literary and Political Journal*, LIII, 1859, p. 400.

[218] *The English Woman's Journal*, I, 1858, p. 344; VI, 1861, p. 354.

Things of Time have voices: speak and perish.
Art and Love speak – but their words must be
Like sighings of illimitable forests,
And waves of an unfathomable sea.

(p. 147, ll. 33-36)

The reviewer of the 'Second Series' is, however, keen to dissociate Procter
from the emotions expressed in the poem 'Envy' which is quoted in the
review. Procter is credited with 'divining thoughts and feelings' which were
'foreign' to her experience.[219] The strength of the poem is recognised,
though, and it is worth quoting this powerful and disturbing lyric in full:

Envy

He was the first always: Fortune
    Shone bright in his face.
I fought for years; with no effort
    He conquered the place:
We ran; my feet were all bleeding,
    But he won the race.

Spite of his many successes
    Men loved him the same;
My one pale ray of good fortune
    Met scoffing and blame.
When we erred, they gave him pity,
    But me – only shame.

My home was still in the shadow,
    His lay in the sun:
I longed in vain: what he asked for
    It straightway was done.
Once I staked all my heart's treasure,
    We played – and he won.

Yes; and just now I have seen him,
    Cold, smiling, and blest,
Laid in his coffin. God help me!
    While he is at rest,
I am cursed still to live: – even
    Death loved him the best.

(pp. 166-167)

---

[219] ibid., 1861.

'Envy' might have been quoted as the epigraph to this book as Procter's struggle to emerge from beneath the shadow of several male authorities, which she did perhaps envy, is at the centre of the discussion. Procter's poetic reserve does at times succeed in diverting attention from the strong emotions which are often conveyed in her poems. *The English Woman's Journal* reviewer preferred to locate the disturbing emotion of envy in a projected outsider who is apparently unknown to the gentle lyric poetess. It is, however, Procter's exploration of anonymous protagonists and their unnamed emotions which lies at the heart of her work. These explorations demonstrate the extent to which Procter did emerge from the shadow of the authorities she both revered and from which her poetry struggles to free itself to achieve fuller expression.

Twentieth Century Reviews and Reassessments

Ferdinand Janku's monograph of Procter, *Adelaide Anne Procter. Ihr Leben Und Ihre Werke* was published in 1912. Janku's account of Procter's life and work is fairly sketchy in terms of biographical detail and his readings and summaries of the poems focus on Procter's religious attitude and social conscience but with little discussion. He does, though, make some interesting comments on Procter's conversion to Catholicism in the context of the Tractarian or Oxford Movement. Janku states that a combination of the increased tendency towards materialism resulting from the Industrial Revolution, combined with the 'rationalist tendency' of the Anglican Church, had produced the 'apparently so reactionary Catholicising movement'.[220]

Janku also provides a very useful bibliography of the folktales Procter might have read and used as sources for some of her narrative poems. He writes 'She must have read all available collections'.[221] The monograph is, however, mostly vague and very speculative. He reads Procter conventionally and with admiration as a Victorian poetess who was in touch with the religious sentiments of her readers.

It is only in the last thirty years that Procter's name has begun to be heard again. In 1965 an article by Margaret Maison appeared in *The Listener*. It is titled 'Queen Victoria's favourite poet' and is an account of the life and work of Adelaide Procter. Maison draws attention to the 'complete obscurity' into which Procter has sunk and reminds her readers that she was Queen Victoria's favourite poet. She quotes from the poem 'The Angel of

---

[220] Janku, op. cit., p. 7.
[221] ibid., p. 14.

Death' which the Queen had admired. The temptation to view Procter as a 'perfect period piece' is, though, Maison argues, 'a superficial and unrewarding view'. She goes on to pay tribute to Procter's 'excellently terse' religious poetry which 'at its best ... soars into that pure felicity characteristic of the finer seventeenth century devotional poets'.[222]

The poem 'A Doubting Heart' provides an excellent example of the 'felicity' Maison admires and may be likened to George Herbert's 'The Flower':

> How fresh, O Lord, how sweet and clean
> Are thy returns! ev'n as the flowers in spring;
> To which, besides their own demean,
> The late-past frosts tributes of pleasure bring.
> Grief melts away
> Like snow in May,
> As if there were no such cold thing.
> ('The Flower')[223]

> Why must the flowers die?
> Prisoned they lie
> In the cold tomb, heedless of tears or rain.
> Oh doubting heart!
> They only sleep below
> The soft white ermine snow,
> While winter winds shall blow,
> To breathe and smile upon you soon again.
> ('A Doubting Heart', p. 35, ll. 9-16)

Procter's devotional lyric is similar to Herbert's 'The Flower' in its 'felicity' and form, with the expanding and contracting lines. 'A Doubting Heart', however, has a Keatsian sensuousness ('The soft white ermine snow') which creates the sense of a more material and desiring body being resurrected from 'the cold tomb'.

Maison also admires Procter's love lyrics, some of which, she states, were written after two 'unfortunate love affairs' and show an 'awareness of intense conflict and suffering'.[224] I have not been able to establish with whom Procter had these 'love affairs', but certainly poems such as 'A Love Token', 'A Warning', 'Fidelis', 'Too Late' and 'The Story of the Faithful

---

[222] Maison, op. cit., pp. 636-637.
[223] *A Choice of George Herbert's Verse*, Intro. R.S. Thomas, London: Faber and Faber Limited, 1967, p. 74.
[224] Maison, op. cit., pp. 636-637.

Soul', amongst others, suggest that she may have had reasons to feel cautious and distrustful of love. Finally Maison pays tribute to Procter's work with *The English Woman's Journal* and concludes her article with the poem 'Envy'.

Another account of Procter's life by Susan Drain appeared in the *Dictionary of Literary Biography* in 1984. Drain is less complimentary than Maison about Procter's poetry, referring to Procter's work as 'a curiosity of Victorian taste', but she pays tribute to Procter's 'determination to make her life her own' and goes on to provide an account of her many activities.[225]

In the same year, 1984, Kathleen Hickock's important re-evaluation of women's poetry *Representations of Women: Nineteenth-Century British Women's Poetry* was published. Hickock refers to Adelaide Procter at several points in this study, discussing aspects of her poetry which had not been considered before. Firstly, she draws attention to Procter's irony and refers to the poem 'A Parting'.[226] In this poem the speaker thanks her ex-lover repeatedly and satirically for the lessons in love's generosity he has taught her and for dispelling her illusions:

> I thank you, yes, I thank you even more
>   That my heart learnt not without love to live,
>   But gave and gave, and still had more to give,
> From an abundant and exhaustless store.
> . . .
>
> Yet how much more I thank you that you tore
>   At length the veil your hand had woven away,
> Which hid my idol was a thing of clay,
>   And false the altar I had knelt before.
> (p. 127, ll. 9-12, 17-20)

Hickcock also stresses the importance of Procter's representations of the fallen woman, particularly in 'A Legend of Provence' (1859). She describes the poem as representing 'the apotheosis in women's poetry of the fallen woman redeemed'.[227] She also discusses Procter's representations of the spinster, and the self-sacrifice with which the spinster was associated, referring to the poems 'Three Evenings in a Life' and 'Philip and Mildred'.

---

[225] *Dictionary of Literary Biography. Victorian Poets Before 1850*, Ed. William E. Fredeman and Ira B. Nadel, Detroit: Gale Research Company, Vol. 32, 1984, pp. 232-235.

[226] Kathleen Hickok, *Representations of Women. Nineteenth-Century British Women's Poetry*, Connecticut: Greenwood Press, 1984, pp. 23-24.

[227] ibid., p. 110.

Hickock writes that Procter 'was one of the few women poets who dared on occasion to proselytize against feminine self-denial'.[228] Procter's poetry, in its struggle with religious, poetic and paternal authorities, does indeed speak out against the strictures and repressions of a self-denying position.

In the late 1980s and early 1990s Procter was included in several dictionaries of women writers. Mary G. De Jong, in the *Dictionary of British Women Writers* (Ed. Janet Todd, 1989), describes Procter as a conventional poet whose work is 'touching but not disturbing'. She adds, though, that several poems 'carry the sting of AAP's irony'. In *The Feminist Companion to Literature in English. Women Writers from the Middle Ages to the Present* (Ed. Blain, Clements, Grundy, 1990) the writer pays tribute to Procter's 'excellent narrative poems', in particular 'A Legend of Provence'. There is also an entry on Procter in *The Oxford Guide to British Women Writers* (Ed. Joanne Shattock, 1993).

In anthologies Procter is represented in *The New Oxford Book of Victorian Verse* (Ed. Christopher Ricks, 1987) which includes the poem 'Envy'; in *Sound the Deep Waters. Women's Romantic Poetry in the Victorian Age* (Ed. Pamela Norris, 1991) the poems 'A Love Token' and 'A Lost Chord' appear; Jennifer Breen includes 'A Woman's Question' and 'A Love Token' in *Victorian Women Poets 1830–1900. An Anthology*; and in *Winged Words. Victorian Women's Poetry* (Ed. Catherine Reilly, 1994) the poems 'Envy', 'A Parting', 'A Woman's Question' and 'A Woman's Answer' appear. These anthologies have importantly included some of Procter's finest lyrics and poems in which the women speakers daringly articulate problems which were integral to relationships between women and men at mid-century (see Chapter 3). Absent, though, are some of Procter's more intensely lyrical poems and her extremely interesting narrative poems.

The balance is redressed, however, in two recently published collections. The first is Angela Leighton and Margaret Reynolds's *Victorian Women Poets. An Anthology* (1995) in which the narrative poems 'A Legend of Provence', 'Three Evenings in a Life' and 'Philip and Mildred' appear. Margaret Reynolds, in her introduction to Procter, pays particular attention to 'A Legend of Provence' which she considers to be Procter's 'best and most interesting poem' in its exploration of the 'double' self the nun encounters on the threshold of the convent. Reynolds also sees Procter's complex irony as one 'of her poetic strengths'.[229]

Isobel Armstrong firmly establishes Procter's place as an important

---

[228] ibid., pp. 125–126.
[229] *Victorian Women Poets. An Anthology*, Ed. Angela Leighton and Margaret Reynolds, Oxford: Blackwell Publishers Ltd., 1995, p. 305.

mid-nineteenth-century poet in her section on Procter in the chapter '"A Music of Thine Own": Women's Poetry' in *Victorian Poetry. Poetry, poetics and politics* (1993). Armstrong describes Procter as a poet associated with the 'radical' thinking of Dickens's journals, *Household Words* and *All The Year Round*, in which Procter's work was published. She comments on the wide range of interests expressed in her poetry, referring to poems concerned with 'the oppression and the suffering of the poor' along with the 'magnificently humane lyrics on the Crimean war' and the narrative poems which consider 'displacement' and a 'woman's "place"' or displacement in a culture.'

Armstrong also discusses the apparent conventionality of many of Procter's lyrics which, she argues, provides a 'way of looking at conformity from within', thus enabling Procter to explore and at times convey the 'intense power of sexual love'. Finally Armstrong most importantly draws attention to the problem of a woman's expressiveness which, she states, Procter explores in some of her best lyrics, including 'A Lost Chord', 'Unexpressed' and 'Words'.[230] A selection of Procter's poems (including 'A Tomb in Ghent' and 'The Requital', discussed in Chapters 2 and 5) are published in *Nineteenth-Century Women Poets*, Ed. Isobel Armstrong, Joseph Bristow, Cath Sharrock (1996).[231]

The problematics of expression are central to Procter's poetry. In a letter to Bessie Parkes dated 1862 in which Procter refers to some general disapproval of her behaviour towards Bessie (typically she does not elaborate on the details) she writes that she has a 'morbid terror of being misunderstood and misinterpreted'.[232] Interestingly Dickens had written that she 'never cultivated the luxury of being misunderstood and unappreciated' (p. 8).

Procter's anxiety about being 'misinterpreted' expresses itself in her poetry as a desire for simplicity, directness and clarity of expression. Simultaneously she exercises poetic reserve (discussed in Chapter 2) which precludes the 'luxury' of an elaboration that may be construed as the self-indulgence Dickens deplored. Her struggle for more coherent expression therefore involves both a directness of expression as well as some constraint upon a more uncontained flow of words.

From this reserved position Procter's poetry engages in an impressive negotiation and struggle with several authoritative voices for her own

---

[230] Armstrong, op. cit., pp. 336–339.
[231] *Nineteenth-Century Women Poets*, Ed. Isobel Armstrong and Joseph Bristow With Cath Sharrock, Oxford University Press, 1996.
[232] MS BRP VIII, 24/2, Parkes papers, Girton College Library.

individual voice. Crucial to all her negotiations is the single woman, often depicted as alone, anonymous, without a family and in a foreign country. Procter's narrative poems frequently express the desire to cut off from homelands and she seems metaphorically to be expressing the wish to free herself from the authoritative sources (biographical and textual) which have partly formed her, as seen in 'From Your Own Correspondents in Search for Solitude'. Foreign territories provide her with the means of exploring from a distance emotions which have not yet found a form and an authority of their own.

This 'Introduction' has provided a lengthy account of Adelaide Procter's life and central preoccupations, and also those of her father Bryan Procter whose work and shadow accompany Procter throughout her career. Although this contextual material is important to an understanding of Procter's work her poetry in many ways explores what is missing in biographical accounts and reviews, revealing further complexities of emotion and thought. Angela Leighton has written of the poet's biographical and writing selves:

> The self who lives is not the same as the self who writes, but that is not to say that the first is simply irrelevant and 'dead' . . . From the start, writing creates another self, [233]

The 'self who writes' takes precedence in this discussion, though never forgetting the biographical self. Procter struggles in her writing with the self's inexpressibility:

> No real Poet ever wove in numbers
> All his dream; but the diviner part,
> Hidden from all the world, spake to him only
> In the voiceless silence of his heart.
>
> ('Unexpressed', p. 147, ll. 21-24)

---

[233] Angela Leighton, *Victorian Women Poets. Writing Against the Heart*, Hemel Hempstead: Harvester Wheatsheaf, 1992, pp. 4-5.

Chapter 2

Spiritual Authority: John Keble

Adelaide Procter converted to Roman Catholicism probably in 1851 at the age of 25, six years after the conversion of the Tractarian theorist John Henry Newman in 1845. Strong devotional feeling runs through Procter's poetry and she is a poet who works very much within the ethos of Tractarian poetics and aesthetics.

The Oxford Movement, led by Newman, John Keble and Edward Pusey, sought to restore the authority of the early Church Fathers and stressed the importance of absolute faith and devotional duties. The movement's main tenets are set out in a series of Tracts which were published between 1833 and 1841. In 'Tract 90' (1841) Newman argued that the 39 articles were to an extent compatible with Catholic theology. There was a strong reaction against the catholicising direction Newman was taking which culminated in his conversion.[1]

Although the movement was said to have ended at the point of Newman's conversion, Tractarian ideas, and in particular its poetry, continued to flourish. G.B. Tennyson writes that the literary influence of the Oxford Movement was extensive and evident later in the century in the poetry of writers such as Christina Rossetti and Gerard Manley Hopkins. For the Tractarians, Tennyson argues, the church or religion and poetry are inextricably linked: 'the Church herself is poetry'.[2] John Keble wrote that originality in poetry was less important than poetry's capacity to convey religious feeling. Novelty, he states, consists:

---

[1]   The Oxford Movement was partly a reaction to the Whig government's suppression of Irish bishoprics and pruning of English ones after the first Reform Act in 1832. (See J.W. Burrow, 'Faith, doubt and unbelief', *The Victorians*, Ed. Laurence Lerner, New York: Holmes & Meier Publishers, Inc., 1978.)

[2]   G.B. Tennyson, *Victorian Devotional Poetry. The Tractarian Mode*, Cambridge, Massachusetts: Harvard University Press, 1981, p. 123. Tennyson argues that Tractarian devotional poetry was in the poetic tradition of Wordsworth and Coleridge. Romanticism and Tractarianism, he states, are linked in their treatment of religion and aesthetics as 'kindred fields' (p. 18).

not in the original topic, but in continually bringing ordinary things, by happy strokes of natural ingenuity, into new associations with the ruling passion.[3]

Procter's early poems, which were mostly published in *Household Words* between 1853 and 1855, are nearly all conventional mourning, didactic and devotional lyrics with titles such as 'Friend Sorrow', 'Give' and 'Strive, Wait and Pray'. 'Strive, Wait and Pray' became a hymn in common use, along with 'Per Pacem Ad Lucem', 'Thankfulness', 'One by One', 'Now', 'The Pilgrims', 'Evening Hymn' and 'The Peace of God'. (See Appendix for publication dates.[4]) Bishop Bickersteth (Edward Henry Bickersteth, bishop of Exeter between 1885 and 1900) in his note in the *Hymnal Companion* (1876) praises Procter's poem 'Thankfulness':

> This most beautiful hymn by A.A. Procter (1858), touches the chord of thankfulness in trial, as perhaps no other hymn does, and is thus most useful for the visitation of the sick.[5]

Procter combines a Tractarian concern with ordinary devotions and duties with a more active urging of her readers to seize the moment or day:

---

[3]   John Keble, 'Sacred Poetry (1825)', *English Critical Essays (Nineteenth Century)*, Ed. Edmund D. Jones, London: Oxford University Press, 1916, p. 174.
[4]   *A Dictionary of Hymnology. Setting Forth the Origin and History of Christian Hymns of all Ages and Nations With Special Reference to Those Contained in the Hymn Books of English Speaking Countries, and Now in Common Use*, Ed. John Julian, London: John Murray, 1892, p. 913. Some of these poems/hymns appear under different titles in this dictionary. 'Per Pacem Ad Lucem' is titled 'Resignation'; 'One by One': 'The Links of Life'; 'Now': 'Redeem the Time'; 'The Pilgrims': 'Life a Pilgrimage'; 'Evening Hymn': 'Evening'; and 'The Peace of God': 'Peace with God'. John Julian writes of Procter: 'Sometimes she is truly lyrical, and her verses, "Confido et Conquiedo", would be suitable for congregational singing. The same may be said of "Our Daily Bread". She does not write in the mere routine of pious verse. Her "Sent to Heaven" is lovely of its kind. She is a thinker, but her poetry is more adapted to reading than to practical psalmody. Religion has taken deep root in her mind, and her days were passed in acts of self-denying charity' (p. 975).
     All these hymns may be found in Adelaide Anne Procter, *Legends and Lyrics Together with A Chaplet of Verses* (1914). See the Appendix for dates of first publication.
[5]   ibid., p. 913.

Rise! for the day is passing,
And you lie dreaming on;
The others have buckled their armour,
And forth to the fight are gone:
A place in the ranks awaits you,
Each man has some part to play;
The Past and the Future are nothing,
In the face of the stern To-day.
('Now' p. 44, ll. 1-8)[6]

Ferdinand Janku in *Adelaide Anne Procter. Ihr Leben Und Ihre Werke* (1912) suggests that Procter's religion, which is often expressed in her poetry as a call to active philanthropy, is at times closer to the spirit of the Christian Socialist movement of Charles Kingsley (who was passionately anti-Tractarian).[7] Procter did attend F.D. Maurice's Queen's College in 1850 where Kingsley taught, and the college's ethos would certainly have made some impact on her.

Poems such as 'The Army of the Lord', 'The Homeless Poor' and 'Homeless' (all published in 'A Chaplet of Verses' in 1862) express Procter's concern that her religion be an active one, seeking out 'Where sin and crime are dwelling' ('The Army of the Lord', p. 275, l. 33) and not content to stay complacently within an aesthetically pleasing church:

'Praise with loving deeds is dear and holy,
Words of praise will never serve instead:
Lo! you offer music, hymn, and incense –
When *He has not where to lay His head.*
('The Homeless Poor', p. 315, ll. 135-136)[8]

Music, hymns and incense are very much the concern of the narrative poem 'A Tomb in Ghent' (published in *Household Words* on 29.12.1855) which

---

6   Jessie Boucherett, founder of the Society for Promoting the Employment of Women (1859), quotes the poem 'Now' in her obituary of Procter (*The English Woman's Journal*, XIII, March 1864, pp. 17-21).

7   Ferdinand Janku, *Adelaide Anne Procter: Ihr Leben Und Ihre Werke*, Wien und Liepzig: Wilhelm Braumuller, 1912, p. 89.

8   Bessie Parkes (Belloc) writes that the poem 'Homeless' was written at the special request of Monsignor Gilbert, Procter's confessor and the founder of the Providence Row Night Refuge for Homeless Women and Children. According to Parkes the poem was inserted for years in the annual report and appeal for funds. (*In a Walled Garden*, London: Ward and Downey Limited, 1895, p. 175). 'Homeless' is discussed in Chapter 3.

provides the main focus of this chapter. This poem, which is about a cathedral organist who devotes his life to the church and to the poor, combines Procter's Tractarian respect for devotional duties with her philanthropic concerns. It is perhaps the most significant poem in Procter's corpus. 'A Tomb in Ghent' shows a greater degree of complexity and has a less monologic voice than many of Procter's earlier religious and didactic lyrics.

From readings and re-readings of this poem it becomes apparent that Procter is engaged in responding to and mounting a critique of some central tenets of Tractarian aesthetics which she works both with and against. Simultaneously she raises important questions relating to gender, hierarchy, poverty, war, heroism and nationhood.

The possibility of there being a multiplicity of interpretations and voices which may conflict with one another is raised and undermines a more absolute faith in a given set of interpretations and in harmonious wholeness which is expressed by the Tractarian John Keble. A reading of 'A Tomb in Ghent' and other poems, in the light of Keble's aesthetic theories and his collection of poems, *The Christian Year* (1827), reveals the extent to which Procter is writing under the influence of Keble's pervasive voice and in direct opposition to some of his central tenets.

I have chosen to read Procter's poetry with reference to Keble's theories and poetry as by the end of the nineteenth century *The Christian Year* had become, in Bessie Parkes's words, 'absorbed into our national thought'.[9] By 1873 Keble's nineteenth-century bestseller had run to 158 editions. G.B. Tennyson writes of the immense popularity of *The Christian Year* and cites numerous literary texts in which it is mentioned, ranging from the Tractarian writer Charlotte Yonge's *The Daisy Chain* (1856) to Thomas Hardy's *Jude the Obscure*.[10]

In *The Poets and the Poetry of the Century* (1891) H.J. Gibbs compares Procter's poetry with Keble's. He writes:

---

[9] Madame Belloc (nee Parkes), *The Flowing Tide* (London: Sands & Co., 1900, p. 193). *The Flowing Tide* is an account of the wave of conversions to Roman Catholicism in the nineteenth century from the 1830s.

[10] Tennyson, op. cit., 'Appendix C', pp. 226–232. In *Jude the Obscure* (1896) Jude meets the shades of 'the founders of the religious school called Tractarian' in Christminster, including John Keble who quotes from *The Christian Year* (Hardy, *Jude the Obscure*, Ed. C.H. Sisson, Harmondsworth: Penguin Books Ltd., 1978, pp. 126–129). In George Gissing's *The Odd Women* (1893) two spinster sisters give their younger sister Monica a gift of *The Christian Year* which they hope will be a 'comfort' to her 'from time to time' (*The Odd Women*, Intro. Margaret Walters, London: Virago Press Limited, 1980, p. 29). In George Eliot's *Middlemarch* (1871–2) *The Christian Year* is amongst Dorothea Brooke's 'favourite books' (*Middlemarch*, Ed. Rosemary Ashton, London: Penguin Books Ltd., 1994, p. 474).

> To compare her for a moment with another sweet religious singer of
> this century, – Keble – it might be said that, while she instils the same
> precepts and inculcates the same duties, she has never attained to his
> height.[11]

The strength of Procter's lyric poetic voice in fact far surpasses that of the
more conservative Keble, but there are similarities between the two poets.
Like Keble, Procter was a popular poet with a simplicity of style and
language which clearly appealed to a wide audience. Procter was also, like
Keble, an intensely religious poet with an apparently simple message. An
avid and intelligent reader of a very wide range of literary texts, Procter
would undoubtedly have been familiar with both *The Christian Year* and
Keble's aesthetics theories.[12]

Procter would have been eight years old when Keble gave his 'Sermon on
National Apostasy' in 1833 which was said to have inaugurated the Oxford
Movement.[13] In this sermon Keble refers to the 'fashionable liberality' of
those who no longer saw the necessity of adhering to the traditions and
authority of the Church.[14] He urges his audience to return to their daily
devotional duties, which he describes as 'ordinary' duties compared with the
public commitments 'ecclesiastical or civil' preoccupying too many men. He
notes a growth of hostility towards the Church and a 'triumph of disorder
and irreligion'.[15]

Keble's most important theoretical works are 'Tract 89. On the Mysticism
attributed to the Early Fathers of the Church' (1840), and *Praelectiones
Academicae* (1832-1841), the Lectures on Poetry given by Keble when he
held the Professorship of Poetry at Oxford. In 'Tract 89' Keble outlines the
important Tractarian theory of reserve. He defends the mysticism attributed
to the Fathers of the Church (who include St Augustine, St Irenaeus and St

---

[11] *The Poets and the Poetry of the Century. Joanna Baillie to Mathilde Blind*,
Ed. Alfred H. Miles, London: Hutchinson & Co., 1891, Vol. 7 , p. 364.

[12] Leesther Thomas argues that Procter's poetry is a 'hybrid' of the Tractarian
mode and that it follows some of the basic principles of Keble's aesthetics theories,
particularly those relating to the 'cathartic' benefits of poetry (Thomas, *A Poetry of
Deliverance With Tractarian Affinities. A Study of Adelaide A. Procter's Poetry*
(PhD Dissertation), The Florida State University, College of Arts and Sciences, 1994).

[13] See G. C. Brodrick, 'A History of the University of Oxford', *Epochs of
Church History*, Ed. Rev. Mandell Creighton, London: Longmans, Green & Co., 1886.

[14] John Keble, *National Apostasy Considered in a Sermon Preached in St
Mary's, Oxford, Before His Majesty's Judges of Assize, On Sunday, July 14, 1833*,
Oxford: S. Collingwood, Printer to the University, for J.H. Parker and J.G. and F.
Rivington, London, 1833, p. 16.

[15] ibid., p. 26.

Ambrose), which was criticised for being too allusive and allegorical. Keble argues that their mysticism was exemplified by the 'reverential reserve' which is associated with the mere hint of a sacramental truth.[16] The 'expressive' or 'visible' symbol was the means of expression promoted by the Fathers for the conveying of deeper truths. By spiritual association the 'minds of the baptized' would be recalled to the sacramental truth associated with the symbol, the visible symbol par excellence being the cross.[17]

Holy Scripture confirms, Keble states, that all material things are invested with 'a set of holy and divine associations and meanings'.[18] Symbolical meanings are, Keble asserts, universal in that:

> There is a wonderful agreement among the Fathers, in the symbolical meanings, which they assign to most of the great objects in nature; such an agreement as completely negatives the supposition of the whole having sprung from mere poetical association.[19]

Keble writes in the poem 'Septuagesima Sunday' in *The Christian Year*:

> There is a book, who runs may read,
>   Which heavenly truth imparts,
> And all the lore its scholars need,
>   Pure eyes and Christian hearts.
>
> The works of God above, below,
>   Within us and around,
> Are pages in that book, to shew
>   How God Himself is found.[20]

---

16   John Keble, 'Tract No. 89. On the Mysticism Attributed to the Early Fathers of the Church', *Tracts for the Times by Members of the University of Oxford*, Vols V and VI for 1838–41, London: J.G.F. and J. Rivington; and J.H. Parker, Oxford, 1840–41, p. 13.

17   ibid., p. 31

18   ibid., p. 144.

19   ibid., p. 145. Keble provides a long list of symbols, for example: 'The flight and hovering of birds . . . token that there are Powers in heaven above who watch our proceedings' (p. 153), 'The waters flowing into the sea, are the people gathered into the Church of Christ' (p. 153), 'Herbs again, and flowers, are the life and body of man' (p. 154).

20   [John Keble], *The Christian Year: Thoughts in Verse for the Sundays and Holydays Throughout the Year*, 2 Vols, Oxford: Printed by W. Baxter, for J. Parker; and C. and J. Rivington, London, 1827.

And yet, according to Keble, full meaning and knowledge are extremely difficult, if not impossible, to attain. God, Keble states, is the 'one great and manifold Person' with a 'Poetry of His own,' and in control of its associations and meanings.[21] God's visible symbol served the purpose of not conveying 'more knowledge, than the rule of the Church allowed.'[22] Keble applauds St Irenaeus's sense of the importance of 'ignorance':

> The very attempt to know all – the very dreaming of such a thing – he felt was impiety; a deep sense of our necessary ignorance, and an humble acquiescence in it, the only safeguard of the inquisitive, ingenious mind.[23]

In this account the notion of reserve is inextricably linked to a necessary ignorance. Absolute knowledge is held in reserve by God and the Fathers.

In his *Oxford Lectures on Poetry* Keble applies the theory of reserve to poetry. According to Keble the notion of relief is linked to the notion of reserve. Poetry, he states:

> gives healing relief to secret mental emotion, yet without detriment to modest reserve: and while giving scope to enthusiasm, yet rules it with order and due control.[24]

The leadings of measure and rhythm (which in Keble's terms provide a means of control) are followed like a 'labyrinthine clue' to the point of relief of emotion.[25] Poetry, like music, is harmonious and brings healing and relief. Once the primal chord or keynote of poetry is struck the structure becomes clear and relief is experienced:

> just as they say of Music, that each harmony has its peculiar *motif* and primal chord, which once rightly seized, the whole structure becomes clear: just so does Poetry ever hark back to its prime and peculiar function of healing and relief.[26]

---

21   Keble, 'Tract No. 89', p. 144.

22   ibid., p. 31.

23   ibid., p. 140.

24   *Keble's Lectures on Poetry 1832–1841*, Trans. Edward Kershaw Francis, 2 Vols, Oxford at the Clarendon Press, 1912, 1, p. 22. The lectures were first published in Latin in 1844.

25   ibid., 1, p. 22.

26   ibid., 1, p. 66.

In this account any violent or overwhelming emotion is kept under control and the 'relief' referred to seems to be as much from as 'of' emotion. Keble refers to the lack of restraint in 'decadent and deteriorated' poetry and in his essay 'Sacred Poetry' (1825) refers to 'Leigh Hunt and his miserable followers' (the 'Cockney School' of poetry with which Bryan Procter was associated) whom he considered guilty of such decadence.[27]

Keble also admires reserve in women. In his discussion of Aeschylus Keble cites the 'beautiful trait of reserve' which is found in women and quotes from Aeschylus's play *The Suppliants*, where in an act of prayer the women's faces are shadowed by their suppliant boughs.[28] Keble describes their supplicatory position as combining 'modest reverence' with a 'confidence in prayer' particularly appropriate to women.[29]

Keble quotes these lines without providing any context. The fifty suppliant women, the Danaides, are women on the run, exiles from the aggression of their fifty cousins, the sons of Aegyptus, who wish to marry them. They flee to Argos from Egypt and seek sanctuary there on the grounds that they are descended from Io, the daughter of Inachus king of Argos. Their father Danaus advises them to make sure they behave as suppliants:

> let there follow upon your speech in the first place that which is not rash, but let the countenance which is not vain proceed out of modest foreheads from a tranquil eye . . . and be not forward to speak nor irksome in speech: the race of people in this country is very jealous . . . but remember to give way: thou art a needy stranger in exile: for it doth not become the inferior to be bold of tongue.[30]

In spite of their apparently reserved position the King of Argos almost mistakes them for Amazons and they are impressive as women passionately pleading their cause rather than cowering behind boughs.[31]

'Bold speech' and the tactical manoeuvrings of women would be out of place in Keble's theory of 'relief' which tends towards a passive state of quiescence rather than the relief arrived at after conflict and struggle. The epigraph to *The Christian Year* is a quotation from Isaiah: 'In quietness and in

---

27   ibid., 1, p. 17. Keble, 'Sacred Poetry', p. 168.

28   *Keble's Lectures on Poetry*, 2, p. 84.

29   ibid.

30   *The Prometheus and Suppliants of Aeschylus; Construed Literaly and Word for Word;* The Rev. Dr. Giles, London: James Cornish, [1858], p. 83.

31   ibid., p. 89. After hearing their story the King of Argos expresses surprise that they claim Argive descent:
I should have conjectured strongly you to be Amazons that have no men among them and that feed on flesh, if ye were armed with bows. (p. 89)

confidence shall be your strength' and the 'Advertisement' refers to 'the *soothing* tendency in the Prayer Book, which it is the chief purpose of these volumes to exhibit'.[32] Central to Keble's theorisations are notions of control and reserve which facilitate a state of quiet withdrawal. Strong emotion, like the truths which God is said to hold in reserve, is kept at a distance.

In his *Oxford Lectures* Keble draws up a list of Primary and Secondary Poets which includes Homer, Pindar, Aeschylus, Lucretius and Virgil. His discussion of Virgil and Homer provides an interesting gloss on the quiescent state of relief he advocates. Keble states that Virgil was primarily interested in 'the quiet life of the country'.[33] He asserts that Virgil's characterisation of Aeneas, a man of action, is sketchy and that this hero is barely delineated.[34] Virgil wrote *The Aeneid* against his natural preference for 'rural pleasures' to 'warlike affairs' Keble argues:

> Virgil's distinguishing peculiarity lies in the fact that he not merely passionately and longingly pines after rural pleasures when separated from them, but evinces, moreover, a most absolute loathing and detestation for warlike affairs . . .[35]

In another lecture Keble states that Virgil's attitude to 'religious and eternal things' is exemplified by his rendering of the allegory of the scattered Sibylline leaves which can never be fully recollected. He states that Virgil implies that:

> the sole way by which the knowledge of divine things is conceded to mortal men, is that they shall collect from every quarter the traces and fragments of it which have been thrown into confusion by the storm and stress of our daily lives and have been scattered in all directions. Moreover, he not obscurely implies that there will be no repairing of this disaster, nor will these fragments of truth ever be arranged and made serviceable to mankind, save by constant, devoted prayerfulness.[36]

Keble's emphasis is on a search through prayer rather than the active and tortuous journey towards 'truth' which Aeneas undertakes. Nor does Keble mention Apollo's violent control of the Sibyl which compels her to utter her

---

32 [Keble], *The Christian Year*, I, Frontispiece and p. vii.
33 *Keble's Lectures on Poetry*, 2, p. 257.
34 ibid., pp. 378-379.
35 ibid., p. 388.
36 ibid., pp. 463-464.

prophecies to Aeneas.[37]

By contrast, Keble's account of Homer shows an admiration for an heroic mode characterised by a love of military action. He describes Homer as 'a man to whom battle is delight'.[38] The heroic temper is also, according to Keble, 'wandering, restless, adventuresome' and in Homer's *Odyssey* is seen to co-exist with 'the consuming love and craving for home and native land'.[39] Keble describes Homer as a poet who 'flourished during the decline of the heroic age' and of kingship throughout Greece when there was a general tendency 'towards popular government'. He suggests that Homer would have sided with the aristocracy in their support for 'the ancient form of government'.[40] In the following lecture Keble states:

> it would be little short of a miracle if Homer had not zealously sided with those whose downfall would also involve the destruction of the privileges of the Heroic Kings, of a quiet restful life, of the happiness of the whole State. But, in fact, the plan of the whole *Odyssey* is, I think, ample demonstration of this.[41]

In this account a state of quiescence is secured by the militarism of heroes. Keble contrasts Homer and Virgil as poets who respectively prefer 'adventure' and 'peace and quiet'.[42] In Lecture XI he states he has assigned 'the last place' to Virgil in his Lectures as he believes that Virgil's poems 'would be found the most suitable transition to things more sacred and divine'.[43] It would seem that Keble's argument does rest on his account of the finally quiescent and peaceful Virgilian mode.

Keble's call for a return to devotional duties in his 'Sermon on National Apostasy' suggests a desire to retreat from the public sphere, from disorder and from the uncontrolled expression of emotion (see p. 106). Keble prefers the place of quiet retreat without acknowledging the authoritarian power and violence which secure that peace. The necessary ignorance of God's meanings which Keble advocates may be linked to a fear of revealing and facing the unacknowledged and unexpressed emotions which are held in check by a state of reserve. Keble retreats to a place of safety where dissonant disorder is kept at bay.

---

[37] Virgil, *The Aeneid*, Trans. W.F. Jackson Knight, Harmondsworth: Penguin Books Ltd., 1958, pp. 149–150.

[38] ibid., 1, p. 156.

[39] ibid., p. 202.

[40] ibid., pp. 238–239.

[41] ibid., p. 242.

[42] ibid., 2, p. 257.

[43] ibid., p. 466.

The Christian Year (1827)

The retreat is to a place where devotional duties are religiously observed and where harmony prevails over disorder. Such a place is the terrain of *The Christian Year* which was written, according to Keble in the 'Advertisement', to help his reader bring his 'thoughts and feelings into more entire unison with those recommended and exemplified in the Prayer Book'.[44] *The Christian Year* begins with poems titled 'Morning', 'Evening' and 'Advent Sunday' and then continues with titles naming the various holy and saints days.

The idea of gathering together his readers' thoughts and feelings into harmony with the Prayer Book is reflected in the emphasis placed on harmonising in *The Christian Year*. In the 'Dedication' the 'Fountain of Harmony!' is praised as the spirit which gathers 'into order' the 'troubled waves of earthly sound'.[45] Difficulties relating to understanding will also be resolved and the harmonies of heavenly love learnt. In the poem 'Fourth Sunday in Advent' the speaker states that he has difficulty in tracing or reading the meanings of 'Nature's beauteous book'. Everything is 'misty' to sight and sound but he is confident that a time will come when he will be able to hear and see clearly. Too much curiosity will not lead to knowledge, he states, but a humble receptivity to training in love's harmonies will enable 'inward Music' to rise:

> And thou, too curious ear, that fain
> Wouldst thread the maze of Harmony,
> Content thee with one simple strain,
> The lowlier, sure, the worthier thee;
>
> Till thou art duly trained, and taught
> The concord sweet of Love divine,
> Then, with that inward Music fraught,
> For ever rise, and sing, and shine.
> ('Fourth Sunday in Advent')[46]

Keble describes congregations as children in need of tuning: 'Their lawless cries are tun'd to hymns of perfect love' ('Fourth Sunday After Epiphany'); 'Childlike though the voices be, / And untunable the parts, / Thou wilt own

44 [Keble], *The Christian Year*, 'Advertisement', I, p. vi.
45 [John Keble], *The Christian Year: Thoughts in Verse for the Sundays and Holydays Throughout the Year*, London: James Parker and Co., [1870], p. xi.
46 [Keble], *The Christian Year* (1827), I, pp. 22-25.

the minstrelsy, / If it flow from childlike hearts' ('Palm Sunday').[47] They learn harmony like learning to read. The music and the book are already there and all the child needs to do is to learn the right keys or way of reading: 'There is a book, who runs may read, / Which heavenly truth imparts' ('Septuagesima Sunday').[48]

Keble's 'Two worlds' of heaven and earth are textual worlds to be read and only the presence of 'Sin' obscures the clear view:

> Two worlds are ours: 'tis only Sin
>   Forbids us to descry
> The mystic heaven and earth within,
>   Plain as the sea and sky.
>
> Thou, who hast given me eyes to see
>   And love this sight so fair,
> Give me a heart to find out Thee,
>   And read Thee everywhere.
>   ('Septuagesima Sunday')[49]

The clear view, however, seems to be completely unattainable. In the 'Dedication' Keble writes that he would 'fain / Track to its source the brightness'.[50] In *The Christian Year* light gleams, flashes, blazes and is at times insufferable.[51] People are protected from the force of the light by God's 'softening veil' which prevents the disclosure of 'rude bad thoughts':

> Who would not shun the dreary uncouth place?
>   As if, fond leaning where her infant slept,
> A mother's arm a serpent should embrace:
>   So might we friendless live, and die unwept.
>   ('Twenty-Fourth Sunday After Trinity')[52]

Keble infantilises his readers by stating that God keeps the full impact of their thoughts from His congregation whilst His own capacity for seeing is

---

47 ibid., pp. 72, 120.
48 ibid., p. 83.
49 ibid., p. 85.
50 [Keble], *The Christian Year* [1870].
51 [Keble], *The Christian Year* (1827). For examples see 'Third Sunday after Epiphany' I, pp. 54-55, 'Fourth Sunday after Trinity', II, pp. 14-15, 'The Conversion of St Paul', II, pp. 110-114.
52 ibid., 2, p. 90.

depicted as unlimited. The searching eye of Heaven is the eye of authority and power and its penetrating gaze can search out any sin:

> Eye of God's word! where'er we turn
>   Ever upon us! thy keen gaze
> Can all the depths of sin discern,
>   Unravel every bosom's maze.
>
> ('St Bartholomew')[53]

> In vain: the averted cheek in loneliest dell
>   Is conscious of a gaze it cannot bear,
> The leaves that rustle near us seem to tell
>   Our heart's sad secret to the silent air.
>
> ('Third Sunday After Trinity')[54]

Keble also describes God's strong sense of hearing. In the poem 'The Waterfall' in Keble's *Lyra Innocentium* (1846) the reader is assured that even a 'feeble infant tone' on earth will be heard in Heaven:

> What boots one feeble infant tone
>   To the full choir denied or given,
>   Where millions round the Throne
>   Are chanting, morn and even?
>
> Nay, the kind Watchers hearkening there
>   Distinguish in the deep of song
>   Each little wave, each air
>   Upon the faltering tongue.[55]

If the notes are discordant the strength and disturbance of this sound and emotion will be calmed by mists from heaven:

> What though in harsh and angry note
>   The broken flood chafe high? they muse
>   On mists that lightly float,
>   On heaven-descending dews,[56]

---

[53]   ibid., 2, p. 148.
[54]   ibid., 2, p. 9.
[55]   [John Keble], *Lyra Innocentium: Thoughts in Verse on Christian Children, Their Ways, and their Privileges*, Oxford: John Henry Parker; F. and J. Rivington, London, 1846, p. 209.
[56]   ibid., p. 212.

The lilting and lulling quatrain, with its simple abab rhyme scheme and lines tapering down to the three stress line, palliates and masks the extent of the power and authority which is being described.

Keble's theories of reserve and relief are exemplified by the extent to which the congregation are screened from an omnipotent power and authority which will only reveal itself once all discords are eliminated. Relief is not attained after an expression of strong feeling: it is more a state of relief from entering into strong emotions at all. (Georgina Battiscombe has written of the absence of 'emotion' in *The Christian Year*, and of Keble's own lack of exploration of emotional depths.[57]) It is a state of quiescence which rests on an absolute power, a 'primal chord' which controls the harmonies and disallows any independent expression of emotion that jars with itself as the harmonious and tuneful source. The emotions of the congregation are arrested in a state of infantilism and passivity.

'A Tomb in Ghent' (1855)

In Elizabeth Von Arnim's *The Pastor's Wife* (1914) Ingeborg Bullivant, the central protagonist, asks herself:

> Was the *Christian Year* enough for one in the way of poetry? And all those mild novels her mother read, sandwiched between the biographies of more bishops and little books of comfort with crosses on them that asked rude questions as to whether you had been greedy or dainty or had used words with a double meaning during the day – were they enough for a soul that had, quite alone, with no father giving directions, presently to face its God?[58]

Ingeborg, a young woman in her early twenties and the daughter of an overprotective and disciplinarian bishop, has responded impulsively to an advertisement for a trip to Lucerne. She has met and been proposed to by a Pastor Dremmel, and her reference to *The Christian Year* suggests that she is

---

[57] Georgina Battiscombe writes: 'Thought, learning, observation – *The Christian Year* has all these admirable qualities. What it lacks is emotion and music, and without emotion and music there can be no true poetry.' She adds, 'Many of the letters which passed between him and his family are emotional, but it is a playful, surface emotion which does not explore the depths beneath. Serious feelings are not to be exposed to view, least of all serious religious feelings' (Battiscombe, *John Keble. A Study in Limitations*, London: Constable and Company Ltd., 1963, pp. 105–106).

[58] Elizabeth Von Arnim, *The Pastor's Wife*, Ed. Deborah Singmaster, London: Everyman, 1993, p. 35.

wondering if that text or surrogate paternal authority will provide her with sufficient guidance for her emotions in the present situation.

Adelaide Procter may very well have been asking herself the same question when she wrote 'A Tomb in Ghent' which explores the authority of the Tractarian tenets which inform her poetry, particularly the notions of reserve, the secret and the visible symbol. In this poem Procter questions the absolute authority of those tenets and employs the cathedral in Ghent as a space for an exploration of Tractarian theories and poetics.

'A Tomb in Ghent' was described by Bessie Parkes as one of Procter's 'most highly-finished' legends, and by Ferdinand Janku as one of the best she wrote in what he calls 'the epic lyrical field'.[59] It is certainly one of her most successful, suggestive and exploratory poems.

The poem opens with an introductory verse paragraph in which an unnamed narrator introduces her subject, an unnamed 'maiden' who is of mixed Belgian and English descent. The maiden has caught the narrator's attention by her singing of 'fragments' from Palestrinian chants, the *Laudate* and Scarlatti's minor fugue. She wonders how the young woman, who is engaged with 'household cares', could have learned 'such deep and solemn harmony'. The narrator has 'set in rhyme' what the young woman has told her so that she may 'chronicle the influence, dim and sweet, / 'Neath which her young and innocent life had grown' (pp. 63-64, ll. 1-29).

The maiden's grandfather had been an English artisan who emigrated to Ghent in Flanders to find work, probably in the early to mid 19th century, when Ghent was the centre of a thriving textiles industry.[60] He cuts a solitary figure in Ghent, choosing not to mix with the other workers, and his one joy is to teach his 'sickly boy'. Homesick he tells his son tales of England and 'English heroes' (p. 64, ll. 30-43) He also tells him the tale of the 'gilt dragon' which glares down from the belfry of St Bavon, the cathedral in Ghent. He relates how the dragon had been brought as a trophy from the Crusades to Bruges, and how Ghent soldiers stole it from Bruges. Rumour has it, the father says, that the dragon will one day fly back to his home "'mid palm and cedar trees'. His son, who daily passes the belfry on

---

[59] [Bessie Parkes],'The Poems of Adelaide Anne Procter', *The Month*, IV, 1866, p. 86.

Janku, op. cit., p. 47.

[60] David Thomson writes that there was a dramatic increase in emigration from the 1830s and that the annual average for the three years 1847-1849 was well over 250,000. The reasons for emigration, Thomson states, were economic hardship and increased opportunity to travel with the introduction of railways (Thomson, *England in the Nineteenth Century 1815-1914)*, London: Penguin Books Ltd., 1950, p. 94).

his way to the cathedral, looks up every day to see if the dragon has flown away and is surprised to find it still 'watching there'. (pp. 64-65, ll. 44-63)

The boy falls in love with the Gothic cathedral and its intensely sensuous pleasures – 'silver-clouded incense' and organ music. He watches the sunlight creeping along the marble floor, lighting up shrines 'all rich with gems and flowers', marble saints, strange carvings and 'demon heads grotesque' which glare impotently on all the beauty. When the shade comes down the child leaves the cathedral and comes out into the 'glare' of the square outside. (pp. 65-66, ll. 64-116). (The boy's love of the cathedral is similar to that of a boy depicted in a story by Agnes Loudon published in *Household Words* earlier in 1855. [61])

The cathedral becomes his 'home for rest and play' (p. 66 l. 117) and there is one spot towards which he is particularly drawn – The White Maiden's Tomb. No-one knows who she is and he imagines 'what she thought, and what she felt' (pp. 66-67, ll. 121-148). He develops a 'genius' for music and eventually becomes the cathedral organist. The possibility of 'world-wide fame' is finally relinquished owing to the passage of time and his own fragility. He does, however, become famous in his own sphere and teaches 'the art of harmony'. He is also a counsellor to the poor (pp. 67-68, ll. 149-188). One day he hears an angel voice singing and sees 'His own White Maiden' singing Mozart's *Sanctus*. He marries the young woman who possesses the voice and they have a daughter. His wife, like himself, is drawn to the White Maiden's Tomb, where she waits and prays (pp. 68-69, ll. 189-234).

The mother dies young and the daughter forgets her 'passionate grief in time, and smiled' whilst the father loses his strength and dies a few years later, his head resting on the White Maiden's Tomb. The narrator concludes that, although the musician never achieved universal fame, he is famous 'By poor men's hearths'. His daughter, who is unable to support herself financially, returns to England and strange 'kinsmen' who welcome her. She pays back their love with 'well-taught housewife watchfulness and skill' and remembers her father, proudly keeping 'his fame' (pp. 69-70, ll. 235-284). The poem concludes:

---

[61] Agnes Loudon's tale is of a French orphan boy who lives with a priest and spends much of his time in a Gothic cathedral where he becomes a chorister. Like the boy in 'A Tomb in Ghent' he enjoys listening to the church music:

the church grew darker, and the organ played solemn and grand music, and the odour of incense still rested on the air.

[Agnes Loudon], 'The Little Chorister', *Household Words*, XII, 1855, p. 28. Agnes Loudon was the only child of John Claudius Loudon, the Scottish horticultural writer.

> And while she works with thrifty Belgian care,
> Past dreams of childhood float upon the air;
> Some strange old chant, or solemn Latin hymn,
> That echoed through the old cathedral dim,
> When as a little child each day she went
> To kneel and pray by an old tomb in Ghent.
>   (p. 70, ll. 285-290)

The poem ends as it began with images of fragmentation. The young girl's life of domesticity in England is depicted as shadowy, and her memories of the cathedral are fragmentary, some conscious (those of her father) and some more unconscious – she sings 'as if she did not know / That she was singing' (pp. 63-64, ll. 9-10).

The poem is Tractarian to the extent that it exemplifies many of Keble's theories. The cathedral remains a place of very partially revealed secrets and there are key visible symbols, such as the White Maiden's Tomb and the dragon, which are unexplained with their truths being held in reserve. The unambitious musician demonstrates the type of humility and reserve which Keble would have admired. He is committed to devotional and parochial duties, and does not involve himself in a more public or civic sphere of activity. He is also a master of harmony, with 'master-power' (p. 67, l. 167). He controls the music and within the cathedral confines there are no obviously discordant notes. A quiescent space has apparently been secured from which the 'rude, bad thoughts' referred to by Keble are excluded and a more active life of heroic and manly action, which is associated with the dragon, is kept at a distance. The musician is depicted as having withdrawn from a more hostile outside world to a place of prayer.

However, the images of fragmentation which begin and end the poem, along with the young woman's displacement, undermine the sense of harmony and quiescence which is suggested by the cathedral's interior. The symbolic tomb and dragon are less visible symbols which fit into a whole than nodal points exerting a hypnotic and magnetic attraction which is destabilising. They undermine the notion of an harmonious whole within which all parts coalesce unproblematically.

By leaving so many fragments floating in mid-air Procter invites enquiry and research, demonstrating the curiosity which Keble disliked. These more active modes of search contrast with the 'devoted prayerfulness' Keble advocates as a means of retrieving the scattered Sybilline leaves.

I shall discuss the poem under various headings – the cathedral, the musician, the White Maiden's Tomb and the dragon – and I shall consider the means by which Procter undermines and unsettles key tenets of Keble's

Tractarian theories. From her revisionary poetics a powerful critique of Keble's authoritative voice is seen to emerge.

The Cathedral

Central to Keble's theorisations is the notion of a place which is reserved from a more disturbing outside world – a place which is rural and English. In *The Christian Year* there are frequent references to rural scenes and home, and although these locations are depicted by Keble as transient compared with heaven they do nonetheless mark out the terrain of the poems. G.B. Tennyson has noted that the landscape of Gloucester and the West Country were the source for most of the descriptions of nature in *The Christian Year*. It is a 'gentle' English landscape which is described by Keble, Tennyson states.[62]

By contrast the location in 'A Tomb in Ghent' is foreign, as it is in many of Procter's narrative poems. Although the musician is depicted as parochial to the extent that his domain is limited, his and his family's displacements, and his father the artisan's alienation from the other workers in Ghent, contrast with Keble's notion of parochial contentment and repose, the 'Sweet' home and 'household nook, / The haunt of all affections pure'.[63]

The Catholic location of Ghent is depicted less as a place to settle than as a site of exploration and discovery. In a letter to Bessie Parkes (undated) Procter wrote that she envied Bessie her visit to Belgium:

> I envy you in Belgium. I've always had a great wish to go there – greater than for greater places – perhaps because it was so practicable, as to come into the domain of what might be.[64]

So Ghent, for Procter, is a place suggestive of possibilities. Bessie Parkes describes Procter as having resembled a 'foreign Catholic' and her choice of a 'foreign' religion, with its visible symbols and sung liturgies, would have provided Procter with rich resources for the imagination and the senses. J.H. Newman, in his account of a conversion to Roman Catholicism, *Loss and Gain* (1848), describes the discovery of the Roman Catholic faith as resembling the discovery of a 'home' by a man who is out in a dark night with a lamp. Newman describes the house of faith as a place of 'glittering

---

62 Tennyson, op. cit., p. 112.
63 [Keble], *The Christian Year* (1827), 'First Sunday in Lent', I, p. 100.
64 MS BRP VIII, 39, Parkes papers, Girton College Library.

chandeliers,' and 'bright ladies' – a 'glorious scene'.[65]

Procter had discovered the rich Catholic location of Ghent. Elizabeth Dhanens in her monograph of Hubert and Jan Van Eyck, *Van Eyck: The Ghent Altarpiece*, states that Ghent was a 'centre where creative thought and art flourished'.[66] St Bavon's was renowned from the sixteenth century for being 'exceptionally rich in works of art', which included the Ghent Altarpiece. Ghent was also well known for its many libraries and scriptorium.[67] And yet Procter, who surely would have known of the Van Eyck Altarpiece and the reputation of Ghent, with Tractarian reserve does not describe any paintings in the poem, and barely refers to the location of Ghent.

The aesthetic wealth of the cathedral is depicted by Procter, but it is glimpsed rather than described as a 'glorious scene'. Procter questions the permanence of access to the beauties of the 'foreign' church she has discovered, and to Newman's religous 'home'. She is asking questions about what kind of 'home' the church provides.

The artisan's son (the musician) comes to a foreign country and discovers a home full of beautiful but strange delights: 'A home for him – mysterious and his own' (p. 65, l. 63). His father's past in England is not referred to and it is as though the boy is homeless up to this point. His actual home in Ghent is not described. Instead the cathedral becomes a kind of domestic space for him. It is 'home' in Keble's sense in that, although mysterious, it is a place which is primarily reassuring as it comforts the boy. But despite the musician's long residence there it is a temporary abode and place of work, and not his actual home.

The description of the cathedral suggests both the strength of the cathedral 'home' and its immense fragility and impermanence:

> Dim with dark shadows of the ages past,
> St Bavon stands, solemn and rich and vast;
> The slender pillars, in long vistas spread,
> Like forest arches meet and close o'erhead;
> So high that, like a weak and doubting prayer,
> Ere it can float to the carved angels there,
> The silver-clouded incense faints in air:
> Only the organ's voice, with peal on peal,

---

65 [John Henry Newman], *Loss and Gain*, London: James Burns, 1848, pp. 181-182. Although Newman converted to Catholicism in 1845 he states that *Loss and Gain* is not autobiographical (see 'Advertisement').

66 Elisabeth Dhanens, *Van Eyck: The Ghent Altarpiece*, Ed. John Fleming and Hugh Honour, London: Allen Lane, 1973, p. 19.

67 ibid., p. 22.

Can mount to where those far-off angels kneel.
Here the pale boy, beneath a low side-arch,
Would listen to its solemn chant or march;
Folding his little hands, his simple prayer
Melted in childish dreams, and both in air:
While the great organ over all would roll,
Speaking strange secrets to his innocent soul,
Bearing on eagle wings the great desire
Of all the kneeling throng, and piercing higher
Than aught but love and prayer can reach, until
Only the silence seemed to listen still;
Or gathering like a sea still more and more,
Break in melodious waves at heaven's door,
And then fall, slow and soft, in tender rain,
Upon the pleading, longing hearts again.

(p. 65, ll. 64–86)

It is interesting to compare this extremely sensuous description of St Bavon's
with A.W. Pugin's description of what he refers to as 'those stupendous
Ecclesiastical Edifices of the Middle Ages' in *Contrasts* (1836). Pugin seeks
to convince his readers of the superiority of medieval architecture (he and
his revival of Gothic architecture are often linked to the aims of the Oxford
Movement[68]):

Here every portion of the sacred fabric bespeaks its origin; . . . the
brazen font where the waters of baptism wash away the stain of
original sin; there stands the gigantic pulpit, from which the sacred
truths and ordinances are from time to time proclaimed to the
congregated people; behold yonder, resplendent with precious gems, is
the high altar, the seat of the most holy mysteries, and the tabernacle
of the Highest! It is, indeed, a sacred place; and well does the fabric
bespeak its destined purpose: the eye is carried up and lost in the
height of the vaulting and the intricacy of the ailes; the rich and
varied hues of the stained windows, the modulated light, the gleam of
the tapers, the richness of the altars, the venerable images of the
departed just, – all alike conspire to fill the mind with veneration for
the place, and to make it feel the sublimity of Christian worship.[69]

---

[68]   Tennyson, op. cit., 'Ch. V. Isaac Williams: Reserve, Nature, and the Gothic
Revival'.
[69]   A. Welby Pugin, *Contrasts: or, A Parallel Between the Noble Edifices of
the Fourteenth and Fifteenth Centuries, and Similar Buildings of the Present Day;
shewing the Present Decay of Taste*, London: Printed for the Author, and Published
by Him, at St Marie's Grange, Near Salisbury, Wilts., 1836, p. 2.

Both descriptions inspire awe and solemnity, but Procter's depiction emphasises the fragility as well as the solemnity of the cathedral. The pillars are 'slender' and the eye is carried down the 'vistas' which suggest a receding and narrowing. Prayer is described as 'weak and doubting' and incense 'faints' in the huge space. And yet immense strength is suggested by the phallic 'organ' and its 'secrets' which inspire the sickly boy, who is supported by its strength, and like the congregation is carried away by the 'desire' it seems to accommodate. The breaking of the waves of 'love and prayer' at Heaven's door demonstrates the gap between the 'hearts' below and heaven above (recalling Keble's poem 'The Waterfall').

By contrast Pugin's description emphasises the bullying and grandiose aspect of the edifice. The font is 'brazen' and the pulpit 'gigantic'. The place conspires to 'make' the mind feel its sublimity. Conspires not inspires, suggesting that the sacred place is indeed a place designed to scare. The descriptions create the sense of an overwhelming power as they accumulate. In Procter's description adjectives and nouns are broken up by conjunctions and prepositions ('solemn and rich and vast'; 'weak and doubting'; 'peal on peal'; 'love and prayer'; 'more and more'; 'slow and soft') which slow the pace, suggesting less a climactic and bullying power than a potency which is calming and which gently dissolves the pain of those beneath it.

This sense of dissolution undermines the weighty and material presence of the cathedral. The movement of sunlight through the cathedral also suggests an impermanence in that it only momentarily lights up the cathedral's treasures. When the boy comes out into the 'noisy glare' of the 'busy square' there is a sense of having left behind a perhaps non-existent or ephemeral world:

> Then he would watch the rosy sunlight glow,
> That crept along the marble floor below,
> Passing, as life does, with the passing hours,
> Now by a shrine all rich with gems and flowers,
> Now on the brazen letters of a tomb,
> Then, leaving it again to shade and gloom,
> And creeping on, to show, distinct and quaint,
> The kneeling figure of some marble saint:
> Or lighting up the carvings strange and rare,
> That told of patient toil, and reverent care;
> Ivy that trembled on the spray, and ears
> Of heavy corn, and slender bulrush spears,
> And all the thousand tangled weeds that grow
> In summer, where the silver rivers flow;
> And demon heads grotesque, that seemed to glare

In impotent wrath on all the beauty there:
Then the gold rays up pillared shaft would climb
And so be drawn to heaven, at evening time.
And deeper silence, darker shadows flowed
On all around, only the windows glowed
With blazoned glory, like the shields of light
Archangels bear, who, armed with love and might,
Watch upon heaven's battlements at night.
Then all was shade; the silver lamps that gleamed,
Lost in the daylight, in the darkness seemed
Like sparks of fire in the dim aisles to shine,
Or trembling stars before each separate shrine.
Grown half afraid, the child would leave them there,
And come out, blinded by the noisy glare
That burst upon him from the busy square.

(pp. 65–66, ll. 87–116)

The transience of wealth as the 'shade' comes down is depicted in this sensuous description. There is a wealth of natural description which also undermines the permanence of the cathedral's features and of its stoniness ('heavy corn', 'slender bulrush spears', 'the thousand tangled weeds'). The immediacy of time ('Now ... Now ... Then ...') which passes is linked to natural death and decay. The 'glare' of the 'demon heads grotesque' is less threatening to this passing beauty than the 'glare' of the external world which blinds the boy when he goes outside.

The external glare contrasts with the 'rosy sunlight glow' inside the cathedral which moves up to the windows glowing 'like the shields of light / Archangels bear'. The remaining 'glow', which is likened to 'blazoned glory', suggests a strong desire to protect the cathedral contents which are only momentarily lit up and revealed. The 'silver lamps', compared to 'trembling stars', suggest vulnerability. The 'glare' outside, which is linked alliteratively to the 'glow' inside, is strong and harsh by contrast.

The sublime and awesome power of the Gothic cathedral which Pugin describes as bespeaking 'its origin' is depicted as less controlling and fixed in 'A Tomb in Ghent'.[70] The weight of Keble's omnipotent and overbearing God with his keen and penetrating 'Eye' is absent. The musician is the only

---

[70] Christina Rossetti in *Time Flies* asks why the 'room' of the church should be contemplated as 'a lofty and vast palace of well-nigh uninhabitable grandeur'. Rossetti contrasts loftiness with homeliness: 'a nest is surely the very homeliest idea of a home'. *Time Flies: a reading diary* consists of short poems and passages, one for each day of the year (Rossetti, *Time Flies. A Reading Diary*, London: Society for Promoting Christian Knowledge, 1885, p. 164).

one who is clearly in possession of 'master-power' and he is described as vulnerable and human. The 'noisy glare' outside does not suggest a divine source. It is not a light or illumination which, Keble writes, when tracked 'to its source' leads to God.[71] It rather suggests the materiality of a busy and noisy city centre. The outside world is depicted as a threat or a 'blind' to the inner resources of faith (p. 66, l. 115).

It is interesting to note that Dante Gabriel Rossetti describes the same St Bavon's in his poem 'Pax Vobis' which was published in the short-lived pre-Raphaelite journal *The Germ* in 1850.[72] Rossetti had visited Ghent in 1850 and Procter may have had a first hand account of the trip as the Rossettis visited the Procters.[73] The poem is about a priest who is losing his faith and the loss of his faith is likened to losing a recently potent music:

> The organ and the chaunt had ceased:
> A few words paused against his ear,
>   Said from the altar: drawn round him,
>   The silence was at rest and dim.
> He could not pray. The bell shook clear
> And ceased . . .

The poem concludes with the priest sadly acknowledging 'There is a world outside'.[74]

The 'glare' of the 'world outside' in 'A Tomb in Ghent' seems to shock the reader temporarily into an awareness of the strength of an external reality. The natural light is harsh and disconcerting rather than suggestive of the bright picture book illuminations depicted by Keble in *The Christian Year*.

1855, the year 'A Tomb in Ghent' was published, also saw the publication in *Fraser's Magazine* of Matthew Arnold's seminal poem about loss of faith,

---

[71] 'Dedication', [Keble], *The Christian Year* (1870).

[72] *The Germ* was edited by W.M. Rossetti and ran for only four issues, from January, 1850 to May, 1850. The first two issues were titled *The Germ: Thoughts towards Nature in Poetry, Literature, and Art*, and the last two *Art and Poetry: Being Thoughts towards Nature*. D.G. Rossetti's 'The Blessed Damozel' was published in the journal, along with poems by Christina Rossetti, Coventry Patmore and W.B. Scott (*The Germ. The Literary Magazine of the Pre-Raphaelites*, Preface. Andrea Rose, Oxford: Ashmolean Museum and Birmingham City Museums & Art Gallery, 1979).

[73] Oswald Doughty gives an account of Rossetti and Holman Hunt's 'foreign tour' of Europe, which included Ghent, in 1849–1850. Doughty describes the poem 'Pax Vobis' as dramatising Rossetti's inner conflict about a religious tradition he was leaving behind (Oswald Doughty, *A Victorian Romantic – Dante Gabriel Rossetti*, Oxford University Press, 1949, p. 136).

[74] *The Germ*, op. cit., pp. 176–177.

'Stanzas from the Grande Chartreuse'. In this poem the spiritual life of Carthusian monks is contrasted with the speaker's loss of faith through his recent education and learning. He feels himself to be 'Wandering between two worlds, one dead, / The other powerless to be born'. His faith has been exposed by the world as a dream: 'For the world cries your faith is now / But a dead time's exploded dream'.[75] Like Arnold, Procter appears to be 'Wandering between two worlds', or more than two, in that the external 'glare' (including the dragon's 'glare' which I shall discuss later), the shadowy domesticity to which the musician's daughter returns and her fragmentary memories undermine the certainties of Keble's faith which posits the two clearly demarcated worlds of heaven and earth.

There are no overt expressions of religious doubt in the poem but there is a strong underlying uncertainty about the permanence of the cathedral and the faith it represents. The cathedral by the conclusion of the poem has become dreamlike: 'Past dreams of childhood float upon the air' (p. 70, l. 286) but the chronicler/narrator has attempted to provide the young woman with a history and a narrative within which the cathedral and her past have a place.

Two months before the publication of 'A Tomb in Ghent' Procter's poem 'A Dream' was published in *Household Words* (6.10.1855). In this beautiful lyric the speaker recounts the tale of yesterday's 'spinning' of a dream while she was sitting on a hill. The 'spinning' has preoccupied her for the entire day:

---

[75] Matthew Arnold, *Selected Poetry*, Ed. Keith Silver, Manchester: Carcanet Press Limited, 1994, pp. 120-126.
Procter would have read Arnold's poem 'The Church of Brou', a poem about a church in the Savoy valleys which is depicted as a beautiful but deathly retreat from the world. The section of the poem 'The Tomb' includes some passages which are very similar to the descriptions of St Bavon's, for example:
On the carv'd Western Front a flood of light
Streams from the setting sun, and colours bright
Prophets, transfigur'd Saints, and Martyrs brave,
In the vast western window of the nave;
And on the pavement round the Tomb there glints
A chequer-work of glowing sapphire tints,
                    ... and on the walls
Shedding her pensive light at intervals
The Moon through the clere-story windows shines,
And the wind washes in the mountain pines.
Then, gazing up through the dim pillars high,
The foliag'd marble forest where ye lie,
(Arnold, *Poems*, London: Longman, Brown, Green, and Longmans, 1853, pp. 150-152)

> I took the threads for my spinning,
>   All of blue summer air,
> And a flickering ray of sunlight
>   Was woven in here and there.
>
> The shadows grew longer and longer,
>   The evening wind passed by,
> And the purple splendour of sunset
>   Was flooding the western sky.

When she returns to the hill in the morning she notes 'There was nothing but glistening dew-drops / Remained of my dream to-day'. (pp. 76-77) Procter's poem 'Dream-Life' (1859) concludes:

> Which, you ask me, is the real life,
>   Which the Dream – the joy, or woe?
> Hush, friend! it is little matter,
>   And, indeed, – I never know.
>   (p. 197, ll. 25-28)

The poem ends on a relatively light note. Although anxious, the speaker is prepared to live with the not knowing. The problem with Procter's consideration of dreams is that it is not clear what remains that is substantial (see Chapter 4). In 'A Tomb in Ghent' there is a sense of a retreat from the richness of a cathedral space, which has become dreamlike or a place of dreams, into an ill-defined domesticity. The title of the poem is after all 'A Tomb in Ghent' which draws attention to some kind of death. The title of the poem does not promote the authority of the building or church itself.

John Keble used the calendar of the Christian year and the Book of Common Prayer to structure *The Christian Year*. Isaac Williams, another important Tractarian poet and theorist, wrote a series of poems called *The Cathedral* (modelled on George Herbert's *The Temple* (1633-1679)) and he uses the cathedral as the structuring principle for these poems. In the 'Advertisement' to the first edition of *The Cathedral* (1838) Williams refers to Wordsworth's 'Preface' to *The Excursion* in which Wordsworth suggests that his poems 'might be considered as capable of being arranged as parts of a Gothic Church'.[76] In this 'Preface' Wordsworth refers to 'The Recluse'

---

[76] 'Advertisement', [Isaac Williams], *The Cathedral, or the Catholic and Apostolic Church in England*, Oxford: John Henry Parker, F. and J. Rivington, London, 1848, pp. v-vi.

and 'The Excursion' and draws attention to the ecclesiastical structure of his works:

> the two works have the same kind of relation to each other, if he may so express himself, as the ante-chapel has to the body of a Gothic church. Continuing this allusion, he may be permitted to add, that his minor pieces, which have been long before the public, being now properly arranged, will be found by the attentive reader to have such connexion with the main work as may give them claim to be likened to the little cells, oratories, and sepulchral recesses, ordinarily included in those edifices.[77]

The parts come together in Wordsworth's rather grandiose account of his sacred corpus, but in 'A Tomb in Ghent' Procter is questioning the young woman's complex relationship to the edifice of the cathedral. Like D.G. Rossetti and Matthew Arnold she is indirectly questioning her relationship to her faith, which was apparently so strong. She is also asking questions about the substance of her corpus of poetry and about the strength of her commitment to her work.

The Musician

The interior space of St Bavon's is shown to be primarily under the control of the musician. In Tractarian poetic terms the church is poetry. Bessie Parkes describes the cathedral as a 'sculptured song' in a poem titled 'The Cathedral'.[78] To that extent the musician controls the music or poetry of faith.

Procter's commitment to the church may be likened to her commitment to her own poetry. In 'A Tomb in Ghent' she subtly questions a young woman's relationship to the 'song' which is under the control of the father – a father to whom the daughter is strongly attached and devoted. Staying inside the church is depicted as staying within the authority or domain of a father who, although attractive, may mute and suppress the daughter's potentiality for expression. Uncertainty regarding her faith (or the church) may be linked to doubts about the respective position of the father and daughter who live within its precincts.

Procter's depiction of the musician father is extremely sympathetic. Unlike

---

[77] *The Poetical Works of Wordsworth*, London: Frederick Warne and Co., [no date], p. 335.

[78] Bessie Rayner Parkes (Belloc), *Poems*, London: John Chapman, 1855, p. 80.

Keble's Fathers of the Church the father figure, although in possession of 'master-power', is depicted as sickly and mortal. Like the church itself he is shown to be both weak and strong. The cathedral organist who entrances his congregation may have represented various 'fathers' in Procter's life. Her actual father did not achieve the status of a major poet, or 'Primary Poet' in Keble's terms, and the 'gentle friend and guide' (p. 68, l. 181) and teacher of harmony in 'A Tomb in Ghent' strongly suggests the figure of Bryan Procter.

The organist also suggests the figure of Father Faber of the London and later the Brompton Oratory. John Julian in *A Dictionary of Hymnology* describes Faber as being responsible for the growth of congregational singing amongst Roman Catholics in Britain. Faber also translated Latin hymns into English, as well as writing hymns in English.[79] Procter had enthusiastically recommended his sermons in a letter to a friend Richard Monckton Milnes – a letter which was written in 1855, the same year as the publication of 'A Tomb in Ghent'.

Procter may also have been thinking of John Pyke Hullah, who pioneered music teaching for the public and initiated popular singing classes in Exeter Hall, London in 1841. Hullah taught at Queen's College, attended by Procter in 1850. (In 1860 Procter wrote to Hullah asking for his advice about the 'capabilities for music' of the legend 'The Story of the Faithful Soul', which is a poem that also expresses doubt, both religious and romantic; see Conclusion.[80])

All these 'fathers' exemplify notions of sharing and a diffusion of knowledge along with the conveying of pleasure. They are unlike Keble's Fathers of the Church in that they are not distant and they seem to have been more admired than feared by Procter.

Procter's depiction of this son of an artisan also exemplifies the quality which Keble refers to in his *Oxford Lectures* as the poetical in 'common daily life'.[81] He describes the poetic feeling and appreciation which the lower classes often demonstrate more than the 'wealthy and the privileged' who, he states, are prone to fall in with 'fashionable convention' rather than express themselves with sincerity.[82]

But Keble's account is patronising. He is opposed to democracy on the grounds that distinction between classes under a democracy will be based on wealth which will then become the dominant principle in people's lives.[83]

---

[79] Julian, op. cit., p. 975. Julian writes 'The congregation to which he was attached entered into his hymns fervently'.

[80] MS, A.A. Procter to J.P. Hullah (23.7.1860), University of Iowa Libraries.

[81] *Keble's Lectures on Poetry*, 1, p. 25.

[82] ibid., p. 28.

[83] ibid., p. 257.

Keble writes: 'poetry will be unappreciated under a democracy'.[84] His position is anti-Utilitarian and he sees the poet as set apart from the 'ignorant many' of whatever class who have come under the sway of utilitarianism. The poet, he states, will incline to that party in the state which 'is furthest removed from them'.[85]

Implicit in Keble's critique is a belief in a hierarchy within which the masses, even if capable of poetic appreciation, will know their place. Keble's pantheon of Primary and Secondary Poets, and his pantheon of heroes, suggest a love of hierarchy within which there is not much room for too many poets or heroes. Isaac Williams in 'Tract 87' describes the revelation of the holiest mysteries which is granted to the faithful only after 'long previous preparation'.[86] Similarly, the writing of poetry, in Keble's account, appears to be reserved for the privileged few.

Procter by contrast provides a critique of Keble's notion of an hierarchical status awarded to the known and approved 'Poet' or 'Hero'. The musician, like his father, is a skilled worker and, although there is a sadness expressed at his lack of wider fame, his skill is still recognised by his congregation, who, like Keble's humble folk, can appreciate his art. The fact that the musician is unnamed and not widely known (and all the protagonists are anonymous) locates him, in class terms, much closer to his unnamed artisan father and to the people who enjoy his music. Procter's critique of Keble's position lies in her suggestion that the musician, under more favourable conditions, may have achieved 'world-wide fame' (p. 68, l. 176). He does not exist at a vast distance from the idealised Poet or Hero of Keble's imagination.

It is a sympathetic and poignant portrait. In a later narrative poem by Procter, 'True Honours' (1858; pp. 24–30), a blind poet recounts how his three brothers have all achieved greater fame than himself. One is a philanthropist, the second a soldier and the third a poet. The blind poet is cheered by the thought that his 'humble verses' are appreciated by the poor (p. 30, l. 239). Procter invokes the figure of Homer (admired by Keble) to draw attention to the relatively anonymous poet – Homer as the wandering minstrel – rather than the poet institutionalised by Keble within a hierarchy of poets.

In several poems Procter rejects the notion of the value which attaches to

---

[84]   ibid.
[85]   ibid., p. 259.
[86]   [Isaac Williams], 'Tract No. 87', *Tracts for the Times. By Members of the University of Oxford*, Vol. V for 1838–40, London: J.G.F. & J. Rivington, 1840, p. 6.

the status of the recognised artist. In the poem 'My Picture' (1854) the speaker describes a picture in her 'garret'. It is a portrait of someone who has 'a student air; / With a look half sad, half stately, / Grave sweet eyes and flowing hair'. The picture becomes a friend, inspiration and support in her struggle as a writer (pp. 20–21), but it is not held in reverential awe:

> Little care I who the painter,
>   How obscure a name he bore;
> Nor, when some have named Velasquez,
>   Did I value it the more.
>   (p. 20, ll. 9–12)

The speaker goes on to say that she would not exchange the picture 'For the rarest piece of art' (p. 20, l. 14).

By invoking Velasquez Procter draws attention to the 'realism' with which Velasquez was associated. *The Oxford Companion to Art* describes his work as follows:

> In such paintings as *The Old Woman Cooking Eggs* . . . and *The Water Carrier* . . . Velasquez gave this kind of subject a new seriousness and dignity. Each object is treated as of value in itself.[87]

Procter draws attention to what she considers the 'real' 'value' of a work of art which is its ability to communicate and show sympathy. The fact that a painting is 'rare' may rarefy or reify it, which does not add to and may well detract from the qualities which she values. It is as if she deliberately chooses not to explore its provenance, a knowledge of which may interfere with her relationship to the picture.

There is a notable absence of works of art by named artists in St Bavon's. The boy has a familiar relationship with the pictures ('The pictured faces that he knew so well'; p. 66, l. 119) which detracts from any sense of awe and the detailed descriptions of the cathedral carvings draw attention to the anonymous craftsmen who worked in the cathedral rather than to the famous artist.[88] Procter would probably have read John Ruskin's 'The Nature of Gothic' in *The Stones of Venice*, published two years earlier in 1853, in

---

[87] *The Oxford Companion to Art*, Ed. Harold Osborne, Oxford at the Clarendon Press, 1970.

[88] See A.A. Procter, 'The Carver's Lesson', pp. 198–199.

which the importance of the workman's close and involved relationship to his labour is discussed.[89]

In 'My Picture' Procter draws attention to the 'poor' writer whose creativity is enabled by the picture watching over her paternally only so long as she is not distracted or intimidated by it as a work of art framed by its fame and status. In 'A Tomb in Ghent' it is significant that it is only when the young woman has left the cathedral setting, or frame, and her father that her song is actually heard and 'valued' by her chronicler. In spite of Procter's sympathetic treatment of the musician father (which contrasts with Keble's representations of the omnipotent Father) the musician's daughter, whilst remaining in the cathedral, stays within the father's shadow and the precincts of his 'home'. If the 'home' the church provides is read as poetry in the Tractarian sense it may be understood to represent the place of her father's poetry and its preoccupations, along with the authority these exert over the daughter.

The White Maiden's Tomb

The young woman's relationship to her song is explored further through the use of key Tractarian visible symbols. The idea that poetry, particularly the symbol, is an expression of theological and spiritual truth was widespread in the nineteenth century.[90] Procter employs visible symbols to convey deeply spiritual meanings whilst simultaneously deploying them to unsettle her reader and to question the truths the symbols embody.

Procter's deployment of these symbols further undermines Keble's notion of a safe, secure and unthreatened space. She also draws attention to a potential for appropriation and violence which is masked by the apparently benign face of a fragile father who actually controls the space and the song within it.

One such symbol is the White Maiden's Tomb. The title of the poem emphasises the importance of the tomb which is a nodal point in the poem.

---

89   In his discussion of the Gothic workman in *The Stones of Venice* Ruskin writes that 'to the Gothic workman the living foliage became a subject of intense affection, and he struggled to render all its characters with as much accuracy as was compatible with the laws of his design and the nature of his material' (Ruskin, *The Stones of Venice* in *Victorian Prose and Poetry*, Ed. Lionel Trilling and Harold Bloom, New York: Oxford University Press, 1973, p. 186).

90   The symbol as a means of expressing spiritual truths and of interpreting facts is discussed in M. Jaduiga Swiatecka, *The Idea of the Symbol. Some Nineteenth Century Comparisons with Coleridge*, Cambridge University Press, 1980.

The boy, the musician he becomes, and his wife are all drawn down the winding stairs to the site of the tomb in the crypt which suggests the presence of a cryptic message or secret:

> The people call it The White Maiden's Tomb:
> For there she stands; her folded hands are pressed
> Together, and laid softly on her breast,
> As if she waited but a word to rise
> From the dull earth, and pass to the blue skies;
> Her lips expectant part, she holds her breath,
> As listening for the angel voice of death.
> None know how many years have seen her so,
> Or what the name of her who sleeps below.
> And here the child would come, and strive to trace,
> Through the dim twilight, the pure gentle face
> He loved so well, and here he oft would bring
> Some violet blossom of the early spring;
> And climbing softly by the fretted stand,
> Not to disturb her, lay it in her hand;
> Or, whispering a soft loving message sweet,
> Would stoop and kiss the little marble feet.
> So, when the organ's pealing music rang,
> He thought amid the gloom the Maiden sang;
> With reverent simple faith by her he knelt,
> And fancied what she thought, and what she felt;
> 'Glory to God,' re-echoed from her voice,
> And then his little spirit would rejoice;
> Or when the Requiem sobbed upon the air,
> His baby tears dropped with her mournful prayer.
>   (pp. 66-67, ll. 124-148)

It is as though the boy is drawn by the maiden's simple, innocent and blank state. She is associated with the music and he imagines that she sings. His contact with the tomb appears to enable his own creativity. The following verse paragraph describes the rousing of his 'artist-soul' and the flaming of his 'genius' (p. 67, ll. 151-152). The White Maiden is depicted as holding within her the source or breath of song whilst she awaits the angel of death: 'Her lips expectant part, she holds her breath'. The boy is shown attempting to 'trace' her face and by association the source of her song. He is depicted as innocently attempting to penetrate her 'secret' by imagining her thoughts and feelings.

The anonymity of this source of song ensures that the musician need make no acknowledgement. When the musician meets his 'own White Maiden',

'Her eyes raised up to Heaven, her lips apart, / And music overflowing from her heart', the notes of her song die under his admiring gaze:

> Perplexed and startled at his wondering look,
> Her rustling score of Mozart's Sanctus shook;
> The uncertain notes, like birds within a snare,
> Fluttered and died upon the trembling air.
>   (p. 68, ll. 193–202)

Although she joins him as pupil and wife, it is his music which predominates and is recognised, whilst her song is arrested in flight. She is identified with the White Maiden's Tomb where she often kneels 'Waiting and praying' in the 'gloom', and she dies young (p. 69, ll. 233–236). Both the tomb and the musician's wife are models of an exemplary womanly 'reserve' in Keble's sense. They remain in the shadows of male authority.

Isaac Williams, often referred to as the 'Apostle of Reserve', describes in 'Tract 87' the Disciplina Arcani (the Discipline of the Secret). This 'Discipline' was instituted by the Fathers of the Ancient Church and only a few initiated in the 'higher doctrines' of the Faith might penetrate the 'Secret'.[91] The difficulties encountered when attempting to understand the 'Secret' are described by Williams as being:

> like the hardness of an external covering, which preserves and guards
> the most precious fruits of nature, and affords trouble at arriving at
> them.[92]

In the poem *The Cathedral* (1838) Williams describes the 'ancient Discipline' which guards her treasures.[93] These treasures or truths are held within the symbolic forms presented by the cathedral structure, and at one point in the poem they are described as embryonic:

> Their embryo forms in secret lie . . .[94]

The White Maiden's Tomb as a model of 'reserve' is presented as having lost the capacity for development. Her reserve is depicted less as a hard 'covering' to be penetrated than as a reserve which has totally hardened and become petrified. Whatever might have been embryonic has been lost or

---

91 [Williams], 'Tract No. 87', p. 6.
92 ibid., p. 44.
93 [Williams], *The Cathedral*, p. 6.
94 ibid., p. 110.

unconsciously appropriated by the musician. An intense anxiety about being heard at all is being expressed.

In the section titled 'The Lady Chapel' in *The Cathedral* the poem 'The Song of the Blessed Virgin' describes the Virgin as paradoxically having a song but 'no voice':

> We seize her mantle, ere she heavenward springs,
> And wait her voice, – from her no accent breaks,
> Her voice is with her God, her silence speaks.[95]

God as the supreme authority has appropriated her song, as the musician with 'master-power' unwittingly appropriates the White Maiden's and his wife's song.

From Procter's exploration of the White Maiden's Tomb and women's song within the cathedral a powerful critique of Tractarian reserve emerges. Procter depicts the fatal consequences of 'reserve' for a woman and seeks a way for her protagonist to escape silence and stoniness.

The daughter, who is the only female depicted as lively – as she climbs, roams and plays in the cathedral – appears to be unaware of the deadening of women's creativity which surrounds her. She is resilient when her mother dies – 'Forgot her passionate grief in time, and smiled' (p. 69, l. 239). Financial circumstances, when her father dies, compel her to return to England where her voice is heard, even though fragmentarily. The enforced return appears to represent a way out of some kind of deadlock as residence within the cathedral may lead to petrifaction.

Procter is likely to have read Caroline Bowles Southey's narrative poem 'The Legend of Santarem', another poem about petrifaction. In this Catholic tale orphan twin sisters find sanctuary in a Portuguese cathedral. The cathedral becomes their home and they are one day visited by Jesus who asks them to eat with him the next day. The Dominican father who is the Catholic priest of the cathedral begs to join them, and the three are led by a ray of sunlight to a small chapel where they meet Jesus: 'Like a golden clue / Streamed on before that long bright sunset ray'. The next day they are found turned to stone and their petrifaction is hailed as a miracle:

---

[95]   ibid., p. 234 and p. 236.

> Suffice it that with Him they surely were
>   That night in Paradise; for those who came
> Next to the chapel found them as in prayer,
>   Still kneeling, stiffened every lifeless frame,
> With hands and eyes upraised as when they died,
>   Toward the image of the Crucified.[96]

The 'sunset ray' provides a 'golden clue', which is like the 'labyrinthine clue' Keble describes – the 'clue' which is provided by the measure and rhythm of poetry. Keble's clue leads to 'healing relief' to 'secret mental emotion', and Keble adds that relief is attained 'without detriment to modest reserve: and while giving scope to enthusiasm, yet rules it with order and due control.' When they follow the 'golden clue' or eye of God the sisters and priest in 'A Legend of Santarem' find scope for their 'enthusiasm' for Jesus (and the church where he metaphorically resides) and the final relief of petrifaction when in the presence of God's controlling authority.

In 'The Legend of Santarem' and 'A Tomb in Ghent' the women poets Bowles and Procter express a fear of petrifaction within the domain of God's or male authority. This fear may be read as a generalised fear of the deadening of women's creativity depicted in well-known myths. Daphne was transformed into a laurel tree by her father Peneus to save her from the all-consuming love of Apollo, and Galatea is given life by Venus when Pygmalion falls in love with the statue he preferred to a real woman.[97] In both cases a woman's petrifaction and animation are dependent upon male potency and desire, and in Daphne's case a father's potency ensures that the daughter becomes an emblem of male triumph, signified by the laurel.

These powerful myths suggest that a woman, particularly a woman who attracts male attention, is in serious danger of being petrified by the potency of male desire for her. The woman poet who attempts to realise her own potential as a poet, and as a woman expressing desires, is faced with the myths which people her imagination. T.S. Eliot, in his essay 'Tradition and the Individual Talent' (1919), writes that the poet and artist need to develop a 'consciousness of the past' in the present, in the presence of which the individual artist surrenders himself:

---

[96] Caroline Bowles (née Southey), *The Birth-Day; A Poem in Three Parts: to which are added Occasional Verses*, London: William Blackwood and Sons, 1836, pp. 276-283.

[97] *The Metamorphoses of Ovid*, Trans. Mary M. Innes, Harmondsworth: Penguin Books Ltd., 1955, pp. 41-44, 231-232.

What happens is a continual surrender of himself as he is at the moment to something which is more valuable. The progress of an artist is a continual self-sacrifice, a continual extinction of personality.[98]

In 'A Tomb in Ghent' Procter explores the 'monuments' in her imagination which include the 'tomb' of a petrified woman whose potential is frozen and incorporated within the song of the father (both the literal father and God). The 'surrender' and 'extinction of personality' which Eliot advocates are extremely problematic for the woman poet who is faced with her own monumentalised surrender. She has already been extinguished. In 'A Tomb in Ghent' the solution to the woman poet's dilemma is metaphorised by the young woman's departure or escape from the father's church which has become a potentially deadening location.

The presence of a longing to escape the place of death is also seen in Procter's poem 'The Two Interpreters' which was published in *Household Words* on 15th December 1855, just two weeks before the publication of 'A Tomb in Ghent'. This poem suggests that two readings may exist simultaneously. 'The Two Interpreters' takes the form of a dialogue between father and son who are shown reading the sky in Tractarian fashion. The mother, who is dead, is seen in the sky by the father as a 'shadowy form', smiling down, and as a white form being carried away by angels.

The son by contrast sees movement and change:

> 'The clouds are fleeting by, father,
>   Look in the shining west,
> The great white clouds sail onward
>   Upon the sky's blue breast.
> Look at a snowy eagle,
>   His wings are tinged with red,
> And a giant dolphin follows him,
>   With a crown upon his head!'

He sees the clouds changing and red and purple ships sailing 'in a sea of fire!', an azure lake and a castle peopled by knights and ladies (pp. 144–145).

The poem describes a father's grief and mourning and a child's resilience in the face of loss (similar to the resilience of the daughter in 'A Tomb in Ghent') and in a more general sense the poem suggests the existence of a struggle between liveliness and deadliness. What has been excluded from the cathedral in 'A Tomb in Ghent' is an adult woman's liveliness. Within the

---

[98] T.S. Eliot, *Selected Essays*, London: Faber and Faber Limited, 1932, p. 17.

cathedral adult women are reserved and deadened and the daughter's liveliness is that of a child's (accommodated by the father) before entering into an adult woman's world.

This exclusion of adult liveliness assumes yet greater significance in the light of Procter's possible exclusion of most of the narrative of the Belgian folktale upon which 'A Tomb in Ghent' may very well have been based, according to F. Janku.[99] This tale provides a further gloss on the extent to which Procter adopted a position of Tractarian poetic reserve. It is worth giving a detailed synopsis of the tale.

The Catholic folktale 'Der Drache auf dem Belfried (Gent)' ('The Dragon upon the Keep') is included in Maria von Ploennies's *Dies Sagens Belgiens* (1843).[100] Set at the time of a crusade it tells the story of Blanka, the king of Jerusalem's daughter. Blanka and some ladies-in-waiting wander off one day and are captured by Balduin (probably Balduin IX of Flanders who led the 4th Crusade in 1202-1204) who imprisons them in a tower. One of the ladies escapes and rides to Jerusalem to seek help from Blanka's father, who dispatches a dragon to watch over the tower. He also offers a ransom for his daughter, which is refused by the Ghent knights but accepted by the Bruges knights.

On receipt of the ransom money they murder the messenger, kill the dragon, and load Blanka and the dragon onto a brace of horses. They then race to the sea where they disembark. Blanka and the leader of the Bruges crusaders fall in love and the crusader succeeds in converting her to Christianity. Having landed on a high sand dune concealing a chapel Blanka asks the name of the place and the knight names it 'Blankenberg' after Blanka. Eager to be baptised, having been strongly impressed by the beautiful ceremony of the mass, Blanka climbs into the broad font for her baptism a few days later. On the same day the priest blesses her marriage to the knight.

The couple return to Bruges with the dragon, which is hung in iron chains from the top of the Church of St Donatius. The iconclasts (the anti-Catholics) burn him and the craftsmen of Bruges make a replica of the dragon out of heavy sheets of bronze. The dragon is eventually reclaimed by Ghent under the leadership of Artevelde the brewer.[101]

---

[99] Janku, op. cit., p. 39.

[100] Maria von Ploennies, *Die Sagen Belgiens*, Koln: F.C. Gifen, 1846, pp. 93-99. (Trans. Philip Jenkins).

[101] Jacob Van Artevelde, a legendary Captain of Ghent (1338-1345). He was assassinated in 1345 by weavers in revolt against his rule (David Nicholas, *The Metamorphosis of a Medieval City. Ghent in the Age of the Arteveldes, 1302-1390*, University of Nebraska Press, 1987, pp. 3-4).

If Procter did draw on this Catholic folktale it is extraordinarily suggestive in terms of what may have been excluded from 'A Tomb in Ghent' and from St Bavon's Cathedral. The lively heroine Blanka contrasts dramatically with the dead White Maiden (and the name Blanka may have influenced Procter's choice of the anonymous White Maiden). Blanka is depicted as a woman on the move, adventurously and comically adopting a new religion, husband and country. As her name suggests she enters into a new, blank and unknown future without reserve. Her career is closely linked to that of the dragon (the loading of Blanka and the dead dragon onto the horses would surely have appealed to Procter's sense of the absurd). But unlike the dragon she appears to survive her appropriation as though through sheer energy. She also survives the dragon as angry woman in that her energies and passions have been channelled in a new direction and she does not apparently end up in chains like the dragon.

The dragon itself provides a further clue as to the passions and emotions which may have been excluded from the cathedral. It is the visible symbol par excellence, which the boy glimpses on top of the cathedral. Like a weather cock (and the actual golden dragon on top of St Bavon's looks like a weathercock) it signals the possibility of new directions – the coming 'into the domain of what might be' which Procter associated with Belgium. It also suggests the presence of a potential for extreme liveliness and destructiveness which has been arrested or rigidified.

'The Gilt Dragon'

In his childhood the musician's artisan father had told him stories of 'English heroes' and the tale of the dragon:

> to him he talked
> Of home, of England, and strange stories told
> Of English heroes in the days of old;
> And (when the sunset gilded roof and spire,)
> The marvellous tale which never seemed to tire:
> How the gilt dragon, glaring fiercely down
> From the great belfry, watching all the town,
> Was brought, a trophy of the wars divine,
> By a Crusader from far Palestine,
> And given to Bruges; and how Ghent arose,
> And how they struggled long as deadly foes,
> Till Ghent, one night, by a brave soldier's skill,
> Stole the great dragon; and she keeps it still.
> One day the dragon – so 'tis said – will rise,

Spread his bright wings, and glitter in the skies,
And over desert lands and azure seas,
Will seek his home 'mid palm and cedar trees.
So, as he passed the belfry every day,
The boy would look if it were flown away,
Each day surprised to find it watching there,
Above him as he crossed the ancient square,
To seek the great cathedral, that had grown
A home for him – mysterious and his own.
                                        (pp. 64-65, ll. 41-63)

The dragon, like the White Maiden's Tomb, is an unsettling nodal point in the poem. The eye is drawn both down into the crypt and up towards the belfry and the dragon, whose presence disturbs rather than frightens, inspiring emotions of wonder, curiosity and surprise at its incongruity rather than the astonishment or terror often associated with sublimity. Edmund Burke in A Philosophical Enquiry into the Origin of our Ideas of the Sublime and Beautiful (1757) writes that 'Astonishment, . . . is the effect of the sublime in its highest degree' and he cites the serpent as capable of 'raising ideas of the sublime, because they are considered as objects of terror'.[102]

Procter's dragon is not a pinnacle denoting sublimity in Burke's sense. It 'glares fiercely down', suggesting a weighty presence, but the reason for its angry look appears to be associated with its displacement. The desire to return home, as opposed to being stuck as a war trophy on top of a foreign cathedral, suggests a desire to lift a weight of some kind.

If read as a conventional visible symbol the dragon might be translated as the demon described in 'The Revelation of St John the Divine', where the dragon or Devil is described as a great red dragon who is preceded by a pregnant woman 'travailing in birth, and pained to be delivered'. The dragon waits for the delivery in order to devour her child. When the woman gives birth her child is taken up to God and she flies into the wilderness, but she is still persecuted by the dragon who attempts to drown her and 'went to make war with the remnant of her seed'.[103]

Inside the cathedral The Singers Panel one of the panels of the Van Eyck altarpiece (which has been installed in the Vijd chapel in St Bavon's Cathedral since 1432) depicts the dragon of the Apocalypse on the side of the Singers' lectern. It is shown 'rearing its head even in defeat' as the

---

[102] Edmund Burke, A Philosophical Enquiry into the Origin of our Ideas of the Sublime and Beautiful, Ed. Adam Phillips, Oxford University Press: 1990, p. 53.

[103] 'The Revelation of St John The Divine', The Holy Bible, Authorized King James Version, London: Collins' Clear-Type Press, 1957, Ch. 12.

Archangel Michael pierces him with his sword. In the picture the richly attired choir of women singers appear to dominate and weigh down on the carving of the dragon. Their music is figured as overpowering, channelling in a more creative direction the destructiveness and hate exemplified by the prostrate dragon.[104] (Interestingly, the 'gilt' dragon may still be associated with the Van Eyck altarpiece and a fascinating contemporary mystery.[105])

In the account in 'Revelation' and in the depiction on The Singers Panel the dragon is demonised. In the 'Twenty-Fourth Sunday After Trinity' (p. 114 in *The Christian Year*) Keble likened the revelation of 'rude bad thoughts', which are usually kept secret, to seeing a 'serpent':

> Or what if Heaven for once its searching light
>   Lent to some partial eye, disclosing all
> The rude bad thoughts, that in our bosom's night
>   Wander at large, nor heed Love's gentle thrall?
>
> Who would not shun the dreary uncouth place?
>   As if, fond leaning where her infant slept,
> A mother's arm a serpent should embrace:
>   So might we friendless live, and die unwept.[106]

The cathedral (which suggests the security of a mother's arms or womb) does have a serpent, but it is a displaced serpent whose external presence is only briefly glimpsed. Procter very cleverly draws attention to something which has been excluded from St Bavon's. With Tractarian reserve she throws out a few hints, leaving the rest to her readers. The presence of the dragon suggests the presence of some strong emotions which are not being

---

104 Dhanens, op. cit., p. 92, p. 114.

105 Elizabeth Dhanens writes 'Several panels were dispersed in the nineteenth century but were reunited in 1920 and the altarpiece is now intact, except for the predella (lost before 1550) and one panel which was stolen in 1934 and is replaced by a copy' (Dhanens, op. cit., Foreword).

The mystery of the stolen panel (depicting the Just Judges) provides an uncanny parallel to the stolen dragon and its displacements. In an article in *The Guardian*, 'Arsene and an old case' (27.12.1995), Stephen Bates investigates 'Ghent's 61-year-old case of the stolen Van Eyck . . . worthy of Hercule Poirot'. Bates reports that Karel Mortier, a Ghent police chief, who has written three books on the case, is convinced that 'the panel is still in the cathedral'. The cathedral tower, Bates writes, 'has never been searched properly'. Karel Mortier looks to the tower to solve the mystery of the displaced or stolen panel, whilst the dragon on the tower provides a clue to something displaced or appropriated in Procter's Tractarian mystery story. Uncannily, the date of Procter's poem is 29.12.1855 whilst the date of Bates's article is 27.12.1995.

106 [Keble], *The Christian Year* (1827), II, p. 90.

fully expressed. Although these emotions are associated with the dragon, a conventionally demonic figure, the dragon's displaced and homeless status counters its bad reputation. Passionate emotions, in the form of the dragon, are depicted as displaced and seeking a home which will accommodate them.

Many of Procter's poems consider the problem of expressibility and she works well within Tractarian aesthetic theory when she states her belief that incompleteness, even if troubling, is accepted in the knowledge that people's lives form fragments of a harmonious whole in Keble's sense:

> Thy heart should throb in vast content,
> Thus knowing that it was but meant
> As chord in one great instrument;
>
> That even the discord in thy soul
> May make completer music roll
> From out the great harmonious whole.
>   ('Light and Shade', p. 212, ll. 40–45)[107]

The number of poems which consider incompleteness, though, suggests a strong desire for fuller and more complete expression. The titles of poems such as 'Unexpressed' (1858), 'Unseen' (1859), 'Incompleteness' (1858) and 'A Lost Chord' (1860) point to an absence which draws attention to itself, and in 'A Lost Chord' (a later poem published in *The English Woman's Journal* in March 1860) the search for meaning becomes urgent and paramount.[108] The one chord is found and lost: 'I struck one chord of music, / Like the sound of a great Amen ... I have sought, but I seek it vainly, / That one lost chord divine'. It is the speaker's discordant ('ill at ease') emotions which predominate, signified by 'the noisy keys' of the organ over which the speaker's fingers wander (pp. 177–178).

The boy (later the musician) in 'A Tomb in Ghent' comes out into the 'noisy glare' of the square and the dragon glares down. The discordant emotions with which the dragon is associated are not resolved within an harmonious whole and Procter leaves the fragment in mid-air. Neither is it a secret encased by the 'hard covering' Isaac Williams describes. It is not a fixed point as the boy expects it to fly away. Its covering of 'gilt' suggests a

---

107 MS BRP X 80/1, Parkes papers, Girton College Library.

108 'Incompleteness' is included in Mrs William Sharp's anthology, *Women's Voices. An Anthology of the Most Characteristic Poems by English, Scotch, and Irish Women*, Ed. Mrs William Sharp, London: Walter Scott, 1887, pp. 198–199.

thin coating rather than the denseness and impenetrability of Williams's 'hard covering'.

If the surface is scratched its 'secret' may be uncovered. Significantly Christina Rossetti wrote the short story 'The Lost Titian' in the same year (1855) as 'A Tomb in Ghent' was published. In this fictional story a picture of a 'flaming, clawed, preposterous' dragon is painted over a Titian master-piece after Titian has lost the painting at dice to his friend Gianni, whose debtors come to claim the painting in payment.[109] Both Procter and Rossetti use a dragon to top or cover something more aesthetically beautiful.

In Longfellow's poem 'The Belfry of Bruges' (1847), which Procter may be invoking, the belfry, where the dragon was situated prior to being stolen by the Ghent military, is described as 'the Golden Dragon's nest'.[110] To this extent the dragon in 'A Tomb in Ghent' may be read as a guardian or enabler of undisturbed goodness – its golden eggs. Its status as dragon, though, draws attention to a destructiveness which has been excluded from the nest.

Joan Riviere, in an article titled 'The unconscious phantasy of an inner world reflected in examples from literature', published in the *International Journal of Psychoanalysis* (1952), discusses the signification of the cathe-dral in T.S. Eliot's *Murder in the Cathedral* (1935). She writes:

> The cathedral represents both the person of the thinker in his most precious and valued aspects, his highest aspirations and capacities – love, truth, nobility and so on – as well as the inside of the idealized mother's body.[111]

Riviere states that internalised bad objects, however, break down the 'idealization of creative love' and persecute the good objects.[112]

In 'A Tomb in Ghent' it might be said that the bad objects have been externalised or projected on to the dragon outside. Although unconscious appropriations and metaphorical deaths are taking place beneath it, they take place under the guise of innocence and benignity – free of the 'gilt'/guilt with which the dragon is coated. In its position at the crux of the cathedral

---

[109] *Christina Rossetti. Poems and Prose*, Ed. Jan Marsh, London: Everyman, 1994, pp. 305–313, p. 311. Jan Marsh states that Rossetti wrote 'The Lost Titian' towards the end of 1855 and that it was first published in 1856 in the American magazine *The Crayon*. p. 305.

[110] Henry Wadsworth Longfellow, *The Belfry of Bruges and Other Poems*, Cambridge, Mass.: John Owen, 1846, p. 15.

[111] 'The unconscious phantasy of an inner world reflected in examples from literature (1952)' in *The Inner World and Joan Riviere. Collected Papers: 1920–1958*, Ed. Athol Hughes, London: Karnac Books for The Melanie Klein Trust, 1991, p. 325.

[112] ibid., p. 326.

the dragon's position is like that of a martyr. The 'gilt'/guilt may be read as thinly coating a passionate woman's anger at the appropriation of women's songs which is taking place beneath her. Passionate womanliness is rendered dragonish and is blamed or assumes the burden of guilt for its very expressiveness – expressiveness which is more unreserved and out in the open (perhaps about to take flight) than the reserve which has a place inside the cathedral.

The anger and passion associated with the dragon are also subtly expressive of strong disapproval of the multiple appropriations of the dragon itself (by a Crusader, by Bruges, by Ghent) which may be linked to the appropriations of women's songs. The passionate woman is angry about both, but has difficulty in expressing that emotion from such a reserved position.

Procter's use of the dragon motif also subtly, almost imperceptibly, points her readers in an easterly direction towards the dragon's home. Earlier in 1855, according to Asa Briggs, an article had appeared in the *Sheffield and Rotherham Independent* which boasted: 'All Asia lies before us'. The Crimean War, it stated, would provide a better route to India via Syria and Mesopotamia.[113]

Just before recounting the narrative of the dragon the narrator states that the boy's father (the artisan) talked to him of 'home, of England, and strange stories told / Of English heroes in the days of old' (p. 64, ll. 42–43). Procter's veiled reference to the Crimean War and English heroism needs to be read in the context of her Crimean War poems, some of which I shall discuss later in this chapter. Procter's lyrics are humane and angry, deploring the consequences of war and showing concern for its victims rather than any desire for military glory.

In 'A Tomb in Ghent' Procter draws attention to the glory which is associated with the war trophy. The golden dragon fascinates the boy and Procter's repeated use of the conjunction 'And' along with the caesuras create the sound of the boy's excited voice and the impression that he is repeating his father's story ('which never seemed to tire') (pp. 64–65, ll. 44–57). The force of the verb 'Stole' at the beginning of the line 'Stole the great dragon' (p. 65, l. 53) suggests the compelling attraction of the appropriation.

The dragon with its comprehensive view also suggests an omnipotence which may be won, ensuring that a race of heroes will be immaculately preserved and displayed like the golden trophy the dragon is. But its 'gilt' status and its temporary and unwished for position undermines any sense of

---

[113] Asa Briggs, *Victorian People. A Reassessment of Persons and Themes 1851–67*, London: Penguin Books Ltd., 1990, p. 74.

omnipotence. The status of the English artisan as an emigrant in search of work, along with the cloistered life of his fragile and 'sickly' son, also undermine the notion of a consolidated, strong and masculinised English heroism.

It is interesting that Procter chose the recently independent and neutral country of Belgium for the location of this poem. It is as though she needed to consider the Crimean War and the notion of English heroism at a distance from an independent and neutral position.[114] From this position Procter very tentatively and allusively mounts a critique of the notion of heroism and its 'strange stories' (p. 64, l. 42). The mythological status of the dragon suggests that the history of heroism creates its own myths or 'strange stories'.

Procter's description of the dragon contrasts with Longfellow's in 'The Belfry of Bruges' (1847), a poem Procter was likely to have read. In this poem the speaker stands on the belfry of a cathedral in Bruges, probably the 14th century Church of Notre Dame. He refers to the belfry having been 'Thrice consumed and thrice rebuilded' but still able to watch over the town. The belfry's tower is described as having 'a heart of iron beating' which triggers off a train of historical memories in the speaker: 'They who live in history only seemed to walk the earth again':

> All the Foresters of Flanders, – mighty Baldwin
>   Bras de Fer,
> Lyderick du Bucq and Cressy, Philip, Guy de
>   Dampierre.
>
> I beheld the pageants splendid, that adorned
>   those days of old;
> Stately dames, like queens attended, knights who
>   bore the Fleece of Gold;
> . . .

---

[114] In 1839 South Netherlands was recognised by the Great Powers as the independent and neutral kingdom of Belgium with Leopold of Saxe-Coburg as King. Ghent had a reputation for independence and self-sufficiency (Nicholas, op. cit.). A poem titled 'Ghent', published in *Fisher's Drawing Room Scrap-Book*, 1851, celebrates Ghent's honesty and integrity:

> Its sturdy citizens, self-taught, self-ruled,
> And self-supported by integrity, . . .
>
> In ages semi-barbarous and oppress'd,
> Such homes and hives of honest working men.
>   (p. 49)

I beheld the Flemish weavers, with Namur and
    Juliers bold,
Marching homeward from the bloody battle of
    the Spurs of Gold;

Saw the fight at Minnewater, saw the White
    Hoods moving west,
Saw great Artevelde victorious scale the Golden
    Dragon's nest.[115]

The speaker is in full possession of his historical memory despite the
repeated destruction of its core (the heart of iron beating in the belfry). The
history is largely one of violence and war, and the pomp, ceremony and
glory which surround them. The strength, wealth and continuity of the past
and its glories is asserted and reasserted, like the belfry which is 'thrice
rebuilded'. It is as though the history of Bruges has a heart of iron and a
weighty significance.

The dragon as a trophy of war has a permanent place in this roll-call of
history, even if it has been displaced and appropriated by Ghent. By contrast
the dragon in 'A Tomb in Ghent' is depicted as having a chequered history,
like the young woman's history which is presented as fragmented and in
need of chronicling. Procter provides little detailed knowledge of its history,
as though she is expressing the difficulty of locating it in time and place.

Procter's account of a woman's and a dragon's displacements is at a far
remove from Keble's belief in an heroic tradition which secures a quiet retreat
from the world. There is no clear sense in 'A Tomb in Ghent' as to what kind
of space has been secured, if at all. Procter undermines Keble's notion of a
quiescent state secured by the strong arm of heroism, and she employs the
Tractarian theories of reserve and the visible symbol to destabilise and
question Keble's certainties. In a veiled manner she suggests that Keble's
idealised world rests on the exclusion of strong emotions, particularly those
of women, and on a belief in an unproblematic and unquestioned heroic
tradition.

Procter's critique only emerges when the poem is subjected to scrutiny and
research. It needs to be read with Tractarian eyes if it is to be understood in
all its subtlety. At this point in her career Procter still exercises a
considerable amount of reserve, and there is a sense of her searching to find
a voice which will free her into greater expressiveness.

'A Tomb in Ghent' is an important poem, suggestive of exploration and

---

115 Longfellow, op. cit., pp. 11-16.

incubation (with the cathedral space as a metaphorical womb) – a working through of ideas, from which her critique of Tractarian theories emerges. These ideas would finally bear fruit two years later in 1858 when a new voice, more expressive and emphatic, is heard in some of her poems.

Crimean War Poems

The emergence of this new voice was also beginning to be heard in Procter's Crimean War poems, published in 1854 and 1855 (the year 'A Tomb in Ghent' was published). Some of these poems demonstrate a loosening of Procter's more monologic voice (exemplified by the short lyrics, didactic and purely lyrical, of her early period) and a movement away from the reserved position adopted in 'A Tomb in Ghent'. The poems are notable for a greater emotional expansiveness and for the presence of voices in conflict and in dialogue. These lyrics show the extent to which Procter was emerging from the shadows of a reserve which muted a potentially strong critical voice.

The poems include 'Words Upon the Waters' (1854), 'The Unknown Grave' (1855), 'The Two Spirits' (1855) and 'The Lesson of the War' (1855). All these poems were published in *Household Words* and *Legends and Lyrics*, with the exception of 'Words Upon the Waters' which was published in *Household Words* only. These lyrics foreground the shattering and explosive violence of war and the totality of its extinctions. In 'The Unknown Grave' only 'the grass's wave, / Over a mound of earth' marks the tomb of the unknown soldier (p. 80, ll. 4-5). The only lesson which may be learned from war, Procter writes in 'The Lesson of the War', is that class and party differences may be forgotten in the face of a shared 'dread' and suffering:

> The rich man who reposes
>   In his ancestral shade,
> The peasant at his ploughshare,
>   The worker at his trade,
> Each one his all has perilled,
>   Each has the same great stake,
> Each soul can but have patience,
>   Each heart can only break!

Hushed is all party clamour;
  One thought in every heart,
One dread in every household,
  Has bid such strife depart.
England has called her children;
  Long silent – the word came
That lit the smouldering ashes
  Through all the land to flame.
(pp. 116-117, ll. 33-48)

Procter focuses on the fears for their 'children' of those at home, and by definition particularly the women. She succeeds in conveying the force of the obliterations and devastations wreaked by a war which is no respecter of class:

The bullet comes – and either
A desolate hearth may see . . .
(p. 116, ll. 25-26)

The simplicity of the words 'The bullet comes –' and the pregnant silence created by the caesura evokes a visceral and emotional response.

Procter focuses on the struggle of the women at home to understand the rationale behind sending children to war. In the 'Two Spirits' her treatment of the war is passionately critical of a dehumanising heroic tradition (admired by John Keble) which sends its children into battle without flinching. The poem takes the form of a dialogue between the Spirits of the Past and Present and Procter cleverly creates the sense of the painful confusion and struggle faced by the humane individual who abhors war's wanton cruelties.

The dialogue between the Spirits of Past and Present is introduced by a narrator who listens to the debate. The voice of the Spirit of the Past is the voice of an heroic tradition:

My deeds are writ in iron;
  My glory stands alone;
A veil of shadowy honour
  Upon my tombs is thrown;
The great names of my heroes
  Like gems in history lie;
To live they deemed ignoble,
  Had they the chance to die!
(pp. 117-118, ll. 7-14)

The Past is characterised by an 'iron' determination which, like the 'heart of iron' beating in the belfry tower in Longfellow's 'The Belfry of Bruges', secures for its glittering heroes a place in an ineffaceable and permanent history. The voice of the Past is also notable for its isolated position: 'My glory stands alone'.

By contrast the Spirit of the Present refers to its many 'children' whose memory will be held 'Dear'. In spite of their respect for 'life' they, like the past's heroes, will obey the call of 'duty' and 'rush into the strife!' (p. 118, ll. 15-22). The past honours the mothers who willingly sacrifice their children:

> Fearless and glad, those mothers,
>   At bloody deaths elate,
> Cried out they bore their children
>   Only for such a fate!
>
>   (p. 118, ll. 27-30)

The Present refers to the 'mourning mother' who sadly submits to a grief which results from the recognition of her own inculcation of heroic virtues in her child:

> The heroes of the fight
> Learnt at her knee the lesson,
>   'For God and for the Right!'
>   (p. 118, ll. 31-38)

To which the Voice of the Past scornfully replies, 'No voice there spake of sorrow' (p. 118, l. 39). The Voice of the Present then shifts the debate to the actual war which is being fought in the Crimea, and to the reality of war's desolations:

> Grief dwells in France and England
>   For many a noble son;
> Yet louder than the sorrow,
>   'Thy will, O God, be done!'
> From desolate homes is rising
>   One prayer, 'Let carnage cease!
> On friends and foes have mercy,
>   O Lord, and give us peace!'
>   (p. 119, ll. 47-54)

By contrast the Past, instead of referring to any specific war situation, speaks of the numbers sacrificed to 'spread their country's glory, / And gain her south or north' (p. 119, ll. 57–58). The imperialist aims of the heroic past are countered by the Present's justification of the Crimean War, which she asserts is fought for freedom from oppression rather than the glory of conquest:

> And now from France and England
>   Their dearest and their best
> Go forth to succour freedom,
>   To help the much oppressed;
> Now, let the far-off Future
>   And Past bow down to-day,
> Before the few young hearts that hold
>   Whole armaments at bay.
>
> (p. 119, ll. 63–70)

This is clearly a reference to the 'Charge of the Light Brigade' that had taken place in 1854, the previous year, and had been commemorated by Tennyson.[116]

The Past concludes with a paeon to 'Fame', which is the chief motivator of the hero, it states:

> They longed that in far ages
>   Their deeds might still be told,
> And distant times and nations
>   Their names in honour hold.
>
> (p. 120, ll. 75–78)

The Present apparently has the last word:

> Though nursed by such old legends,
>   Our heroes of to-day
> Go cheerfully to battle
>   As children go to play;
> They gaze with awe and wonder
>   On your great names of pride,
> Unconscious that their own will shine
>   In glory side by side!
>
> (p. 120, ll. 79–86)

---

116 'The Charge of the Light Brigade', Tennyson, *Poems and Plays*, Ed. T. Herbert Warren, Oxford University Press, 1971, pp. 206–207.

The narrator concludes that she thinks she saw 'in the dim morning grey' the paling of the Past's 'bright diadem' before the 'glorious Present' (p. 120, ll. 87–90).

This is not specifically an anti-Crimean War poem in that Procter does justify the war on the grounds of freedom from oppression. As a Catholic she was likely to have supported the cause on the grounds that it was ostensibly fought for the protection of holy places claimed by Roman Catholic monks in Jerusalem from the Greek Orthodox Church. Her mention of France might also be an acknowledgement of Napoleon III's patronage of the Catholic Church.[117]

The poem is, however, anti-war in the widest sense. It is a scathing indictment of an heroic past which places fame and glory above any more humane considerations. The poem also provides a critique of the egotistical notion of individual destiny ('My glory stands alone') which encompasses a greed for empire that will go to any lengths to secure its territories at whatever the cost in lives.

The relentless tone of the voice of the Past does not admit confusion or deviation. The Present is heard as a voice which is attempting to come to terms with its confusions. There is regret that the mother who now grieves is in fact partly responsible for instilling in her child the virtue of heroic sacrifice. Procter powerfully depicts the struggle of the voice of sadness with the manic voice of the mothers' elation at the 'bloody deaths' of their children. This madness is linked to the unconsciousness of the children who are prepared to go into battle as if into a child's game ('As children go to play'). Deluded by the 'old legends' and mesmerised by fame ('They gaze with awe and wonder / On your great names of pride') they are unaware that they too will soon be 'writ in iron' by the bullet over which they have no control.

Procter draws attention to a lack of boundaries which links the heroic Past and its desire for conquest, the mother's lunatic emotions which know no limits, and the child's lack of consciousness which does not distinguish between playing and reality. The voice of sadness and of vulnerability (the repetition of 'Dear' suggests the softness which is exposed) counters the voices of military and maternal manias, and just wins through in conclusion. Procter does not, however, present the dialogue as fully resolved. The voice of the Present's predominance may be short-lived and there is a sense that the struggle will continue.

'The Two Spirits' explodes the myth expounded by Keble of a heroism which can 'delight in battle' (see p. 111), detaching itself from the childlike

---

117 Briggs, op. cit., p. 65.

masses it seeks to control and bring into harmony with its aims. Procter enters into dialogue with a voice which she recognises as not solely external and omnipotent. She presents the struggle of voices which have become internalised and compete to be heard.

'Words' assumed paramount importance in Procter's poetry of a later period and 'The Two Spirits' stresses the need to engage with competing languages which create a sense of disharmony rather than the harmony promoted by Keble.[118] Ironically it is as though the impact of an actual war and its violence gives Procter a context for an exploration of the power of her own words and dissonances. Listening to news of the war may be understood as a metaphorical listening to news from a more distant part of the self. In 'The Lesson of the War' England is depicted as waiting 'Breathless':

> and listens
> For every eastern breeze
> That bears upon its bloody wings
> News from beyond the seas.
> (p. 116, ll. 9-12)

Like the bullet ('The bullet comes –') 'word' of war comes ('Long silent – the word came') (pp. 17-18, l. 25, l. 46) and it ignites the passions of 'Long silent –' children:

> England has called her children;
> Long silent – the word came
> That lit the smouldering ashes
> Through all the land to flame.
> (p. 117, ll. 45-48)

The silence (emphasised by the caesura) of England's children is the silence of those 'who toil and suffer' (p. 117, l. 49). It suggests the passivity and reserve of an oppressed class which may be likened to the reserve exemplified by the White Maiden in 'A Tomb in Ghent'. The strength of Procter's womanly and passionate voice breaks the silence, as does the 'word' which ignites the poor.

In the poem 'Words upon the Waters' the language of passionate expression and the flow of words becomes confused with the language of violence and of war. The speaker urges her audience to listen for any words of greeting carried across the sea from the Crimea 'On the rushing waves'.

---

[118] See discussion of Procter's poem 'Words' (1858) in Chapter 3.

The soldiers in the Crimea are likened to children who anticipate victory before the 'strife is yet begun' and the emotions ('Hope, regret, and joy and sorrow') conveyed by the words are identified with the 'water's roar' with which they 'mingle'. The noise of children rushing to be heard is contrasted with the held breath of the listeners in England who wait for news of victory:

> Hush! amid the din of waters
>   Let us hold our breath, and hear,
> If the thunder of the cannon
>   Be not borne towards us here;
> If the deadly sound of battle
>   Come across the waters free,
> And the English cry of 'Victory!'
>   Be not echoed by the Sea![119]

The held breath of the listeners suggests the deadliness and fear which are associated with war and victory. Procter shows the extent to which an involvement in war evokes 'deadly' passions, and paradoxically the way that the flow of words and strong emotions may momentarily dissolve the pain of war and conflict and detract from the harsh reality.

In 'A Tomb in Ghent' the held breath of the White Maiden is described as signifying an expectancy ('Her lips expectant part') (p. 67, l. 129). Her place is in the crypt, a site of secrets, and she is located below in direct opposition to the dragon above. It is as though she is shown to be waiting in the shadow of reserve (or death) to be freed into a more passionate form of expressiveness hinted at by the dragon. Passion is associated with war and ugliness and Procter draws attention to the danger of aggressive and violent emotion which may attach to more open and unreserved forms of expression.

'A Tomb in Ghent' and the Crimean War poems mark a crucial phase in Procter's development as a poet. The poems express her concern with the importance of entering into dialogue and into freer and more open forms of expression, along with the concomitant dangers. The poems struggle with the Tractarian notions of reserve and the visible symbol: notions which in Keble's theoretical texts and in his poetry primarily fix and deaden rather than free the capacity for expressiveness.

---

[119] 'Words upon the Waters', *Household Words*, IX, 1854.

Chapter 3

Poetic Authority: Robert Browning

In the years 1856 and 1857, following the publication of 'A Tomb in Ghent' at the end of 1855, Procter's poetic output decreased. Ten poems were published in *Household Words* in 1856 but only one in 1857 (see Appendix). In these years Procter may have been suffering as a result of a broken engagement. Some of her poems suggest that this was the case. The poem 'A Chain' (14.6.1856) expresses an anxiety that the chain of love may be broken: 'And see, though slender, it is made / Of Love and Trust, and can they fade?' (p. 92, ll. 25–26); and in 'Fidelis' (6.12.1856) the speaker states that the chain has been 'broken' and a 'promise' retracted (p. 113, ll. 1–8).[1] In the poem 'A Dead Past' (1.8.1857) the speaker mourns a dead past which she cradles like a baby in her arms: 'You know you laid her, / Long years ago, then living, in my arms' (p. 34, ll. 19–20).

This image of dead or stillborn love may also be read as the death of Procter's writing. 'A Dead Past' expresses emotions of desolation and emptiness ('I have nothing more'; p. 34, l. 24) which, however, precede a surge of creativity in 1858 and 1859 when nineteen poems were published in *Household Words* (ten in 1858 and nine in 1859) and four in *The English Woman's Journal*. 1858 was also the year when the 'First Series' of *Legends and Lyrics* was published and when *The English Woman's Journal* was launched, with Procter's two close friends, Bessie Parkes and Matilda Hays as its co-editors.

Procter's status as a poet was established and her voice was clearly being heard, along with those of her fellow women campaigners of the Langham Place Circle. Later in the year, on the 11th October 1858, the *National Association for the Promotion of Social Sciences* held its Second Annual Meeting in Liverpool, and in an announcement of the meeting in *The English Woman's Journal* (1.10.1858) the writer states that the Association had 'assumed the right of woman ... to express her opinion in that assembly if

---

[1] 'A Chain' was published in *Household Words* as 'The Chain' and 'Fidelis' as 'Patient and Faithful'.

she chooses', and that several women, including Louisa Twining and Florence Nightingale, were to give papers.[2]

Earlier in 1858, as a result of the strength of the voices and opinions of women campaigners (notably those of Caroline Norton) the Matrimonial Causes Act had become law on the 1st January 1858. This Act secured property rights for the woman separated from her husband (a femme sole), but the married woman who stayed with her husband still had none. Under the Act divorce became easier as secular courts were established to grant divorces, but there was still 'inequality of grounds by which men and women could sue for absolute divorce' in that a man could sue for adultery whilst a woman could sue only on the grounds of 'aggravated' adultery (adultery combined with incest, bigamy, desertion or cruelty).[3]

An increased sense of the power of women's voices and the changes women might effect existed simultaneously with an awareness of continuing inequalities under the law. It was in this climate that Procter's poems became increasingly concerned with love and relationships, and with the risks women faced on entering into marriage.

In her discussion of *The English Woman's Journal*, Jane Rendall states that the founders of *The English Woman's Journal* enjoyed 'a circle of friendship' which 'could provide the basis for the choice of a single life'.[4] Many of Procter's poems published in 1858 and in subsequent years suggest that, even if remaining single was not necessarily a positive choice, it may certainly have been in many ways preferable to marriage, which in the poem 'The Bride's Dream' the speaker describes as a 'life-long chain' of sorrow (p. 259, l. 58). In the poem 'A Warning' (1859) an adult speaker urges a young girl to exercise 'double caution' when it comes to love – to 'treasure' it and to try to establish a relationship on an equal footing:

---

[2] 'Social Science', *The English Woman's Journal*, II, 1858, pp. 124–125. Louisa Twining was the originator of Workhouse Reform and her campaigning led to the establishment of a Workhouse Visiting Society in the 1850s and to the 1875 Act enabling women to be Poor Law Guardians (Ray Strachey, *The Cause. A Short History of the Women's Movement in Great Britain*, (1928) London: Virago Limited, 1978, pp. 80–82).

[3] Mary Poovey, *Uneven Developments. The Ideological Work of Gender in Mid-Victorian England*, London: Virago Press Limited, 1989, p. 84.

[4] *Equal or Different. Women's Politics. 1800–1914*, Ed. Jane Rendall, Oxford: Basil Blackwell Ltd., 1987, p. 13. Rendall states that women's friendships provided a 'kind of informal network that might be found in the common educational experiences and male clubs of their fathers, sons and brothers'.

> Measure all you give – still
> Counting what you take;
> Love for love: so placing
> Each an equal stake.
>
> (pp. 170-171, ll. 21-24)

Procter sets a high standard of love in the poem 'True or False' (pp. 152–154) which was published in *Good Words* in 1862. The speaker lists the counterfeit loves (love of Self, Pleasure, Power, love of Love) which are difficult to distinguish from true love. True love is depicted as being outside the speaker's experience – 'I have heard' (p. 153, l. 49), '(they tell me)' (p. 154, l. 67) – and it is characterised by its 'inner life' (p. 153, l. 60). She asks her lover if he can offer her this 'true Love' and concludes on a teasing note:

> Neither you nor I can answer;
> We will – wait and see!
>
> (pp. 152-154)[5]

These poems combine a sense of despair at ever finding a 'true' love based on equality with a growing sense of Procter's increasing confidence in articulating her ideas and feelings about entering into relationships and marriage.

There is a sense that Procter is enjoying the sound and strength of her own voice as she enters into the marriage debate. She has lost the earlier Tractarian reserve which seemed to preclude a more direct engagement with topics relating to love and sexuality. In *Browning and Conversation*, E.A.W. St George writes:

> Those with loud voices may grow used to having themselves heard
> and to hearing themselves . . . Browning certainly spoke loudly, as if
> in public . . .[6]

It is Procter's response to Browning's 'loud' and 'large' poetic voice which provides the focus of this short chapter. Hearing her own voice more clearly coincides with Procter's critical response to Browning's lyric poetry and his concern with the relationships of 'men and women'.

Procter responds to Browning the love poet, and in particular to some of

---

[5] Published as 'True or False?' in *Good Words. For 1862*, Illustrated by A.B. Houghton, III, pp. 721-722.

[6] E.A.W. St George, *Browning and Conversation*, London: The Macmillan Press Ltd., 1993, p. 44.

the lyrics published in *Men and Women* in 1855. The poems 'A Woman's Question' (1858), 'A Woman's Answer' (1861) and 'A Woman's Last Word' (1861), a revision of Browning's poem of the same title, repeat the 'Women' formula established by Browning in *Men and Women* with poems such as 'Women and Roses', 'A Pretty Woman', 'A Woman's Last Word' and 'A Light Woman'.[7] Procter's women speakers are centre stage and notable for the extent to which they appear to enjoy entering into a dialogue which seems to be more public than private.

The confident tone of these poems may well have been inspired by the vigorous powers of speech of some of Browning's 'men and women' speakers. Her father Bryan Procter's admiration of Browning's poetry may also have encouraged Adelaide to take more risks with her own poetry. Bryan Procter was a close friend of Browning (who was twenty-five years younger), whom he encouraged and advised from early in his poetic career. The Preface to *Selections from the Poetical Works of Robert Browning* (1863), edited by Procter and John Forster, states that:

> The volume originated with two friends who, from the first appearance of 'Paracelsus,' have regarded its writer as among the few great poets of the century . . .[8]

In a letter to Browning, dated 23rd May 1851, he expressed the opinion that 'a friend of mine has more of the material of a great poet in him' than the recently appointed Poet Laureate Tennyson.[9]

In another letter to Browning, dated the 5th November 1851, Bryan Procter wrote:

> I should like to see a book of your lyrics – any book of yours indeed – but lyrics (like your others) indicative of your different moods of thought & feeling – would draw less upon your time than any long elaborate poems – & might be quite as popular perhaps. They might be dotted down at once as the easy expression of your mood – one at a time – & would amount to a book before you would be aware of it. (Here Mrs Browning joins me, I know, in urging you to this pleasant little task.) – How many things you will see where you are – how

---

[7]   Robert Browning, *Men and Women*, 2 Vols, London: Chapman and Hall, 1855.

[8]   *Selections from the Poetical Works of Robert Browning*, [Ed. J. Forster and B.W. Procter], London: Chapman & Hall, 1863, p. vi.

[9]   MS, B.W. Procter to Robert Browning (23.5.1851), University of Iowa Libraries. Tennyson succeeded Wordsworth as Poet Laureate in 1851.

many things you *are* seeing now – how many dreams – every one of which shall suggest a poem to you. There is one crossing your brain at this moment . . .[10]

It was in Paris in the New Year of 1852 that Browning decided to write a poem a day, and in the first three days he wrote 'Love Among the Ruins' (1st January), 'Women and Roses' (2nd January) and 'Childe Roland' (3rd January).[11] It seems probable that Browning wrote in direct response to his mentor's letter.

This kind of enthusiastic advice would surely have made an impact on Adelaide who more obviously follows her own 'thought and feeling' in the poems discussed in this chapter, 'A Woman's Last Word' (pp. 268–269) and 'Three Roses' (pp. 199–200).

'A Woman's Last Word', published in the 'Second Series' of *Legends and Lyrics* in 1861, boldly revises Browning's poem (published in *Men and Women* in 1855).[12] In Browning's poem the woman speaker tries to return herself and her husband or lover to a state of calm after some contention between them. By contrast, the woman speaker in Procter's revision tries to make the break from her lover. Her spare, forceful rhetoric counters the language of an idealised love which temporarily silences more conflictual emotions in Browning's poem. Although Browning questions the idealisations of romantic love he still depicts the exclusive love relationship as possessing an enthralling and overwhelming power, whilst Procter's woman speaker attempts to cut through and free herself from the beguilement of the language of romantic love.

By contrast, Procter's 'Three Roses', published in *Household Words* on 21st August 1858, which I shall contrast with Browning's 'Women and Roses' (*Men and Women*, 1855), depicts a silent exchange of love which is initiated by the woman.[13] The control which is exerted through the power of a woman's speech in 'A Woman's Last Word' is lost when a woman attempts to enter into an expression of her own desires. Procter implicitly challenges Browning's idealisation of women in 'Women and Roses' in which poem the male ego defines itself in relation to a powerful and resilient female presence. The woman who is always there, either as one of a couple or as muse to

---

[10] MS, B.W. Procter to Robert Browning (5.11.1851), University of Iowa Libraries.

[11] William Irvine and Park Honan, *The Book, the Ring, and the Poet. A biography of Robert Browning*, London: The Bodley Head Ltd., 1975, p. 293.

[12] Browning, *Men and Women*, pp. 31–34.

[13] *The Poetical Works of Robert Browning*, 3 Vols, I, *Lyrics, Romances, Men, and Women*, London: Chapman and Hall, 1863, pp. 137–139.

Browning's imagination, is shown to be extremely vulnerable in Procter's
'Three Roses'.

Procter demonstrates that a woman's acquisition of a more articulate
language of desire, spoken or silent, places her either in an ambivalent
position ('A Woman's Last Word') or excludes her from relationship ('Three
Roses').

'A Woman's Last Word'

Eleven years before the publication of 'A Woman's Last Word' in *Men and
Women* (1855) Browning's play 'Colombe's Birthday' was published in 1844.
The play was dedicated to Barry Cornwall (Bryan Procter). The dedication
reads:

> No One Loves and Honours Barry Cornwall More Than
>   Does Robert Browning;
> Who, Having Nothing Better Than This Play To Give
> Him In Proof of It, Must Say So.[14]

'Colombe's Birthday' is concerned with the nature of love and its capacity for
an instinctual generosity – how much love is prepared to 'Give' or give up.
The play is set in seventeenth-century Germany on the day of Colombe's
birthday (Colombe is the Duchess of Juliers and Cleves). It is also the first
anniversary of her accession to the duchy and Colombe is faced with
choosing to marry Prince Berthold, a claimant to the duchy, or Valence, a
representative of 'all who starve / at Cleves'.[15] Berthold is primarily
interested in expanding his power and his love is depicted as 'calculating': he
lists Colombe's lineage, virtue, truth, intellect and beauty as the qualities
which attract him and states 'A further love I do not understand.'[16] By
contrast Valence is shown to elicit an instinctual response from Colombe: 'I
am first her instinct fastens on.'[17] Valence describes himself as possessing a
'lover's instinct' which recognises that Berthold's love is not true.[18] Colombe
finally gives up her status and her power to marry Valence, but the outcome

    14 Robert Browning, *Bells and Pomegranates*, 'No. VI. Colombe's Birthday. A
Play, in Five Acts', London: Edward Moxon, 1844, p. 2.
    15 ibid., p. 5.
    16 ibid., p. 18.
    17 ibid., p. 12.
    18 ibid., p. 15.

of their marriage and whether the risk was worth it is unknown.[19]

Procter would surely have read 'Colombe's Birthday', a play dedicated to her father. The title points to the birth of love – a love which cannot be calculated or quantified and is prepared to take huge risks. Like Browning she is concerned with love's capacity for generosity and her poem 'A Woman's Question' (1858) (pp. 32–33) – to which 'A Woman's Answer' is the reply and 'A Woman's Last Word' perhaps a final word – considers the risks that love is prepared to take.[20]

The poem invokes Elizabeth Barrett Browning's poem 'A Woman's Short-comings' which describes a woman who enters into the superficial forms of courtship but falls short of a love one should 'die' for.[21] The speaker in Procter's poem questions her lover prior to trusting herself to a future which will 'give colour and form' to hers (p. 32, l. 4). She asks him if, like her, he is prepared to break the links with the past and commit himself to her absolutely. She states that she has 'staked the whole' and needs to know if in the future he might be diverted from such undivided love by 'The demon-spirit change' or 'withdraw' his hand, blaming 'Fate' and 'today's mistake' for his breaking of his pledge (pp. 32–33). The poem concludes with an ironic twist:

> Nay, answer *not* – I dare not hear,
> The words would come too late;
> Yet I would spare thee all remorse,
> So, comfort thee, my Fate –
> Whatever on my heart may fall – remember, I *would* risk it all!
> (p. 33, ll. 36–40)

The final stanza is missing from the *Household Words* version. If Dickens edited it out it was perhaps because it is in this stanza that the speaker

19 It is interesting that Browning chose to dedicate 'Colombe's Birthday' to Bryan Procter, who, in spite of his Whig sympathies, was keen to dissociate himself from politics. John Woolford writes that in abdicating power in favour of Berthold, an 'ancien regime' despot, Colombe 'renounces the defiance of tyranny she had earlier expressed' (John Woolford, *Browning the Revisionary*, London: The Macmillan Press Ltd., 1988, p. 20). Browning was perhaps thinking of Procter's desire to avoid the political arena.

20 'A Woman's Question' attracted Emily Dickinson's attention when it was published in the *Springfield Republican* in 1865. According to Karen Richardson Gee, Dickinson cut out the poem when it appeared. (Gee, *'Kinswomen of the Shelf': Emily Dickinson's Reading of Women Writers*, PhD dissertation, The University of Tennessee, 1990, p. 74)

21 Elizabeth Barrett Browning, *Poems*, 2 Vols, London: Chapman & Hall, 1850, II, pp. 398–399.

suggests that a woman 'would / risk it all!' if she married. If the word 'would' which is italicised for emphasis is understood in its conditional tense the speaker is saying she is not prepared to risk an 'I will'.

Procter's speaker is like an ironic priest officiating at her own marriage: 'Speak now – lest at some future day my whole life wither / and decay' (p. 32, l. 25). Although the speaker apparently addresses a lover she is more impressive as a solo speaker who rises above the rhetorical and hypothetical questions she asks. The expansion and contraction of the lines suggest a growing capacity for emotional expansiveness, with the very long concluding line suggesting an expulsion of energy as the speaker dramatises and ironises her 'Fate'.

The opening of the companion poem 'A Woman's Answer' (1861) (pp. 251–252) gives a categorical answer to the question the speaker in 'A Woman's Question' has put to her lover, imaginary lover, or perhaps her own alter ego:

> I will not let you say a Woman's part
> Must be to give exclusive love alone;
> Dearest, although I love you so, my heart
> Answers a thousand claims besides your own.
> (p. 251, ll. 1–4)

Procter's speaker questions the role, the 'part' women play in the 'exclusive' love relationship. Her litany of loves, which exclude him, suggest promiscuous and wide-ranging desires which include 'myriad things' (p. 251, l. 6): the summer, the winter, the Stars, the Flowers, people and poetry (pp. 251–252).

Whilst expressing these desires the woman reassures her lover (for whom she has often waited a long time) that all her loves are in fact subordinate to her love for him. The poem concludes:

> Will you be jealous? Did you guess before
> I loved so many things? – Still you the best: –
> Dearest, remember that I love you more,
> Oh, more a thousand times than all the rest!
> (p. 252, ll. 45–48)

Despite this apparent reassurance, the strength of her catalogue of desires, along with the rhetorical forcefulness of the language and the teasing questions which conclude her speech, suggest both defensiveness and aggression which preclude absolute commitment. The speaker's expression of limitless love is shown to overcompensate for the anger at his absence which she is clearly feeling. She also suggests that he is not particularly interested in her loves which exist outside her love for him:

> I love – what do I not love? earth and air
> Find space within my heart, and myriad things
> You would not deign to heed, are cherished there,
> And vibrate on its very inmost strings.
> (p. 251, ll. 5-8)

Whilst expressing a veiled anger the speaker's rhetorical question suggests the fear of a possibly antagonistic response from her lover. When she asks, 'I love – what do I not love?' the words echo the Duke of Ferrara's description of his dead duchess in Robert Browning's poem 'My Last Duchess':

> She had
> A heart ... how shall I say? ... too soon made glad,
> Too easily impressed; she liked whate'er
> She looked on, and her looks went everywhere.
> Sir, 't was all one![22]

The confidence of Procter's woman speaker masks an anxiety relating to a response which may attempt to silence her.

The speaker also refers to Elizabeth Barrett Browning's long narrative poem *Aurora Leigh* (1857) as a favourite book which her lover 'used to read' to her in the summer. She anxiously asks him if he remembers why she prizes this book above the rest:

> But most of all I think Aurora Leigh,
> Because – because – do you remember why?
> (p. 252, ll. 41-44)

In *Aurora Leigh* Aurora rejects her cousin Romney's marriage proposal because he scorns her ambition to become a poet. She does finally marry him, but only after ten years, by which time she has become a successful writer.[23]

In 'A Woman's Answer' the anxiety which is expressed in her hesitant speech ('Because – because – ') suggests that the speaker may, like Aurora, reject her lover so that she is freer to pursue her ambitions. The position

---

[22] *The Poetical Works of Robert Browning* (1863), I, p. 160.
[23] Elizabeth Barrett Browning, *Aurora Leigh*, London: Chapman and Hall, 1857.

depicted in the poem is one of ambivalence. The speaker's apparent generosity in love appears to be more a generosity with words which masks a strong desire to escape absolute commitment. It is in the context of the 'Question' and 'Answer' posed in these poems that 'A Woman's Last Word' needs to be read. In both poems the power of the speaking voice is heard, but there is a sense that the words in fact conceal more than they reveal and that the women speakers have opened themselves up to debate but not to love.

By contrast, Robert Browning, in some of the poems in *Men and Women*, depicts the power of words to cut into the bower of love. In 'A Lover's Quarrel' the male lover blames a 'word' for cutting through the lover's romantic idyll: 'See a word, how it severeth!' The 'word' is also described as penetrating – it pierces their 'ingle-glow'.[24] The lover remembers the time when he and his lover were immersed in each other under cover of the snow ('the mesmeriser Snow') which suggests an imagined blanking out of any differences between the lovers under the screening whiteness.[25]

The desire to erase difference and avoid the pain of 'contention' or 'talking' under cover of a blanketing is also explored in Browning's 'A Woman's Last Word', where the woman speaker longs for the blanket of sleep:

> Let's contend no more, Love,
>   Strive nor weep –
> All be as before, Love,
>   – Only sleep![26]

Words are aligned with the wildness of predatory nature, which may strike at any moment:

> What so wild as words are?
>   – I and thou
> In debate, as birds are,
>   Hawk on bough![27]

The birds and the hawk share the same syntax, and 'debate' encompasses the violent attack of the bird of prey.

The word is also aligned with the knowledge of good and evil; truth and

---

24 Browning, *Men and Women*, pp. 12–13.
25 ibid., p. 12.
26 ibid., p. 31.
27 ibid., p. 31.

falsehood become interchangeable words and hard to distinguish when it is recognised that entering into dialogue or 'debate' means entering into the wildness and unpredictable nature of the self:

> What so false as truth is,
>   False to thee?
> Where the serpent's tooth is,
>   Shun the tree – 28

'Truth' cannot avoid the insidious 'tooth' which cuts into it. There is also the suggestion here that the words, like Cadmus' dragon's teeth, may spring up and onto the attack with redoubled vigour. To avoid this pain the woman longs for her lover to be both a god and a man who will envelop her in his power and with whom she may become fully identified: 'I will speak thy speech, Love, / Think thy thought –'.29 The fact that she defers this absolute immersion until the next day ('That shall be to-morrow / Not to-night') suggests that she is aware that the 'debate' will be resumed.30 The blanket of sleep will provide only a temporary respite.

By contrast the speaker in Procter's revision of 'A Woman's Last Word' attempts to use words to make a clean break from her lover:

'A Woman's Last Word'

> Well – the links are broken,
>   All is past;
> This farewell, when spoken,
>   Is the last.
> I have tried and striven
>   All in vain;
> Such bonds must be riven,
>   Spite of pain,
> And never, never, never
>   Knit again.
>
> So I tell you plainly,
>   It must be:
> I shall try, not vainly,
>   To be free;

---

28 ibid., p. 32.
29 ibid., p. 33.
30 ibid., p. 34.

Truer, happier chances
  Wait me yet,
While you, through fresh fancies,
  Can forget; –
And life has nobler uses
  Than Regret.

All past words retracing,
  One by one,
Does not help effacing
  What is done.
Let it be. Oh, stronger
  Links can break!
Had we dreamed still longer
  We could wake, –
Yet let us part in kindness
  For Love's sake.

Bitterness and sorrow
  Will at last,
In some bright to-morrow,
  Heal their past;
But future hearts will never
  Be as true
As mine was – is ever,
  Dear, for you . . .
. . . Then must we part, when loving
  As we do?

(pp. 268–269)

The poem opens on a note of fatigue following struggle. Although the speaker says she has made the break her expression of desperate determination that the bonds will 'never, never, never' knit again suggests that she feels an anxiety that she will not be able to make the break. A clean break spoken in plain language ('I tell you plainly') is desired, however, and the noble woman speaker attempts to rise above both her own and her lover's pain ('Truer, happier chances . . . Than Regret.').

In the third stanza the speaker wavers when she invokes a dream state which threatens to undermine her determination to make the break. Having said that she has broken with her lover she now declares, 'Oh, stronger / Links can break!' The lines 'Had we dreamed still longer / We could wake' are ambiguous. Either they assert that the lovers could wake up after a longer dream; or that it is pointless to remain in a dream world from which they are incapable of waking up, even though they dreamed they could. Parting seems the only way out.

The bright voice which believes healing will take place is countered dramatically in the final stanza when syntax breaks down, tenses become confused and plain speech is broken up and disrupted by the speaker's desire to stay with her lover. Procter has cleverly invoked the voice of the speaker in Browning's 'The Lost Mistress' (1845): 'I will hold your hand but as long as all may, / Or so very little longer!' The beginning is also an echo from that poem: 'All's over, then-'.[31]

In Browning's 'A Woman's Last Word' the woman appears to be preoccupied with placating and reassuring her lover under cover of a lulling, soft and mesmeric voice. In Procter's version the woman struggles to free herself from the hypnotic or dream state of love through the power of incisive and penetrating rhetoric. She is well aware, though, that the break has not been made.

Procter does, though, attempt to stay with the contention or dialogue. The simplicity of the clean rhetoric provides a possible means to cutting through or shedding the phantasies attached to love, perhaps making it possible to communicate more directly.

In the final stanza of Procter's 'A Woman's Last Word' the pain of separation is felt as the speaker gropes for a language of love which has been discarded. Browning's poem ends with a falling into sleep, a temporary state of quiescence, and the speaker's reassurance that she is 'Loved' by her lover. Procter depicts a state of wakefulness, and active and painful 'loving', which disturbs any notion of gaining respite in sleep. Her poem draws attention to the woman's capacity to struggle with the 'dream' and to take full responsibility for breaking away from romantic love and its idealisations. Her position, though, is problematic in that the 'plain' speaking woman risks creating a split within herself by throwing out the totality of love's languages. As in 'A Woman's Question' and 'A Woman's Answer' the strength of the woman's voice and her rhetoric predominate over and exclude a more lyrical and vulnerable voice.

---

[31] Robert Browning, *Bells and Pomegranates*, 'No. VII, Dramatic Romances & Lyrics', London: Edward Moxon, 1845, p. 8.

'Three Roses'

In Procter's three 'Women' poems the women speakers are located on the cusp of relationship in a defensive position. The speaker in 'A Woman's Answer' holds on to her love for the flowers which are depicted as hoarding and holding on tight to her memories:

> I love the Flowers; happy hours lie
>   Shut up within their petals close and fast:
> You have forgotten, dear: but they and I
>   Keep every fragment of the golden Past
> (p. 252, ll. 21-24)

Similarly the speaker holds the book, or the words, *Aurora Leigh*, closely to her. These images of retention suggest a fear of opening up. The spareness of the skeletal language of 'A Woman's Last Word' suggests that the struggle with the 'dream' of romantic love may lead to a difficulty with allowing the full flowering or luxuriance of sexual desire and love. Holding on to her words bars fuller expression.

Procter explores the problems of expression in the poem 'Unexpressed' which was published in the 'First Series' of *Legends and Lyrics* in 1858, the same year as the publication of 'A Woman's Question' and 'Three Roses'. It was also quoted in *The English Woman's Journal* review of *Legends and Lyrics* (see Chapter 1). In this poem the speaker states that the artist, the thinker, the musician, the poem and Love itself are all incapable of expressing themselves fully:

> Dwells within the soul of every Artist
> More than all his effort can express;
> And he knows the best remains unuttered;
> Sighing at what *we* call his success.

The 'dream' of the Poet is described as 'Hidden' and speaking only 'In the voiceless silence of his heart' (p. 147, ll. 21-24).

In another poem published in *Household Words* in the same year, 'Words' (1858), Procter explores the paradox of the lightness and insubstantiality of 'Words' which coexist with the potential of 'living' words to both 'sting' and bring joy (pp. 98-99). The paradox is also seen in Procter's assertion that the life of the 'rose-leaf' is stronger than the 'word', whilst Procter's own words resonate with great power:

> And the rose-leaf that we tread on
> Will outlive a word.
>
> (p. 98, ll. 7-8)

The life which is trodden on in the form of the resilient rose-leaf finds an echo in the speaking silence of the White Maiden's Tomb which suggests both a deathliness and a potentially powerful expressiveness (see Chapter 2).

In Procter's beautiful and moving lyric, 'The Carver's Lesson', which was admired by Thackeray and published in the *Cornhill* in May, 1860, the speaker refers to a 'hidden spirit, / That we may, or may not, understand' (p. 198, ll. 3-4).[32] The 'spirit' is found in the 'fragments' of the carvings of flowers and angels which 'Hide' a meaning (p. 198, ll. 5-12). The carving may open its 'stony hands' and disclose its secret – teaching a 'weary soul' how to 'solve the problem of his pain' (p. 199, ll. 25-36). The hidden power of the carver is aligned with immense vulnerability – the vulnerability and the pain of expressivity.

'The Carver's Lesson' comes just before the lyric 'Three Roses' in the 'Second Series' of *Legends and Lyrics* (1861) which suggests that Procter had established a link between the two poems. The opening of 'stony hands' described in 'The Carver's Lesson' may be read as an opening up and disclosure of a more vulnerable and secret self: 'the rose-leaf that we tread on', the White Maiden's hidden expression.

In 'Three Roses' there is a sense that Procter is struggling to locate a self and form of expression which she 'may, or may not, understand' ('The Carver's Lesson'; p. 198, l. 4). It is worth quoting the poem in full:

Three Roses

> Just when the red June Roses blow
> She gave me one, – a year ago.
> A Rose whose crimson breath revealed
> The secret that its heart concealed,
> And whose half shy, half tender grace
> Blushed back upon the giver's face.
> A year ago – a year ago –
> To hope was not to know.

---

[32] *The Cornhill Magazine*, I (1860), p. 560. Thackeray teased Procter by sending her a sketch of a chicken being carved with an invitation to dinner: 'The Editor of the Cornill Magazine presents his compliments to the Author of the Carvers Lesson and requests the honor of her company at dinner'. *The Letters and Private Papers of W.M. Thackeray*, Ed. Gordon N. Ray, 4 Vols, London: Oxford University Press, 1945, IV, p. 182.

Just when the red June Roses blow
I plucked her one, – a month ago:
Its half-blown crimson to eclipse,
I laid it on her smiling lips;
The balmy fragrance of the south
Drew sweetness from her sweeter mouth.
          Swiftly do golden hours creep, –
          To hold is not to keep.

The red June Roses now are past,
This very day I broke the last –
And now its perfumed breath is hid,
With her, beneath a coffin-lid;
There will its petals fall apart,
And wither on her icy heart –
          At three red Roses' cost
          My world was gained and lost.
                    (pp. 199–200)

The poem invokes Elizabeth Barrett Browning's poem 'Change upon Change' (1846) which begins 'Five months ago' (in May). The speaker refers ironically to the change in her lover's affections mirroring the changes in nature:

The flowers have dried down to the root;
And why, since these be changed since May,
          Shouldst *thou* change less than *they*?

The speaker's cheeks blushed five months ago, like the speaker's in 'Three Roses', but now they are pale. She blames her lover for his false love and asks why she should change any less than him: 'And why, since these be changed, enow, / Should *I* change less than *thou*?'[33]

In 'Three Roses' the lovers appear to be caught up in a cycle of sexual exchange, flowering and death. It is beyond their control or power to 'change' or reverse this cycle. Procter is posing the question which Browning asks in 'Two in the Campagna': 'How it is under our control / To love or not to love?'[34] She is concerned with the split second timing of the moments of giving love and its reception: 'Just when ... Just when ... The red June Roses

---

[33] Elizabeth Barrett Browning, *Poems* (1850), II, pp. 405–406.
[34] *The Poetical Works of Robert Browning*, I, p. 117.

now are past'. Similarly Browning in 'Two in the Campagna' is concerned
with the passing of the 'good minute':

> > > - I pluck the rose
> > And love it more than tongue can speak -
> > Then the good minute goes.[35]

The speaker is forever losing the 'thread' of his loved one:

> > Just when I seemed about to learn!
> > > Where is the thread now? Off again!
> > The old trick! Only I discern -
> > > Infinite passion, and the pain
> > Of finite hearts that yearn.[36]

Procter echoes Browning's words 'Just when'. She is also concerned with the
finite moment. But whilst Browning struggles to fix the moment and
describes actively plucking 'the rose', the woman in 'Three Roses' is so
closely identified with the rose that her attempt to take control is depicted as
doomed from the start.

Literary associations of the rose with wasting and death ('Go, lovely
Rose - / Tell her that wastes her time and me'; 'O Rose, thou art sick!')
emphasise the mortality of a woman's sexual promise which is signified by
the rose. [37]George Meredith in 'Modern Love' (1859) considers the problem
of mortality when the husband states 'I cannot be at peace / In having Love
upon a mortal lease.'[38] In 'Three Roses' desire is shown to run its fatal
course as time ticks away (' . . . a year ago . . . a month ago . . . This very
day I broke the last -').

The fact that the woman initiates the cycle of desire appears to implicate
her even more clearly in love's demise. She is shown to reveal the sexual
secret - 'The secret that its heart concealed' - rather than conceal it under
cover of a woman's natural reserve, or under cover of defensive words.
William Blake describes the dangers of revelation in his poem 'Never Seek
to Tell Thy Love':

---

[35]   ibid., p. 118.
[36]   ibid., p. 118.
[37]   Edmund Waller, 'Go, Lovely Rose'; William Blake, 'The Sick Rose', *The
New Oxford Book of English Verse 1250-1950*, Ed. Helen Gardner, Oxford
University Press, 1972, p. 276, p. 483.
[38]   George Meredith, *Modern Love and Poems of the English Roadside, With
Poems and Ballads*, London: Chapman & Hall, 1862, p. 61.

> I told my love, I told my love,
> I told her all my heart,
> Trembling, cold, in ghastly fears –
> Ah, she doth depart.[39]

A woman's revelation of the rose's 'secret' doubly burdens her with guilt as to live *sub rosa* was conventionally to live under an injunction to secrecy. In Roman myth the rose is described as sealing the lips:

> Cupid presented a Rose to Harpocrates, the grave god of silence, and thus made the flower a symbol of secrecy and silence.[40]

Revealing her secret exposes the woman to the full force of culpability for breaking the taboo. The fact that she is identified with the rose renders her initiative more shameful as she explores the desire at the heart of a woman's mythic reserve and secrecy.

Desire and guilt are shown to feed off each other in 'Three Roses'. The expression of desire is followed by a repercussive blushing 'back upon the giver's face' with the blush suggesting both the desire and her guilt. The 'sweetness' of her secret which 'Drew sweetness from her sweeter mouth' appears to eat her up.

Her lover's laying of the rose 'on her smiling lips', although denoting reciprocity, also suggests that it may have been better if her lips had remained sealed. In Victorian flower language touching an offered flower with the lips implies an affirmative 'Yes', but in 'Three Roses' the woman's breaking of the *sub rosa* injunction excludes her from the formal niceties of a ritual exchange of flowers.[41] Desire and shame are shown to suffuse her face to the extent that the boundaries which constitute a more formal exchange break down. The woman's blushing face and 'smiling lips', and the sense of her sexual pleasure which is created by the repeated assonantal 'o', appear to exceed any boundary set between the lovers.

The fact that the speaker, the initial recipient of the rose, is ungendered adds to the confusion about boundaries. This suggests that Procter is also exploring an alter ego, a shadowy figure, who may be an observing self watching on as the more vulnerable persona is fated by the strength of an

---

[39] Gardner, op. cit., p. 485.
[40] *The Language of Flowers with Illustrative Poetry; To Which are now First Added The Calendar of Flowers and The Dial of Flowers*, London: Saunders and Otley, 1835, p. 113. 'The Dial of Flowers' is a poem by Felicia Hemans.
[41] Laura L. Valentine, *The Language and Sentiment of Flowers and the Classical Floral Legends*, London: Frederick Warne & Co., 1860, p. 49.

involuntary emotion that is too strong for the more conscious self.

Like the male speaker already posited the observer cannot control 'the rose-leaf' or sexual desire which is trodden into the ground or grave. Martyred by her desires (and the red rose symbolises martyrdom) the blush suggests that the woman is both conscious and unconscious of her martyrdom.

In *Keats and Embarrassment* (1974) Christopher Ricks states that the blush may be read as both an involuntary expression of emotion as well as an embarrassed self-consciousness. In his discussion of the frequency of the nineteenth century blush Ricks refers to Darwin's discussion of the blush in *The Expression of the Emotions in Man and Animals* (1872) which refers to 'involuntary' expression and 'self-attention'.[42] Darwin draws attention to the importance of the blushing face:

> Of all parts of the body, the face is most considered and regarded, as
> is natural from its being the chief seat of expression and the source of
> the voice.[43]

The face is therefore the primary focus of 'self-attention' and most liable to blush, Darwin argues.[44] The woman's martyrdom depicted in 'Three Roses' is linked to the absence of the 'voice' of the self which is expressing emotion involuntarily, with the blushing face signifying her emotion. Even though there is a controlling consciousness, which receives the message (in the form of the rose) from the silent self, the unspoken words and a painful self-consciousness – 'the rose-leaf that we tread on' ('Words', p. 98, l. 7) – are more resonant than the controlling voice of the poem.

This silence is figured in Elizabeth Barrett Browning's poem 'Lady Geraldine's Courtship' (1844).[45] In this poem Bertram, a self-educated and 'low-born' poet, falls in love with Lady Geraldine.[46] They stand one day in Lady Geraldine's garden by a sculpture which Lady Geraldine describes as 'marble Silence' holding a 'symbol rose' slackly between its fingers. She expresses the opinion that the sculpture and the slackly held rose suggest 'That the essential meaning growing, may exceed the special symbol'.

---

[42] Christopher Ricks, 'Darwin, Blushing, and Love', *Keats and Embarrass-ment,* Oxford University Press, 1974, pp. 50–53.

Charles Darwin, *The Expression of the Emotions in Man and Animals,* Ed. Francis Darwin, London: John Murray, 1892, pp. 328–329.

[43] ibid., p. 347.
[44] ibid.
[45] Elizabeth Barrett Browning, *Poems* (1850), II, pp. 97–128.
[46] ibid., p. 100.

Bertram disagrees, arguing that "'Tis the substance that wanes ever, 'tis the symbol that exceeds'. The fact that 'Silence' holds onto the rose, if slackly, denotes its silence: 'Yet *she holds it* – or would scarcely be a Silence to our ken' he states.[47]

Bertram's hidden agenda is his love for Lady Geraldine and his fear that she may be silent, or empty of substance, when it comes to him. The obeying of the external forms of her social class may be more important than any love for him. 'Silence' stands between them, a third party to their discussion.

In 'Three Roses' the woman speaker appears to have no external form other than the rose. Her silence speaks and is suggestive of the vulnerability which the stoniness of a womanly reserve has allowed to slip away from its pedestal.

Bertram and Lady Geraldine stay within the bounds of formal debate and dialogue (this is further exemplified by the formal garden and its statues). They are able to displace their silent love and their vulnerability on to the symbol. Even though Lady Geraldine says she prefers the substance, and by implication the substance of her love, she conveys her meaning by reference to the statue.

By contrast, Procter's speaker appears to have become detached from and drifts away from external forms. With reference to symbols and the form they take it is interesting to note that the complete quotation from R.W. Emerson's essay 'Gifts' (1844), which Procter quotes from in her dedication to Matilda Hays in *Legends and Lyrics* reads:

> our tokens of compliment & love are for the most part barbarous. Rings and other jewels are not gifts, but apologies for gifts. The only gift is a portion of thyself. Thou must bleed for me. Therefore the poet brings his poem; the shepherd, his lamb; the farmer, corn; the miner, a gem; the sailor, coral & shells; the painter, his picture; the girl, a handkerchief of her own sewing.[48]

Procter's quotation reads:

> Our tokens of love are for the most part barbarous. Cold and lifeless, because they do not represent our life. The only gift is a portion of

---

47   ibid., pp. 106-107.
48   'Gifts', 'Second Series' (1844), *The Essays of Ralph Waldo Emerson*, Intro. Edward F. O'Day, San Francisco: John Henry Nash, 1934, p. 212.

thyself. Therefore let the farmer give his corn; the miner, a gem; the sailor, coral and shells; the painter, his picture; and the poet, his poem.
– Emerson's Essays   A.A.P.[49]

In her quotation Procter excludes the words from Emerson's essay, 'Thou must bleed for me', 'the shepherd, his lamb' and 'the girl, a handkerchief of her own sewing.' The 'gift' of the rose in 'Three Roses' suggests the blood or passion of the woman who cannot find a form or voice which will hold and contain the desire that martyrs her. The vulnerability of both the 'lamb' and the 'girl' consigned to her 'sewing' are edited out by Procter who chooses not to include the more disturbing aspects of Emerson's text.

The external forms which metaphorically hold Bertram and Lady Geraldine contrast with the sense of a groping for a form which is presented in 'Three Roses'. The 'blush' which suffuses the poem blurs any distinction between the subject and object, donor and recipient. This formless self appears to slip away from and resist entering into a relationship with another person.

The voices of the women on the interstices of and pulling away from marriage (depicted in the 'Women' poems) find an echo in the voice of a woman whose desire leads to her falling away from conventional forms (and she may be read as a fallen woman – she certainly falls as a result of her sexual initiative). In a powerful lyric by Alice Cary called 'The Bridal Veil' (1866) the speaker threatens:

> And spite of all clasping, and spite of all bands,
> I can slip like a shadow, a dream, from your hands.[50]

It is this 'dream' which Robert Browning seems to be extremely anxious to keep hold of in his poem 'Women and Roses' published in *Men and Women* in 1855. Procter's 'Three Roses' has a dreamlike quality with the roses moving between the parties, as though in the dark and free from any rootedness or context. By contrast, the roses and women in Browning's lyric are paradoxically both firmly attached to and detached from the central male speaker whose rose tree represents him ('They circle their rose on my rose tree.').[51]

A reading of 'Three Roses' by contrast with 'Women and Roses' shows

---

[49] 'Dedication', Adelaide Anne Procter, *Legends and Lyrics. A Book of Verses*, Intro. Charles Dickens, London: George Bell and Sons, 1882.
[50] Alice Cary, *Ballads, Lyrics, and Hymns*, New York: Hurd and Houghton, 1866, p. 144.
[51] *The Poetical Works of Robert Browning*, I, pp. 137–139.

the extent to which Procter responds to the strength of Browning's lyric voice whilst implicitly providing a critique of his depiction of women as strong, resilient and powerfully present, even in their absence, in his imagination. She attempts to locate the woman who is not formed and present for the male imagination, and who may seek to 'slip' away from more conventional representations of women.

'Women and Roses' was one of the lyrics written by Browning in Paris early in January 1852, very probably in response to Bryan Procter's advice to Browning to write more lyrics. The poem was suggested by a dream Browning had about some roses Elizabeth Barrett Browning had received the previous day.[52] The poem begins:

> I dream of a red-rose tree.
> And which of its roses three
> Is the dearest rose to me?[53]

The speaker describes the women circling the rose tree as its guardians. They are women from the past seen in engravings and in poetry. They are followed by the living, loving and loved women of the present and finally multitudes of future 'Beauties unborn'. The second stanza is followed by a tercet stating that the rose's term has been reached and no longer attracts the bees.[54] In Stanza IV the speaker longs for possession of the women from 'the antique time!':

> How shall I fix you, fire you, freeze you,
> Break my heart at your feet to please you?
> Oh, to possess and be possessed![55]

But the women keep circling. A tercet celebrating the rose's present brimming joy follows. In Stanza VI the speaker's sexual desire is barely containable – like a bee sucked in by a hyacinth he longs to 'bury' himself in the woman ('Eyes in your eyes, lips on your lips! / Fold me fast where the cincture slips').[56]

In the following tercet the speaker addresses the rose of the future, 'First streak of a new morn'. The poem concludes with the speaker longing for

[52]   William Clyde DeVane, *A Browning Handbook*, New York: Appleton-Century-Crofts, Inc., 1955, p. 259.
[53]   *The Poetical Works of Robert Browning*, I, p. 137.
[54]   ibid., p. 137.
[55]   ibid., p. 138.
[56]   ibid.

wings to enable him to rise above the women and get a clearer perspective so that he may 'conquer' what 'is near.' He simultaneously pays tribute to the resilience of the rose which will spring from 'the dust where our own flesh moulders'. The poem concludes:

> What shall arrive with the cycle's change?
> A novel grace and a beauty strange.
> I will make an Eve, be the artist that began her,
> Shaped her to his mind! – Alas! in like manner
> They circle their rose on my rose tree.[57]

As in many of his love lyrics Browning is exploring the desire to possess and know women. This desire is shown to exist in creative and dynamic tension with the women's measured and repetitive circling. The question in the final stanza, 'What shall arrive with the cycle's change?', and the speaker's desire to be the artist who will begin 'her' according to his own 'mind!', are answered by the continued circling.

The 'novel grace' and 'beauty strange', which the speaker anticipates will arrive at 'the cycle's change' are contrasted with the repetitive cycles of time and tradition (exemplified by the women written in history and literature). The artist is shown struggling with notions of creativity. The yearning for novelty and strangeness is countered by archaic and antique rhythms, which are associated with 'nature' (the women and the roses).

The intensity of the speaker's explicit sexual feeling ('Fold me fast where the cincture slips') is enabled by the ritualised circling. Male sexuality finds release and pleasure in the 'one' sexual moment ('Drink once and die! –' . . . 'Girdle me once!'[58]). His sexuality exists in tension with the 'dazzling drift' and ephemerality ('like a dance of snow') of the women's sexuality, which is depicted as strong through repetition and resilience.[59]

The male speaker seeks to rise above the women, the roses and the cyclicality of time. Christ-like he longs for a 'far' off eternity whilst simultaneously yearning for the 'eternities of pleasure' which exist within the 'old measure' of earth-based past, present and future time.[60] His struggle to rise above the women may be read as an attempt to avoid the women's powerful triple presence.

The triple presence of women is discussed by Freud in his essay 'The Theme of the Three Caskets', where he explores the choosing of the three

---

[57] ibid., pp. 138–139.
[58] ibid., p. 138.
[59] ibid., p. 137.
[60] ibid., p. 138.

caskets in Shakespeare's *The Merchant of Venice*. He reads the caskets as women:

> If what we were concerned with were a dream, it would occur to us at once that caskets are also women, symbols of what is essential in woman, and therefore of a woman herself – like coffers, boxes, cases, baskets, and so on.[61]

In *The Merchant of Venice* Bassanio chooses between the three women and in choosing the lead casket he chooses silence or dumbness, Freud writes:

> That is to say: 'Thy plainness moves me more than the blatant nature of the other two.' Gold and silver are 'loud'; lead is dumb . . .[62]

Freud writes that 'in dreams dumbness is a common representation of death'.[63] The choice of death is unconscious, he states, and reflects an 'ancient ambivalence' which is associated with a primeval identity whereby Mother goddesses, 'The great Mother-goddesses of the oriental peoples', were both creators and destroyers.[64] Freud concludes his essay with the suggestion that the three female figures represent the 'three inevitable relations that a man has with a woman':

> the woman who bears him, the woman who is his mate and the woman who destroys him; or that they are the three forms taken by the figure of the mother in the course of a man's life – the mother herself, the beloved one who is chosen after her pattern, and lastly the Mother Earth who receives him once more. But it is in vain that an old man yearns for the love of woman as he had it first from his mother; the third of the Fates alone, the silent Goddess of Death, will take him into her arms.[65]

In his dream of 'women and roses' Browning depicts a speaker who seeks to transcend the women of the past, present and future and their cyclicality. He reverses the cycle of birth, mating and death by beginning with the rose of

[61] 'The Theme of the Three Caskets' (1913), *The Standard Edition of the Complete Psychological Works of Sigmund Freud*, Ed. James Strachey, 24 Vols, London: The Hogarth Press and the Institute of Psycho-analysis, 1958, Vol XII (1911–1913), p. 292.
[62] ibid., p. 294.
[63] ibid., p. 295.
[64] ibid., p. 299.
[65] ibid., p. 301.

the past, moving on to present joy and concluding with an image of the unborn child: 'Thy bud's the babe unborn'.[66] There is a return to the moment of the birth of sexual desire when the cycle may be repeated.

The women's silence is depicted as less deathly than suggestive of creative possibilities. The male artist's struggle is shown to be enabled by his recognition that he can never fully know the women. Morse Peckham has written of 'Browning's rather remarkable insight that to want to know everything, to be forever restless, is to deny the redemptive power of tradition.'[67] This reading of Browning is confirmed in 'Women and Roses', with the women being presented as guardians of the strength of tradition suggested by the 'red-rose tree', which roots both the male speaker and the women ('They circle their rose on my rose tree.') The restless male is depicted as both deeply attached to and detached from the tree. As a restless and enquiring artist he plays with the choices which present themselves ('which of its roses three is the dearest rose to me?'), and although he cannot avoid coming to 'term' he is not shown to be wholly and irrevocably in the arms of the 'Fates' as suggested by Freud.

In Procter's 'Three Roses' the triple movement towards death and burial agrees much more completely with Freud's theory of the 'Three Caskets'. The woman gives birth to desire, the lovers mate, but she not he is destroyed. She appears to be fated to a coffin or 'casket'. Paradoxically, by choosing to initiate the exchange of roses she breaks with the tradition which places her in the role of woman as 'Fate' who holds the secrets of life and death. Her 'secret' redounds on herself once it is exposed, and it is as though she cannot escape the silence she represents.

This silence also suggests the absence of a more articulate language of love. 'Three Roses' echoes Robert Browning's poem 'In a Year' (*Men and Women*, 1855). In this poem the woman speaker struggles to understand why her lover has turned cold on her:

> Strange! that very way
>   Love begun:
> I as little understand
>   Love's decay.[68]

She asks why generosity should be her lover's preserve:

---

66 *The Poetical Works of Robert Browning*, I, p. 138.
67 Morse Peckham, 'Browning and Romanticism', *Writers and Their Background. Robert Browning*, Ed. Isobel Armstrong, London: G. Bell & Sons, 1974, p. 68.
68 *The Poetical Works of Robert Browning*, I, p. 134.

> Why should all the giving prove
> His alone?[69]

Her gift, as in 'Three Roses', is shown to dispossess her of love. In 'In a Year', a poem which ironises romantic love, Browning gives the woman speaker an articulate voice and language which attempts to make sense of her experience. By contrast the woman's silence in 'Three Roses', and her merging with the rose, depict her as caught up in a cycle of 'nature' and fate, which precludes any more conscious articulation of her problems.

Interestingly 'Three Roses' appeared in *Household Words* following an article by Eliza Lynn entitled 'Our Vegetable Friends', which is a tribute to Jane Loudon for her popularisation of botany and for developing a taste for flowers.[70] Ironically, it is a deep fear of becoming a silent 'vegetable friend' which Procter is expressing. Very few of her poems directly express sexual or romantic desires, which suggests how deep her fear may have been – the fear that the expression of sexual desire might be fated to silence and deadening.

Although Procter's treatment of sexual desire is bold in 'Three Roses', and in spite of the fact that she had entered into the marriage debate in the 'Women' poems and in other poems, there is a sense that Procter herself had in fact given up on the idea of sexual love and marriage. Her women protagonists in the narrative poems are often single and in the 'Women' poems the women are shown to exist within the interstices of relationship. Even though the speaker in 'A Woman's Answer' attests to a 'thousand' loves it is as though Procter nips them in the bud.

In Procter's poem 'From "Lost Alice"' (1861) the speaker states that she and her lover have 'killed our Love,' and that 'No longing can restore / Our dead again.':

> Our buried Love: its grave lies dark and deep
> Between us evermore.
>
> (p. 210)

'From "Lost Alice"' may well be a reference to a story of the same title by Mary W.A. Gibson which was published in *Household Words* (24.4.1858).[71]

---

[69] ibid., p. 135.

[70] *Household Words*, XVIII, 1858, p. 228. Jane Loudon (née Webb) (1807–1858) was the wife and amanuensis of the horticultural writer, John Claudius Loudon. She wrote botanical books, her most successful work being *The Ladies Companion to the Flower Garden* (1841).

[71] [Mary W.A. Gibson], 'Lost Alice', *Household Words*, XVII, 1858, pp. 438–445.

In this story Alice marries a man several years older than herself. She is described as having charmed a 'thousand hearts' and having had a 'thousand fancies'.[72] She views herself as a rebel who gratefully submits to her 'master's chains'.[73] Her husband schools himself to withdraw from the warmth of her emotions and Alice's love for him dies: 'My love is dead and buried.'[74]

Procter's short poem focuses on the death of love, and a woman's warm emotions and multiple desires, depicted in Gibson's 'Lost Alice' and in 'A Woman's Answer', are not described. In other later poems such as 'Three Evenings in a Life' (1858) (pp. 233-244), 'Philip and Mildred' (1861) (pp. 187-194), and 'The Story of a Faithful Soul' (1861) (pp. 253-255) the death of love and the faithlessness of male lovers provide the main focus.

Procter remained single, and it is the difficulties encountered by the single woman in her negotiations of the love relationship which are the central concern of the poems discussed in this chapter. Procter's response to Browning (and it is a brief and limited response – to an extent nipped in the bud) is to a voice which assumes a powerful presence, even in her absence, of the woman who is often depicted as one of a couple.

Many of Browning's poems in *Men and Women* are inevitably concerned with the couple, for example 'Love Among the Ruins', 'A Lover's Quarrel', 'Two in the Campagna', 'By the Fireside'. Browning's twinning of poems stresses the importance of the pair: 'Meeting at Night' and 'Parting at Morning'; 'Home-Thoughts, from Abroad' and 'Home-Thoughts from the Sea'; 'One Way of Love' and 'Another Way of Love'; 'Love in a Life' and 'Life in a Love'.[75]

By contrast Procter is concerned with the single woman who is often depicted as the shadowy third party to a couple, for example in 'Three Evenings in a Life', 'A New Mother', 'The Story of a Faithful Soul'. In 'By the Fireside' Browning refers to a 'shadowy third' person who is often in the presence of the couple:

> If you join two lives, there is oft a scar,
>   They are one and one, with a shadowy third;
> One near one is too far.[76]

---

72   ibid., p. 441.
73   ibid., p. 442.
74   ibid., p. 443 and p. 445.
75   All these poems are in *The Poetical Works of Robert Browning*, I.
76   Browning, *Men and Women*, p. 78.

This third party, which I shall refer to in later chapters, may be read as the shadowy presence of Procter herself who places herself at a distance from, and in tentative dialogue with, the poetry of Robert Browning and Elizabeth Barrett Browning.

Elizabeth Barrett Browning's seminal work, *Aurora Leigh* (1857), was praised by Bryan Procter. He wrote to his Boston publisher, James Fields:

> The most successful book of the season has been Mrs Browning's 'Aurora Leigh'. I could wish some things altered, I confess; but as it is, it is by far (a hundred times over) the finest poem ever written by a woman. We know little or nothing of Sappho, – nothing to induce comparison, – and all other wearers of petticoats must courtesy to the ground.[77]

Procter's praise of *Aurora Leigh* and his immense respect for Browning's poetry place the Brownings' work at quite a distance above the poetry of his daughter who is struggling for her own form of expression.

In *Aurora Leigh* it is the figure of Marion Erle who figures as the third party to the central couple Aurora and Romney. The intensity and potential violence of sexual desires – desires which are postponed by Aurora in favour of her writing career – seem to be projected on to the third party, Marion, who is raped, has a child and chooses to remain single.

Marion, who has been described as a Christ-like martyr, is associated with 'nature' throughout the poem.[78] By contrast, Aurora tears herself away from the garden and its June roses where Romney proposes to her. She fears that she may become aligned with a 'nature' which will prevent her from pursuing her poetic ambition:

---

[77] James T. Fields, *Old Acquaintance. Barry Cornwall and Some of His Friends*, Boston: James R. Osgood and Company, 1876, p. 115. Joan Hedrick writes that James T. Fields was himself 'known for his generosity, particularly to struggling women writers' and that unlike 'most of the men in his circle he supported women's suffrage' (Joan D. Hedrick, *Harriet Beecher Stowe. A Life*, Oxford University Press, 1994, p. 294).

[78] Elizabeth Barrett Browning, *Aurora Leigh*. Marion Erle, a destitute 'drover's daughter' (p. 112), is befriended by Romney Leigh, Aurora's cousin and future husband. She leaves England after rejecting marriage with Romney. Marion is raped on her way to Australia and has a child. Aurora finds Marion in the 'Market-place of Flowers' in Paris (p. 244); she describes her as fluttering 'like a cyclamen' (p. 245) at her approach. Aurora also refers to Marion's 'broad wild woodland eyes' (p. 378) and 'impassioned spaniel head' (p. 379), and describes her as a 'leaping fawn' (p. 379). Romney describes Marion's father as 'a woodland boar' (p. 388).

We all begin
By singing with the birds, and running fast
With June-days, hand in hand: but once, for all,
The birds must sing against us ...[79]

When Aurora reunites with Romney ten years later the feared rose is translated into a rose which, according to Romney, combines spiritual and natural qualities. He delivers a speech worshipping the rose which is depicted as powerfully symbolic of 'Loves filial, loves fraternal, neighbour-loves, / And civic'; Aurora comments that Romney had not so long ago sworn that 'this very social rose smelt ill' to which Romney replies 'is it a rose at all? / The filial's thankless, the fraternal's hard'. But he still invokes the 'Flower of Heaven' as the ideal of love and his tone is religious.[80] The book concludes on a climactic and transcendent note with Aurora and Romney metaphorically rising above both 'ill' smelling roses and the bruised Marion who remains in the shadows of, and subsidiary to, the central couple.

Aurora has in a sense projected her more vulnerable and exposed self onto Marion. Her surname Leigh, which will be her married name as she and Romney are cousins, finally eclipses Marion's surname which denotes the early (or Erle/Leigh) part of Aurora – the desiring self which is exposed too early and does not appear like the triumphant dawn suggested by the name 'Aurora'.

In 'Three Roses' Procter depicts the 'fate' of the single woman who is too closely identified with the roses. The fear of a 'vegetable' nature and of silence, which may result from too early exposure of the desiring self, is powerfully expressed. There is a sense of a shadowy sexual and single self who is attempting to find a form and a voice. This appears to be the voice of a critical third party who is located either within the interstices or on the threshold of relationship; or the voice of the third woman (or rose) – Browning's 'shadowy third' person who 'scars' the couple in their apparent unity – the oneness for which Browning strives but which always eludes him.[81]

---

79 Elizabeth Barrett Browning, *Aurora Leigh*, p. 70.
80 ibid., p. 400.
81 op. cit., Browning, *Men and Women*, p. 78.

Chapter 4

Paternal Authority: Bryan Procter

The voice of a third party – the 'shadowy third' person posited at the end of the last chapter – may also be the voice of the daughter. In this chapter I shall consider Adelaide Procter's response to and negotiation of Bryan Procter's authority and influence as a poet. Unlike the 'strong' poets Harold Bloom posits in *The Anxiety of Influence* (1973) Bryan Procter was a relatively 'weak' poet who chose not to develop his poetic strengths.[1] His work and preoccupations are, however, central to Adelaide's development as a poet. Her poetry negotiates Bryan Procter's constructions and thematic concerns, which are at times potent but also present her with many problems.

The main focus of the chapter is Procter's narrative poem 'A Legend of Provence' (1859) which is considered in relation to Bryan Procter's poem 'The Girl of Provence' (1823). Before discussing these poems, however, it is important to consider the relationship between father and daugher, the kind of poetic precedents Bryan Procter provided for Adelaide and the ways that her poetry responds to her father's.

The relationship between father and daughter seems to have been close. Bryan Procter held up Adelaide as a role model for her sister Edith in the poem 'To Edith. 1845': 'May'st thou take note – as a good child should do, / Of all things best in her'.[2] The poems he wrote to Adelaide as a child ('Golden-Tressed Adelaide. A Song for a Child.', 'To Adelaide') suggest that his eldest child occupied a very special place in his affections.[3]

In biographical material there are very few references to Bryan Procter's

---

1   Harold Bloom, *The Anxiety of Influence. A Theory of Poetry*, New York: Oxford University Press, 1973. Bloom is interested in the 'strong' poet's anxiety and his struggle with the influence of his precursors.

2   Barry Cornwall, *English Songs and Other small Poems*, London: Chapman and Hall, 1851, p. xxiii.

3   ibid., pp. 197, 199. 'Golden-Tressed Adelaide' was set to music by Sigismund Von Neukomm (Chevalier Neukomm) (1778-1858). Neukomm was a pupil of Haydn and composed songs and oratorios which achieved great popularity. The MS of 'To Adelaide' is titled 'To my Child written on her Birthday. Oct 30th 1825' (MS, University of Iowa Libraries).

specific views of his daughter's poetry, but he appeared to encourage and applaud her writing. Jane Brookfield (p. 90, note 56) referred to the 'beautiful attachment' between the father and his 'bright, enthusiastic daughter' and to 'each poet with critical approbation' admiring the other's work.[4] In a letter to William Brookfield dated 1858 (the year the 'First Series of *Legends and Lyrics* was published), Bryan Procter wrote:

> We are still 'climbing trees in the Hesperides,' as you will see. The difference is that the daughter is now the active person, and not the father, whose poor old verses you so good-naturedly wrap up in your lawn.[5]

Bryan Procter was surely addressing Adelaide when he wrote in an untitled and unpublished poem 'You are soaring in the sun; / I rest in shade'.[6]

Bryan Procter had apparently taken to the 'shade' early on in his poetic career when he married Anne Skepper and concentrated his energies on his work as a lawyer and Commissioner for Lunacy. His popular *English Songs* (1832) are presented by him as a 'farewell offering' to a kind public.[7] He was only 45 years old, and his own recognition that his poetry was minor, along with a well documented lack of ambition, seem to have contributed to his relinquishing the desire to become a more successful poet.

As the daughter of an apparently unambitious and frequently self-denigrating father Adelaide would almost certainly have faced many difficulties in articulating the desire to make her mark as a poet. Like her father Adelaide employed a pseudonym (Miss Berwick). According to Dickens, in his 'Introduction' to *Legends and Lyrics*, she had said that she feared he might publish her poems 'for papa's sake, and not for their own' if he did not like them (p. 2). Adelaide may also have employed a pseudonym to free herself from guilt if she were to succeed and also perhaps from too close an association with her father's poetry.

The name Miss Berwick, with its sharp, crisp tone, contrasts with her father's pseudonym Barry Cornwall which evokes a softness and gentleness, perhaps the honeyed feel identified by the actress Fanny Kemble. A running away into strange, dreamlike states and into exile is often apparent in Bryan

---

4   Charles and Frances Brookfield, *Mrs Brookfield and Her Circle*, 2 Vols, London: Sir Isaac Pitman and Sons Ltd., 1905, II, pp. 460–461.

5   ibid., p. 460.

6   MS III, University of Iowa Libraries.

7   Barry Cornwall, *English Songs and Other Small Poems*, London: Edward Moxon, 1832, p. xvi.

Procter's work, for example in poems such as 'Marcian Colonna' (pp. 57–58), 'The Girl of Provence' and 'Midsummer Madness' (discussed in this chapter). By contrast, poetic reserve and control are the hallmarks of Adelaide Procter's poetry, and it would seem that she sought to curtail what she may have considered to be her father's poetic excesses. Her poetry is also notable for its clarity by contrast with her father's work which is often confused and unclear.

It is important to consider in more detail the dreamlike and often night-marish states Bryan Procter depicts. It is significant that many of his poems are concerned with madness ('Tartarus', 'A Sicilian Story' and the poems mentioned above amongst others) and as a Commissioner for Lunacy madness clearly interested him. In his essay 'On English Poetry' (1825) Bryan Procter wrote of poetry as a solution to madness. He writes of 'the harmony of the mind . . . which embraces and reconciles its seeming discords'.[8] In another essay, 'A Defence of Poetry' (1828), he makes a distinction between poetic 'visions' and 'delusions', stating that the 'visions':

> form, in fact, a wholesome cessation from our reasoning habits, like sleep, or a quiet landscape; but enjoyed when sleep will not come to us, and when there is no beauty of landscape actually near, to relieve the fatigue of our brain, or induce pleasurable and gentle emotions.[9]

Poetry provides an experience which is equivalent to having a pleasant dream.

In 'A Defence of Poetry' Bryan Procter describes poetry as a study of:

> the movements of the human mind, – to see how it is affected by certain causes, and how it adapts itself to various contingencies, – to contemplate it when under extraordinary depression, or when lifted to a state of perilous excitement . . .[10]

This state of mind is depicted in 'Marcian Colonna' (1820), Bryan Procter's most convincing, if confused, study of madness which may have influenced the writing of Browning's 'Porphyria's Lover'. In this poem the protagonist Marcian moves in and out of a state of lunacy and finally poisons his lover Julia, his brother's widow. At one point he refers to his love as 'A strange

---

[8]   Barry Cornwall, *Essays and Tales in Prose*, 2 Vols, Boston: Ticknor, Reed and Fields, 1853, II, p. 132.

[9]   ibid., pp. 187–188.

[10]   ibid., pp. 189–190.

and sad perverseness'.[11]

The poem is an immensely sympathetic account of the protagonist's painful condition but to what extent a poem such as this is designed to 'relieve the fatigue of our brain, or induce pleasurable and gentle emotions' is not clear. The poem does promote sympathy, but the fragmented, disrupted and nightmarish life the deluded Marcian leads is depicted as extremely unsettling. The reader is left with a sense of acute disturbance and the presence of unresolved emotions in conclusion rather than with any feeling of relief.

In Bryan Procter's poetry there is evidence of a struggle to articulate extremely painful and disturbing emotions along with the desire to escape from and obliterate them. Marcian seeks to escape his complex emotional state by crossing the sea (which suggests a solution or a place of immersion for his madness) only to find himself back at the original site of his lunacy and its confinement, the 'convent prison' in the Appenines.[12]

Benign 'vision' and more malign 'delusion' (which in his essay Procter is keen not to confuse) are seen to struggle for precedence in some of his poems. In 'Michael Angelo', one of Procter's 'Four Dramatic Scenes' (1853), this struggle takes the form of a dialogue between Angelo and Raffaelle. Angelo is urged by the Pope to 'dream' for him in the form of a painting. Angelo replies that he will do his best but that he cannot control the thought that 'strikes which way it will through the dark brain'. Raffaelle, who comes to look at Michael's paintings, has to leave as he finds his art too disturbing:

> Thy figures haunt me, like Disease.
> I must go hear some Roman melody,
> Accomplish'd music, and sweet human words,
> And bask beneath the smiles which thou dost scorn.[13]

---

[11] *The Poetical Works of Milman, Bowles, Wilson and Barry Cornwall*, Paris: A & W Galignani, 1829, p. 94, xv. 'Marcian Colonna' is prefaced by an 'Advertisement' (p. 90) which states that the story was suggested by a paper called 'Extracts from Gosschen's Diary' in *Blackwood's Magazine*. The extract is from the diary of a German priest called to the death-cell of a young man condemned for murdering his mistress in a fit of insanity (*Blackwood's Edinburgh Magazine*, III, 1818, pp. 596–598). Procter writes that 'his original intention was to paint the fluctuations of a fatalist's mind, – touched with insanity' (p. 90). Michael Mason compares Procter's depictions of Marcian's mania with Browning's more 'rational' lunatic in 'Porphyria's Lover'. Mason discusses the contemporary debate concerning the notion of 'rational lunacy' (Mason, 'Browning and the Dramatic Monologue', *Writers and Their Background. Robert Browning*, Ed. Isobel Armstrong, London: G. Bell & Sons, 1974).

[12] ibid., p. 92, v; p. 102, xiii.

[13] Cornwall, *Essays and Tales in Prose*, II, pp. 202–206.

Bryan Procter admired both artists, but his affection was reserved for Raffaelle, and perhaps for what he perceives to be his more benign vision. In his essay 'A Chapter on Portraits' (1829), Procter describes 'the grace, and intelligence, and unequalled propriety of Raffaelle!'[14]

His poetry, however, is more often concerned with 'diseased' and troubled figures. For example, in 'The Two Dreams' (1819), one of his many poems based on a tale from Boccaccio's *Decameron*, a married couple relate their dreams the morning after a night in which Andreana has excluded her husband, Gabriello, from her bed. Her dream was of a creature which seized Gabriello and jumped with him into a gulf. Gabriello dreamt first of a fawn and later of a black greyhound like a wolf which attacked him:

> it seized
> My side (my left side here), and gnaw'd its way
> In a moment to my heart: the blood gush'd out,
> And once methought so freely that the dog
> Was blinded with it, but he shook't away
> And came with fiercer appetite.

Gabriello concludes:

> Now, Andreana, learn how little hath
> A dream to do with life, and yet life is
> Itself a dream perhaps ...

At the moment of proving the fallacy of dream to his wife Gabriello dies.[15]

In Bryan Procter's poem 'I and My Dream' the speaker states his belief that his benign and gentle 'dream' is the truth: 'who hath aught beside him / Truer than a dream?'[16] The relief that we 'Are of such stuff / as dreams are made of; and our little life / is rounded with a sleep!' (quoted from Prospero's speech in Procter's 'Memoir and Essay on the Genius of Shakspere', 1853) is, however, countered by the terror of the disruption of nightmare (seen in

---

[14]   ibid., I, p. 166. Bryan Procter had a collection of Italian masters which included works by Domenichino, Fra Bartolomeo and Raffaelle. According to Richard Armour his collection 'has disappeared very mysteriously, only an unfinished head, attributed to Raphael, having come down to the grandchildren' (Armour, *Barry Cornwall A Biography of Bryan Waller Procter With a Selected Collection of Hitherto Unpublished Letters*, Boston: Meador Publishing Company, 1935, Footnote 2, p. 91).

[15]   Barry Cornwall, *Dramatic Scenes and Other Poems*, London: Printed for C. and J. Ollier, 1819.

[16]   Cornwall, *English Songs and Other Small Poems* (1851), p. xxii.

'The Two Dreams') which might prove to be the 'truth'.[17]

In an article entitled 'A May Dream', published in *The London Magazine* in May 1821, Bryan Procter describes the impasse he has reached in his relationship to dreams:

> We protest that we hate to dream; for if it be unpleasant, it *is* unpleasant, and therefore not to be desired; and if it be pleasant, then is the waking therefore a pain. We hate dreams, therefore . . .[18]

In 'A May Dream' Bryan Procter dreams of his sleeping self surrounded by a mass of literary figures from the past (Marlow, Lyly, Drayton, Decker, Massinger, Jonson, Spenser, Webster, Beaumont and Fletcher, Shakespeare). All these figures bow down before 'Shakspeare' whose touch awakes Procter 'like an electric shock'. The account of the dream concludes with the assurance that the dream holds no 'hidden purpose' or 'concealed drug in the sugar'.[19]

Procter seeks to dispose of the significance of his own 'purpose' or place in the dream. The account begins with an epigraph from Spenser's *The Shepheardes Calendar*: 'we here sitten as drowned in a dream'.[20] Procter introduces himself as 'pleasant and anonymous' and as one who does 'not profess to lead thee direct to any of the public-houses of knowledge'.[21] In his memoir of Charles Lamb, Procter referred to himself as being one of 'the crowd of contributors' to *The London Magazine* and as now being under the protection of 'that great Power which is called "Oblivion"'.[22] He presents himself in the memoir and in 'A May Dream' as being 'drowned' out by his literary peers.

The 'concealed drug in the sugar' which Procter denies is present is a problematic desire to enter into a dream of immersion within his group of peers as a way of losing any sense of his own importance, along with any responsibility for his writing and for his dreams which may involve some pain. The epigraph from Spenser does draw attention to the problem of being

---

[17] Barry Cornwall, *Essays and Tales in Prose*, I, p. 61. Procter slightly misquotes; Prospero says 'We are such stuff / As dreams are made on' (Shakespeare, *The Tempest*, Ed. Anne Righter, Penguin Books, 1968, IV.I, p. 120).

[18] *The London Magazine*, III, 1821, p. 478.

[19] ibid., pp. 479–483.

[20] ibid., p. 477. The shepherd Alsus is chiding Damoetas fo his Melancholy Disposition (Edmund Spenser, *The Shepherd's Calender* (1579), Dublin: R. Smith, 1758?).

[21] ibid., p. 478.

[22] Barry Cornwall, *Charles Lamb. A Memoir*, London: Edward Moxon & Co., 1866, p. 153.

a melancholic dreamer but Procter typically does not elaborate on the quotation.

In his biography of Bryan Procter, Richard Armour writes that Procter was 'too self-effacing for good autobiography' and that *An Autobiographical Fragment* 'breaks off abruptly before having carried the life story much beyond boyhood'.[23] Many of Procter's poems and plays have the same fragmentary quality and the titles of the collections, *Dramatic Scenes* and 'Dramatic Fragments', suggest that Procter did prefer to express himself in terms of fragments which may be lost.[24] Escaping into states of anonymity and fragmentation, and a dreamlike world for which he does not take full responsibility, would seem to free him from the more disturbing implications of the madness and violence which are depicted as overwhelming in many of his poems.

By contrast, Adelaide Procter in her poetry is not on the whole overtly concerned with an exploration of either 'visions' or states of delusion. A cluster of short lyrics which relate to dreams dramatically contrast with her father's more dreamlike world. In 'A Dream' (1855) the speaker describes herself as spinning out a dream whilst she sits on a hill. She relinquishes the dream when:

> At last the grey shadows fell round me,
>   And the night came dark and chill,
> And I rose and ran down the valley,
>   And left it all on the hill.

When she returns the next morning nothing 'but glistening dew-drops' remain of a dream which has not been described. (pp. 76–77)

In another lyric, 'In the Wood' (1861), the speaker recounts how she met with a fairy 'Where the wild wood-strawberries cluster' who leads her to a fairyland palace:

> And I stood in a strange enchantment;
>   I had known it all before:
> In my heart of hearts was the magic
>   Of days that will come no more,
> The magic of joy departed,
>   That Time can never restore.

---

[23] Armour, op. cit., pp. 16–17.
[24] Cornwall, *Dramatic Scenes and Other Poems* (1819) (1857); Cornwall, 'Dramatic Fragments', *English Songs and Other small Poems* (1851), pp. 217–284.

> That never, ah, never, never,
>   Never again can be:–
> Shall I tell you what powerful fairy
>   Built up this palace for me?
> It was only a little white Violet
>   I found at the root of a tree.
>
> (pp. 186–187)

'In the Wood' conveys a sense of both the intense grief which is evoked by recalling the 'magic' of the past, as well as the joy associated with the memory which forms part of a process of grief. The speaker does not need to be overwhelmed by magical visions of the past to remember it. The wood and the 'root of a tree' in a sense root her grief and provide it with a ground. The violet in Victorian flower language signifies modesty, and there is a sense of Adelaide Procter, the poet, modestly refraining from entering into the overly elaborate fantasy world of visions and delusions often favoured by her father.

This restraint (or poetic reserve in Tractarian terms) is seen again in the poem 'From "Phantastes"' (1859) where it proves to be more problematic. This poem is the second of a series of four poems which are entitled 'Borrowed Thoughts' (pp. 209–210). Unlike her father, Procter hardly ever presents her poetry in the form of 'fragments'. Her lyrics are often crisp and finished, with the verse and language tightly controlled. The 'Borrowed Thoughts' are an exception in that they are presented as thoughts borrowed from a complete work, but they are still complete poems in themselves.

'From "Phantastes"' is a poetic thought from George Macdonald's *Phantastes*, published in 1858. *Phantastes*, the source text for C.S. Lewis's *The Lion, The Witch and The Wardrobe*, is subtitled *A Faerie Romance for Men and Women*.[25] It is the story of Anodos, a young man who journies through fairyland. Throughout his journey he is accompanied by a shadow which is associated with a feeling of 'anxiety and fear' that Anodos cannot account for.[26] At one point he sees the shadow's eyes which seem to express a 'gnawing voracity'.[27] He also encounters a beautiful white woman who keeps eluding him. At one juncture he frees her through the power of his song from a block of alabaster (like Pygmalion giving life to Galatea), which he describes as an 'antenatal tomb':

---

[25] George Macdonald, *Phantastes. A Faerie Romance for Men and Women*, Ed. Greville MacDonald, London: Arthur C. Fifield, 1905.
[26] ibid., p. 49.
[27] ibid., p. 52.

> I sat down on the ground by the 'antenatal tomb', leaned upon it with
> my face towards the head of the figure within, and sang . . .[28]

The white woman is contrasted with The Maid of the Alder whose
impression of 'intense loveliness' changes to that of 'a living, walking
sepulchre, faithless, deluding, traitorous'. Anodos asks, 'How can beauty and
ugliness dwell so near?'[29]

Anodos's journey is presented as an attempt to work through the extremes
of beautiful and ugly thoughts and emotions, which are allowed their fullest
expression in his fantasy world. He enters into his fantasies so that he may
learn to bear them:

> Afterwards I learned, that the best way to manage some kinds of
> painful thoughts, is to dare them to do their worst; to let them lie and
> gnaw at your heart till they are tired; and you find you still have a
> residue of life they cannot kill.[30]

It is this point which Procter isolates in her poem 'From "Phantastes"'. The
poem opens:

> I have a bitter Thought, a Snake
>   That used to sting my life to pain.
> I strove to cast it far away,
> But every night and every day
>   It crawled back to my heart again.

The speaker allows the 'Thought' to 'Gnaw' at her heart, and 'do its worst':

> And so I let it have its way.

She determines never to fall 'Into a false and dreaming peace' from which
she will wake to the pain. Now that she has allowed the pain a place in her
heart it 'can never cease' she states. The poem concludes:

> But I gained more; for I have found
>   That such a snake's envenomed charm
> Must always, always find a part,
> Deep in the centre of my heart,
>   Which it can never wound or harm.

---

[28]   ibid., p. 69.
[29]   ibid., p. 83, p. 87.
[30]   ibid., p. 101.

It is coiled round my heart to-day.
It sleeps at times, this cruel snake,
And while it sleeps it never stings:–
Hush! let us talk of other things,
Lest it should hear me and awake.
(pp. 209–210)

The speaker expresses a 'deep' love for the snake and its 'envenomed charm' whilst simultaneously dreading its 'sting'.

The poem provides a dramatic contrast to Macdonald's 'Faerie Romance'. By facing evil Anodos's creativity is enabled. Anodos is proud of his singing voice, which he describes as 'undulating, like a serpent of sound'.[31] By contrast the speaker, or singer, in 'From "Phantastes"' is presented as existing in a precarious position. She cannot sleep or dream in the presence of the potency signified by the snake. The intensity of Procter's focus on the snake suggests a fear of a phallic power which is both loved and dreaded.

Anodos, whilst under threat, can still utilise the power of song which is phallicised as 'a serpent of sound'. In freeing the white woman from her 'antenatal tomb' Anodos is shown to enable the birth of a beautiful thought. In 'From "Phantastes"' the speaker is presented as totally paralysed by the presence of the snake and its power.

It is significant that Procter draws attention to the dream world of *Phantastes* in the title of her poem whilst focusing on a state of alert wakefulness: 'I shall never fall / Into a false and dreaming peace'. It is as though she is resisting her father's seductive and potent, but often violent and disturbing 'visions' and 'delusions'.

She is also resisting the seductions of his literary language. The spareness, simplicity and tight control of Procter's language suggest the extent to which she is attempting to free herself from her father's much more ornate, wordy and allusive language. Her poems are notable for the relative absence of classical allusion and ornate description. Unlike her father, she never employs epigraphs and rarely draws attention to a source text. Even when she mentions *Phantastes* she does not supply Macdonald's name.

To an extent Procter attempts to effect what Harold Bloom terms 'Kenosis' – a movement of the imagination which empties itself of its precedents (see Bloom's *The Anxiety of Influence* (1973)). In her poetry Procter attempts to free herself of a world of delusions, dreams and literary allusions, along with her father's submerged position within that world which may have appeared dreamlike and indefinable to her. She therefore resists both her father's poetic fantasies and the dreamlike quality of the father himself.

---

[31]   ibid., p. 190.

Procter attempts to find a poetic voice which is independent of her father's poetic authority and her desire is anticipated in a very interesting poem by Bryan Procter called 'Home (A Duet)'.[32] The poem is a reworking of Mignon's song 'Kennst du das Land?', the song from Goethe's *Wilhelm Meister's Apprenticeship* which enjoyed such enormous popularity in the nineteenth century.[33]

> '*Home (A Duet)*'
>
> He.   Dost thou love wandering? Whither would'st thou go?
>   Dream'st thou, sweet daughter, of a land more fair?
>   Dost thou not love these aye-blue streams that flow?
>   These spicy forests? and this golden air?
>
> She. O, yes, I love the woods, and streams, so gay:
>   And, more than all, O father, I love *thee*;
>   Yet would I fain be wandering – far away,
>   Where such things never were, nor e'er shall be.
>
> He.   Speak, mine own daughter with the sunbright locks!
>   To what pale banished region would'st thou roam?
>
> She. O father, let us find our frozen rocks!
>   Let's seek that country of all countries, – Home!
>
> He.   See'st thou these orange flowers! this palm, that rears
>   Its head up tow'rds Heaven's blue and cloudless dome?
>
> She. I dream, I dream: mine eyes are hid in tears:
>   My heart is wandering round our ancient home.
>
> He.   Why, then, we'll go. Farewell, ye tender skies,
>   Who sheltered us, when we were forced to roam!
>
> She. On, on! Let's pass the swallow as he flies!
>   Farewell, kind land! Now, father, *now*, – for Home!

---

[32] Cornwall, *English Songs and Other small Poems* (1851), p. 118.

[33] *Wilhelm Meister's Apprenticeship and Travels*. Trans. Thomas Carlyle (1824), 3 Vols, London: Chapman and Hall, 1842, I, Book III, p. 163. Carolyn Steedman writes of the nineteenth-century fascination with Mignon and with her song 'Kennst du das Land?' – most famously set to music by Schubert (Steedman, *Strange Dislocations. Childhood and the Idea of Human Interiority. 1780-1930*, London: Virago Press Limited, 1995).

In this dialogue Bryan Procter is surely addressing his young daughter Adelaide of the 'sunbright / locks!' There is a sense of the daughter's confusion and the pain she feels at not being able to locate her 'home'. The 'home' the father provides is a place of balmy romanticism, with its 'spicy forests', 'golden air' and 'orange flowers'. It is a place of tenderness ('ye tender skies') and of shelter but it is not apparently their actual home.

Father and daughter are depicted as wanderers, like Oedipus and Antigone, Wilhelm and Mignon, and even though the poem concludes 'Now, father, *now*, – for / Home!' there is a sense that it is the wandering which provides a more definite location than the 'home' which is apparently sought: 'Dost thou love wandering?', 'Yet would I fain be wandering–', 'My heart is wandering'.

It is also a place which may only exist in a dream: 'Dream'st thou sweet daughter . . . ?', 'I dream, I dream:'. The daughter's struggle to escape the dream in which she and her father wander, as well as the dream she wanders towards, is seen in her sudden stark delineation of 'home' midway through the poem which disrupts the poem's surface:

> O father, let us find our frozen rocks!
> Let's seek that country of all countries, – Home!

The 'pale banished region' evoked by the father suddenly emerges as a hard, rocky and 'ancient' place which may be the only ground possible for a daughter who seeks a way out of her father's more dreamlike world. Unlike Mignon, the daughter is attempting to move away from 'the land where citron-apples bloom'.[34] It is also a poignant depiction of a father and daughter who are mutually struggling to find their way.

The difficulty with finding a 'Home' may also suggest that there is a confusion about the kind of home the absent mother or adult woman provides. In many ways the woman depicted in Bryan Procter's poems is his element, as are the dreams and nightmares in which he immerses himself.

Many of his poems express the desire to submerge himself in a female element, along with the fear of becoming overwhelmed by an element which may prove deadly. In the poem 'Hereafter', headed by an epigraph from Wordsworth, 'The glory and the freshness of a dream', the speaker describes seeing 'a Shape of beauty in a dream' which is separated from him by 'an icy bar'. He finally flies through the bar which shatters to fragments:

---

34 *Wilhelm Meister's Apprenticeship and Travels*, p. 163.

> How I flew! the bar was shatter'd
> To fragments in a moment . . .

The 'beauty' reveals herself as 'Death' and the speaker wakes alone.[35]

In the poem 'Midsummer Madness', published in *The Literary Gazette* (1820), the speaker expresses the desire to free himself of 'poetic sin' by immersing himself in the sea and air:

> Now will I plunge, and bathe my brain therein,
> And cleanse me of all dull poetic sin.

He concludes, though, that he is in fact incapable of scaling the 'heights which the great poets pass along' and that:

> 'Tis enough for me,
> That I can bask in woman's star-like eyes,
> A slave in that love-haunted paradise,
> Without a wish ever to wander free.[36]

Freedom and success as a poet are associated with the ability to rise above the 'love-haunted paradise'. It is not clear, however, if the madness is identified with the desire to be free of a woman or with becoming her 'slave', or both.

In her discussion of Keats in *Romanticism and Gender* (1993) Anne Mellor refers to the 'extreme anxiety Keats felt toward his feminine subject matter, even as he could not turn away from it'.[37] Bryan Procter seems both anxious about his 'feminine subject matter' and confused by his close identification with it. The longing to 'bask' in a woman's element may have provided Procter with a means of escaping an unwelcome adult masculinity associated with a more robust forcefulness Procter seems to have lacked.

Bryan Procter's immersion within a crowd of literary precursors and peers may be likened to his losing himself within what he identifies as a female element. It is a place where he loses distinction as both a man and a poet, in the sense of distinguishing himself from (women and other poets) and attaining distinction. The loss of a distinct form is also suggestive of the

---

[35] *The Poetical Works of Milman, Bowles, Wilson and Barry Cornwall*, pp. 150-151.

[36] *The Literary Gazette and Journal of Belles Lettres, Arts Sciences, etc. For the Year 1820*, p. 173.

[37] Anne K. Mellor, *Romanticism & Gender*, New York & London: Routledge, 1993, p. 184.

dreamlike state he often depicts. It is as though he prefers to remain submerged and anonymous.

In a very interesting poem, 'The Sexes', published in *Dramatic Scenes With Other Poems* in 1857, the immense difficulty of 'difference' is explored by Bryan Procter:

> Strange, inborn, profound attraction!
> Not the Poet's range of soul,
> Learning, Science, sexless Virtue,
> Can the gazer's thought control.
>
> But, thro' every nerve and fancy
> Which the inmost heart reveals,
> Twined, ingrained, the Sense of difference,
> Like the subtle serpent, steals.[38]

This poem may well have influenced Adelaide Procter's writing of 'From "Phantastes"'. Living with the snake of 'difference' clearly preoccupied both father and daughter. Their work differs profoundly, however, in that Bryan Procter's solution is often to dissolve or immerse himself in a depicted feminine element (a woman, a dream, the sea) whose difference he fears, whilst his daughter seeks to find a form and a poetic 'home' which is free from the overwhelming immersion or solution her father depicts.

The Fallen Woman

Bryan and Adelaide Procter's shared concerns, and their differences, come together in their treatment of the fallen woman and their concern with the fallen woman may be linked to Bryan Procter's preoccupation with dreams. Adelaide Procter's negotiation of her father's poetic authority is again apparent.

Like many other writers at mid-century father and daughter responded to an increased concern with the figure of the fallen woman. Bryan Procter admired Nathaniel Hawthorne's tale of a fallen woman, *The Scarlet Letter* (1850), and James T. Fields of Ticknor and Fields, the Procters' Boston publishers, writes of a dinner at which Adelaide Procter 'sat for some time in

---

[38] Barry Cornwall, *Dramatic Scenes With Other Poems*, London: Chapman and Hall, 1857, p. 312.

earnest talk with Hawthorne'.[39]

Bryan Procter wrote a series of poems on the fallen woman, most of which were published in *English Songs*. They include the poems 'Within and Without. A London Lyric', 'Thirteen Years Ago', 'On a Lady Slandered' and 'A Song; On an Old Subject'.[40] Two poems, 'Verdict – "Found Dead"' and 'The Mother's Last Song', were published in the 1850 and 1851 editions of *The Keepsake* (edited respectively by the Countess of Blessington and her niece Marguerite Power).[41] All these poems show immense sympathy for the fallen woman.

In 'Within and Without. A London Lyric' the 'world's poor child' who sobs outside is contrasted with the idle rich feasting inside. The speaker reveals that the child, who may be the rich man's mistress or bastard child, has been 'forsaken' by him and that even though 'his deeds are all trumpet-sounded' he is not in any way blamed.[42]

In 'Thirteen Years Ago' a beggar girl confronts the shamed mother who had thrown her out thirteen years ago. The mother takes her back and the child states that even though death seems near she will 'struggle – not to die'.[43] In the poem 'On a Lady Slandered' the speaker defends the lady and the 'Shadow' she now lives under.[44] 'A Song; On an Old Subject' is a plea for the fallen woman and for people to listen to her story: 'Let's not tell her story / A thousand times in vain!'[45]

The poem 'The Mother's Last Song' depicts a mother who urges her child to 'Sleep!' in the face of the suicide she is determined on:

> Sleep! – The ghostly winds are blowing:
> No moon's abroad; no star is glowing:
> The river is deep, and the tide is flowing
> To the land where you and I are going![46]

As in 'Within and Without' the father, a 'heartless sire', and his 'man's desire' are blamed for the woman's fall in this poem, and the woman is depicted as being caught up in what Lynda Nead has referred to as the

39   James T. Fields, *Old Acquaintance. Barry Cornwall and Some of His Friends*, Boston: James R. Osgood and Company, 1876, pp. 103, 66.
40   Cornwall, *English Songs and Other small Poems* (1851), pp. 8–9, 18–20, 38–39, 49–50.
41   *The Keepsake*, 1850, pp. 37–39. *The Keepsake*, 1851, p. 101.
42   Cornwall, *English Songs and Other small Poems* (1851), pp. 8–9.
43   ibid., pp. 18–20.
44   ibid., pp. 38–39.
      ibid., pp. 49–50.
      The Keepsake, 1851, p. 101.

'seduction to suicide mythology' epitomised in Thomas Hood's poem 'The Bridge of Sighs' (1844).[47] A contempory of Hood's (some of his poems were published in *Hood's Magazine and Comic Miscellany*), Bryan Procter also appears to be caught up in this mythology in that although he is sympathetic to the fallen woman she is depicted as doomed.[48]

The extent to which Procter blames the seducer is interesting. The flowing verse, with its rhyming quatrains and tercets, creates the sense of a desire which knows no limits and flows inevitably, like the fallen woman, to its death. Procter's sympathy for the fallen woman seems to be an expression of his own desire to escape or absent himself from what is depicted by him as an unfeeling and hard masculinity.

The sense of an uncontained flow of desire is also apparent in an unpublished poem 'The Rationale of Love'.[49] The poem takes the form of a dialogue between mother and daughter. It begins:

Mother.
'Love not, my daughter of the golden hair!
Love not. In man dwells nought of true or fair,
To meet *thy* truth – to claim thy love or care.'

The daughter protests that she loves as her mother 'hast done', to which the mother replies that man 'strides a tyrant thro' the dream of life, / His friend

---

[47] Lynda Nead, *Myths of Sexuality. Representations of Women in Victorian Britain*, Oxford: Basil Blackwell Ltd., 1988, p. 169. Nead writes 'A woman's "fall" from virtue was frequently attributed to seduction and betrayal which set the scene for her representation as victim' (p. 95). In Thomas Hood's 'The Bridge of Sighs', the drowned body of a woman, identified as fallen by the speaker, is retrieved from the river:

> The bleak wind of March
> Made her tremble and shiver;
> But not the dark arch,
> Or the black flowing river:
> Mad from life's history,
> Glad to death's mystery,
>   Swift to be hurl'd –
> Any where, any where
>   Out of the world!

Hood's Magazine and Comic Miscellany, I, 1844, pp. 414–417.

[48] The poems 'A Song for Greybeards', 'The Flax Spinners' and 'The Last Stave' appeared in *Hood's Magazine and Comic Miscellany*, I, 1844, pp. 169, 395–396, 423.

[49] *Bryan Waller Procter (Barry Cornwall). An Autobiographical Fragment and Biographical Notes With Personal Sketches of Contemporaries, Unpublished Lyrics, and Letters of Literary Friends*, [Ed. Coventry Patmore], London: George Bell and Sons, 1877, p. 235.

a martyr, and his slave a wife'. The daughter replies that her love for him is ubiquitous: 'I hear, I see, I love him – everywhere.'[50] Desire is shown to exceed all boundaries.

The 'daughter of the golden hair!' is surely Adelaide, of whom Bryan Procter is apparently very protective. As in 'The Mother's Last Song', the speaker is a woman and, by adopting a female voice, Bryan Procter aligns himself closely with a femininity which he perceives to be both martyred and enslaved to men's tyranny. The 'friend a martyr' may be read as the more feminine friend of the masculine 'tyrant'. The line 'Man strides a tyrant thro' the dream of life', suggests that Bryan Procter's preference is for the apparently benign dream world which excludes violence and the 'strife' which he identifies with men, who are described as 'Stern, selfish, coarse, inconstant, nursed in strife'.[51]

The daughter and her desires would seem to be fated by the extent to which her parent is caught up in a dream world, 'the dream of life' which excludes both an unfeeling masculinity and the woman's love and desire it enslaves. A more feminised sexual desire is expelled, martyred and doomed in the forms of both the fallen woman and of the daughter who may fall prey to men's desires. The woman becomes a part of Bryan Procter's world of 'visions' which exist beyond the materiality of the 'real' world.

Adelaide Procter, like many philanthropic women at mid-century, was concerned to provide a concrete home for the women 'outside'.[52] In 1862 Procter's 'A Chaplet of Verses' was published to raise funds for the Providence Row Night Refuge for Homeless Women and Children. Although the Refuge made 'character' a condition of entry (p. 342), the women admitted would almost certainly have included some fallen women and their children.

The extent to which society 'did not forgive, forget and reclaim its fallen women', a view which was reflected in the literature of the period, has been explored by Kathleen Hicock in *Representations of Women* (1984). Hicock argues that women poets in particular treated the subject with a great deal of 'emotional commitment' and singles out Procter's seminal poem 'A Legend of Provence' as epitomising such commitment.[53]

---

[50] ibid.

[51] ibid.

[52] Christina Rossetti became a voluntary worker at the St Mary Magdalene Penitentiary for Fallen Women in Highgate in 1859 (Jan Marsh, *Christina Rossetti – a literary biography*, London: Jonathan Cape, 1994, pp. 218-219).

[53] Kathleen Hickock, 'The Fallen Woman', *Representations of Women. Nineteenth-Century British Women's Poetry*, Connecticut: Greenwood Press, 1984. Hickock discusses poems by Jean Ingelow, Dora Greenwell and Mary Howitt amongst others.

The poems by Procter which may also be read as treatments of the fallen woman are 'Home at Last', 'Three Roses', 'Too Late' and 'Homeless' (pp. 148, 199-200, 178-179, 338-339). These poems are notable for their not naming the women depicted as fallen. By contrast with her father's poems Procter is more concerned with the women's formlessness. Her father's poems are much more explicit about the 'Old Subject' of the fallen woman, and the 'tyrant' male seducer is also named. By contrast Adelaide Procter's poems explore the 'fallen' woman's anonymous status and what it suggests.

In 'Home at Last' (published under the title 'Home and Rest' in *Household Words* on 24th April 1858) a mother reassures her child that they will find their 'home' in the 'calm, cold, purple depths' of the sea where they will 'sleep' (p. 148, ll. 32-33). The poem invokes Bryan Procter's poem of seven years earlier, 'The Mother's Last Song', in which the mother urges her child to 'Sleep!' as they approach the river and suicide.

'The Mother's Last Song' conveys a sense of desperation and drama as the mother and child approach death. They are depicted in flight from tyrants and the world's cruelty: 'The world is cruel; the world's untrue: / Our foes are many; our friends are few'.[54] In 'Home at Last', by contrast, the speaker is depicted as less caught up in a drama than sadly resolved in the face of death which is presented as a refreshing and calming sleep:

> And lay thy head on my breast:
>   Child, do not weep;
> In the calm, cold, purple depths
>   There we shall sleep.
>   (p. 148, ll. 30-33)

In 'The Mother's Last Song' mother and child face a river and flowing tide which contrast with the calm depths of the sea depicted in 'Home at Last'. Adelaide Procter creates a sense of the 'depth' of an unexplored emotion which remains unexpressed.

The flow of the river, and of the speaker's emotion, in 'The Mother's Last Song' are a means of expelling the fallen woman along with the poet's emotions – a catharsis is therefore enabled. By contrast, the reader is left with a stillness at the end of 'Home at Last' which suggests that the emotion has not been expelled. It has become residual and dormant, metaphorically lying on the sea bed where it may be reactivated and awakened from its 'sleep'.

The *Household Words* title 'Home and Rest' suggests that what remains –

---

54 *The Keepsake*, 1851, p. 101.

the unexplored residue of emotion or the 'rest' – is more important in Procter's poem than making an identification with a fallen woman who, by definition, has often been expelled from the 'home' along with her unruly passions. Procter is subtly exploring the problem of expression.

Like 'Home at Last', the poems 'Three Roses' (1858) and 'Too Late' (1860) do not name the women depicted as fallen, although they may well be. In 'Three Roses' it is the helplessness of the speaker in the face of the death of his lover which is depicted – he is not blamed for the 'fall' of the rose. The image of the rose which passes between the lovers suggests the presence of a resilient sexual feeling and, although it finally dies, there is a strong suggestion that the rose, a shrub which repeats itself endlessly, may reassert itself and that a fuller expression of desire may be achieved (pp. 199–200).

The poem 'Too Late' (pp. 178–179) depicts a dead woman with 'wan, worn features' who is described as having led a 'Restless, helpless, hopeless' existence, but has now been received back into a wealthy household:

> She who toiled and laboured
>   For her daily bread;
> Sees the velvet hangings
>   Of this stately bed.
>
> (p. 178, ll. 1–16)

She has been forgiven by those who are now keen 'to cover over / Their relentless past' (p. 178, ll. 19–20). The speaker then states that if the woman had lived longer she would have received a letter from a man whom one assumes was her lover, but the nature of their relationship is not actually specified in the poem. The extent of his attempted communication is suggested by the speaker:

> For one word she hungered –
> There are thousands here.
>
> (p. 179, ll. 47–48)

The speaker states that she can 'almost pity' the lover and mourns 'his fate' when he shall hear that he was 'too late' (p. 179, ll. 37, 57–60).

The absence of any explicatory context in 'Too Late' creates a sense of total disconnection. The woman, her (probable) lover and it would seem her family (although even that information is not supplied) are depicted as anonymous and shadowy. Their anonymity is linked to the total breakdown in communications or connectedness which has taken place: the woman cut off from her family and from her lover. The only concrete image of communication is the letter which is placed in the dead woman's 'cold white hand':

> If she could but hear it,
>   Could but understand;
> See – I put the letter
>   In her cold white hand.
>
> (p. 179, ll. 49–52)

The 'thousands' of words the letter contains are self-consciously sealed away from the reader by the speaker:

> Yet she never blamed him:–
>   One day you shall know
> How this sorrow happened;
>   It was long ago.
>
> (p. 179, ll. 41–44)

As in 'Home at Last' Procter is more concerned with what has not been expressed than with the specific plight of the fallen woman. It is the breakdown in communication which interests her, and the 'thousands' of words remaining unheard by their recipient, rather than the 'blaming' of the lover or seducer (a word Procter never uses) – the seducer who is blamed by her father.

The final poem in this cluster is the poem 'Homeless' which is unlike the other three in that it does express strong anger (pp. 338–339). The poem is concerned primarily with homelessness and the speaker blames the rich with their 'silken spaniels' for ignoring the homeless whilst their dogs are sheltered. Even the Criminal finds shelter in the prison, the speaker states (p. 338, ll. 1–6, 19–20).

The 'homeless children', even though 'wandering to and fro', are named by the speaker as 'homeless' and to that extent they also have a place of sorts outside the home (p. 338, ll. 11-12). By contrast the homeless woman depicted is described as a 'shadow':

> Look out in the gusty darkness –
>   I have seen it again and again,
> That shadow, that flits so slowly
>   Up and down past the window pane:–
> It is surely some criminal lurking
>   Out there in the frozen rain?

> Nay, our Criminals all are sheltered,
>> They are pitied and taught and fed:
> That is only a sister-woman
>> Who has not neither food nor bed –
> And the Night cries 'sin to be living',
> And the River cries 'sin to be dead'.
>> (p. 338, ll. 13–24)

The woman is depicted as having no place, either inside or outside the home, and she exists as a 'shadow' on the threshold of life and death. A woman of the 'Night' and of the 'River' she may easily be read as a fallen woman.

In the next stanza she is described as looking like a 'pack' forgotten by a pedlar, which is sharply delineated against a 'blank and bare' wall:

> Look out at that farthest corner
>> Where the wall stands blank and bare:-
> Can that be a pack which a Pedlar
>> Has left and forgotten there?
>> (p. 338, ll. 13–24)

But, the speaker states, goods are not left to 'grow rotten' by 'thrifty England' who knows the market value 'Of silk or woollen or cotton' (p. 339, ll. 31–34).

The poem is a powerful indictment of homelessness, but it is the 'shadow' of the woman which seems to interest Procter above all – the shadow of a woman whose pain and fragility is suggested by 'the window pane' she passes. The window also suggests that the woman outside is looked through rather than at, and that her deprivation has not assumed an identifiable form.

'Homeless' recalls Bryan Procter's poem 'Within and Without. A London Lyric'. In this poem the child outside sobs her 'grief' and 'pain' but is not heard by the rich feasters inside. Her seducer is, however, named and blamed and she is defined to the extent that she has a narrative and a voice.[55] What is interesting about 'Homeless' is the woman's lack of any definition, her shadowy status.

In these poems Adelaide Procter explores the anonymity of the fallen woman and what is not being expressed by or about her. By not naming her as fallen, Procter opens up a suggestive space for a wider exploration of a woman's desires.

Procter attempts to free her protagonists from the category of fallen woman which forms an integral part of Bryan Procter's imagination. She is

---

55 Cornwall, *English Songs and Other small Poems* (1851), pp. 8–9.

also concerned not to be drowned out by his fantasies which include the dreamlike and doomed fallen woman. A preoccupation with locating a home, as depicted in 'Home at Last', 'Homeless' and in Bryan Procter's 'Home – A Duet' (a search at the core of many of Adelaide Procter's poems), suggests that Adelaide Procter was engaged in a metaphorical search for a place where a less dreamlike form might be found – where the 'shadow' or the dream might assume some substance.

These poems present problems in that so many explicatory details are omitted or withheld by Procter. However, the formlessness and total anonymity of her fallen women suggest that Procter was searching for her own distinct form of poetic expression. In these poems Procter also expresses an anxiety relating to the anonymity her father anticipated, whilst paradoxically developing her own stronger poetics. An original and striking form is assumed in Procter's narrative poem 'A Legend of Provence'. This poem combines simplicity and clarity of language with lyric and rhetorical intensity to create a striking and compelling narrative of a fallen woman redeemed.

'A Legend of Provence'

'A Legend of Provence' was published in the 1859 Christmas number of *All The Year Round*, edited by Dickens. It is a narrative poem in which a legend is remembered as if it were a dream and it is the only poem by Procter in which she overtly enters into an elaborate dream world.

Procter's depictions of dreams either seek to dispel illusion, as seen in poems such as 'A Dream' and 'In the Wood', or show restraint and some fear in terms of entering into fantasy or dream states, as seen in 'From Phantastes'. 'A Legend of Provence', the tale of a fallen woman, is significantly the only poem by Procter which openly explores a woman's 'deviant' sexuality, and it is as though it is only by way of entering into a rich fantasy world, her father's preferred medium, that a woman's sexuality may be more fully explored and named. A comparison of 'A Legend of Provence' and Bryan Procter's 'The Girl of Provence' (1823) shows the extent to which Adelaide was working with her father's tropes and constructions whilst making radical departures from them.

'A Legend of Provence' is one of a series of narratives which make up 'The Haunted House', the title of the *All The Year Round* Christmas number. Dickens wrote the frame narrative, 'The Mortals in the House', the mortals being friends of the protagonist, John, who is staying in an apparently haunted house. He has asked them to come so that they may establish

Figure 3: 'A Legend of Provence', Illus. George Du Maurier, 1866

whether or not it is in fact haunted. When they meet to report on any ghosts, the ghost of each guest's room proves to be attributable either to the imagination or to the memory of each guest.[56]

The narrator/Dickens describes the friends and includes a portrait of Belinda Bates who is a thinly disguised Adelaide Procter. This cameo frames Procter (and significantly she has been allocated the 'Picture Room') as an 'intellectual, amiable, and delightful girl' who is businesslike and apparently obsessed to absurdity with 'everything that is Woman's with a capital W', particularly women's employment issues.[57]

In the conclusion of 'The Haunted House' Dickens pairs Belinda off with a ludicrous young man, Alfred Starling, to whom she becomes engaged. Dickens concludes that it is a 'wholesome union' with Alfred needing 'a little poetry' and Belinda 'a little prose'.[58] Belinda's obsession with 'Woman's Rights' is linked by Dickens to an unhealthily poetic temperament.

The curbing of what Dickens perceives to be her political and poetic excesses is dramatically countered by the poem which Belinda narrates. Dickens's lead into her account of her night spent in the Picture Room begins:

> Belinda, with a modest self-possession quite her own, promptly answered for this Spectre in a low clear voice . . .[59]

The suggested containment of Belinda's self is juxtaposed to the discontent figured in the opening lines of the poem:

> The lights extinguished, by the hearth I leant,
> Half weary with a listless discontent.
> (p. 156, ll. 1–2)[60]

The speaker sits in the dark and the fire momentarily lights up a picture showing 'The likeness of a Nun' which is likened to a Rembrandt (p. 156, ll. 3–11). The portrait triggers the memory of a legend the speaker once heard, and in a dreamlike state she is transported to Provence where she meets a

---

[56] *The Haunted House. The Extra Christmas Number of All The Year Round*, II, 1859, pp. 1–48.

[57] ibid., p. 7.

[58] ibid., p. 48.

[59] ibid., p. 19.

[60] All references (page and line numbers) to 'A Legend of Provence' refer to Adelaide Anne Procter, *Legends and Lyrics Together with A Chaplet of Verses* (1914).

storyteller who narrates a legend relating to the nearby convent, 'Our Lady of the Hawthorns' (p. 156, ll. 15-42).

The convent's prized possession is a young orphaned woman, Sister Angela, who is described as virginal, childlike and accomplished in singing and flower arranging. Some soldiers wounded in a crusade (perhaps the 13th century Albigensian crusade) seek aid in the convent and a young foreign knight is nursed by Angela (pp. 157-159, ll. 43-132).[61] As he recovers, she recounts legends to him and describes various festivals. He reciprocally describes tournaments and pageants, and, amazed that the rumoured 'hideous charm' of the world is absent from his descriptions of loveliness, she asks for more (pp. 159-160, ll. 133-168). She and the knight subsequently elope, very much in the style of the lovers of Keats's 'The Eve of St Agnes':

> Across the moonlit grass, with stealthy tread,
> Two silent, shrouded figures passed and fled.
> And all was silent, save the moaning seas,
> That sobbed and pleaded, and a wailing breeze
> That sighed among the perfumed hawthorn trees.
> (p. 160, ll. 181-185)

Angela's fantasy is quickly dispelled by her realisation that the knight's love for her is 'slight' and 'frail' (p. 161, l. 199). Disillusioned, she becomes an outcast (and perhaps a prostitute) and finally crawls back to the convent, where she begs to be admitted. Looking up, she sees 'Herself', now 'a grave woman, gentle and serene: / The outcast knew it – *what she might have been*' (p. 162, ll. 252-257). 'Herself' proves to be the Virgin Mary who has taken Angela's place in her absence. Angela resumes her old position, with only a 'shadow' of a difference: 'Not trouble – but a shadow – nothing more' (p. 165, l. 295). Before she dies, years later, she tells her story from her death bed. The narrator concludes: 'But still *our place is kept*' (p. 166, l. 327).[62]

The poem unconventionally allows the fallen woman to resume her 'place' and she is not blamed for her fall. Kathleen Hickock has written that 'A Legend of Provence' represented the 'apotheosis in women's poetry of the

---

[61] Marina Warner writes that the Albigensian crusade was fought between 1209 and 1213 against the Cathar heresy, 'a fierce and ascetic form of Manichaeism' (Warner, *Alone of All Her Sex. The Myth and the Cult of the Virgin Mary*, London: Picador, 1985, pp. 143-147).

[62] 'A Legend of Provence' may have been suggested by Robert Browning's poem 'The Boy and the Angel', published in *Hood's Magazine* in 1844. In this poem the angel Gabriel takes the place of a young craftsman, Theocrite, who becomes the new Pope. He resumes his old place as God misses Theocrite's 'human praise' (*Hood's Magazine and Comic Miscellany*, II, 1844, pp. 140-142).

fallen woman redeemed'. 'In the light of nineteenth-century attitudes toward the fallen woman', Hickock writes, 'this total reclamation is "miraculous" indeed'. She adds that, even though the poem is deeply religious and conventional in its expression of religious sentiment, the narrator's assertion that 'We always may be what we might have been' in conclusion 'was extraordinary' when applied to the fallen woman.[63]

Procter's sympathy for the fallen woman reflects and far surpasses that of her father in this poem. By allowing Angela full reinstatement and a return to her past self, her fall becomes an episode for which she is not blamed, although incarceration within a convent may be considered sufficient punishment. She is not, however, the object of either castigation or of a double-edged sympathy, such as Bryan Procter's, which uses the figure of the fallen woman as a means of effecting his own emotional catharsis.

She is allowed a 'place', and it is the search for a place or home that will give her a clearer definition which is central to this poem. The name 'Provence' may be linked to the name 'Procter' and the search for some kind of poetic origin or provenance is evident in the poem. At the beginning of the poem it is a picture in shadow which is depicted and there is a sense of something or someone which is beginning to take shape.

Procter may be invoking Tennyson's poem 'The Day Dream' (1831) where the speaker daydreams until 'The reflex of a legend past, / And loosely settled into form'.[64] The dream is of the Sleeping Beauty whose figure Angela's clearly suggests:

All dull, all dark; save when the leaping flame,
Glancing, lit up a Picture's ancient frame.
Above the hearth it hung. Perhaps the night,
My foolish tremors, or the gleaming light,
Lent power to that Portrait dark and quaint –
A Portrait such as Rembrandt loved to paint –
The likeness of a Nun. I seemed to trace
A world of sorrow in the patient face,
In the thin hands folded across her breast –
Its own and the room's shadow hid the rest.
I gazed and dreamed, and the dull embers stirred,
Till an old legend that I once had heard
Came back to me ...

(p. 156, ll. 5-17)

[63] Hickock, op. cit., pp. 110-111.
[64] Tennyson, *Poems and Plays*, Ed. T. Herbert Warren, Oxford University Press, 1971, p. 97.

Likened to a Rembrandt, the picture lies in the 'shadow' of a named and well known painter. The name Rembrandt suggests that the association with a named artist may help the speaker remember and give some form to a shadowy and anonymous self which as yet has no clear shape or history.

Procter draws attention to the gap between the known and anonymous artist as well as to the unknown subject of the painting in the shadows. It is the picture's lack of provenance which is interesting to Procter, and its association with the name of Rembrandt provides a suggestive Tractarian hint as to its potential value.

Procter's depiction of the picture, and her exploration of pictures in other poems (for example 'My Picture' and 'My Picture Gallery' in which she stresses the uncommercial value of a work of art as distinct from the value its status awards it) provides an interesting comparison with her father's treatment of art in his life and in his poetry.

As a connoisseur and collector of paintings Bryan Procter surrounded himself with the work of named artists as he does with the writers he reveres in 'A May Dream'. In his essay 'A Chapter on Portraits' (1829), Procter lists the artists he admires with great delight and relish: Massaccio, Perugino, Leonardo, Michael Angelo, Giorgione, Titian, Correggio, Raffaelle, Guido, Domenichino, Annibal, Fra Bartolomeo, Claude, Salvator Rosa.[65] In the poem 'Seeing' the speaker points out the nation's pictures to his interlocutor:

> You will see
> Gems to make rich a nation's treasury.[66]

In 'A Chapter on Portraits' Procter expresses a preference for the portrait to the history painting. He writes that a portrait of a lady 'without a name' or 'one of Titian's piercing heads' is preferable to 'the most elaborate composition of history'.[67] Bryan Procter prefers the portrait, he states, as it enables intimacy 'and becomes our friend'.[68] There is no sense, though, that the subject's anonymity needs to be explored. It becomes a friend who is known and familiar. In his poem 'The Picture' (1857), which may well have influenced Adelaide's writing of 'A Legend of Provence' two years later,

---

[65]   Cornwall, *Essays and Tales in Prose*, I, p. 166.

[66]   Cornwall, *Dramatic Scenes With Other Poems* (1857), p. 318.

[67]   Barry Cornwall, *Essays and Tales in Prose*, I, p. 163. Andrew Moore writes of the 'era of heroic portraiture' following the Napoleonic Wars (Moore, *Family and friends. A Regional Survey of British Portraiture*, Norfolk Museums Service, HMSO, 1992, p. 135). Procter wrote of his dislike of the notion of heroism in *The Life of Edmund Kean* (1835).

[68]   ibid.

the speaker describes the picture, a 'thousand-guinea panel' of a soldier and his lady, which had once hung in 'the great old Moro palace' near the Adriatic. The 'Strangers' who went to view it became involved in the romance which is suggested by the picture:

> Strangers, all who thronged to see it,
> Vowed the soldier's coal-black eyes
> Burned beneath the lady's beauty,
> Glowing there with sweet surprise.

Although the pair are anonymous, and their future life unknown, the speaker, as though intimate with them, wishes them happiness, and there is a sense that they have been placed by Procter in the scheme of things. The picture has a monetary value (with its 'thousand-guinea panel') and it is described as making a striking impression when lighting up 'the golden room' at sunset in the Moro Palace.[69]

The anonymous picture of 'The likeness of a Nun' in 'A Legend of Provence' is notable for its lack of prominence within the Picture Room which frames it. Its actual 'ancient frame' is less defining than suggestive of a past which needs to be explored. Its place in the Picture Room is not clear and the legend it triggers provides the key to its history. On recalling the legend there is a sense of the narrator entering into a painted world which slowly comes to life:

> In the far south, where clustering vines are hung;
> Where first the old chivalric lays were sung,
> Where earliest smiled that gracious child of France,
> Angel and knight and fairy, called Romance,
> I stood one day. The warm blue June was spread
> Upon the earth; blue summer overhead,
> Without a cloud to fleck its radiant glare,
> Without a breath to stir its sultry air.
> All still, all silent, save the sobbing rush
> Of rippling waves, that lapsed in silver hush
> Upon the beach; where, glittering towards the strand,
> The purple Mediterranean kissed the land.
> All still, all peaceful; when a convent chime
> Broke on the mid-day silence for a time,
> Then trembling into quiet, seemed to cease,
> In deeper silence and more utter peace.
>
> (pp. 156-157, ll. 19-34)

---

69 Barry Cornwall, *Dramatic Scenes With Other Poems* (1857), pp. 286-288.

The entry into Keats's 'warm South' – the land of Romance and the Provencal courtly love lyric – is depicted as an entry into a silent, motionless and strikingly beautiful world.[70] The narrator/Procter finds (and will perhaps discover) herself – 'I stood one day' – in her father's Romantic and dreamlike landscape.

The Mediterranean landscape and the silence which pervades it, along with the 'dense and flowering wood' (p. 157, l. 43) which surrounds the convent, suggest both an impenetrability and a creativity which flourishes. Angela, the 'Convent-Child' (p. 157, l. 72) at the wood's centre, is depicted as both impenetrable and anonymous to the extent that there appears to be nothing to penetrate or know, as well as creative in the impression she makes on others:

> Of all the nuns, no heart was half so light,
> No eyelids veiling glances half as bright,
> No step that glided with such noiseless feet,
> No face that looked so tender or so sweet,
> No voice that rose in choir so pure, so clear,
> No heart to all the others half so dear,
> So surely touched by others' pain or woe,
> (Guessing the grief her young life could not know) ...
> (p. 157, ll. 63–70)

Angela is depicted ironically as both priceless and without value since she lacks a history and a definition. The repetition of 'No' renders her almost absent, and she becomes a repository for the others' lack, need and pain. Without any firm ground, she is a a figure of infinite malleability:

> She had known
> No home, no love, no kindred, save their own.
> An orphan, to their tender nursing given,
> Child, plaything, pupil, now the Bride of Heaven.
> (p. 158, ll. 73–76)

The most defined expression of her emotions is seen in the floral vocabulary with which she is associated:

---

[70] 'Ode to a Nightingale', *The Poetical Works of John Keats*, London: Edward Moxon, 1846, p. 209.

Thus Angela loved to count each feast the best,
By telling with what flowers the shrine was dressed.
In pomp supreme the countless Roses passed,
Battalion on battalion thronging fast,
Each with a different banner, flaming bright,
Damask, or striped, or crimson, pink, or white,
Until they bowed before a new born queen,
And the pure virgin Lily rose serene.
Though Angela always thought the Mother blest
Must love the time of her own hawthorn best,
Each evening through the year, with equal care,
She placed her flowers . . .
                         (p. 158, ll. 87–98)

This passage has an obsessive quality which creates a sense of the intensity of Angela's repeated placing of the flowers (the name Angela suggests the chimes of the angelus which would have punctuated her day). The placing of the flowers repeats the multiple moments of pleasure and simultaneously marshals her desires with military precision. The roses in battalions mirror the regimentation and strength of her arrangements, with the flaming roses suggesting passionate and triumphant love. An immaculate and self-regenerating nature is suggested by the 'new born queen' and the 'virgin Lily', but it is a nature which is well contained.

The robustness of the flower imagery momentarily counters Angela's lack of definition. The passion associated with the flowers speaks against the silence of the archetypal nun who, for example, is depicted in Alice Meynell's beautiful lyric 'Soeur Monique' (1875) as a 'vague reality' whom the speaker may 'guess' the memory of in the form of a single white violet.[71] The flowers in 'A Legend of Provence' speak loudly through the silence which is suggested by the roses and their association with the *sub rosa* injunction to secrecy.

Angela's position is similar to that of the speaker in Christina Rossetti's poem 'The Iniquity of the Fathers upon the Children' (1866). In this poem an illegitimate daughter wonders about her origins and what lies under her 'simple-seeming state'.[72] Angela, though, is depicted as less rooted and without a ground to delve into. To an extent she *is* the cut flowers laid on the shrine, suggesting that she is cut off from the strength of the passion the flowers signify.

---

[71] Alice Meynell, *Poems*, London: Burns & Oates, 1919, pp. 26–27.
[72] Christina Rossetti, *Poems and Prose*, Ed. Jan Marsh, London: Everyman, 1994, p. 203.

The hawthorn wood which names the convent is more suggestive of an uncontrolled living nature with a potential for both pleasure and pain. The virginal impenetrability signified by the hawthorn, the 'May' or Mary's flower, is countered by the possibility of a thawing, but the thorn also suggests martyrdom.

The knight metaphorically cuts through the wood and thorns into Angela's contained and ritualised silence and he prompts her to an unfamiliar eloquence. At this point in the narrative Procter employs humour and irony to question Angela's apparent naivety and innocence:

> What could she speak of? First, to still his plaints,
> She told him legends of the martyred Saints;
> Described the pangs, which, through God's plenteous grace,
> Had gained their souls so high and bright a place.
> This pious artifice soon found success –
> Or so she fancied – for he murmured less.
>
> (p. 159, ll. 135-140)

Her question is teasingly rhetorical and the images of martyrdom suggest a poignant awareness of her ludicrous position. She enjoys her own loquacity as she proceeds to elaborate on the festivals, and a reference to the showering hawthorn in the Virgin Mary's procession sounds sexually provocative:

> They struck the hawthorn boughs, and showers and showers
> Of buds and blossoms strewed her way with flowers.
>
> (p. 160, ll. 155-156)

Her access to speech is depicted as freeing her into the spontaneity of her desires.

In the folk-tale sources for this legend (identified by Ferdinand Janku) the nun's lover is either a cleric or devil in disguise, and the nun is often depicted as being subjected to temptation, succumbing to her seducer only after a struggle to control her desires. The following is an extract from a Cistercian monk, Caesarius Heisterbacensis's version, 'Item de Beatrice custode', in *Dialogus Miraculorum* (1851):

> the ancient serpent so vehemently took hold of her heart, that she could not bear the flame of love. Going to the altar of the blessed Virgin, protectress, thus she said: Lady, how much I have devoted myself to you and served you, here I give up to you your keys, I am

not able to control for long the temptations of the flesh. And having placed the keys above the altar, she secretly accompanied the cleric.[73]

By excluding the temptation and struggle Procter emphasises the attraction of the knight's proposition and Angela's lack of guilt. Her sexual desire appears to be natural, and she responds to a man who is 'foreign' but not a devil or seducer in disguise. She responds to the pageantry of 'Tourney, and joust' (p. 160, l. 159) which he describes to her – imagery which is mirrored in her flower arranging (the roses in battalions). Her erotic desires displaced on to the flowers are thus associated with the knight's ambitious desire for glory.

In 'A Legend of Provence' Procter poses the problem of the *sub rosa* desires of a young woman whose 'place' is depicted as ephemeral and fragile. The virginal/fallen woman's cut off and displaced self is depicted as coexisting alongside the self which confidently and with ironic humour expresses her desires.

The return of the young, homeless nun to some kind of 'place' in the convent is poignant. Procter depicts the struggle for a form which exists beyond the exiled and dreamlike figure of the fallen woman described by her father (whose apotheosis is seen in his poem 'The Girl of Provence') and beyond the figure of the inspirational woman who only functions in relation to the needs of others. The final inclusion of the fallen woman, along with her active desires, was a bold move by Procter, countering the expulsion of both the fallen woman and other doomed lovers who figure in her father's poetry.

In poems by Bryan Procter such as 'Marcian Colonna' and 'Lysander and Ione' the fated lovers are exiled from the home. In 'Marcian Colonna' the lovers end up in a cave where Marcian poisons Julia, and in 'Lysander and Ione' the naiad Ione lives in her 'ocean cave' all day, and can only come out at night to meet Lysander.[74] A cave is also the final home of Isabella in Bryan Procter's 'A Sicilian Story' (1820) which is a version of Boccaccio's tale of the pot of basil.[75] Although this poem is often unfavourably

---

[73] Caesarius Heisterbacensis, *Dialogus Miraculorum*, 2 Vols, Ed. Joseph Strange, Cologne, Bonn and Brussels: J.M. Heberle (H. Lempertz & Comp.), 1851, II, p. 43. Several sources are quoted in Janku, op. cit., pp. 55-56. Janku states that in the many medieval versions of the story the nun is called Beatrice and that she is usually the gatekeeper of the cloister (p. 55). He states that in most versions her seducer is a cleric (p. 56).

[74] *The Poetical Works of Milman, Bowles, Wilson and Barry Cornwall*, pp. 103, xvi, 10.

[75] *The Decameron of Boccaccio*, London: Charles Daly, [1845], pp. 221-223.

compared with Keats's 'Isabella or the Pot of Basil', 'A Sicilian Story' was praised for its beauty and lack of affectation in a review in *The London Magazine*.[76] There is certainly much that is impressive and striking in the poem, and Bryan Procter's treatment of a woman's doomed love provides an interesting comparison with 'A Legend of Provence'.

In 'A Sicilian Story' Bryan Procter shows a particular interest in Isobel's intermittent madness which is caused by the murder of her lover Guido (Lorenzo in Keats's version as in Boccaccio's tale). He is concerned to recount the story of Isabella's madness and the 'heart' she has lost. Significantly it is Guido's 'heart', and not the more phallic 'head' of Keats's version, which she cuts from him and buries.[77] The image of the basil and the potted and festering head of Lorenzo is central to Keats's 'Isabella and the Pot of Basil'. By contrast in 'The Sicilian Story' it is the narrative of Isabella, a woman who goes mad and tries to find a place for the 'heart' (and the love and desire it suggests), which is prominent. Keats's 'Isabella' concludes with the words 'O cruelty, / To steal my Basil-pot away from me!' whereas Procter's 'The Sicilian Story' ends 'This is the tale of Isabel / And of her love the young Italian'.[78]

'The Sicilian Story' records the suffering of a woman whose desires which have gone mad or 'silly' in its root definition of *unhappy* (unsoelig, Gmc.) Isabel finally comes to rest in the cave:

> And in the solitude she found a cave
> Half hidden by the wild-brier blossoming . . .[79]

This retreat may be likened in microcosm to the convent in 'A Legend of Provence', which is almost concealed by the flowering hawthorn wood. Yet, Isabel, like Bryan Procter's other doomed lovers, is depicted as finally exiled and alone, along with her unbearable emotions.

---

[76] 'His poetry is of the true and natural class, in opposition to the false and artificial' (*The London Magazine*, I, 1820, pp. 85-86). John Wilson (?) wrote that 'A Sicilian Story' was 'very delicately and beautifully finished – and full everywhere of the spirit of nature' (*Blackwood's Edinburgh Magazine*, VI, 1820, p. 643).

Dorothy Hewlett writes that 'A Sicilian Story' is told 'in a much more "gentlemanly" manner' than Keats's 'Isabella or the Pot of Basil'; and Aileen Ward writes of Procter's 'sentimental and decorous version' (Dorothy Hewlett, *Adonais. A Life of John Keats*, London: Hurst & Blackett, Ltd., 1937, p. 369; Aileen Ward, *John Keats. The Making of a Poet*, London: Secker & Warburg, 1963, p. 352).

[77] *The Poetical Works of Milman, Bowles, Wilson and Barry Cornwall*, p. 79, xiv.

[78] *The Poetical Works of John Keats*, p. 147; *The Poetical Works of Milman, Bowles, Wilson and Barry Cornwall*, p. 80, xxi.

[79] ibid., xviii.

Bryan Procter's interest in the intensity of a woman's love is seen again in the poem 'The Girl of Provence' (1823) which provides a striking comparison with 'A Legend of Provence'.[80] In this poem Bryan Procter again shows immense sympathy for his female protagonist whilst customarily exiling her and her madness to a dreamlike location beyond the confines of any place of safety or security. He also explores the fallen woman's relationship to the inspirational woman.

There is an introduction to the poem which quotes a passage from George D. Collinson's 'Essay on Lunacy' which is included in *A Treatise on the Law Concerning Idiots, Lunatics and Other Persons Non Compotes Mentis* (1812). The passage provides a strange account by a German lady, Madame de Haster. She records that whilst visiting the Salle d'Appollon in the National Museum in Paris, she saw a beautiful girl standing 'electrified' before the statue of Apollo, having 'imbibed' a 'fatal passion' for the god. She is told by the attendants that the girl came every day and that in May she brought flowers to the statue. One morning, the attendant relates, they found the girl had tried to get in before opening time:

we found her within the grate, sitting within the steps almost fainting, exhausted with weeping. The whole Hall was scented with the perfume of flowers, and she had elegantly thrown over the statue a large veil of India muslin, with a golden fringe.

On further enquiries Madame de Haster found out that the girl had been taken to the country and 'died raving'.[81]

The poem opens with a tribute to the 'Provencal maid' who loved Apollo. The speaker refers to the maid both as a 'rich inspiration' whose embrace he longs for, and as 'a shadow'.[82] He then narrates the history of the girl Eva who had a scornful and cruel father and a sister Heloise whom the father favoured. Her mother died young and Eva, neglected, took to excessive reading of 'radiant' fables which included 'Apollo's page'. Apollo's beauty is described by the narrator as 'tyrannic' and he apostrophises Eva, declaring her to be:

Self-martyred in thy green Provencal bowers,
Consumed to dust before Apollo's powers.[83]

---

80 ibid., pp. 115-123.
81 ibid., p. 115 (*A Treatise on the Law Concerning Idiots, Lunatics and Other Persons Non Compotes Mentis*, London: W. Reed, 1812, pp. 496-498).
82 ibid., p. 115, iv-v.
83 ibid., pp. 116-118, vii-xxxviii.

The story of her seduction by Apollo follows. The god's seductive power and that of his entrancing surroundings are powerfully evoked. His 'crystal palace' is described as a textual paradise:

> The pictured rooms, all fair (and some divine)
> With skiey stories since made plain by song . . .[84]

The 'bright Dream' which has seduced Eva finally burns 'Madness upon her' when a scornful Apollo (mirroring her father's scorn) rejects her after the seduction.[85] The poem ends with Madame de Haster's account of seeing Eva in the museum in Paris which is followed by the narrator's description of Eva's death:

> She died at morning when the gentle streams
> Of day came peering through the far east sky,
> And that same light which wrought her maddening dreams,
> Brought back her mind. She awoke with gentle cry,
> And in the light she loved she wish'd to die:−
> She perished, when no more she could endure,
> Hallow'd before it, like a martyr pure.

Eva dies in the light she loves but cannot bear, unlike Clytie who flowers in the presence of Apollo's rays.[86]

Before considering the many comparisons which may be made with 'A Legend of Provence' it is important to ask who the 'Girl of Provence' may have been for Bryan Procter. She may be read as 'the girl' of the father − the poet daughter to whom he almost certainly looked for inspiration. In 'The Girl of Provence' Procter describes a martyred and masochistic relationship to such poetic inspiration. The poet looks to the 'girl' for inspiration but simultaneously consigns her to madness and the shadows:

---

[84]   ibid., p. 119, l, lviii.

[85]   ibid., p. 120, lxviii, p. 121, lxxxi.

[86]   ibid., p. 123, c. 'The Girl of Provence' is a reworking of the Clytie myth in which Clytie is 'mad with love' for Apollo who has rejected her. After long waiting and gazing 'on the face of the sungod' she finally becomes 'rooted to the earth' and 'a flower like a violet' grows across her face: 'Though held fast by its roots, this flower still turns to the sun, and although Clytie's form is altered, her love remains' (*The Metamorphoses of Ovid*, Trans. Mary M. Innes, Harmondsworth: Penguin Books Ltd., 1955, p. 101).

> Let thy dark odorous hair be round me flung
> And twined (rich inspiration!) till I die
> For love of thee – a shadow . . .[87]

The only place the girl may signify is in the museum (a place of deadness) where she is noticed and recorded as an object of both sympathy and curiosity. Like Apollo she has become an icon of sorts. The only moment of sanity is when she is illuminated by Apollo's light, and the moment of illumination is also the time of her death. The light of Apollo is described as phallic in that it metaphorically pierces her dreams – it comes 'peering through'.[88] The light which in one sense might free her from her dark obsessions is in fact the medium of her obsession. The only place left for the girl is the dark place of death.

Inspiration and illumination are described as potent but they are also associated with excessive male violence and deadliness. Eva traces Apollo's 'violet veins' and is clearly fascinated by the *vio*lence they suggest.[89] As a woman who is inspirational she is identified with Apollo but her inspirational status is linked to that of 'a martyr pure'. It is her sacrifice to Apollo and her fall in the presence of male potency which 'hallow' her as a source of inspiration.[90]

Bryan Procter seems to be exploring his own confused state of mind as a male poet who was sympathetic to and in this poem seeks inspiration from the fallen woman. The 'Girl' or daughter becomes the repository of an unresolved struggle with ideas about inspiration and the masculine violence which is depicted as inhering to the creative process. The woman whose 'inspiration' the poet longs for is depicted, as in many of Bryan Procter's poems (for example, 'Hereafter', 'Midsummer Madness'), as an element associated with madness:

> She died, mad as the winds, – mad as the sea,
> Which rages for the beauty of the moon,
> Mad as the poet is whose fancies flee
> Up to the stars to claim some boundless boon,
> Mad as the forest when the tempests tune
> Their breath to song and shake its leafy pride,
> Yet trembling like its shadows: – So she died.[91]

---

[87]   ibid., p. 115, v.
[88]   ibid., p. 123, c.
[89]   ibid., p. 121, lxxix.
[90]   ibid., p. 123, c.
[91]   ibid., p. 122, xcix.

The male 'poet' is feminised by his association with the girl's madness and with the elements of the sea and the forest which cannot bear being under the sway of the 'moon', 'stars' and 'tempests'. These latter are masculinised through their association with Apollo who, like them, exists above in the spheres and is depicted as a destructive source of inspiration. As a poet Bryan Procter appears to be exploring his own femininity and its complex relationship to both masculinised and feminised forms of inspiration.

Adelaide Procter clearly seeks to escape or avoid her father's poetic dilemma and her own involvement in it. In 'A Legend of Provence' Angela is shown to avoid madness and petrifaction by temporarily escaping from the convent, a museum of sorts where Angela, like Eva, becomes an iconic source of inspiration whilst not possessing an identity of her own.

She goes to a place with the knight which is never described and she is defined more by her sudden accession to lively speech and by her rapid movement away from the flowers and her displaced desires. Her movement back to the convent and her dramatic re-entry also provide her with a sharper definition. She escapes the fixed category of the iconic and inspirational woman, as well as that of the unredeemed fallen woman consigned to darkness (literal and psychological). Angela's movements outwards and back are suggestive of a woman's exploratory and perhaps transitional movements which cannot yet be more fully described and named.

Like those of the fallen women in the poems discussed earlier, the full extent of Angela's desires and fantasies remains unknown and to that extent she is still anonymous. Unlike Eva she has not become mythologised as a source of inspiration, nor has she been written up as a case history. She is allowed a 'place' of sorts and Procter/Belinda's attempt to remember her may be understood as an attempt to connect up with a more anonymous and unplaced self.

Angela also falls in love with a very ordinary man, who is blamed only a little for his abandonment of her. There is nothing overwhelmingly seductive about what he has to offer and, although she suffers acutely, there is no overt enactment of a sado-masochistic relationship with the knight as there is in 'The Girl of Provence'. Her response to the knight, which importantly frees her into speech and some humour, does not involve her in any elaborate recourse to fantasy. She is caught up in a 'charmed dream' (p. 160, l. 178), but wakes from it to a realisation that his love for her has been 'slight' (p. 161, l. 199), and the image of the knight recedes even further from the reader's view, unlike that of Apollo whose maddening power is depicted as overwhelming to the last.

Although the convent is depicted as the site of the deadening idealisation and infantilisation of Angela, her return to it is depicted as a relief from her vagrant existence. The location is important and it is worth considering the implications of Procter's choice of the convent setting.

Bryan Procter described the convent at Laverna in 'Marcian Colonna' as a 'convent prison' where Marcian and his madness are incarcerated. It is also set in a sublime landscape, with 'dizzy' precipices and 'yawning' chasms.[92] Bryan Procter associates sublimity, and by association the sublime inspiration of Romantic poets, with madness and the need for containment. By contrast 'Our Lady of the Hawthorns' is depicted as a more benign location. Although it is a place of often monotonous and tedious work no sense of acute despair is conveyed. It is described as a place where a single woman may in some sense signify in that it is a place of employment. As a single, educated woman Adelaide Procter was concerned to find work for both herself and others. The nuns are workers, skilled in medicine and nursing, and involved in the local community settling 'cottage strife or village brawl' (p. 157, l. 51). They provide counselling for young people and shelter for the homeless.

The location of 'Our Lady of the Hawthorns' may derive from Anna Jameson's depiction of an Italian refuge in her lecture 'The Communion of Labour' (reprinted in 1859). Jameson describes 'Il Refugio' in Turin which had 'a manufactory of artificial flowers' and received women back after two departures, but not three.[93] Procter, who had stayed in Turin with her aunt Emily de Viry early in the 1850s, may have visited 'Il Refugio' herself.

By setting the action in France Procter is also reflecting a contemporary view of France as a place associated with women's industry. Many articles in *The English Woman's Journal* praised France for the enterprise and skill of its women workers and managers: 'In France women have far more energy, and constantly undertake the whole management of shops.'[94] In an article entitled 'What Can Educated Women Do?', published in *The English Woman's Journal* in 1859, Bessie Parkes argues for women's management of hospitals, prisons, workhouses, schools and factories.[95] The depiction of the

---

92   ibid., p. 91, iii.
93   Mrs Jameson, *Sisters of Charity and The Communion of Labour. Two Lectures on the Social Employments of Women. With a Prefatory Letter to The Right Hon. Lord John Russell, President of the National Association for the Promotion of Social Science. On the Present Condition and Requirements of the Women of England*, London: Longman, Brown, Green, Longmans, and Roberts, 1859, p. 108. The first edition of *Sisters of Charity* was published in 1855, and *The Communion of Labour* in 1856.
94   'On the Choice of a Business' (published in *The English Woman's Journal* in November 1862), *Barbara Leigh Smith Bodichon and the Langham Place Group*, Ed. Candida Ann Lacey, Routledge & Kegan Paul, 1987, p. 262.
95   ibid., pp. 150–162.

Virgin Mary on the threshold of the convent (who has taken Angela's place while she has been away) provides an example of the 'maternal management' of institutions which was being advocated in the journal.[96]

Procter's attempt to render the convent more ordinary, as a place of work and flirting, contrasts with her treatment of the Virgin Mary who presents such an extraordinary figure. However, in what may be termed a near blasphemous portrayal of the Virgin, Procter manages to unite the ordinary and extraordinary – the figures of maternal manager and miraculous and inspirational mother along with her angelic and fallen daughters.

Significantly the 'immaculate conception' of the Virgin Mary had been proclaimed in 1854, and the Catholic Procter's fascination with and adoration of this figure (which is seen in her many paeons to the Virgin published in 'A Chaplet of Verses') is matched by her evident desire to both penetrate and demystify it.[97]

The closest literary equivalent to this meeting, which I have identified, is in Elizabeth Gaskell's *Mary Barton* (1848) in which Esther, Mary Barton's aunt and a prostitute who has been exiled from her family, returns home. Mary momentarily mistakes Esther for her dead mother and throwing herself into her arms, cries out 'Oh! mother! mother! You are come at last!'[98] Mary rejects Esther, though, when she realises she is not Mary, her actual mother. By contrast, Procter merges the sexualised daughter with the mother Mary. It is worth quoting the passage in full:

> She raised her head; she saw – she seemed to know –
> A face that came from long, long years ago:
> Herself; yet not as when she fled away,
> The young and blooming novice, fair and gay,
> But a grave woman, gentle and serene:
> The outcast knew it – *what she might have been.*
> But, as she gazed and gazed, a radiance bright
> Filled all the place with strange and sudden light;
> The Nun was there no longer, but instead,
> A figure with a circle round its head,
> A ring of glory; and a face, so meek,
> So soft, so tender ... Angela strove to speak,

---

[96] Anna Jameson advocates '*maternal* management' of hospitals, prisons and workhouses in the Letter to the Right Hon. Lord John Russell prefaced to *Sisters of Charity and The Communion of Labour*, op. cit., p. xxxv.

[97] Marina Warner, *Alone of All Her Sex. The myth and the cult of the Virgin Mary*, London: Picador, 1985, p. xxii.

[98] Elizabeth Gaskell, *Mary Barton: A Tale of Manchester Life*, Ed. Stephen Gill, London: Penguin Books, 1970, p. 287.

And stretched her hands out, crying, 'Mary mild,
Mother of mercy, help me! – help your child!'
And Mary answered, 'From thy bitter past,
Welcome, my child! oh, welcome home at last!
I filled thy place.

(p. 162, ll. 252–268)

It is a moment of magic and madness and to that extent this depiction brings
Procter's work close to that of her father. Paradoxically, however, this
moment of transfiguration also marks a movement away from her father's
tropes.

Bryan Procter's exiled lovers and women fated by love find it impossible
to return to an original home. Even when lovers survive, as in 'The Flood of
Thessally', they awake cleansed from the deluge to create a new world.
Pyrrha and Deucalion produce a new race from the stones they throw and
the men and women are described as rising from 'the fragments'.[99] The
'fragments' do not so much come together as magically assume a new and
independent form, like a phoenix rising from the ashes.

In 'A Legend of Provence' Procter attempts to find a home which will
accommodate different versions of a woman, whereby a fragmented self
may in some way coalesce. The return to a place or home which has always
been there, along with its frustrations and sense of emptiness (*'thy place was
kept'*, p. 162, l. 271), is an attempt to locate a more secure ground for the
self. This ground contrasts with the places of exile and totally new ground
often envisaged by her father.

In other poems by Adelaide Procter single women protagonists are
depicted returning home with immense difficulty. In 'A Legend of Bregenz'
(1854) the return home is to a metaphorised mother country (Austria) which
is associated with the constancy of the 'heart' – the 'blue heart' of Lake
Constance where Bregenz has stood 'A thousand years and more.' (pp. 71–
72, ll. 1–16) The protagonist who has fled Bregenz (perhaps another fallen
woman) returns to save her country from attack by neighbouring Switzerland
(where she has been living). The poem concludes at the point of her entry to

---

⁹⁹ *The Poetical Works of Milman, Bowles, Wilson and Barry Cornwall*, pp.
113–114.

> And ever where they cast the fragments rose
> Men, strong and young, or women beautiful,–
>   ... He awoke:–
> And o'er him, gently bending, children hung
> (He their creator), and a new-born world
> Opened upon his sense ...

the town and the image of the 'old stone gateway' which memorialises her deeds (p. 76, l. 171). She is metaphorically petrified at the point of re-entry.

In 'A Tomb in Ghent' (see Chapter 1) the return is to her father's home in England and to a state of shadowy domesticity, and the mother has died young. There are few depictions of mothers or of domesticity in Procter's poetry, and there would seem to be a difficulty in envisaging her own mother city, London, apart from its shadowy streets and alleyways (in poems such as 'Homeless' and 'The Angel's Story'). In her factual or fictional trip to the Lakes London is mentioned but not described in any detail, although she does finally long to return there.

The absence of mothers and the difficulty with returning to a 'home' may indicate a difficulty Procter had with her own mother Anne Skepper, whom many described as biting and satirical. Without more evidence of the relationship between mother and daughter it is, however, impossible to reach any conclusion. It is interesting, though, to consider the return to and through the mother depicted in 'A Legend of Provence' as Procter's attempt to negotiate her father's dreamscapes and visions by entering into the dream of Provence as the metaphorised mother.

In George Du Maurier's illustration of the poem, Angela is depicted gazing up at the Virgin Mary/'Herself' who is framed by the branches of a dense wood (see Figure 3).[100] The wood in Freudian terms may be read as the 'materia' of the mother's body, and thus creates a powerful sense of her materiality.[101] J.B. Pontalis, in *The Dream Discourse Today* (1993) writes:

> Dreaming is above all an effort to maintain the impossible union with the mother, to preserve an undivided totality.[102]

Madelon Sprengnether in *The Spectral Mother* (1990) refers to the body of the mother as 'the carnal origin of every human subject' which represents

---

[100] Adelaide Anne Procter, *Legends and Lyrics*, Intro. Charles Dickens, London: Bell and Daldy, 1866, p. 193.

[101] 'Symbolism in Dreams', *The Standard Edition of the Complete Psychological Works of Sigmund Freud*, Ed. James Strachey, London: The Hogarth Press and the Institute of Psycho-analysis, 1963, XV (1915-16), p. 160. Freud writes 'For in the Portuguese language "*madeira*" means "wood". You will notice, however, that "*madeira*" is only a slightly modified form of the Latin word "*materia*", which once more means "material" in general. But "*materia*" is derived from "*mater*", "mother": the material out of which anything is made is, as it were, a mother to it. This ancient view of the thing survives, therefore, in the symbolic use of wood for "woman" or "mother".'

[102] J-B. Pontalis, 'Dream as an object', in *The Dream Discourse Today*, Ed. Sara Flanders, London and New York: Routledge, 1993, p. 113.

both 'the dream of plenitude and the recognition of its impossibility'.[103]

The wood as signifier of the mother's body and the wood as Belinda's dream landscape doubly suggest the importance of both the dream and the mother in Procter's imagination. The moment of merger on the threshold may be understood as an attempt to penetrate and demystify the powerful dream of union with and immersion in the 'plenitude' with which the mother is associated.

It is also a moment of intense anxiety. Angela Leighton, in her discussion of 'A Legend of Provence' in the article '"Because men made the laws": The Fallen Woman and the Woman Poet', writes:

> the threshold of the convent seems to be a threshold of the self, marking a split in consciousness which echoes the moral divisions of the age. If the place of the Romantic imagination is that of a border-line between the known and the unknown, the border-line of the Victorian female imagination is the same, but fraught with social and sexual anxieties.[104]

The desire for a magic or miraculous mother who will dissolve anxiety and resolve the problem of crossing the threshold is clearly strong in 'A Legend of Provence', but by entering into the anxiety of the moment Procter momentarily breaks the spell of the mother's magical status. It is this anxiety which Bryan Procter frequently seeks to escape by exiling his protagonists, along with their emotions, and by seeking refuge in mythical and haunting visions from which there is often no return.

Angela is, however, left with a 'shadow' (p. 165, l. 295) which precipitates her death. Despite the complex and dramatic struggle for a place and a form there is a sense that finding a more substantial form for the young woman, or daughter, still escapes Procter.

It was in the following year 1860 and in 1861 that Procter's monograph of Juliette Récamier (or Madame Récamier), the French salon hostess and friend of Madame de Staël, appeared in three parts in *The English Woman's Journal* (December 1860, January and February 1861).[105] Procter's monograph was one of several versions of Juliette Récamier's life, and Procter's

---

[103] Madelon Sprengnether, *The Spectral Mother: Freud, Feminism and Psychoanalysis*, Ithaca and London: Cornell University Press, 1990, p. 230.

[104] Angela Leighton, '"Because men made the laws": The Fallen Woman and the Woman Poet', *Victorian Poetry*, 27, 1989, pp. 118-119.

[105] *The English Woman's Journal*, VI, 1860, pp. 225-237; VI, 1861, pp. 197-305, 373-383.

interest in this figure suggests that she was still exploring an anonymous and elusive figure or self which had not yet found a form.

At the age of fifteen Juliette Récamier (1777–1849) had married a man who, according to Mary Clarke Mohl, may have been the lover of her mother, Madame Bernard, and Juliette's father.[106] Procter recounts that Juliette was renowned for her wide circle of friends and male admirers, who included Napoleon, and for her ability to exert an influence over 'men and women of all shades of political opinion, of all diversities of character, habit, and feeling'.[107] A Russian, Madame Swetchine, wrote to Juliette that she had an:

> indefinite penetrating charm by which you subjugate even those about whom you do not concern yourself.[108]

Procter views Juliette as an enigma who inspired devotion and attachment but who escaped definition herself:

> But what was she herself? Was she anything besides a source of inspiration to others? Where did her singular power of enchantment reside? And did she use the strange charm voluntarily and intentionally or not?[109]

After moving around Europe from one location to another, Juliette finally retreats, after financial setbacks and her husband's death, to a small cellule on the third floor of the Convent of the Abbaye du Bois where she is visited by her lover François René Chateaubriand.[110] Procter quotes the 'words of Chateaubriand himself'. He describes her room as follows:

---

[106] Madame M*** [M.E. Mohl], *Madame Recamier with A Sketch of the History of Society in France*, London: Chapman & Hall, 1862, pp. 6–7. Mohl writes: 'if Madame Recamier was his daughter, he might have thought the mere legal form of marriage the only chance of securing his fortune to her, and that his death would soon restore her to freedom'.

[107] *The English Woman's Journal*, VI, 1860, p. 228. According to Procter, Juliette Recamier's admirers included the Prince of Wurtemburg and the hereditary Grand Duke of Mecklenburg Strelitz. Despite the admiration of Napoleon her salon 'was reported as a place of meeting for those disaffected to the government, and that to frequent it was therefore likely to be displeasing to Napoleon'. (ibid., p. 234) Juliette was exiled from Paris after visiting the exiled Madame de Staël in Coppet by Lake Geneva (ibid, VI, 1861, p. 299).

[108] ibid., VI, 1861, p. 380.

[109] ibid., VI, 1860, p. 227.

[110] François René Chateaubriand (1768–1848) achieved celebrity with his work *Le Genie du Christianisme* (1802), a work of Christian apologetic.

The bedroom was furnished with a bookcase, a harp, a piano, a portrait of Madame de Stael, and a view of Coppet by moonlight. When, quite out of breath from having climbed three flights of stairs, I entered the *cellule* at evening, I was enchanted: the windows looked on the garden of the Abbaye, and in the green space nuns were walking and schoolgirls playing.[111]

This is a place occupied by an intellectual, musical and artistic woman, but she is inaccessible and imprisoned within a retreat.

Juliette is described as a woman with whom Adelaide Procter may well have identified, and it is her apparent lack of a substantial core, as with the nun Angela, which interests Procter. The convent may be the only place where she can truly signify, and the concrete objects which surround her in the small 'cellule' do give Juliette some materiality.

Juliette's relationship to a man who may be both her husband and her father is also interesting in that Procter's almost certainly close identification with her father as a poet may very well have led to confusion about the kind of poetic place she herself might occupy. I am not suggesting that her relationship with her father was incestuous, but it may well have been difficult to disentangle herself from his preoccupations.

In this monograph Procter explores and queries the 'charm' which attracts, but also repels, in that it mystifies Juliette and renders her an enigma. In the process she is querying her father's commitment to the charm of the 'vision' which distances him as a poet from harsher materialities. Bryan Procter is less interested in exploring the anonymous and excluded outsider than in romanticising and dramatising her or his position. Similarly he dramatises his own position as a minor and in his own view 'anonymous' poet, almost making a virtue out of his submerged position.

His daughter, despite her disclaimers, was more interested in establishing a prominent position as a poet. 'A Legend of Provence', with its dazzling lyricism and unsettling epiphanies, marks a significant moment and climactic point in Procter's career. She explores the problems for the woman, iconic and fallen, of establishing a more material base for herself. As a poet she had ensured that her place would indeed be 'kept'.

---

[111] *The English Woman's Journal*, VI, 1861, p. 374.

Chapter 5

Editorial Authority: Charles Dickens

'A Legend of Provence' was the last of Procter's narrative poems published in the Christmas numbers of *Household Words* and *All The Year Round*. Only two more poems, 'Too Late' and 'My Will', were published in *All The Year Round* in 1860, the latter sadly anticipating Procter's impending death in 1864.

The publication of 'A Legend of Provence' marks the culmination of a long and productive working relationship with her editor Charles Dickens. This final chapter considers the narrative poems which were published annually in the *Household Words* Christmas numbers between the years 1853 and 1858. Of especial interest is the relationship and tension between these poems and the narrative voice of Dickens who wrote the frame narratives of these Christmas numbers.

In response to Dickens's editorial authority Procter's poetry challenges implicitly his authoritative voice through her choice of themes and tropes and in her resistance to the narrative frameworks devised by Dickens. These frame narratives, and the place of Procter's poems within them, provide a powerful metaphor for the states of inclusion and exclusion which are central concerns in Procter's poetry. The narrative poems published are concerned primarily with excluded parties, particularly the figures of the child and the single woman, along with their often complex emotional states. These figures invariably exist in tension with, and at times in direct opposition to, the narrative resolutions and conclusions provided by Dickens: for example the solution and conclusion provided by Christmas itself; final inclusion within marriage and the family as solutions to individual loneliness and isolation; and enclosure within a secure household, which is suggested by the title of Dickens's journal. Although Dickens's narratives and their conclusions are far from free from their own ambiguities and tensions, they impose a form of control over the other contributions. Procter's poetry responds to Dickens's voice and concerns whilst subtly resisting the control he exerts.

The chapter concludes with a discussion of Procter's poem 'The Requital' which was published in 1860 in *The English Woman's Journal*, an alternative and different kind of home for Procter's poems. The extreme emotions expressed in this poem may not have found a place on Dickens's journal. Before discussing these poems, however, it is important to establish the extent to which Procter had assumed a place in Dickens's imagination by 1859 when 'A Legend of Provence' was published.

'The Letter B'

By the time 'The Haunted House' (HH), the 1859 Christmas number of *All The Year Round*, was published Procter had clearly assumed quite a prominent place in Dickens's thoughts. His description of Belinda Bates/ Adelaide Procter in the frame narrative is of a woman whose 'fine genius for poetry' and 'business earnestness' are respected, whilst her commitment to 'woman's' issues is depicted as overly zealous. Dickens, the narrator, respects the need for more 'employments' for women but berates Belinda for seeing the oppressor in 'the unfortunate men' who support their families and are not all playing 'Wolf' to vulnerable Red Ridings Hoods (see Chapter 1).

Dickens had either read 'A Legend of Provence' before writing the frame narrative and was teasing Procter about Angela's adventures in the hawthorn wood, or Procter wrote the poem partly as a comment on and in flight from the 'Belinda Bates' persona imposed upon her by Dickens. Whatever the case, Procter's ironic treatment of the nun Angela's flirtatious response to the young knight counters Dickens's caricature and shows the extent to which she was capable of the 'drollery' and humour which Dickens admired in her.

The poem also expresses the subversive desire to find a place for a single woman's strong sexual desires which are not necessarily accommodated within a marriage. The poem resists Dickens's pairing of Belinda and the ridiculous Alfred Starling, who have become engaged by the conclusion of Dickens's narrative. Dickens's choice of Alfred Starling for Belinda's lover, a man plagued by incapacitating ague-fits of love and with a penchant for strenuous Lancashire clog dancing, was surely designed to tease and irritate Procter (HH, p. 48).

The extent to which Dickens may have been teasing Procter is also seen in the introductory part of the frame narrative where Dickens describes 'The Mortals in the House' and the reported haunting of the house by 'Master B', an 'owl' and a 'hooded woman': 'According to the accounts, we were in a perfect Convent of hooded women' (HH, pp. 3-5). The reference to the convent playfully invokes the Catholic Procter's description of 'Our Lady of the Hawthorns' and its hooded women.

In the narrative of 'The Ghost in Master B's Room', written by Dickens, the narrator recounts his meeting with Master B who turns out to be his younger self. He says that 'from the first, I was haunted by the letter B' and it transpires that 'B' stands for his boyhood (HH, p. 27). He returns with his ghost to a time when he was about eight and recalls organising a 'Seraglio' in the style of 'the good Caliph Haroun Alraschid'. The 'Ladies of the Hareem' consist of eight girls from an 'establishment', probably a school, near Hampstead Ponds (HH, pp. 28–30).

Both Dickens's and Procter's narratives are linked to the extent that they recall a time of youthful pretence and play. In 'A Legend of Provence' Angela, the 'Convent Child' (HH, p. 19) appears to be playing with the idea of a sexual relationship, although playing and reality finally become confused. There is the added adult frisson created by Dickens's imagined seraglio and Procter's convent. (Roy Porter and Lesley Hall write that in the nineteenth century 'Nuns, convents and the confessional . . . seem to have been capable of generating erotic frissons in a Protestant nation.'[1])

In Dickens's account, however, childhood is clearly differentiated from adulthood – the adult male narrator who is returned to at the conclusion of the narrative. By contrast 'A Legend of Provence' ends on a note of uncertainty as to whether a transition has in fact been made from girlhood to adulthood. The 'shadow' (HH, p. 21) which remains suggests the ghost of a single, young woman's newly found and unconventional sexuality which has not been accommodated in adulthood. The letter 'B' may also stand for 'Belinda Bates' in Dickens's imagination, and a haunting which has not been recognised or named by him.

Woman and Poetess

By contrast Dickens's posthumous 'Introduction' to *Legends and Lyrics* (1866) does not in any way suggest that Dickens felt haunted or disturbed by Procter (pp. 1–10). It is a glowing tribute. Michael Slater states that it was his 'only extended public tribute to a literary woman'.[2] Dickens admires Procter's 'honesty, independence, and quiet dignity' along with her many accomplishments and intellectual ability (pp. 2–3). He also pays tribute to her philanthropic work:

---

[1]   Roy Porter and Lesley Hall, *The Facts of Life. The Creation of Sexual Knowledge in Britain. 1650–1950*, Yale University Press, 1995, p. 153.

[2]   Michael Slater, *Dickens and Women*, London and Melbourne: J.M. Dent & Sons Ltd., 1983, p. 320.

Now, it was the visitation of the sick, that had possession of her; now, it was the sheltering of the houseless; now, it was the elementary teaching of the densely ignorant; now, it was the raising up of those who had wandered and got trodden under foot; now, it was the wider employment of her own sex in the general business of life; now, it was all these things at once. (p. 9)

He adds that such 'incessant occupation' (p. 9) was likely to undermine and wear her down, and this description recalls his account of the energetic Belinda Bates persona.

Dickens also admired Procter's poetry, recalling her early contributions under the Miss Berwick pseudonym, which he recognised as 'possessing much more merit' than the 'shoal of verses' passing through the *Household Words* office (p. 1). Dickens wrote to Procter in 1854 expressing his pleasure with 'the sentiment and grace' of her verses.[3] The extent to which he was committed to her poetry is seen in his joint authoring of the poem 'Hidden Light' (26.8.1854), a poorly written early poem which seems to have been the only poem by any writer published in *Household Words* with Dickens as joint author.[4]

Despite his recognition of the 'merit' of her work in his 'Introduction' Dickens is keen to dissociate Procter from the 'gloomy or despondent' state of mind, which may be assumed from the tone of her poetry, he writes (p. 8). Central to his 'Introduction' is the tribute Dickens pays to Procter's 'unusual vivacity, enjoyment, and sense of drollery'. He writes:

She was exceedingly humourous, and had a great delight in humour.
(p. 8)

Nearly half of his 'Introduction' is taken up with two extracts from letters she wrote home to England from Turin, where she was staying with her aunt Emily de Viry between 1853 and 1854. The two pieces, 'A Betrothal' and 'A Marriage', are wry and amusing accounts of the betrothal and marriage of a local Piedmontese couple. Adelaide and Emily are invited to the betrothal ball where Adelaide dances 'seven or eight dances' and clearly

---

3   *The Letters of Charles Dickens*, Ed. Walter Dexter, Bloomsbury: The Nonesuch Press, 1938, II (1847–1857), p. 609.

4   *The Uncollected Writings of Charles Dickens. Household Words 1850–1859*, 2 Vols, Ed. Harry Stone, London: Allen Lane, The Penguin Press, 1969, II, p. 511. Stone writes 'According to the Office Book, "Hidden Light" is the only *Household Words* poem with Dickens as joint author. Perhaps the last three stanzas are by him.'

enjoys herself (p. 6). She comments on the incongruity of some of the pictures on the wall of the kitchen where the party is being held:

> I distinguished the Martyrdom of Saint Sebastian, and the others appeared equally lively and appropriate subjects.   (p. 5)

The account of the wedding is equally humourous, with Procter describing it as a 'melancholy affair', with the bridegroom getting drunk and dancing a 'Monferrino' with her, and the 'bride crying the whole time' (p. 7).

Dickens's choice of these extracts suggests that he was keen to counter any notion of Procter as a disaffected and melancholy poetess. Procter's ironic noting of 'Saint Sebastian' and her sensual enjoyment of the engagement party works against any idea of a martyred and joyless spinster.

Dickens follows these two extracts with an impassioned account of the qualities he most respected in Procter:

> She was a friend who inspired the strongest attachments; she was a finely sympathetic woman, with a great accordant heart and a sterling noble nature. No claim can be set up for her, thank God, to the possession of any of the conventional poetical qualities. She never by any means held the opinion that she was among the greatest of human beings; she never suspected the existence of a conspiracy on the part of mankind against her; she never recognized in her best friends, her worst enemies; she never cultivated the luxury of being misunderstood and unappreciated; she would far rather have died without seeing a line of her composition in print, than that I should have maundered about her, here, as 'the Poet,' or 'the Poetess'.   (p. 8)

This is an attack on the grandiose, paranoid and isolationist position Dickens associated with Byron. He wrote to an S. Harford, an aspiring poet, in 1840:

> It is not the province of a Poet to harp upon his own discontents, or to teach other people that they ought to be discontented. Leave Byron to his gloomy greatness . . .[5]

It would seem that above all Dickens admired Procter's 'sterling noble nature' and her good humour. By dissociating these qualities from what he identifies as the 'conventional poetical qualities' he runs the risk, however, of excluding Procter the 'poetess' altogether. The fact that Dickens gives no

---

[5]   Dexter, op. cit., I (1832–1846), p. 279. Dickens writes that S. Harford's verse has 'more agonies of despondency than suit my taste'.

account of the content, style or themes of Procter's poetry suggests that, although he liked her work, there may have been some aspect of it which did indeed 'haunt' him. His foregrounding of the cheerful Procter excludes the melancholy persona he is so keen to erase from the picture.

Dickens also chooses not to mention the organisations with which Procter was involved. *The English Woman's Journal*, The Society for Promoting the Employment of Women and the Providence Row Hostel are not named, although he does mention her devotion to 'the wider employment of her own sex in the general business of life' and to 'the sheltering of the houseless' amongst her many other philanthropic activities (p. 9). By naming these organisations Dickens would perhaps have felt that he was recognising Procter's official positions and her public as opposed to her philanthropic roles.

Kate Flint has argued that ample support can be found to substantiate the widely held view that Dickens had little 'sympathy for women who busied themselves with public causes'. Flint states that his response to 'Bloomerism' was typical of many commentators of the period.[6] She refers to an article by Dickens entitled 'Sucking Pigs', published in *Household Words* (8.11.1851). In this article Dickens describes Bloomerism and women's espousal of public causes as resembling the condition of 'sucking pigs' in that the movement had not yet gone the 'whole hog'.[7] He writes:

> ... should we love our Julia better, if she were a Member of Parlia-
> ment, a Parochial Guardian, a High Sheriff, a Grand Juror, or a
> woman distinguished for her able conduct in the chair?[8]

Flint adds that Dickens was, however, sympathetic to working and fallen women, such sympathy being exemplified by his support for the Govern-esses' Benevolent Institution and his work with Angela Burdett-Coutts in the establishment and management of Urania Cottage, a home for fallen women.[9]

In 1859, the same year as the publication of 'A Legend of Provence' and the creation of the Belinda Bates persona (a woman busy with causes), Dickens asked his sub-editor W.H. Wills to write to Adelaide Procter who was supporting female education at the Royal Academy. He writes:

---

6   Kate Flint, *Dickens*, The Harvester Press, 1986, pp. 112, 123.
7   HW, IV (1851), pp. 145–147.
8   ibid., p. 145.
9   Flint, op. cit., p. 124. Angela Burdett-Coutts was the grand-daughter of Thomas Coutts, the founder of the London banking house, Coutts & Co. She established Urania Cottage in 1847 in Shepherd's Bush.

Hullah's daughter (an artist, who is here), tells me that certain female students have addressed the Royal Academy, entreating them to find a place for *their* education. I think it a capital move, for which I can do something popular and telling, in the 'Register'. Adelaide Procter is active in the business, and has a copy of their letter. Will you write to her for that, and anything else she may have about it: telling her that I strongly approve, and want to help them myself.[10]

Dickens is obviously keen to support Procter's 'public cause' in this instance, although he clearly has an eye on a potential story for *Household Words*. There is just a hint of distaste conveyed in the words 'in the business', suggesting the busyness he associated with Belinda Bates. In his cameo of Procter Dickens had in fact recognised the 'great necessity . . . for more employments being within the reach of Woman than our civilisation has as yet assigned to her' (HH, p. 7).

These accounts do suggest that Dickens felt a fair amount of ambivalence towards Procter's involvement in 'Women's' issues. He seems, though, in his 'Introduction' to *Legends and Lyrics*, less concerned to exclude the busyness of a zealous philanthropist and campaigner than to discount the existence of a gloomy, melancholy poetess and perhaps what that melancholy might suggest, hint at or threaten.

Interestingly, Thackeray, another of Procter's editors, romanticised Procter's melancholy in a letter to her dated 4th June 1858, written on the publication of the 'First Series' of *Legends and Lyrics*. He drew attention to the 'very grey and sad' verses of a melancholy, withdrawn and celibate poetess:

> you sit in your poems like a grey nun with three or four little prattlers nestling round your knees, and smiling at you, and a thin hand laid upon the golden heads of one or two of them: and having smoothed them and patted them, and told them a little story, and given them a bon bon the grey nun walks into the grey twilight, taking up her own sad thoughts and leaving the parvulos silent and wistful.[11]

The poetess literally fades into 'grey' in this account. She presents a spectral figure who is sweetly and gently haunting in the half-light.

By contrast Dickens does award Procter an adult and womanly status. He

---

[10] Dickens to W.H. Wills (28.4.1859), *Charles Dickens as Editor*, Ed. R.C. Lehmann, London: Smith, Elder & Co., 1912, p. 267.

[11] *The Letters and Private Papers of William Makepeace Thackeray*, Ed. Gordon N. Ray, 4 Vols, Oxford University Press, 1945-46, IV, pp. 87-88.

avoids romanticising and infantilising Procter and is keen to dispel the illusion of the recessive poetess. He links Procter's enthusiasm for poetry as a child to the energetic pursuits of the adult woman, with poetry being just one of her many achievements. Her poems are not shown to isolate and render her invisible as they are in Thackeray's account.

It is paradoxical, therefore, that whilst Dickens admired her poetry and encouraged her writing he nonetheless distances himself from what he identifies as the gloom or melancholy of the poetess. It is also a paradox that the more Procter was included by Dickens on his journal, and established as his most frequent contributor (approximately one-sixth of the poems published were by Procter), the more her narrative poems, in particular, were concerned with tropes of exclusion and loneliness.[12] The extent to which she was included seems to have accentuated by contrast what remained excluded and in the shadows.

The following discussion of the *Household Words* Christmas numbers will explore the tensions between states of exclusion and inclusion in Procter's narrative poems when read in the context of Dickens's narratives and other contributions. Procter's poetry is shown to resist Dickens's frameworks and to challenge implicitly the conventional solutions which Dickens seeks to impose. Procter draws attention to the concerns of the single woman poet and her melancholy (and what that suggests) which have not been fully accommodated within Dickens's schema.

The *Household Words* Christmas Numbers (1850–1858)

The Christmas numbers of *Household Words* ran from 1850 to 1858 and they were extremely successful with circulation figures at times reaching 250,000.[13] The first two numbers were primarily concerned with Christmas itself. 'The Christmas Number', 1850, includes accounts of Christmas in different parts of the world, and the 'Extra Number for Christmas', 1851, consists of reflections on different kinds of Christmases.[14]

From 1852 the numbers were made up of stories, which in the 1852 and 1853 numbers were fairly random. Many of the stories were not concerned

---

[12] *Household Words. A Weekly Journal. 1850–1859. Conducted by Charles Dickens.* Table of Contents. Compiled by Anne Lohrli, University of Toronto Press, 1973, p. 405.

[13] *Dickens. The Critical Heritage,* Ed. Philip Collins, London: Routledge and Kegan Paul, 1971, p. 402.

[14] 'The Christmas Number', HW, II, 1850; 'Extra Number for Christmas', HW, IV, 1851.

with Christmas.[15] From 1854, however, the stories were brought together within an overall narrative framework usually written by Dickens and sometimes by Wilkie Collins, Dickens's closest collaborator on the Christmas issues. Dickens would set an overall theme and his usual strategy was to bring together a group of strangers who would pass the time telling stories. Percy Fitzgerald, one of the contributors, wrote:

> It was amazing how he worked on the theme, what variety and dramatic feeling he infused into it, how systematically he carried it out, and how the public never seemed to tire of the subject.[16]

In a letter to Angela Burdett-Coutts dated 4th December 1856, enclosing the 1856 Christmas number, 'The Wreck of the Golden Mary', Dickens writes:

> I am the Captain of the Golden Mary; Mr Collins is the Mate.[17]

The extent to which Dickens's was the central narrative voice, the 'Captain' of these narratives, has been discussed by Deborah Thomas in *Dickens and the Short Story* (1982). She identifies in the Christmas numbers Dickens's increasing foregrounding of a 'talkative first-person narrator' whose primary purpose 'is a revelation of his or her distinctive self'.[18]

Dickens's narrative voice is dominant and the pieces he wrote have come to exist independently of the numbers. From 1858 the stories 'The Poor Traveller' and 'Boots at the Holly-Tree Inn' were adapted for public readings by Dickens, and many of his stories and frame narratives were collected as independent pieces in later editions of the *Christmas Stories*.[19] Deborah Thomas has noted that the stories are now, however, largely ignored in critical discussions and that 'the conventions that originally governed them have largely been forgotten'.[20]

The place of Procter's poetry within Dickens's frame narratives is

---

[15] 'A Round of Stories by the Christmas Fire', HW, VI, 1852; 'Another Round of Stories by the Christmas Fire', HW, VIII, 1853.

[16] Percy Fitzgerald, *Memories of Charles Dickens*, Bristol: J.W. Arrowsmith Ltd., 1913, pp. 146–147.

[17] Dexter, op. cit., II, p. 814.

[18] Deborah A. Thomas, *Dickens and the Short Story*, Philadelphia: University of Pennsylvania Press, 1982, p. 81.

[19] Norman Page, *A Dickens Companion*, London: The Macmillan Press Ltd., 1984, p. 264.

Charles Dickens, *Christmas Stories*, Intro. Margaret Lane, London: Oxford University Press, 1956.

[20] Thomas, op. cit., pp. 62–63.

therefore very uncertain. On the one hand her narrative poem, usually the only poem, stood out in a sea of prose. However, it also ran the risk of losing significance in the face of the dominance and centrality of Dickens's narrative voice. As a struggling poet writing under a pseudonym in the early days Procter may well have felt extremely anxious and ambivalent about her position. In the following discussion the presence of tensions and ambivalent feelings becomes increasingly apparent.

'The Angel's Story'

The 1853 Christmas number of *Household Words* was entitled 'Another Round of Stories by the Christmas Fire' (ASCF) and it consists of stories which are unconnected to any framework other than the 'Christmas Fire' around which they are told. Miss Berwick (Adelaide Procter) and Eliza Lynn were two new contributors and the other contributors were George Sala, Elizabeth Gaskell, Edmund Dixon, W.H. Wills and Samuel Sidney. Dickens wrote the first and the concluding narratives, 'The Schoolboy's Story' and 'Nobody's Story', which enclose the other narratives and confirm his position as First narrator and editor.[21]

'The Angel's Story', Procter's intensely lyrical and dramatic narrative poem, is the fourth story in the sequence and it is narrated in the third person. The poem opens with the death of a rich child:

> Silken curtains fell around him,
>   Velvet carpets hushed the tread,
> Many costly toys were lying,
>   All unheeded, by his bed;
> And his tangled golden ringlets
>   Were on downy pillows spread.
> (ASCF, p. 18)

An angel arrives, folds the 'sick child' in his arms and flies with him 'through the air'. In flight the angel places a 'red branch of blooming roses' on the child's heart and tells him the story of a 'little sickly orphan' who had wandered through the narrow streets and 'crowded city's pathways'. He relates how the orphan had come to a beautiful mansion surrounded by a garden wall:

---

21 'Another Round of Stories by the Christmas Fire', HW, VIII, 1853.

Figure 4: 'The Angel's Story', Illus. G.H. Thomas, 1866

> There were trees with giant branches,
>   Velvet glades where shadows hide;
> There were sparkling fountains glancing,
>   Flowers whose rich luxuriant pride
> Wafted a breath of precious perfume
>   To the child who stood outside.
>
> He against the gate of iron
>   Pressed his wan and wistful face,
> Gazing with an awe-struck pleasure
>   At the glories of the place;
> Never had his fairest day-dream
>   Shone with half such wondrous grace.
>   (ASCF, p. 18)

The angel tells the child in his arms, 'You were playing in that garden, / Throwing blossoms in the air' and that he had pitied the poor orphan. He had passed him 'the reddest roses' through the 'stern grating' which surrounded the garden, and bid him 'Farewell!' The poor child had joyfully accepted 'the loving word' and crawled back to his garret where with the next day's dawn 'Child and flowers both were dead'. The rich child in the angel's arms wonders what is the 'mystery' of the 'blooming roses' which have now been laid at his heart (ASCF, 18–19).

The *Household Words* version of the poem concludes with the angel announcing that he himself was the poor child who had died and that God has granted him leave to take the rich child to heaven before 'Sin and the hard world' defile him (ASCF, p. 19). In the *Legends and Lyrics* version the poem concludes with an additional stanza in which the two boys' graves, one a marble tomb and the other a pauper's grave, are seen side by side:

> In the churchyard of that city
>   Rose a tomb of marble rare,
> Decked, as soon as Spring awakened,
>   With her buds and blossoms fair –
> And a humble grave beside it –
>   No one knew who rested there.
>   (p. 18, ll. 196–201)

Procter may well have had in mind Dickens's short story 'A Child's Dream of a Star' (1850) when she was writing 'The Angel's Story'. In this story a boy, whose sister has died and gone to heaven, longingly watches the star at whose entrance his sister waits for him: 'His sister's angel lingered near the entrance of the star.' He watches as she is joined by his baby brother, his mother and his own daughter. With relief he at last joins her.[22]

Procter's younger brother Edward died at the age of six in 1835 and the poem may well be expressing a desire to join him as well as providing a possible means of reconciling herself to his early death. Procter may also have been anticipating her own early death and a reuniting with her brother.

The choice of death as preferable for the child in a suffering world was a common Victorian theme which Procter expresses in the lyric 'The Cradle Song of the Poor' (1855) in which a mother, unable to feed her child, longs for its early death, thus avoiding the pain she herself has suffered:

> Better thou shouldst perish early,
> Starve so soon, my darling one,
> Than in helpless sin and sorrow
> Vainly live, as I have done.
>
> (p. 54, ll. 21–24)

Procter's concern with child poverty, along with her awareness of gross disparities in wealth, is also seen in her lyric 'God's Gifts' (1855). In this poem the speaker expresses strong disapproval of a world which brands the depraved and deprived child from birth whilst rewarding the 'noble' child who is already favoured: 'Let added honours now be shed / On such a noble heart and head!' (p. 63, ll. 50–51).

Child poverty and deplorable housing were particularly acute in London, the 'great City' where 'The Angel's Story is presumably set (ASCF, p. 18). In 1851, two years before the publication of 'The Angel's Story', Henry Mayhew's *Morning Chronicle* articles were published as *London Labour and the London Poor*. Mayhew records the appalling conditions in 'Low Lodging-Houses':

> Every Londoner must have seen numbers of ragged, sickly, and ill-fed children, squatting at the entrances of miserable courts, streets and alleys, engaged in no occupation that is either creditable to themselves or useful to the community. These are, in many cases, those whose sole homes are in the low lodging-houses . . .[23]

---

[22] *The Ghost Stories of Charles Dickens*, Ed. Peter Haining, 2 Vols, Sevenoaks: Coronet Books, Hodder and Stoughton, 1982, Vol. 2, pp. 115-117.

[23] Henry Mayhew, *London Labour and the London Poor*; A Cyclopaedia of the Conditions and Earnings of Those that *Will* Work, those that *Cannot* Work, and those that *Will Not* Work, 3 Vols, London: George Woodfall and Son, 1851, I, p. 257.

Hugh Cunningham in *Representations of Childhood since the Seventeenth Century* (1991) refers to Lord Ashley's speech to Parliament in 1848 when he stated that there were probably more than 30,000 lawless and roaming children in and around London.[24] By mid-century, Cunningham states, 'the children of the streets' were seen as a threat:

> The fear was that the children, represented as disorderly and dirty, were a threat to the future of the race unless something was done about them.[25]

The conditions these children lived in were often deplored in the pages of *Household Words*. In one issue, dated 3rd September 1853, Bryan Procter's close friend James Leigh Hunt describes a London rookery in Kensington as a 'sore' where roughly a thousand people were living 'crammed, perhaps, into a place which ought not to contain above a hundred'.[26]

Disease and insanitary conditions were rife, and the cholera outbreak of 1853–1854 is recorded in 'Miasma', a poem by George A. Cape published in *Household Words* on 10th December 1853: 'He had stolen their breath, / And had wrapped them in Cholera's cloak of death.'[27] At the beginning of 1854 an article by Henry Morley about the working of the recent Common Lodging-Houses Act refers to 'the army of dead men claimed yearly by King Dirt'.[28]

'The Angel's Story' was therefore an extremely topical poem and it expresses many of Dickens's own concerns. He may even have specifically briefed Procter. The poem is not, however, a Christian indictment of child poverty and deprivation only. It also expresses the desire to fuse forcibly states of wealth and poverty, and draws attention to the extreme tensions which exist between these states. The gift of the roses cannot merely be construed as a benign wish to alleviate poverty. It has a very ambiguous status.

The roses, which signify both passionate love and martyrdom, in one sense appear to kill the poor recipient who dies the day after receiving them. His determination to repay the gift and to claim the rich child, ostensibly to

---

[24]   Hugh Cunningham, *The Children of the Poor. Representations of Childhood since the Seventeenth Century*, Oxford: Basil Blackwell Ltd., 1991, p. 106.

[25]   ibid., pp. 4–5.

[26]   [James Leigh Hunt], 'Kensington', HW, VIII, 1853, p. 16.

[27]   HW, VIII, 1853, p. 348. George Cape was the secretary to the Lambeth Baths and Wash Houses Co.

[28]   [Henry Morley], 'Your Very Good Health', HW, VIII, 1854, p. 526.

save him from adult suffering, is a gesture which borders on a vindictiveness which is veiled by his angelic status.

The veiled threat, referred to by Cunningham, which is posed by the street child turned angel in 'The Angel's Story', is seen more clearly in illustrations of the poem later in the century. Charles O. Murray's illustration of 'The Angel's Story' depicts the angel as stern and looming. His fixed gaze suggests fixation rather than tenderness.[29] In an illustration by Ida Lovering the angel is depicted deluging the child with roses. The angel's face is hidden and the pair are lit up by the starlight which spotlights them. It is a strange, unsettling picture suggesting the presence of uncanny feeling and dramatic emotion – it is not in any way reassuring.[30]

It is significant that 'The Angel's Story' comes just after George Sala's 'Over the Way's Story' in the sequence of stories. This is an urban fairy tale of a young girl, a little Nell, living in poverty with a weak father. She goes to work for a harsh warehouse owner, termed 'The Beast', and inevitably transforms him into a gentler man. Her marriage to his son concludes the 'old, old story of Beauty and the Beast' (ASCF, pp. 9-17). In an article entitled 'Little Children', published in *Household Words* a month earlier on 26th November 1853, Sala stressed the innocence of the child and the loving feelings with which the child is born.[31] 'Over the Way's Story' illustrates his point that a child's nature is essentially generous. 'Children love to give' Sala states in 'Little Children'.[32] Sala also writes that 'The avaricious child is a monster'.[33] The idea that the angel in 'The Angel's Story' may not harbour strictly angelic feelings would surely have been anathema to Sala, and the positioning of the story after his would perhaps have muted the potential threat hinted at in the poem.

'The Angel's Story' is, however, also framed by Dickens's opening and concluding narratives, 'The Schoolboy's Story' and 'Nobody's Story'. These stories, which exhibit their own interesting tensions and ambiguities, work in tension with 'The Angel's Story' in ways which draw attention to the problematic relationship between states and feelings of inclusion and exclusion, with the 'inside' and the 'outside' being locations which shift according to the vantage point taken.

---

[29] Adelaide Anne Procter, *The Angel's Story*, Illus. Charles O. Murray, London: George Bell and Sons, [1881], p. 15.

[30] Adelaide Anne Procter, *Legends and Lyrics. A Book of Verses*. Intro. Charles Dickens, London: George Bell and Sons, 1895, p. 4.

[31] HW, VIII, 1853, pp. 289-293.

[32] ibid., p. 292.

[33] ibid., p. 292.

'The Schoolboy's Story' is the tale of Old Cheeseman, a Latin master in a boys' school, and also an ex-pupil (ASCF, pp. 1–5). As an orphan he stayed at the school during the holidays, and he is depicted as a solitary, lonely figure:

> In the Midsummer holidays, some of our fellows who lived within walking distance, used to come back and climb the trees outside the playground wall, on purpose to look at Old Cheeseman reading there by himself.   (ASCF, p. 1)

When Old Cheeseman becomes the second Latin master the boys ostracise him as a traitor. An inheritance from his grandfather frees him from the school, but he comes back to share the news with the boys without blaming them for their former treatment of him. Moved by his generosity and by feelings of guilt the boys cheer him and the episode concludes with a celebratory meal. Cheeseman then asks if there is any boy who stays at school in the holidays, and at this point in the story the narrator reveals that he is the boy Cheeseman and his wife took home to stay with them in the holidays: 'So I went to their delightful house, and was as happy as I could possibly be' (ASCF, p. 5).

The story ends with the boy's apparently happy inclusion within Cheeseman's family. He does, however, express some uncertainty about his status as a child. The story begins:

> Being rather young at present – I am getting on in years, but still I am rather young – I have no particular adventures of my own to fall back upon.   (ASCF, p. 1)

When the boy narrator (whose life has been lived as an orphan) states that he is 'rather young' but 'getting on in years', one is reminded of Cheeseman who was called 'Old Cheeseman' even when he was a boy and who is depicted reading rather than playing in the playground.

The isolation of the child who has not yet accumulated adult experiences or 'adventures', but who seems prematurely old, is the isolation of the child who is neither fully child nor yet an adult. This position is contrasted with that of Cheeseman the adult, who has apparently made the transition from an isolated boyhood to a married life which includes the 'play' he never fully had: 'When they take a boy to the play, for instance, they *do* take him' remarks the schoolboy narrator about Cheeseman and his wife (ASCF, p. 5).

Malcolm Andrews in *Dickens and the Grown-up Child* describes 'the integration of child-like sensibility and worldly maturity' which is achieved in

Dickens's fiction both in his depictions of characters and in the form and expression of the novels themselves.[34] In 'The Schoolboy's Story', 'integration' is achieved to the extent that Cheeseman unites a child's delight in feasting and play with an adult maturity that can forgive and forget episodes from his past. The image of the lonely Cheeseman in the playground lingers, however, along with the rather disembodied voice of the orphan child narrator who is unsure about just how substantial his narrative is. The story concludes:

> So, now I have told you all I know about Old Cheeseman. And it's not much after all, I am afraid. Is it?   (ASCF, p. 5)

At the point of happy conclusion and apparent inclusion within a happy home the narrative voice uncertainly questions whether the story was worth the telling. It is as though the narrative of orphanhood and an echoing loneliness undermine the domestic narrative the boy has secured.

Stories which are not fully recognised and accommodated are the concern of the concluding story of the Christmas number, Dickens's 'Nobody's Story'. In this story Dickens satirises the English class system within which the Bigwigs, the industrial and mercantile bourgeoisie, refuse to educate, provide sanitation and supply 'mental refreshment and recreation' for the poor. The Bigwigs also blame the Nobodies for a pestilence which kills their children. Dickens concludes the story with a strongly rhetorical appeal to his readers to think of the 'Nobodies':

> So Nobody lived and died in the old, old, old way; and this, in the main, is the whole of Nobody's story.
>
> Had he no name, you ask? Perhaps it was Legion. It matters little what his name was. Let us call him Legion. . . . The story of Nobody is the story of the rank and file of the earth. They bear their share of the battle; they have their part in the victory; they fall; they leave no name but in the mass. The march of the proudest of us, leads to the dusty way by which they go. O! Let us think of them this year at the Christmas fire, and not forget them when it is burnt out.
>
>   (ASCF, pp. 34–36)

Margaret Lane has written that readers looking for Christmas cheer 'must have been chilled and disappointed by "Nobody's Story", for this is

---

[34] Malcolm Andrews, *Dickens and the Grown-up Child*, London: The Macmillan Press Ltd., 1994, p. 174.

Dickens's angry voice'.[35] Certainly the 'Christmas fire' which concludes the story is not very consolatory in the knowledge that a wilderness of nobodies exists just beyond the hearth.

Dickens was fascinated and concerned with the notion of nobodies – seen, for example, in his creation of the character Nemo, the impoverished law-writer in *Bleak House* (1852–3), and the 'Nobody' who shadows Arthur Clennam in *Little Dorrit* (1855–7), along with the articles on 'blank' or foundling children published in *Household Words* such as 'Received, a Blank Child' (19.3.1853).[36] He also explored the ambiguity of the concept of 'nobody' in an article titled 'Nobody, Somebody, and Everybody' published in *Household Words* (30.8.1856), in which 'nobody' is shown to take respon-sibility. Dickens writes:

> My heart, as the ballad says, is sore for Somebody. Nobody has done more harm in this single generation than Everybody can mend in ten generations. Come, responsible Somebody; accountable Blockhead, come![37]

The categories of Nobody and Somebody are depicted as interchangeable, and in 'Nobody's Story' the Christmas fire around which 'somebodies' presumably congregate is depicted as precarious in that its demise is antici-pated in the act of invoking it ('and not forget them when it is burnt out') (ASCF, p. 36).

The tensions explored in Dickens's stories are between states of exclusion and inclusion, the child and the adult, nobodies and somebodies. These categories or states are represented as existing in fragile opposition. Dickens does nonetheless attempt to achieve some harmony and a sense of conso-latory resolution in 'The Schoolboy's Story' and 'Nobody's Story'. The home, adulthood and a place by the Christmas fire are, if very precariously, his final resting point. The title 'Another Round of Stories by the Christmas Fire' also provides the consolation that the 'old, old' story of the Nobodies and their perennial problems will occur cyclically and inevitably, as though in the final analysis nothing will actually change or disturb the cycle.

---

35 Lane, op. cit., p. vi.

36 Charles Dickens and W.H. Wills, 'Received, a Blank Child', HW, VII, 1853, pp. 49–53. This article refers to the Founding Hospital in London established by Thomas Coram in 1722. Dickens and Wills describe the basket for depositing children outside the hospital gate and add that receipt of the 'blank' children is recorded officially: 'The blank day of blank, Received a blank child.' Dudley Costello's article 'Blank Babies in Paris' gives an account of the Paris Founding Hospital founded in 1800 which also had a 'basket for babies' (HW, VIII, 1853, pp. 379–382).

37 HW, XIV, 1856, pp. 145–147.

'The Angel's Story', particularly the *Household Words* version, refuses any such consolatory resolutions. The *Household Words* version concludes with a depiction of the angels in mid-air at the point when the poor child/angel reveals his identity to the rich boy he has claimed:

> Then the radiant angel answered,
>   And with holy meaning smiled:
> 'Ere your tender, loving spirit
>   Sin and the hard world defiled,
> Mercy gave me leave to seek you;–
>   I was once that little child!'
>   (ASCF, p. 19)

The poem begins with the preposition 'Through' ('Through the blue and frosty heavens') suggesting that something is perhaps being worked through by Procter rather than fully resolved (ASCF, p. 17). The fact that there is an alternative ending, along with the depiction of the two adjacent graves, suggests the presence of a doubleness which refuses any cosy resolution. A somebody and a nobody are brought very close together, either at a point of transition (in mid-air) or in their adjacent graves. An uncertainty about the possibility of making a transition is shown to culminate in death. The uneasy tensions between inside and outside locations, expressed in 'The Schoolboy's Story' and 'Nobody's Story', become much more acute in 'The Angel's Story' where the final location is depicted as either an in-between place or the grave. The angel, as an intermediary figure between heaven and earth, powerfully suggests the presence of an ambivalent feeling about life and death.

The red roses also denote a full-blooded passion for life as well as a deathly martyrdom. Interestingly roses figure in a story in the *Household Words* number published on 31st December 1853 during the Christmas period in which 'The Angel's Story' was published. 'Amy the child', written by an unidentified writer named 'Townsend', depicts a seven year old girl Amy who is saddened by the fact that her poverty does not enable her to do much good. She looks for things to do and washes dust from a 'languishing rose bush in a brook'. When she returns home her stepfather hits her on seeing her torn frock and leaves her for dead. At this point in the story:

an Angel came gliding in, through the low door of the little chamber and in his hand he held a garland of fresh fragrant roses. These he laid against the cheek of the pale child; and lo! they restored to it the hues of life, and they bloomed again. And the flowers seemed to whisper: 'This we do unto thee, in return for the good thou didst unto us!'[38]

Amy revives, but it is unclear whether this is a temporary revival only. As in 'The Angel's Story', the child seems to exist half-way between life and death, with the roses suggesting both intense pleasure in life as well as its pain.

This ambivalent position, suggested by the depiction of the angels frozen in mid-air at the end of the poem, may also be seen as a point of arrested development. In an essay by Dickens entitled 'Where We Stopped Growing', published in *Household Words* on the 1st January, 1853, which was, like 'The Angel's Story', published on the cusp of the New Year (a year earlier), the adventures of childhood are described by Dickens as points of arrested growth.[39]

Dickens states that it is important that at certain points in childhood growth is arrested, so that the experience remains in the memory of the adult who never outgrows it. The essay concludes:

Right thankful we are to have stopped in our growth at so many points – for each of these has a train of its own belonging to it – and particularly with the Old Year going out and the New Year coming in.[40]

Points of arrested growth are viewed and valued by Dickens from the vantage point of his adulthood (or the New Year). He draws a fine line between the adult whose growth has been arrested at particular points and the mature adult who incorporates that memory – the balance would seem to be precarious. There is, however, a general confidence in imaginative 'growth' expressed, even when, paradoxically, memories have been arrested in the imagination. This would seem to partially counter the more negative connotations of the notion of stoppage.

In 'The Angel's Story' the depiction of the angel and boy in mid-air suggests the presence of an arrested condition which has not been resolved, incorporated or left behind, leading to a state of impasse. At this point in her career, when she had only just started contributing to *Household Words*,

---

[38]   HW, VIII, 1853, pp. 431–432.
[39]   HW, VI, 1853, pp. 361–363.
[40]   ibid., p. 363.

Procter may well have felt that she was half-way between being a 'Nobody' and a 'Somebody'. She may also have felt tentative about directly expressing strong feelings both inside and outside Dickens's literary 'garden'.

The children in the story become the repository and screen for some strong and unresolved emotions. Penny Brown in *The Captured World. The Child and Childhood in Nineteenth-Century Women's Writing in England* (1993) states that the childhood self and suffering child were powerful resources for women writers in 'articulating their responses to a society that marginalised and repressed them'.[41] Writing about boys early in her career enabled Procter to express strong emotions at a distance from an imagined place outside the 'garden'. A sweet poem about children and angels may well have been the poem Dickens welcomed aboard his journal. Anger, passion and feelings of impoverishment and exclusion as a woman he may well not have asked inside.

It is interesting to note that the only other story in the Christmas number which expresses such unresolved doubleness is 'The Old Lady's Story' by Eliza Lynn (a regular contributor to *Household Words*). It is a story of two sisters, Lizzie and Lucy. In a game one Allhallows' Eve Lizzie, when looking into a mirror for her future husband (which is the aim of the game) sees a strange man's face staring at her contemptuously. The man then appears in the neighbourhood and Lizzie agrees to elope with him. Her sister distrusts him and on interceding between sister and lover dies in the act. The story concludes with Lizzie, an old woman who has never married, saying she will join her sister soon (ASCF, 5-9).

The 'Old Lady's Story' clearly prefigures Christina Rossetti's 'Goblin Market' (1862) in that it expresses the desire to explore a sexual attraction which is depicted as frighteningly compulsive. The story also figures two sisters, one of whom places herself between the other sister and temptation.[42] The tension between this attraction and the longing for a quiet life finds resolution only in death.

'The Angel's Story' may also be read as a narrative of displaced sexual

---

[41] Penny Brown, *The Captured World. The Child and Childhood In Nineteenth-Century Women's Writing in England*, Hemel Hempstead: Harvester Wheatsheaf: 1993, pp. 136-137.

[42] Christina Rossetti, *Poems and Prose*, Ed. Jan Marsh, Everyman, 1994, pp. 162-176. In 'Goblin Market' the sisters are called Lizzie and Laura. Laura yields to the goblins, who tempt the sisters with fruit, and falls sick from pining for more. Lizzie saves her sister by carrying her the juices of the fruits which the goblins smear over her face when she resists them. The juices act as an antidote and revive Laura.

Eliza Lynn (Linton) (1822-1898) was a novelist and journalist who became well known for her attack on the 'New Woman' in *The Girl of the Period* (1883).

---

desire which is signified by the red rose. Sexual desire is just held on to with the angel depicted 'sub-rosa' and in arrested flight (in Freudian terminology flight signifies sexual excitement[43]).

Procter's Tractarian reserve (the key visible symbol in the poem being the rose) holds many secrets in store, but 'The Angel's Story' is suggestive of a resistance to Dickens's editorial authority. Dickens's 'Nobody's Story' has far outlived 'The Angel's Story' and is still published in editions of the *Christmas Stories*.[44] It is ironic that it is Dickens's 'Nobodies' who have survived, perhaps at the expense of the 'Somebody' struggling for a place on the inside of his journal. This 'Somebody' strongly resists the garden's 'gate of iron', which may ensure that her place in the garden is protected but may also bar entrance to the strong emotions of the poetess self who partly remains on the outside.

'Poor Travellers'

Dickens's contribution to the 1854 Christmas number, 'The Seven Poor Travellers' (SPT), has also survived in editions of the *Christmas Stories*.[45] In this number the First Poor Traveller (Dickens) introduces the six other travellers. He recounts how he had been wandering about Rochester on Christmas Eve when he came upon an inscription over a 'quiet old door' which read:

> RICHARD WATTS, Esq.
> by his Will, dated 22 Aug. 1579,
> founded this Charity
> for Six poor Travellers,
> who not being ROGUES, or PROCTORS,
> May receive gratis for one NIGHT,
> Lodging, Entertainment,
> and Four-Pence each
> (SPT, p. 1)

The narrator decides that he is not a 'Proctor' and wonders if he is a 'Rogue' (SPT, p. 1). He goes on to seek out the house and decides to treat the

---

[43] 'Symbolism in Dreams', *The Standard Edition of the Complete Psychological Works of Sigmund Freud*, Ed. James Strachey, London: The Hogarth Press and the Institute of Psycho-analysis, 1963, XV (1915–16), p. 155.

[44] Lane, op. cit.

[45] ibid.

resident 'Poor Travellers' to a Christmas 'supper and a temperate glass of hot Wassail' (SPT, p. 3). After supper it is agreed that each traveller will tell a story in turn, beginning with the narrator (SPT, p. 4).[46]

Dickens as narrator and 'First' traveller clearly enjoys teasing Procter and mistreating his travellers, or fellow contributors. He describes painting 'their portraits' in his mind and in anticipation of their arrival states:

> I made them footsore; I made them weary; I made them carry packs and bundles; I made them stop by finger-posts and mile-stones, leaning on their bent sticks and looking wistfully at what was written there; I made them lose their way, and filled their five wits with apprehensions of lying out all night, and being frozen to death.   (SPT, p. 3)

Adelaide Procter had recently reached a 'milestone' in her career as a poet as Dickens had just discovered her identity. She had been welcomed by him as one of the *Household Words* contributors and metaphorically she became one of the 'poor travellers' who are entertained by Dickens in both senses of the word. As editor Dickens is in the forefront of this entertainment and he kicks off with the story of Richard Doubledick, with the protagonist's tautologous name playfully providing a sense of Dickens's own self-importance. Dickens is identified with both the hero of his story and with the founder of the 'Richard Watts' charity. The metaphorical 'rich'ness of the editor and proprietor is contrasted with the poverty of his contributors or 'travellers'.

The story of Richard Doubledick recounts the protagonist's progress from wild and dissolute private in a cavalry regiment to Captain in the Napoleonic Wars. His rapid ascent through the ranks is aided by Doubledick's friendship with a Major Taunton who is later killed in the Peninsula War. Doubledick decides to take revenge on the French officer he saw kill his friend. After the wars Doubledick meets the officer while he is staying in France, but when it transpires that he is a friend of Taunton's mother he decides to forgive and forget. The story concludes on a note of reconciliation and a reference to the contemporary alliance of England and France in fighting the Crimean War – 'like long-divided brothers whom the better times have brought together, fast united' (SPT, pp. 4–10).

In a letter dated 3rd January 1855 to M. De Cerjat (a friend Dickens had met when he stayed in Lausanne in 1846) Dickens writes:

---

[46]   The narrator/Dickens says to the travellers: 'Our whole life, Travellers . . . is a story more or less intelligible – generally less; but, we shall read it by a clearer light when it is ended' (SPT, p. 4).

I hope you will find, in the story of the soldier which they contain, something that may move you a little. It moved me *not* a little in the writing, and I believe has touched a vast number of people. We have sold eighty thousand of it.[47]

Dickens refers to the Christmas Number as though his story is indeed the only one that counts, and certainly its topicality would have appealed to readers.

The number does, however, also include some interesting and striking stories by George Sala, Wilkie Collins, Eliza Lynn, and two important narrative poems by Adelaide Procter, 'The Sailor Boy' and 'A Legend of Bregenz'. These poems are, however, subject to Dickens's playful double exclusion. In the letter to Procter, in which he expresses his amazement at his discovery of her identity, he concludes:

So pray accept the blessing and forgiveness of Richard Watts, though I am afraid you come under both his conditions of exclusion.[48]

Dickens is joking about Richard Watts's 'conditions of exclusion' which were that applicants should not be 'ROGUES, or PROCTORS' (SPT, p. 1). 'The Sailor Boy' and 'A Legend of Bregenz', a pair of poems primarily concerned with states of exclusion and exile, convey a sense of this double barring and Dickens's light-hearted bantering takes on a rather less playful aspect when the implications of these poems are considered.

A reading of the poems shows the extent to which Procter was questioning the centrality and dominance of Dickens's narrative which overshadows and partly obscures her poems – poems which are themselves concerned with issues relating to creativity and accession to fame.

The narrator of 'The Sailor Boy' is a twelve year old boy, the 'Third Poor Traveller', and the poem begins with the boy declaring that he is setting off on his 'first voyage':

> For the first time I venture forth,
> From our blue mountains of the north.

He describes his home as a 'lodge' near a wood which is shared with his kinsman Walter. It is adjacent to a 'stone gateway' carved with 'quaint

---

[47] *The Letters of Charles Dickens*, Ed. His Sister-in Law and His Eldest Daughter [Georgina Hogarth and Mary Dickens], London: Chapman and Hall, Limited, 1882, p. 389.

[48] Dexter, op. cit., II, p. 609.

devices' and 'dragons'. The boy recalls the times when the stern landowner Earl, who lived in the castle which towered over the land, would come down to hunt deer. He describes the Countess who accompanied him as possessing a 'soft sad glance' and as seeming to be disassociated from the present and oblivious to her child, 'the little lord upon her knee' who resembles the Earl (SPT, p. 16).

The boy is drawn to the Countess and learns through a network of gossip that she was apparently a 'low-born bride' who had been widowed and lived alone with her baby by her first husband. The Earl had fallen in love with her but married her on the condition that she part from her child and never see him again. The Countess had agreed and:

All links of the low past were broken ...

After their marriage the lady appears to be 'Still living in some weary dream' and she is depicted as being disassociated from giving birth to an heir to the Earl. Her emotion of overwhelming despair is expressed metaphorically in the salute the birth is given:

She heard, with face of white despair,
The cannon thunder through the air,
That she had given the Earl an heir.
(SPT, p. 16)

The sailor boy, who is never actually identified as her first son, finds it strange that the lady loves him with such tenderness:

I never heard
Such tender words as she would say,
Or murmurs, sweeter than a word,
Would breathe upon me as I lay.
(SPT, p. 17)

Her attention is especially strange, he states, as others consider him peculiar:

Our neighbours said that none could see
In me the common childish charms,
(So grave and still I used to be,)
And yet she held me in her arms,
In a fond clasp, so close, so tight, –
I often dream of it at night.
(SPT, p. 17)

The boy, an orphan who has never known his mother, describes being able to 'pour' his 'fancies' before the lady's 'loving face' (SPT, p. 17).

The Countess's guilt appears to be overwhelming when she almost reveals the truth of her abandonment of her child. She narrates the story of a mad woman who 'coined the life-blood of her child', but reassures the boy that it was only a dream (SPT, p. 17). On another occasion the boy wakes to find the lady, dressed for a feast, bending over him:

> Arrayed for some great feast she came,
> With stones that shone and burnt like flame.
> Wound round her neck, like some bright snake,
> And set like stars within her hair ...
>   (SPT, p. 18)

She kisses the boy and he cries out 'O if my mother were not dead!'. On her asking him if she is not the same as a mother to him, he replies 'I love you, too; / But it can never be the same'. His remark appears to devastate the Lady and finally the boy is summoned to her bedside where she expresses her confidence in his bravery and truth 'where'er thy life may go'. After her death the boy feels a 'strange grief' and finally sets out on his journey whilst retaining the 'guiding memory' of the lady's belief in him:

> One guiding memory I shall take
> Of what She prayed that I might be,
> And what I will be for her sake!
>   (SPT, pp. 18-19)

The boy's hope that he will retain the thread provided by this memory appears to be extremely tenuous. His planned journey into the unknown seems to be more an expedition into the blank space suggested by the sea than a voyage of discovery. His lack of consciousness as to his origins (Dickens refers to 'the unconscious little sailor-boy' in the conclusion of the frame narrative) appears to preclude his linking up to a more conscious entering into the world and a future (SPT, p. 36).

In his letter to Procter on discovering her identity, Dickens had welcomed 'The Sailor Boy' as 'the little sailor's song'. Dickens also refers to the 'tears' he has shed on reading her 'verses'.[49] The sweetness of the 'little sailor's' innocence, and his 'unconsciousness' of his past and of his mother's guilt, clearly appealed to Dickens, and to that extent his response appears to

---

[49] ibid., pp. 608-609.

have been to Wordsworth's 'Romantic Child', the possessor of original innocence.[50] This innocence is described by Rousseau in his seminal text *Emile* (1762):

> There is no original perversity in the human heart. There is not a single vice to be found in it of which it cannot be said how and whence it entered.[51]

Elizabeth Barrett Browning wrote in the poem 'A Child Asleep', 'He is harmless – ye are sinful, – / Ye are troubled – he, at ease!'.[52] Along with many other writers Barrett Browning was taking up a position within the 'Original Innocence' (Rousseau, Wordsworth & c.) versus 'Original Sin' (Wesley, Barbauld, Trimmer & c.) debate which continued to dominate representations of children at mid-century, as critics such as Penny Brown and Peter Coveney have explored.[53]

In 'The Sailor Boy' the 'innocent' child is depicted on the brink of a more adult or manly existence. By contrast Dickens's narrative 'The Tale of Richard Doubledick' is concerned with Doubledick's successful transition from an irresponsible youth ('this relative of mine had gone wrong and run wild' the narrator states; SPT, p. 5) to mature adulthood. Doubledick apparently makes the transition from his earlier dissipation to Captain of his regiment through the rigours and comradeship of war. He is shown to enter into and achieve integration within his own adult experiences. At the conclusion of 'The Sailor Boy' there is little sense that the boy will continue to grow and make a successful transition to adulthood, as the link with the past and to his mother appears to be so tenuous. (The Lady is not even actually identified as his mother in the poem but we assume she is.)

Interestingly, the story of the Fifth Poor Traveller, a journeyman watch-maker from Geneva, written by George Sala, recounts the traveller's meeting with two 'odd little people' in charge of a public house in an isolated spot in France. A boy of eight is described as looking 'at least

---

[50] In 'Ode. Intimations of Immortality from Recollections of Early Childhood' Wordsworth writes that the child comes 'trailing clouds of glory ... From God, who is our home: / Heaven lies about us in our infancy!' (*The New Oxford Book of English Verse. 1250–1950.*, Ed. Helen Gardner, Oxford University Press, 1972, p. 509).

[51] Jean-Jacques Rousseau, *Emile or On Education*, Trans. Allan Bloom, London: Penguin Books, 1991, p. 92.

[52] Elizabeth Barrett Barrett, *Poems*, 2 Vols, London: Edward Moxon, 1844, II, p. 126.

[53] Brown, op. cit.

Peter Coveney, *The Image of Childhood: The Individual and Society: A study of the theme in English literature*, Harmondsworth: Penguin, 1967.

thirty-seven years of age' and his sister, who is blind, is referred to as a 'little blind fairy'. Their role is to take care of 'poor travellers', and it is as though they have become permanent fixtures who, by dint of their strangeness, are arrested in a condition which is neither one of youth nor adulthood. In conclusion the narrator confirms Sala's belief in an unproblematic childhood innocence when he prays that he 'may have a boy and girl, as wise, and good, and innocent as I am sure those little children were' (SPT, 26–29). However, a watchmaker's narration of the story draws attention to the time which appears to have stopped for the children. Like the sailor boy, and the boy and the angel in 'The Angel's Story', these children are depicted as arrested in time.

Dickens may have welcomed Sala's story and Procter's poem as tales of childhood innocence and arrested growths which might be incorporated within his more adult framework. It is important, therefore, to consider to what extent 'The Sailor Boy' disturbs the apparently unproblematic and childlike 'sentiment' which Dickens so admired in Procter's work.

The sailor boy is notable for his strangeness and stillness ('So grave and still') and for a lack of passionate emotion (SPT, p. 17). He only shows some strong feeling when regretting the Lady's death and on setting out to sea. There is an uncanniness about his state of dissociation which is reminiscent of Wordsworth's depictions of children in *Lyrical Ballads*, for example in 'The Idiot Boy' and 'We are Seven'.[54] Robert Rosenblum, in *The Romantic Child. From Runge to Sendak* (1988), describes the 'uncanny loneliness' which is suggested in some of Phillip Otto Runge's paintings at the turn of the century.[55] In the painting 'The Artist's Wife and Son' (1802) (a picture of Runge's wife Pauline holding their two-year-old son, Otto Sigismund) the child looks out of the picture at his audience whilst the mother looks towards him. The child's hand is placed on his mother's breast, but its position is ambivalent in that it seems to be both resting on as well as pushing his mother away. The look on the child's face is difficult to read but it may be interpreted as enquiring, suspicious and dissociated.[56]

In 'The Sailor Boy' there is similarly a depiction of a boy's loneliness and of his pulling away from a woman (who may or may not be his mother). He is presented as dissociated from her. Although he loves her 'it can never be the same' as the relationship with the real mother, he states (SPT, p. 18).

---

[54] Wordsworth and Coleridge, *Lyrical Ballads. 1798*, Ed. W.J.B. Owen, Oxford University Press, 1969, pp. 84–101, 63–65.

[55] Robert Rosenblum, *The Romantic Child. From Runge to Sendak*, London: Thames and Hudson, 1988, p. 24.

[56] ibid., pp. 48–49.

In Felicia Heman's poem 'The Adopted Child' a similar longing for the original mother is depicted. The adopted child, a boy, expresses the desire to free himself from a 'Lady' who tells him that his mother died in childbirth and that his brothers have left home. He yearns for the place where 'the waters leap, and the fresh winds blow' and pleads 'Lady, kind lady! O, let me go.'[57]

'The Sailor Boy' also prefigures Christina Rossetti's poem 'The Iniquity of the Fathers upon the Children', written in 1865 and originally called 'Under the Rose'. In this poem the young woman speaker in the care of a nurse wonders:

> Who might my parents be,
> For I knew of something under
> My simple-seeming state.[58]

After her nurse's death a Lady living nearby takes her in as her maid. The Lady's interest in her seems overly intense – she is described as looking 'with a long long look / Of hunger in my face; / As if she tried to trace / Features she ought to know'. The speaker suspects that the Lady is her mother and longs for the 'mask' to drop, but determines to remain 'nameless' so long as her place 'Under the rose' remains a secret.[59]

In these poems the problem with connecting up with a mother, who is described as either dead or unrevealed, metaphorically points to a difficulty with making a connection with the mother as a place of birth and creativity. It is as though the figure of the child is articulating a problem with an expressive flow which has been blocked in some way.

The sailor boy, who is described as 'still', is like a stillborn child who lacks animation (SPT, p. 17). A child cut off from liveliness is also alluded to in 'Adventures of Your Own Correspondents in Search of Solitude', Procter's account of the trip to the Lake District (see Chapter 1). In this account Procter relates how she and 'A' enjoyed 'Mr Brocklebank's Ball', an entertainment put on by a 'travelling dancing-master'.[60] At the ball Procter takes a particular interest in the dancing of one of the girls, 'the dancing master's daughter', whose mother tells Procter and 'A' about her:

---

[57] *The Complete Works of Mrs Hemans*, 2 Vols, Edited by Her Sister [Harriet Hughes], New York: D. Appleton and Company, 1856, II, pp. 158-159.
[58] Rossetti, op. cit., p. 203.
[59] ibid., pp. 206-214.
[60] *The English Woman's Journal*, IV, 1859, pp. 40-43.

She was eleven. She was not 'so strong'. She was a very good musician, and generally played the piano for the others to dance, but to-night she was wanted to complete the number. She had had music lessons in Edinburgh; but they were dear, and *as she was eleven she must now do for herself!*

She is nicknamed 'Mignon' by 'A' and they watch her 'with a painful sort of interest'. Mignon is described as 'leaning wearily against the wall' and as knitting 'her brows' as she watches the others dance. Procter remarks:

What a strange life was before her, and what strange possibilities of romance and pain her future held. Her parents were evidently good, hard-working people: but the vagabond theatrical kind of life, the genius with too much, and yet too little, to feed on! I don't think we shall forget our Mignon of Netherwastdale.

Procter and 'A' then leave, having left 'a little present' for 'Mignon'.[61]

The reference to 'Mignon of Netherwastdale' is to Mignon in Goethe's *Wilhelm Meister's Apprenticeship* (*Wilhelm Meister's Lehrjahre*) (1795-6).[62] Mignon, a figure who became an object of fascination in the nineteenth-century, is a child of about 12 or 13, although she says 'No one has counted'.[63] She belongs to a troupe of rope-dancers and is befriended by Wilhelm for whom she develops an intense affection and devotion. She is particularly skilled in performing 'the egg-dance' which involves dancing though a maze of eggs without touching them: 'Constant as the movement of a clock, she ran her course'. Her movements are described as:

Rigid, sharp, cold, vehement, and in soft postures, stately rather than attractive . . .[64]

Her writing, by contrast, is 'irregular, and her lines crooked', as though her body is contradicting her mind, the narrator states.[65] Mignon is also subject to sudden violent spasms and her love for Wilhelm finally kills her. The physician who attends her comments:

---

61 ibid., p. 43.
62 *Wilhelm Meister's Apprenticeship and Travels.* From the German of Goethe. Trans. Thomas Carlyle, 3 Vols, London: Chapman and Hall, 1842.
63 ibid., Book II, p. 106.
64 ibid., p. 126.
65 ibid., p. 149.

> The strange temper of the child seems to consist almost exclusively of deep longing . . .[66]

The interest Procter takes in 'Mignon', although apparently lighthearted, suggests that she was concerned with the burden which rigorous training and repression of emotion might place on a young woman, and the privations she might suffer. Goethe's Mignon is depicted as having an extremely vulnerable shell, like the eggs she dances round, and Procter points to a possible future death when referring to the girl as 'Mignon of Netherwastdale', as though the danger that she 'never was', the risk of an erasure, is ever present.

At one point in *Wilhelm Meister's Apprenticeship* Mignon is described as wearing a jacket and sailor trousers, and like the sailor boy her gender is depicted as unclear.[67] Although the boy longs to be a sailor, a masculine occupation, he is described by Dickens in the opening section of the frame narrative as:

> a little sailor-boy, a mere child, with a profusion of rich dark brown hair, and deep womanly-looking eyes.   (SPT, p. 3)

His womanliness links him to the poet who tells his story in the first person, suggesting that Dickens the editor has merged the 'poetess' with her production. Through this figure Procter underlines the danger that, as in Mignon's case, the growth of a woman poet may be stunted and perhaps damaged by womanly reserve and the containment of emotions which cannot be fully expressed. The appeal of the 'little' poem which attracted Dickens masks feelings of deadness and blocked creativity.

It may be, however, that Dickens's response to 'The Sailor Boy' was to an extent ambivalent, and that at some level he did recognise its more disturbing aspects. After all, 1854 was the year in which *Hard Times* had been serialised in *Household Words* and the character of Louisa Gradgrind may well have influenced both the writing of 'The Sailor Boy' and Dickens's acceptance of the poem.[68] In *Hard Times*, Louisa, the daughter of the Utilitarian Gradgrind and later the wife of the bombastic Bounderby, a local manufacturer, is depicted as being cut off from her own emotions. She has been deadened and maimed by her Utilitarian upbringing and can only gaze into the 'fire' which suggests the strength of the passion which is repressed

---

[66]   ibid., Book V, p. 279.
[67]   ibid., Book II, p. 128.
[68]   *Hard Times* was serialised in *Household Words* between 1st April and 12th August, 1854.

in her and which may never find expression.[69] James Harthouse, who has come to support Gradgrind's political campaign, is fascinated by Louisa's reserve and impenetrability: 'she baffled all penetration'.[70]

Her unimpassioned state may be likened to the sailor's boy's blankness and strange dissociated condition. Dickens was clearly interested in this state of repression and his treatment of Louisa is sympathetic. He does not, however, allow Louisa fulfilment within a sexual or marital relationship and she remains maimed emotionally. Michael Slater has argued that Dickens's awareness of women's predicament was an uneasy one, and that his passionate women are in fact often punished or neutralised.[71]

Dickens's attitude toward Adelaide Procter also seems to have been an uneasy one. In his discussion of Dickens's 'Introduction' to *Legends and Lyrics* Slater has linked Dickens's description of Procter's involvement in philanthropic works to Esther Summersons's 'childhood resolution' to 'do some good' (*Bleak House*). Slater writes in an earlier chapter that the role Esther adopts 'will involve suppression of her own desires'.[72]

Procter's poetry often explores states of repression and as a poet she exercises considerable reserve in her masking of and hinting at strong emotions. There is, however, always a sense of the Procter who, like Louisa Gradgrind, longs to enter into the 'circus' and who enjoys a more dramatic and performative mode of expression – an expressiveness which Dickens also admired.

Many of Procter's narrative poems have dramatic and performative qualities and in 'A Legend of Bregenz', the tale of 'The Seventh Poor Traveller', a woman is depicted primarily in terms of her mobility and her ability to establish a sound reputation. This poem provides an interesting contrast with 'The Sailor Boy', and by including the pair Dickens may have unwittingly included the two aspects of Procter's persona – the more repressed and the more expressive.

In this poem, set in sixteenth-century Austria and Switzerland, a young Austrian woman is exiled for no apparent reason from her home in Bregenz

---

69   Charles Dickens, *Hard Times*, Ed. David Craig, Penguin Books, 1985, p. 93. Tom, Louisa's brother, remarks that the fire into which Louisa gazes 'looks to me as stupid and blank as everything else looks'. Louisa replies that she doesn't 'see anything in it . . . particularly' but that since looking into it she has wondered about she and Tom being 'grown-up'. Dickens is again exploring the notion of nothingness and 'blank' children.

70   ibid., p. 161.

71   Slater, op. cit., p. 265. Slater writes 'A frozen life, a premature death, a life selflessly devoted to the service of others: such are the fates of Edith Dombey, Lady Dedlock and Louisa Gradgrind.'

72   ibid., pp. 320, 243.

to work in the Swiss Valleys (SPT, pp. 34-35). Like the sailor boy she is depicted as having no known past. She flees Bregenz and there is no reason given for her sudden departure:

> Far from her home and kindred,
>   A Tyrol maid had fled,
> To serve in the Swiss valleys,
>   And toil for daily bread ...

The years erase 'the memory of the Past' until the maid hears some men plotting to attack Bregenz. She immediately rides back to Bregenz on a white charger with an adventurous gallop through the dark and across the Rhine (SPT, pp. 34-35). The swim across the Rhine is depicted semi-comically by Procter and recalls Charlotte Brontë's description in *Shirley* (1849) of Shirley Keeldar and Caroline Helstone crossing the deep flowing beck on their way to Robert Moore's mill to save him from the approaching machine breakers ('on their present errand, a strong and foaming channel would have been a barrier to neither'[73]):

> She strives to pierce the blackness,
>   And looser throws the rein;
> Her steed must breast the waters
>   That dash above his mane.
> How gallantly, how nobly,
>   He struggles through the foam,
> And see – in the far distance,
>   Shine out the lights of home!
>
> Shall not the roaring waters
>   Their headlong gallop check?
> The steed draws back in terror,
>   She leans above his neck
> To watching the flowing darkness,
>   The bank is high and steep,
> One pause – he staggers forward,
>   And plunges in the deep.
>   (SPT, p. 35)

---

[73] Charlotte Brontë, *Shirley*, Ed. Andrew and Judith Hook, London: Penguin Books, 1974, p. 332.

The maid arrives in time to save Bregenz and her action is memorialised in a carving of 'The Charger and the Maid' above a stone gateway. Every night at the stroke of midnight her name is called out by the warden of the city:

> 'Nine,' 'ten,' 'eleven,' he cries aloud,
>   And then (O crown of Fame!)
> When midnight pauses in the skies,
>   He calls the maiden's name!
>   (SPT, p. 35)[74]

The poem is primarily concerned with the maid's accession to fame and memorialisation. It is narrated by the 'Book-Pedlar', who, 'apparently afraid of being forgotten, asked what did we think of his giving us a Legend to wind-up with?' (SPT, p. 34).

In the introductory section of the frame narrative, the Book-Pedlar is described as having a 'quantity of Pamphlets and Numbers with him, and who presently boasted that he could repeat more verses in an evening, than he could sell in a twelvemonth' (SPT, p. 3). Dickens may be playfully addressing Procter in these descriptions, suggesting that she is keen to make her mark and not be 'forgotten'. He may also be alluding to the many 'verses' by Procter which had been published in *Household Words* in 1853 and 1854.

The poem suggests that Procter is playing with the idea of 'Fame!' and is humorously showing the lengths to which a woman might need to go to secure it. 'A Legend of Bregenz' also recalls the infamous charge of the Light Brigade which had been recorded by Tennyson in his poem 'The Charge of the Light Brigade' published in the *The Examiner* on the 9th December 1854.[75] By contrast the Charger and the Maid prevent rather than rush headlong into a line of fire and secure a measure of fame in the process.

---

[74] Procter may be invoking Felicia Hemans's poem 'The Switzer's Wife' in which the wife of Werner, a Swiss confederate, spurs her husband on to deliver Switzerland from Austrian rule:

> 'Go forth beside the waters, and along
>   The chamois paths, and through the forests go;
> And tell, in burning words, thy tale of wrong
>   To the brave hearts that 'midst the hamlets glow.
> God shall be with thee, my beloved! – Away!
>   Bless but thy child, and leave me: I can pray!'
>   (Hemans, op. cit., II, p. 97)

Procter typically chose a single woman and exile for her heroine.

[75] *Tennyson. A Selected Edition*, Ed. Christopher Ricks, Harlow: Longman Group UK Limited, 1989, pp. 508–509.

By placing 'A Legend of Bregenz' as the final contribution Dickens does suggest that the poem might have seemed to be an appropriate companion piece for his own 'Story of Richard Doubledick'. The Book-Pedlar is also the 'Poor Traveller' Dickens parts with last when the travellers take to the road on Christmas morning: 'the book-pedlar accompanied me over the bridge' (SPT, p. 36). By contrast, the sailor boy is paired off with the near insane widow, the narrator of Eliza Lynn's story, 'The Tale of the Sixth Poor Traveller', in the conclusion: 'The widow took the little sailor towards Chatham, where he was to find a steamboat for Sheerness' (SPT, p. 36). It is as though the widow's madness (resulting from her husband's murder of her sister) finds its mate in the strange dissociation of the sailor boy.[76]

Some 'kind of bridge' though has been built between Dickens's and Procter's contributions whilst Procter has subtly challenged the dominant rhetoric of heroic manliness of Dickens's story of Richard Doubledick. Dickens, however, finally turns his back on the travellers and returns to London and the Christmas hearth which awaits him. He concludes:

> And there I told of worthy Master Richard Watts, and of my supper with the Six Poor Travellers who were neither Rogues nor Proctors, and from that hour to this, I have never seen one of them again.
> (SPT, p. 36)

For the moment Dickens conjures his 'travellers'/writers out of existence.

Procter's poems, however, resonate disturbingly. As the third and seventh contributions they are 'odd' poems which raise questions about a woman's ability to link up with sources of creativity (metaphorised by the figures of the sailor boy and his mother, the maid and her mother country) and to establish a reputation. Stone gateways figure in both poems and they point to the presence of a threshold which may be crossed as well as a site of petrification. In 'The Sailor Boy' the gateway appears to lead nowhere (into a wood) and in 'A Legend of Bregenz' it marks the maid's accession to fame but also an end to her story. The poems implicitly challenge the dominance of the double 'D' which Dickens impresses on the Christmas Number by drawing attention to expression which has been muted or blocked – partly perhaps by Dickens's overwhelming desire to control his own production.

---

[76] The widow narrates the tale of 'The Sixth Poor Traveller', written by Eliza Lynn (SPT, pp. 29–34). It is the story of her marriage to a forger who had fallen in love with her sister whom he preferred to his 'doll'-like wife. He kills the sister on her discovery of his 'trade'.

The Music of Anonymity

The Christmas Numbers of 1855 and 1856 were entitled 'The Holly Tree Inn' (HTI) and 'The Wreck of the Golden Mary' (WGM). In 'The Holly Tree Inn' (1855) the occupants of a Yorkshire inn tell stories to the chief 'Guest', the persona assumed by Dickens. Procter's contribution is the intensely lyrical narrative poem, 'The Wayside Inn' (HTI, pp. 30–31). The poem recounts the story of Maurice, a young man living at an inn in Southern France. He watches a young woman going through various stages of her life as she periodically passes the inn door – as a young woman, a bride, a woman grieving and finally at her own funeral. She is depicted as dissociated from any historical and personal context, and from any home. The only exchange which takes place between Maurice and the woman is his giving her a blossom from the Judas tree, the passion flower.

A sense of betrayal and martyrdom pervade the poem, along with a feeling of painful dissociation from expressivity. The woman is shown to go through the motions of life at a distance from the passion suggested by the flower: 'The hanging purple blossoms / Upon the Judas Tree' (HTI, p. 30). The detailed narrative of her life remains unrevealed.

In the lead into the poem Dickens casts Procter as 'The Barmaid' who narrates the story:

> She was a pretty, gentle girl – a farmer's orphan daughter, and the landlord's niece – whom I strongly suspected of being engaged to be married very shortly, to the writer of the letter that I saw her reading at least twenty times, when I passed the bar, and which I more than believe I saw her kiss one night. She told me a tale of that country which went so pleasantly to the music of her voice, that I ought rather to say it turned itself into verse, than was turned into verse by me.
>
> (HTI, p. 30)

As in 'The Haunted House' (1859) Dickens attempts to marry Procter off metaphorically. The farmer's daughter is described as healthily involved in a romance and probably engaged. Her enthusiasm for her lover counters the dissociated state of Maurice and the young woman depicted in 'The Wayside Inn'. Unlike the ghostly presence of the woman who passes Maurice by she is depicted as an 'earthy' farmer's daughter and barmaid. Harry Stone writes that Dickens, in preparation for 'The Holly-Tree Inn', sent out Instructions to contributors, so Procter may well have had sight of 'The Barmaid' before submitting 'The Wayside Inn'.[77] Whether or not she did, there is clearly a tension between her poem and the role Dickens casts for its narrator.

The frame narrative of 'The Wayside Inn' is primarily concerned with 'The Guest', who mistakenly believes he has lost his loved one to another, and is en route via Liverpool to the United States. In conclusion he is reunited with his lover and declares that they have since married and have had eight children. The Guest is shown to be prolific, like the writer Dickens, and his story contrasts strangely with the death of passion and lack of creative connection depicted in 'The Wayside Inn'.

Procter's was usually the only poetry in the Christmas number, and to that extent she must surely have felt both included and prominent as the only poet, but simultaneously perhaps excluded by the prose of the well-known voices of Dickens, Wilkie Collins and others which surrounded her work. It is interesting to note that Dickens's narrator states that the Barmaid's tale, along with 'the music of her voice', rather turned 'itself into verse, than was turned into verse by me' (HTI, p. 30). This may be an indirect reference to Dickens's editing of Procter's verse, and to the 'grace and sentiment' of her poetry which he admired. The description also suggests that it was the lyricism and 'music' of Procter's poetry that Dickens approved, rather than its more disturbing aspects.

In 'The Wreck of the Golden Mary' (1856), one of the most popular of the Christmas numbers, Procter's mournful and dirge-like poem 'Homeward Bound' was published (WGM, pp. 25-27). This poem, which prefigures Tennyson's 'Enoch Arden' (1864) and Elizabeth Gaskell's Sylvia's Lovers (1863), relates the story of an unnamed sailor's total exclusion from his wife and home. Having been away ten years at sea and as a prisoner to 'black Moors' in Algeria he returns to find his wife married to another man and his own child dead.[78] Dickens's lead into the poem reads:

---

[77]   Stone, op. cit., II, p. 661.

[78]   In 'Enoch Arden' Enoch is shipwrecked and absent from home for ten years, in which time he is given up for lost by his wife who marries a close friend Philip (in 'Homeward Bound' an 'ancient comrade'). When Enoch discovers his wife Annie has remarried he does not reveal himself to her and stays in the seaport until his death. As in 'Homeward Bound' Enoch returns to find a baby son dead and the birth of a child by the new father (Tennyson, Poems and Plays, Ed. T. Herbert Warren, Oxford University Press, 1971, pp. 117-129).

Thomas Woolner, sculptor and member of the Pre-Raphaelite Brotherhood, provided Tennyson with the bare bones of the story. He related a 'Fisherman's' story he had first read in the diary of a fellow-passenger on a journey back to England from Australia in 1852 (Leonee Ormond, Tennyson and Thomas Woolner, Lincoln: The Tennyson Society, Tennyson Research Centre, 1981, p. 24).

In Elizabeth Gaskell's Sylvia's Lovers Sylvia, a farmer's daughter living in

An old Seaman in the Surf-boat sang this ballad, as his story, to a curious sort of tuneful no-tune, which none of the rest could remember afterwards.   (WGM, p. 25)

Procter's poetry is described as a kind of undercurrent – a 'tuneful no-tune' which is essentially music, like the 'music' of the Barmaid's voice, but which seems to be present before it takes the form of poetry. Like the rhythms of the sea in which the passengers are stranded, the 'ballad' is important in that it provides an undertow or undertone, but the singer, his subject and the actual poem remain anonymous and quickly forgotten.

Interestingly and sadly 'The Old Sailor's Story' is the only item omitted from the most recent edition of *The Wreck of the Golden Mary* published in 1961. The foreword states:

The present edition has jettisoned from 'The Beguilement in the Boats' one item, a sad tale told in 224 lines of rhyming verse by an old sailor. In other respects the story stands as it came from the hands of two great novelists.[79]

Many of Procter's protagonists are anonymous and the narratives of her poems often exhibit a tension between the pull towards or 'jettisoning' into anonymity and the desire for recognition. In both these poems the fading away or exclusion of the central protagonists is depicted and Dickens is seen to work or 'conduct' this 'music' of anonymity and exclusion in amongst his prose pieces.

'Three Evenings in a House'

In the 1858 Christmas Number of *Household Words*, 'A House to Let' (HTL), Procter's poem 'Three Evenings in a House' appeared. (In the *Legends and Lyrics* version the title of the poem is 'Three Evenings in a Life'.) In this poem Procter's narrative voice changes dramatically. The

---

Monkshaven, loses her lover Charley Kinraid to the press gang. Charley returns to find Sylvia married to her cousin Philip, who has led Sylvia to believe that Charley is dead, although he saw him being pressed. When the truth is known Charley leaves and Philip enlists, to return badly wounded years later. He lives locally, unknown to Sylvia, and watches her and their daughter Bella, whom he one day saves from drowning but dies in the act (Mrs Gaskell, *Sylvia's Lovers*, Intro. Arthur Pollard, London: J.M. Dent & Sons Ltd., 1964).

[79] Charles Dickens and Wilkie Collins, *The Wreck of the Golden Mary*. Illus. John Dugan, London: Methuen & Co. Ltd., 1961, Foreword.

lyricism, mournfulness and melancholia of earlier narrative poems (which often mask more acute and painful emotions) make way for a more discordant, bitter and overtly despairing tone. The poem recounts the life of a single woman, Bertha, who sacrifices herself to the cause of others – her brother, his wife and Bertha's ex-lover who marries her sister-in-law after her brother dies (HTL, pp. 23–26).

1858, the year in which the poem appeared, was, as I have stated in previous chapters, a very important year for Procter, marking the publication of the 'First Series' of *Legends and Lyrics* and the launch of *The English Woman's Journal*. In 1859 she would become a leading committee member of the Society for Promoting the Employment of Women, and, as a single woman, she would have been acutely aware of the 'problem' of single women whose numbers had been numbered as half a million in excess of men in the 1851 Census.[80]

Paradoxically, recognition as a poet and involvement in more 'public' causes seem to have enabled the writing of a bitter poem which, in terms of its poetry is significantly inferior to many of Procter's more lyrical poems. It is, however, a poem which manages to convey despair more directly than in much of her work.

Procter may have felt enabled to express such emotions by her stronger position as both a poet and an activist. She may also have felt freer to challenge Dickens's construction of herself as the noble woman who could rise above feelings of hopelessness and melancholy. In this poem Procter's narrative voice is in direct opposition to the solutions which Dickens provides for the single woman depicted in his frame narrative.

The 'house' of the title of Procter's poem is the central location described in 'A House to Let'. Dickens and Wilkie Collins wrote the frame narrative 'Over the Way' which takes the form of a well plotted story of the house and its series of occupants. Interestingly, Dickens may have derived the idea for 'The House to Let' from Bryan Procter's essay 'The Story of the Back-Room Window', published in 1838. In this essay Bryan Procter recalls the time when the Procters lived in Bedford Square. Their 'back-room window' looked out on to a crescent and a house which had been 'untenanted' for a long time. From the window the family saw the arrival of a young man, his wife and later their baby. They also witness the wife's death, the child's

[80] 'Statistics as to the Employment of the Female Population of Great Britain' (reprinted from *The English Woman's Journal*, March 1860) *Barbara Leigh Smith Bodichon and the Langham Place Group*, Ed. Candida Lacey, New York and London: Routledge & Kegan Paul, 1987, p. 177.

death and finally that of the husband who has taken to drink. The essay concludes with the 'To Let' sign going up again:

> The same board which two years before had been nailed to the wall, with the significant words 'To Let' upon it, was again fixed there.[81]

Dickens had written to Bryan Procter on 15th April, 1854:

> I remember to have read The Back-room Window some years ago, and I have associated it with you ever since. It is a most delightful paper.[82]

The frame narrative of 'A House to Let' recounts the story of the house. A self-designated 'old maid', who regrets not having had children, moves from Tunbridge Wells to London where she lives in a house opposite a dirty and dilapidated ten-roomed house to let. The 'old maid', who is exotically named Sophonisba, suspects that the house is occupied when she sees 'a secret Eye' looking out at her. A friend, Jarber, and her manservant Trottle, who are both competing for Sophonisba's favours, investigate the house's history (HTL, pp. 1-4).

Jarber discovers that it has been occupied by a family from Manchester (their story, 'The Manchester Marriage', is by Elizabeth Gaskell), and by Magsman, a Showman. The story of Magsman, titled 'Going into Society', was written by Dickens and later abridged for a reading by Dickens in 1868 called 'Mr Chops the Dwarf'.[83] Magsman recounts how he rented the house with a dwarf who had won 'Twelve thousand odd hundred pound' in a lottery. The dwarf is enabled by his fortune to 'Go into Society' and he is presented at Court and to George IV. He finally dies, exhausted by the rigours and greed of 'Society' which has fleeced him. Magsman finds the house so 'dismal' without him that he returns to his caravan (HTL, pp. 18-22).

For the dwarf the house represents 'Society' and its exorbitant demands. Withdrawal from the house suggests Dickens's own imaginative retreat from onerous public performances (readings, dinners, talks etc.). By contrast, Procter's 'Three Evenings in a Life' raises the problem for a single woman of actually entering into a role or performance at all, and of her experiencing that role as ghostly and disembodied.

---

[81] Barry Cornwall, *Essays and Tales in Prose*, Boston: Ticknor, Reed, and Fields, 1853, II, pp. 1-11, 9.
[82] Dexter, op. cit., II, p. 551.
[83] Page, op. cit., p. 264. 'Going into Society' was one of the pieces extracted for Dickens's *Christmas Stories* (Lane, op. cit.).

Procter's poem is the record of the third occupant of the house, who has been discovered by Jarber through a Circulating Library:

> Number Three looked like a very short manuscript, and I said as much. Jarber explained to me that we were to have some poetry this time. In the course of his investigations he had stepped into the Circulating Library, to seek for information on the one important subject. All the Library-people knew about the House was, that a female relative of the last tenant as they believed, had, just after that tenant left, sent a little manuscript poem to them which she described as referring to events that had actually passed in the House; and which she wanted the proprietor of the Library to publish. She had written no address on her letter; and the proprietor had kept the manuscript ready to be given back to her (the publishing of poems not being in his line) when she might call for it. She had never called for it; and the poem had been lent to Jarber, at his express request, to read to me. (HTL, pp. 22-23)

Dickens is joking with Procter about the circulating library in West London where Miss Berwick directed letters in her determination to elude the *Household Words* staff. Dickens presents the 'female relative' as a shadowy figure who, like Miss Berwick, prefers not to be identified. She is, of course, the single woman, Bertha, of 'Three Evenings in a House'.

The poem is in three sections which describe three consecutive Christmas Eves. In the first section the narrator describes the 'strange and wild regret' Bertha feels at having given up her 'home' in the country to join and support her brother in London, 'the dull, feverish town' where he is struggling to become an artist. Her 'regret' is even more for a future 'home' with her ex-lover which she has sacrificed for her brother (HTL, pp. 23-24).

The second Christmas Eve marks the death of Bertha's brother Herbert and of his art:

> The studio is deserted,
> Palette and brush laid by ...

Bertha recalls Herbert's marriage to a 'fair young wife' Dora in the past year and Dora's 'poor jealous pride' which distances Herbert from Bertha, depriving him of her 'truth, and power, and strength'. When he dies he asks Bertha to look after Dora, whom Bertha describes as a 'poor weak child' (HTL, pp. 24-25).

In Section Three Bertha recounts how her ex-lover Leonard had returned from 'Indian islands' in the past year, and that her initial relief and raised hopes at his return were superceded by 'sick despair' when she overheard a conversation between Dora and Leonard. Leonard was declaring love to Dora, and on Dora's expressing reservations on account of his former involvement with Bertha, he replied:

> Dearest,
> Bertha is far too cold
> To love; and I, my Dora,
> If once I fancied so,
> It was a brief delusion,
> And over, – long ago.

Although Bertha is devastated she maintains an impenetrable and 'cold' demeanour, and stands as bridesmaid to Dora and Leonard. The poem concludes with Bertha wandering out of the house. In the final stanza the narrator applauds her passage through 'the fire' which will strengthen Bertha and enable her to play 'An earnest noble part'. It is the image of her leaving the house, though, which lingers:

> And now the gloomy evening
> Sees Bertha pale and worn,
> Leaving the house for ever,
> To wander out forlorn.
>   (HTL, pp. 25-26)

Bertha expels herself, along with her despair and feelings of exclusion. It is as though the retiring and modest Miss Berwick persona preferred by Dickens has been replaced by the more disturbing figure of Bertha (and their names are linked), who recalls Bertha Mason of *Jane Eyre* (1847) in that she is depicted as near mad and distraught, although under control, inside a house and not an attic.[84] To this extent she is depicted as being closer to 'home'.

The figures of children and young anonymous women located outside the home depicted in other poems by Procter are replaced by a named woman on the inside of a house. Procter very rarely describes scenes of domesticity, and the result of depicting a woman on the inside of the home appears to be disastrous in this poem. Procter depicts the 'noble' woman Bertha as unable to express herself creatively, other than through facilitating others. She sacrifices her life to her brother, the creative artist, and the infantilised

---

[84] Charlotte Brontë, *Jane Eyre*, Ed, Q.D. Leavis, London: Penguin Books Ltd., 1966.

woman, Dora, who is allowed to enter into the potentially creative relationship of marriage. The name 'Dora' recalls that of Dora Spenlow, David Copperfield's childlike wife.[85]

Procter is bitterly satirising the idealised and noble womanliness which Dickens admired in her, and which in this poem is shown to exclude the adult woman from both creative artistry and her own sexuality. 'Three Evenings in a House' also provides a comment on Procter's own tireless philanthropic work. In September 1860 Procter's poem 'Fate and a Heart' was published in the *Cornhill* (it was later retitled 'The Tyrant and the Captive').[86] In this poem a tyrant voice taunts his captive with her 'compassion' which is now 'impotent' as she lies 'in helpless pain'. Her devotion to the 'welfare' and 'service' of her 'brethren' has been pointless, the tyrant suggests (pp. 197-198). Procter was to die four years later and this poem is perhaps expressing her own torturing feeling of impotence in the recognition that 'compassion' for others has not resolved her own pain, physical or emotional.

In 'Three Evenings in a House' Bertha's pain is to an extent muted by the sense of her dissociation and dislocation. In a review of 'A House to Let' in *The Saturday Review* (25.12.1858) the writer describes Dickens's preoccupation with 'grotesque trifles' in this Christmas number. The writer is referring primarily to Dickens's writing and he states that it is:

> exactly the sort of impropriety which might be expected from a man who looks upon life and death almost exclusively from a theatrical point of view.[87]

The depiction of Bertha in 'Three Evenings in a House' may also be described as distorted and theatrical in that the narrative voice is that of Bertha's dissociated alter ego who watches on as she goes through the motions of her own life, as though playing a part in a three-act play rather than entering into 'the House' of herself. (The *Legends and Lyrics* title, 'Three Evenings in a Life', suggests that Procter had made the connection between the house and the life) (pp. 233-244).

Bertha's dissociated and dislocated state indicates the presence of distorted and unexpressed emotions. In the opening section Bertha's ex-lover's 'words' and their 'well-known tone' echo disturbingly, along with

---

[85] Charles Dickens, *David Copperfield*, Ed. Trevor Blount, London: Penguin Books, 1985.

[86] *The Cornhill Magazine*, II, 1860, pp. 287-288.

[87] *The Saturday Review of Politics, Literature, Science, and Art*, VI, 1858, pp. 644-645.

her own 'words', 'So hard, so cold, so strong' which cut her off from him (HTL, p. 23). It is as though the words have become detached from the speakers and their painful emotions. The third person narration also provides a sense of distance from Bertha's acute pain.

When Bertha listens to Dora and Leonard's conversation she is depicted as a ghostly, eavesdropping presence, hearing but simultaneously cut off from the 'words' on the other side of 'the open'd door'. Again her emotion is partly displaced on to 'The tone – the words – the accents:' she hears:

> Yes, he was there; and pausing
>   Just near the open'd door,
> To check her heart's quick beating,
>   She heard – and paused still more –
> His low voice – Dora's answers –
>   His pleading – Yes, she knew
> The tone – the words – the accents:
>   She once had heard them too.
>   (HTL, p. 25)

Procter is almost certainly invoking Elizabeth Barrett Browning's poem 'Bertha in the Lane' (1844) in which an elder sister overhears her younger sister, Bertha, and the elder sister's lover, Robert, talk in the 'lane' about their new found love, and also their awareness of herself and her claims.[88] As in 'Three Evenings in a House' the speaker's dissociated state is conveyed:

> And I walked as if apart
>   From myself, when I could stand –
> And I pitied my own heart,
>   As if I held it in my hand . . .[89]

A difficulty with really grasping the 'heart' and life is also depicted in Procter's very interesting poem 'Hearts' (1861) which prefigures Christina Rossetti's poem 'Twice' (1864) in which the speaker holds her broken heart in her hand and offers it to God.[90] In 'Hearts' the speaker makes three attempts to hold on to the heart which she persists in allowing to slip away from her, and there is a sense that the speaker is at some level wilfully and perhaps perversely dropping it (or dropping the subject of the heart):

---

88 Barrett Browning, *Poems* (1844), II, pp. 191–202.
89 ibid., p. 198.
90 Rossetti, *Poems and Prose*, pp. 87–88.

> Sailing over the waters,
>   Watching the far blue land,
> I dropped my golden heart, dear,
>   Dropped it out of my hand!
>   (pp. 265–266)

At the end of 'Three Evenings in a House' Bertha slips away from the 'House' or 'Life' she has been unable to enter into fully. In the conclusion of Bryan Procter's story 'The Back-Room Window', the 'To Let' sign appears again after two years. Procter writes that it was as though 'the old time had returned again, and that the interval was nothing but a dream.'[91]

Like her father, Adelaide Procter allows her occupant to slip away as though her life has taken on the semblance of a dream as she moves into the shadows of the 'gloomy evening' outside. It is a dreamlike and haunting state which Dickens, in the frame narrative (co-written by Wilkie Collins), also lets slip. Sophonisba, when she has heard the poem, remarks:

> I could warmly and sincerely praise the little poem … but I could not say that it tended in any degree towards clearing up the mystery of the empty House.   (HTL, p. 26)

In spite of Dickens's suggestion that the poem does not really help, 'Three Evenings in a House' provides its own distinct comment on 'the mystery of the empty House' and exists in sharp tension with Dickens's narrative resolution. In the concluding narrative Trottle, the manservant, finds out that an unknown cousin of Sophonisba, George Forley, owns the house. On visiting the house Trottle discovers a five year old child in the garret:

> Close under this window, kneeling on the bareboards with his face to the door, there appeared, of all the creatures in the world to see alone at such a place and at such a time, a mere mite of a child – a little, lonely, wizen, strangely-clad boy, who could not at the most, have been more than five years old. He had a greasy old blue shawl crossed over his breast, and rolled up, to keep the ends from the ground, into a great big lump on his back. A strip of something which looked like the remains of a woman's flannel petticoat, showed itself under the shawl, and, below that again, a pair of rusty black stockings, worlds too large for him, covered his legs and his shoeless feet.

---

[91]   Cornwall, *Essays and Tales in Prose*, II, p. 9.

The boy is scrubbing the floor obsessively (HTL, p. 29).

It transpires that the boy is the son of Forley's second daughter, who was disowned for running away with a merchant seaman. When the daughter died in childbirth and the husband was drowned the child was registered as still-born so that Forley's other daughter's girls might inherit the family wealth. The house was kept empty, bar the boy's grisly caretakers, a mother and son employed by Forley, to make it 'the surest of all hiding places for the child'. Once discovered, the boy is taken into the care of the 'old maid' Sophonisba, who buys the house and converts it into a Hospital for Sick Children (HTL, pp. 34, 36).

The discovery of deprivation's 'hiding-place' in Dickens and Collins's frame narrative provides the 'old maid' with a noble cause. Sophonisba the spinster is neatly paired off with her 'adopted boy' who is soon reintegrated into the community:

> he came to be pretty, and childish, and winning, and companionable, and to have pictures and toys about him, and suitable playmates.
>
> (HTL, p. 36)

As in 'The Seven Poor Travellers' the child and the single woman, like the boy and the widow, are paired off in conclusion. Dickens is keen to find a resolution for 'solitude' and 'neglect', and a partner for the single woman. The narrator Sophonisba concludes:

> Many an Eye I see in that House now, but it is never in solitude, never in neglect. Many an Eye I see in that House now, that is more and more radiant every day with the light of returning health.
>
> (HTL, p. 36)

And yet the prominence of the solitary and repeated 'Eye' creates a disturbing resonance. Similarly the image of the deprived boy who goes through the motions of his stunted existence, metaphorically 'scouring' himself of the emotions of deprivation, is stronger than that of the 'dear chubby face' of Sophonisba's 'pet' who nods at one of the windows in conclusion (HTL, p. 36).

Dickens's injunction to embrace the points of stopped growth in 'Where We Stopped Growing' (1853) is seen here in inverted form. What has been arrested in the imagination is the boy's state of harsh deprivation instead of a moment of joy. Similarly, the figure of Mr Chops the Dwarf in 'Going into Society' resists Dickens's determination not to 'end the thing with unseasonable grimness'.[92] The dwarf, like the boy, is of stunted growth and, although not a 'grim' figure, he is suggestive of a dwindling within the house which can only find resolution in his poignant death.

Dickens and Procter are both addressing the problem of deprivation, and by locating it within the home they disrupt the notion of the comfortable Victorian home which Jeffrey Weeks has described as a 'microcosm of stable society and a sanctuary from an unstable and rapidly changing one'.[93]

Deprivation, for Dickens, is located at a distance in the figures of a boy and a dwarf. For Procter, however, the figure of the spinster may have been in some aspects uncomfortably close to home, or to her own life. Procter resists Dickens's resolution which seeks to return life to the empty house and to exorcise it of its haunting deprivations. In the following year in 'The Haunted House' (1859) Dickens similarly attempts to free a house of its rumoured 'hauntings', exposing them as none other than the inner hauntings of the guests' lives and memories.

Procter's poetic voice, however, is haunting in its irresolution. Bertha, the single woman, cannot find a place in 'The House to Let', and if the 'House' is read as 'Life' and 'Let' as 'tell', it becomes apparent that there is some doubt as to whether she even has a 'story to tell'. Dickens had filled his 'house' with stories, but Procter's single woman and her abruptly curtailed story finally remain on the outside.

In these Christmas numbers Procter's poems, in their concern with states of deprivation and exclusion, show a close affinity with Dickens's own preoccupations. They also provide a complex response to his editorial authority. Painful feelings remain unresolved and unaccommodated in her poems. In 'The Angel's Story' and 'The Sailor Boy' there is no transition made to an apparently happier adulthood, and the images which continue to disturb are those of the boy angels arrested in mid-air and the sailor boy's impassivity and frozen emotional state.

Emotions are given a freer rein in 'A Legend of Bregenz' but the protagonist cannot escape a legendary status which precludes the telling of a more personal and specific story. In 'Three Evenings in a House' a transition has been made from the depiction of boy children and a legendary maid to

---

92   Dickens wrote to W.H. Wills on 2nd October, 1858: 'I am not clear about following up the old Materials, and making them doomed and destructive. I think it would end the thing with unseasonable grimness. If I could build them into a good school, or infirmary, or child's hospital, or something of that sort, it might be a more pleasant end, and a working round to something brighter' (Dexter, op. cit., III, p. 60).

93   Jeffrey Weeks, *Sex, Politics and Society. The regulation of sexuality since 1800*, London and New York: Longman Group UK Limited, 1981, p. 29.

Figure 5: 'The Requital', Illus. George Du Maurier, 1866

that of a named adult woman on the inside of a house, but no resolution is found for her emotional pain which is evacuated from the house. In 1859 in 'A Legend of Provence' Procter's single woman protagonist is shown to secure a place for herself inside a house, although it is a place of celibacy to which she returns after her 'fall'. Sexuality is, however, allowed expression in this poem.

In the following year, 1860, Procter's poem 'The Requital' was published in *The English Woman's Journal*, and in this powerful lyric the murderous emotions of a girl child and their reception by an adult fallen woman come together to devastating effect.[94] The fact that the poem was published in the household of a women's journal rather than in Dickens's *All The Year Round* suggests that Procter may have chosen to have the poem published in *The English Woman's Journal* as a more receptive space for the expression of such feelings. A reading of this poem provides an interesting comment on what may have been excluded from Dickens's household.

'The Requital'

Michael Slater has written that Dickens would probably have found Elizabeth Barrett Browning's *Aurora Leigh* (1856) 'disagreeably coarse and unwomanly in many places'. Slater also states that Dickens was reported to have declared in 1860 (the year 'The Requital' was published) that he had read neither *Jane Eyre* nor *Wuthering Heights* and that he disapproved of the 'whole school'.[95]

A young girl's extreme anger and rage, which are likely to have been unpalatable to Dickens, are the central motifs of this poem, which is worth quoting in full:

---

[94] *The English Woman's Journal*, V, 1860, pp. 184-185.
[95] Slater, op. cit., p. 320.

The Requital

Loud roared the Tempest,
　Fast fell the sleet;
A little Child Angel
　Passed down the street,
With trailing pinions,
　And weary feet.

The moon was hidden;
　No stars were bright;
So she could not shelter
　In heaven that night,
For the Angels' ladders
　Are rays of light.

She beat her wings
　At each window pane,
And pleaded for shelter,
　But all in vain:-
'Listen,' they said,
　'To the pelting rain!'

She sobbed, as the laughter
　And mirth grew higher,
'Give me rest and shelter
　Beside your fire,
And I will give you
　Your heart's desire.'

The dreamer sat watching
　His embers gleam,
While his heart was floating
　Down hope's bright stream;
... So he wove her wailing
　Into his dream.

The worker toiled on,
　For his time was brief;
The mourner was nursing
　Her own pale grief:
They heard not the promise
　That brought relief.

But fiercer the Tempest
    Rose than before,
When the Angel paused
    At a humble door,
And asked for shelter
    And help once more.

A weary woman,
    Pale, worn, and thin,
With the brand upon her
    Of want and sin,
Heard the Child Angel
    And took her in.

Took her in gently,
    And did her best
To dry her pinions;
    And made her rest
With tender pity
    Upon her breast.

When the eastern morning
    Grew bright and red,
Up the first sunbeam
    The Angel fled;
Having kissed the woman
    And left her – dead.

                                    (pp. 173-177)

The child at the window recalls the spectre of Catherine Earnshaw/Linton
haunting the window of Lockwood's room in Emily Brontë's *Wuthering
Heights*.[96] This heralded the appearance of other similar hauntings in the
texts of women writers such as Elizabeth Gaskell, Harriet Parr and Christina
Rossetti.

In Elizabeth Gaskell's 'The Old Nurse's Story', published in the 1852
Christmas Number of *Household Words*, the ghost of a child, murdered by
the father of a daughter who had married a foreigner, is described as a
Phantom Child with 'little battering hands' beating upon the window glass

---

[96] Emily Brontë, *Wuthering Heights*, Ed. David Daiches, London: Penguin
Books Ltd., 1965, p. 67. Lockwood narrates, 'I discerned, obscurely, a child's face
looking through the window'.

but with 'no sound'.[97] In Harriet Parr's 'Too Late!', published in *Household Words* in 1856, a mother refuses entrance to her daughter who 'presses a face to the streaming glass' and moans and wrings 'its ghastly hands' on the threshold but moves 'with soundless tread'.[98] Christina Rossetti's 'Behold I Stand at the Door and Knock', published in *The English Woman's Journal* in 1861, a year after 'The Requital', figures 'A stunted child, / Her sunk eyes sharpened with precocious care' who stands at a 'Lady's' gate. The Lady refuses her succour on the grounds that she should go and find some work 'instead of cry'.[99]

Procter depicts the child angel in 'The Requital' as both ignored but powerfully present. In the first stanza the opening dactylic metres and the alliterative 'f' ('Loud roared the Tempest, / Fast fell the sleet') create a sense of the strength of the child's emotions. Procter's economic use of language and the pared down form of the poem, with its monosyllables and short 2 2 lines, sharply focus the reader on the child's deprived condition and emotional state.

The beating of her wings 'at each window pane' emphasise the child's physical presence whilst the punning 'pane' suggests both the materiality and the fragility of her suffering. She is depicted less as a ghostly presence than as a little girl in desperate need – more one of Henry Mayhew's 'ragged little felons' wandering the streets of the metropolis than an unearthly being or phantom.[100]

In George Du Maurier's illustration of the poem a woman in black (signifying her sin and impending death) holds out her hand to a dark, straight-haired girl angel who is drawing back from the woman. The child looks both needy and suspicious and in no way presents a picture of angelic innocence (see Figure 5).[101] Procter may even have had in mind the figure of the child prostitute ('I will give you / Your heart's desire') who finds and

---

[97]   HW, VI, 1852, p. 17.
[98]   HW, XIII, 1856, p. 326.

>   There presses a face to the streaming glass;
>   She can see the light in the room;
>   She can see her mother's tall shadow pass,
>   To the inner chamber's gloom.
>   As it duskily glows on the panell'd wall,
>   The fire looks kind and clear,
>   And the peering eye that traces it all,
>   Grows dim with a burning tear.

[99]   Rossetti, *Poems and Prose*, pp. 27–28.
[100] Mayhew, op. cit., I, p. 274.
[101] Adelaide Anne Procter, *Legends and Lyrics*, Intro. Charles Dickens, London: Bell and Daldy, 1866, p. 207.

requites her fallen mother for her sin – perhaps the mother who is totally excluded from the picture in 'A Legend of Provence'.

In 'A Legend of Provence' the state of dream or reverie is suggestive of a maternal plenitude, and there is an attempt to penetrate that dream by confronting the miraculous mother on the threshold of the convent. By contrast, in 'The Requital' the child's dream is shown to have worn very thin ('A weary woman, / Pale, worn, and thin'). The child has no dream or fantasy of the interiors of the houses from which she is excluded by a pane (or pain) which is both transparent but invisible to the occupants. Her wailing is not recognised and it is woven into the male dreamer's dream ('he wove her wailing / Into his dream'), whilst the worker and mourner exclude the promise of relief (or death) which the child holds out. She is both incorporated and barred from their interiors, and she is allowed no place of her own.

The voice of deprivation is only fully recognised by the fallen woman, and the moment of her reception of the child is a moment of intense affectivity and vulnerability. The child submits to the surrogate mother's arms but repays her with death.

Procter has used the idea of requital to draw attention to the problems of female expression. The definition of the verb 'to requite' is to make a return to a person for a kindness or an injury. Its etymology is quietus, the Latin adjective meaning quiet, peaceful, at rest, asleep. Quiet dormant passivity seems to be countered by the notion of active requital, but the act of requital returns its maker to a state of quiescence. The action is self-cancelling at the moment of its most intense activity. Procter is considering the problems of how to express female anger without returning its voice to a state of passivity which sought a means of expression.

The onward mobility of the child prevents a return to a state of total quiescence. She leaps out of the world, upward and onward, unlike Blake's child of experience in 'Infant Sorrow' who leaps into the 'dangerous world' and, although struggling against constraint, is finally bound to his mother's breast:

> Bound and weary I thought best
> To sulk upon my mother's breast.[102]

The child's emotion in 'The Requital' is depicted as being beyond the containment of the mother's arms. Procter draws attention to the rapacious-

---

[102] William Blake, *Songs of Innocence and of Experience*, Intro. Sir Geoffrey Keynes, Oxford University Press, 1970, p. 151.

ness of a child's excessive needs and to a mother who is herself in need and cannot provide the child with a full breast.

In his essay 'Little Children' (*Household Words* 26.11.1853) George Sala describes the mother as 'the centre of love' toward which the child gravitates. He quotes the example of the little boy 'in the Greek epigram' who was 'creeping down a precipice'. The only thing that induces him to return is 'the sight of his mother's breast'.[103]

By contrast the child in 'The Requital' flees away from the mother's worn and thin breast, which she has sucked dry, and up a precipital space into an unspecified location. Heaven is figured as inaccessible. The child was barred from it the previous evening when the moon was hidden and 'the Angels' ladders', the 'rays of light', had disappeared. She flees up the first sunbeam in the bright and red 'eastern morning', which suggests that her destination may in fact be the hell or purgatory of her own murderous and deprived feelings. The flight upwards creates a sense of the vertiginous instability of the girl's emotional state.

Penny Brown has observed that women writers such as Emily and Charlotte Brontë and George Eliot were becoming increasingly concerned with the expression of girls' energies and emotions, and she links the figure of the child to that of the woman: 'the figure of the child can be seen as a paradigm of the condition of womanhood itself'.[104]

Procter's friend Anna Jameson, the art critic and writer, links the emotions of the child and the adult woman in an essay entitled 'A Revelation of Child-hood' (1855). She asks the question 'What do we know of the mystery of child-nature, child-life?'[105] In an account of her own childhood, which she describes as being unexceptional like that of many children, she reveals the existence in herself of the 'capacity of strong, deep, silent resentment, and a vindictive spirit'.[106] The depiction of herself as an average girl counters notions of a passive and angelic femininity. Jameson links the life of the child to that of the adult woman:

> We do not sufficiently consider that our life is not made up of separate parts, but is *one* – is a progressive whole. When we talk of leaving our childhood behind us, we might as well say that the river flowing onward to the sea had left the fountain behind.[107]

---

[103] HW, VIII, 1853, p. 293.

[104] Brown, op. cit., p. 180.

[105] Mrs Jameson, *A Commonplace Book of Thoughts, Memories, and Fancies*, London: Longman, Brown, Green, and Longmans, 1855, p. 117.

[106] ibid., p. 124.

[107] ibid., p. 121.

In 'The Requital' a child's rapacious and murderous emotions and an adult's woman's need are expressed in the form of what might be categorised as a fantasy. The poem is not overtly didactic and its religious significance, although implicit, is not stressed. Similarly, 'The Angel's Story' might also be described as fantastic literature in spite of its conventional religious didacticism.

Penny Brown writes that fantasy fiction (which had been the target of moralists such as Barbauld, Trimmer and More) was being reinstated at mid-century. She refers to Lewis Carroll's *Alice in Wonderland* (1865) which, like 'The Requital', is concerned with whether or not doors will open to a young woman.[108] Brown states that the importance of fantasy is its ability to capture the child's 'joys of a sense of all-powerfulness'.[109] In 'The Requital' the child's omnipotent desires are placed in the context of the fallen woman's deprivation. They are shown to result from need, the sight of which the girl metaphorically kills off.

The depiction of the child's desires provides an interesting contrast with the omnipotence of the child which figures in George Eliot's *Silas Marner* (published in 1861, just a year after 'The Requital'). In this novel Eppie, the golden-haired baby of the lower-class, opium-addicted Molly (the abandoned wife of Godfrey Cass, the local squire's son) crawls into Silas's cottage when Molly dies in the snow outside. Effie appears before Silas as a vision of the gold he has lost: 'Gold! – his own gold – brought back to him as mysteriously as it had been taken away!' The child exerts an omnipotent and magical power over Silas whilst the destitute mother lies dead beyond the threshold.[110] Eliot attributes Molly's destitute condition to her opium addiction rather than to 'her husband's neglect'. She describes her as incapable of 'Just and self-reproving thoughts':

> how should those white-winged delicate messengers make their way
> to Molly's poisoned chamber, inhabited by no higher memories than
> those of a bar-maid's paradise of pink ribbons and gentlemen's
> jokes?[111]

The golden-haired child shines by contrast with the demonised mother (with her 'long black hair'[112]) who is excluded from the home.

108 Brown, op. cit., p. 188.
109 ibid., p. 188.
110 George Eliot, *Silas Marner: The Weaver of Raveloe*, Edinburgh and London: William Blackwood and Sons, 1861, pp. 221–222.
111 ibid., p. 215.
112 ibid., p. 235.

By contrast in 'The Requital' Procter brings the child and the mother together under the same roof and shows that deprivation may exist on either side of the threshold. It cannot be placed at a convenient distance, projected on to the cold outside of domestic warmth. In locating deprivation on both sides of the threshold 'The Requital' expresses concerns which are close to those of Dickens, despite the fact that the poem may not have appealed to him. The poem recalls his last Christmas story, 'The Haunted Man and The Ghost's Bargain' (1848), in which Dickens explores emotional pain and deprivation and the 'Gift' of omnipotence.[113]

'The Haunted Man and The Ghost's Bargain' is the story of Redlaw, a Chemist, who is haunted by the betrayal of a friend who won his own loved one instead of marrying his sister as Redlaw had hoped (interestingly this narrative prefigures Procter's 'Three Evenings in a House'). He is visited by a spectre who grants him the power of oblivion on the condition that this gift is passed on to all whom Redlaw meets. Redlaw's power of forgetfulness has dire consequences in that the erasure of past memories includes the eradication of good and benign feelings and memories.

The only person who is immune to his powers is a deprived and desperate street child who seeks refuge at his door. The child is described as:

A baby savage, a young monster, a child who had never been a child,
a creature who might live to take the outward form of man, but, who,
within, would live and perish a mere beast.[114]

He is also described as a 'baby-monster' with a 'sharp malignant face', and Redlaw is horrified to see that 'the expression on the boy's face was the expression on his own'.[115] It is an expression from which all compassionate and sensitive feeling has been obliterated. It is only when Redlaw appreciates what he has lost, and his memory is restored, that he can feel compassion for the street child who is finally included within the house as a surrogate son for Milly and her husband (the caretaker and his wife) who have no children. Dickens shows how the omnipotent desire to erase painful memories is impotent in the face of a deprivation which cannot be magically wiped away or relocated.

'The Haunted Man and the Ghost's Bargain' depicts the changing locations of the deprived boy who is seen by Redlaw darting back and forth over the threshold of the home. His first sight of the boy is when he rushes into his

---

113 Charles Dickens, *Christmas Books*, London: Chapman and Hall, 1852.
114 ibid., p. 225.
115 ibid., pp. 242–243.

room from outside 'like a wild-cat'.[116] When Redlaw directs the boy to Milly's room down the 'long arched passage' the boy darts outside again.[117] At one point in the narrative Redlaw looks in through the window of Milly's room to see the boy coiled up asleep on the floor. He seems to be looking in on his own deprivation in the form of the boy, and when the boy angrily tries to eject Redlaw with the words 'This is the woman's house – not yours' his exile from 'the woman's house' is keenly felt.[118] Throughout the story the boy is shown to cling to 'the woman's house' with 'The woman's fire', and at one point he asks Redlaw eagerly 'Back to the woman's?'[119]

Although the house of the good angel Milly in one sense provides a haven from the outside world there is always a sense that a place there has not been entirely secured. Even though the strange street child is finally included in her house, the haunting image of Redlaw looking in on his own needy self is resonant and disturbing, despite the reconciliatory Christmas dinner which concludes the narrative.

'The Requital' suggests that looking through the window at the deprived alter ego in the form of a deprived mother may be totally unbearable. Both deprived girl and mother are finally excluded from domestic warmth (through death and flight) as there is no 'good' woman's house to recognise and accommodate their pain and need.

It is as though Procter reaches a state of impasse in her negotiations with the figures of exiled and deprived children and women. Unlike Dickens she is unable to incorporate them or provide for them within a more reassuring narrative structure. Whilst Dickens pairs off widow and sailor boy, spinster and deprived boy, and childless couple and deprived boy in 'The Haunted Man', Procter's protagonists either remain single and exiled, or they are brought or fused together in an extremely uncomfortable or deadly coupling ('The Angel's Story' and 'The Requital').

For Procter the figure of the child seemed to represent emotions which had not been accommodated. Several poems depict a single woman's uneasy and at times extremely ambivalent relationship to the child. In the poem 'A Student' the 'lone student' is depicted ignoring the metaphorical child or alter ego at her elbow, who takes the form of a consolatory 'little hand upon' her arm and 'two blue pleading eyes' (pp. 35–36). It is as though the figure of the child is drawing attention to the vulnerabilities and yearnings which are excluded by the writer's narrow and intense focus on her work.

---

[116] ibid., p. 225.
[117] ibid., p. 225.
[118] ibid., p. 241.
[119] ibid., p. 225, p. 249.

In 'A Comforter', which was published in *The English Woman's Journal* in 1860, the same year as 'The Requital', comfort comes in the form of a child, Effie, whose name and silence suggest the presence of the speaker's ineffable desires and longings. The child is the repository for the 'impossible things' she yearns for (pp. 229–231).[120] In both these poems the child stands outside the adult, either ignored or silent, and although providing comfort and a focus for longings, she is not really embraced or incorporated by the adult speaker.

In the same year, 1860, Procter's remarkable and poignant poem 'The Changeling' was published in the *Cornhill*.[121] In this poem the speaker describes 'A little changeling spirit' who 'Crept to my arms one day'. The child's incessant 'wailing' torments the speaker to such an extent that she buries her and covers her with violets, only to disinter her and once again feel her 'clinging hold' and suffer 'the ceaseless wailing'. Finally she leaves her 'wailing burden' in a church, and she is comforted by the child turned angel who watches over her from heaven (pp. 227–8).

This cluster of poems, the last two published in 1860 when Procter was thirty-five, poignantly suggest that as a single woman Procter may have been mourning the fact that she had not had a child. They also identify the immense difficulty encountered by an adult woman writer who may feel exiled from a more vulnerable, emotionally needy and 'wailing' part of herself, as well as from the comfort that recognition of the child and its vulnerabilities might bring.

In Alice Meynell's 'The Poet to His Childhood' (1875), the speaker blames the child self for choosing the 'destiny' of the poet who is excluded from ordinary domesticity and comfort:

> You will stand upon the thresholds with a face of dumb desire
> Nor be known by any fire.[122]

In 'The Requital' Procter does articulate 'dumb desire' in an attempt to find a place for the child/woman's pain and hunger within a community of people (the worker, the dreamer, the mourner and the fallen woman). The poem may be read as an account of a woman poet, hungry for recognition, who is attempting to find a place within Dickens's house of writers which might accommodate her strong desires and emotions.

Procter and Dickens shared many preoccupations, and Dickens welcomed

---

[120] *The English Woman's Journal*, VI, 1860, pp. 177–178.
[121] *The Cornhill Magazine*, I, 1860, p. 329.
[122] *Victorian Women Poets 1830–1901. An Anthology*, Ed. Jennifer Breen, London: Everyman, 1994, p. 103.

her as his main contributor of poetry despite his reservations about her 'gloom'. He had included 'A Legend of Provence', an unconventional poem about the reinstatement and rehousing of a fallen woman. However, he may very well have barred entrance to a poem about a woman's unresolved rage and pain which might have proved a little too close to his 'home' and comfort.

Abbreviations

ASCF   Another Round of Stories by the Christmas Fire
ATYR   All The Year Round
HH   The Haunted House
HTI   The Holly Tree Inn
HTL   A House to Let
HW   Household Words
SPT   The Seven Poor Travellers
WGM   The Wreck of the Golden Mary

Conclusion: 'The Inner Chamber'

Procter's lyric 'The Inner Chamber' appeared in the 'Second Series' of *Legends and Lyrics* (1861). The speaker sits on the threshold of what appears to be an inner sanctum and the poem provides a striking and poignant image of the woman poet who is still struggling with her relationship to the authorities this 'inner chamber' seems to metaphorise.

A reading of this enigmatic, disturbing and very beautiful lyric provides a means for restating the main points of my discussion and for drawing some general conclusions. It is worth quoting the poem in full:

> *The Inner Chamber*
>
> In the outer Court I was singing,
>   Was singing the whole day long;
> From the inner chamber were ringing
>   Echoes repeating my song.
>
> And I sang till it grew immortal;
>   For that very song of mine,
> When re-echoed behind the Portal,
>   Was filled with a life divine.
>
> Was the Chamber a silver round
>   Of arches, whose magical art
> Drew in coils of musical sound,
>   And cast them back on my heart?
>
> Was there hidden within a lyre
>   Which, as air breathed over its strings,
> Filled my song with a soul of fire,
>   And sent back my words with wings?

Was some seraph imprisoned there,
  Whose Voice made my song complete,
And whose lingering, soft despair,
  Made the echo so faint and sweet?

Long I trembled and paused – then parted
  The curtains with heavy fringe;
And, half fearing, yet eager-hearted,
  Turned the door on its golden hinge.

Now I sing in the court once more,
  I sing and I weep all day,
As I kneel by the close-shut door,
  For I know what the echoes say.

Yet I sing not the song of old,
  Ere I knew whence the echo came,
Ere I opened the door of gold;
  But the music sounds just the same.

Then take warning, and turn away;
  Do not ask of that hidden thing.
Do not guess what the echoes say,
  Or the meaning of what I sing.
                    (pp. 262–263)

Procter, the singer of poems, sits on the threshold of a place which has become precious to her. The 'door of gold' suggests just how much she has invested in the inner sanctum. The authority inside may be God who renders her song 'immortal', or someone who possesses 'magical art'. Her doubts about the inner circle and its secrets, with its interminable 'arches' and 'coils of musical sound', are, however, manifest. Perhaps a 'lyre' or 'liar' sits inside or someone who has become 'imprisoned' by his or her own 'Voice' and 'despair'. Looking into the inner chamber apparently opens the door to both grief and fear, as well as to an increased sense of reverence: 'I kneel by the close-shut door'.

Various authorities – religious, paternal and poetic – are central to Procter's poetics, and 'The Inner Chamber' seems to be asking whether it has been worth opening the door on those authorities and their 'hidden' things. In the final stanza the fear of such knowledge becomes urgent and paramount. But far from seeking to close the door on the search for knowledge ('Do not ask of that hidden thing') the urgency of the speaker's imperative voice actually draws attention to what she longs to reveal, although she fears the yet unknown consequences of such a revelation.

What, then, are the secrets attached to the sanctums or authorities Procter has looked into in her poetry? Chapter 2 states that Procter responded critically to the Tractarian theories of John Keble in her seminal poem 'A Tomb in Ghent'. 'The Inner Chamber' (and the inner space depicted may be read as the huge space of St Bavon's Cathedral in microcosm) draws attention to the Tractarian 'Disciplina Arcana', the discipline of the secret.

In this poem the inner secrets of her faith appear to be in considerable doubt. The singer has not been able to stay within the bounds of the 'reserve' which Keble promotes as a means of restraining the believer from wishing to know too much, and she has momentarily penetrated the sanctum of her religion's secrets. Women, in Keble's account, especially exemplify the principle of reserve. Dora Greenwell, in the essay 'Our Single Women', describes the reserve which 'draws an unseen circle round the Christian and cultivated Englishwoman, never permitting her to overstep the modesty of nature'. In another essay, 'Hardened in Good', Greenwell refers to the 'citadel' of the 'soul' which is guarded 'by some strange and secret spell' as though this inner goodness is unassailable.[1]

When the singer in 'The Inner Chamber' enters into the 'citadel' she looks into what is most precious but 'strange' within herself as well as into the authority which confirms and partly constitutes this inner 'citadel'. By finally remaining outside the door she may hold on to her belief in the omnipotence of her song ('filled with a life divine') and the inner authority which sanctions it. Once she has looked inside and has explored the inner space, fear and it would seem disillusionment ('For I know what the echoes say') set in.

'The Inner Chamber' interestingly prefigures a poem by Agnes Mary F. Robinson, 'God in a Heart'. In this poem the speaker and a companion enter into a temple to find 'evil things . . . Blind, crawling, chill, discoloured, and impure'. The speaker describes the 'foulness of the illumin'd room' which is exposed to view.[2] The singer in 'The Inner Chamber' chooses not to reveal what she has uncovered and, although disillusioned, remains in awe ('I kneel by the close-shut door') of the secrets she has uncovered.

Procter's faith was strong as so many of her religious lyrics testify, but

---

[1]   Dora Greenwell, *Essays*, London: Alexander Strahan, 1866, pp. 15-16, 111.

[2]   *The Collected Poems. Lyrical and Narrative of A. Mary F. Robinson (Madame Duclaux)*, London: T. Fisher Unwin, [1902], p. 155. Agnes Mary Frances Robinson (1857-1944) wrote a biography of Emily Brontë in the 'Eminent Women' series.

there is a strand of doubt, never fully articulated or named, which runs through her work – for example in poems such as 'A Vision', 'Fidelis', 'Illusion', 'Over the Mountain', 'Discouraged', 'A Castle in the Air' and 'An Ideal'. This last poem poignantly depicts a state of uncertainty which has set in:

> Is not a faithful spirit mine –
>   Mine still – at close of day? . . .
> Yet will my foolish heart repine
> For that bright morning dream of mine.
>   (p. 250, ll. 45–48)

This is a similar doubt to that expressed in 'The Inner Chamber' – the doubt that 'that very song of mine', her faith, can be sustained when its secrets, divested of their 'bright' attractions, have been exposed.

'The Inner Chamber' may also be read as the expression of painful doubt and anxiety about romantic love and relationships. The single woman who has looked into the hidden secrets of love and sexuality, having parted the hymeneal 'curtains with heavy fringe', withdraws to her lonely position on the threshold of desire – a Psyche who has 'dared to cross the threshold' of sexual knowledge but, unlike Psyche, retreats from it.[3]

Another later poem by Procter, 'The Story of the Faithful Soul' (1861), provides an interesting gloss on Procter's lack of faith in romantic love (pp. 253–255). The poem also comments more indirectly on her religious faith. In this narrative poem the narrator describes a young woman's sufferings in purgatory. She died the night before her wedding and longs to return to earth to comfort her fiancé. The archangel Michael releases her on Mary's feast day, granting her 'one short minute's space' with her lover on the condition that she returns and pays for her reprieve with 'A thousand years in torment, / A thousand years in pain' (p. 254, ll. 60–64). The 'faithful soul' returns to earth to find that her fiancé has in fact remarried. On her return to purgatory Michael exempts her from further suffering and she is granted passage to Heaven. The poem ends at the point of her passing or transition:

---

    3   Lucius Apuleius, 'Cupid and Psyche (I)', *The Transformations of Lucius Otherwise Known as The Golden Ass*, Trans. Robert Graves, London: Penguin Books Ltd., 1990, p. 71.

'Pass on,' thus spake the Angel:
  'Heaven's joy is deep and vast;
Pass on, pass on, poor Spirit,
  For Heaven is yours at last;
In that one minute's anguish
  Your thousand years have passed.'
                                      (p. 255, ll. 91–96)

In this poem Procter describes the imprisoning position of a woman who is situated in an ambivalent position midway between heaven and earth. Although she has been granted passage to heaven, it is the point of transition which actually concludes the poem. The woman is depicted as being on the threshold of deeper knowledge ('Heaven's joy is deep and vast') which may be understood to be either religious or sexual. The place of the single woman on the threshold in 'The Inner Chamber' may be likened to the ambivalent position of the woman depicted in 'The Story of the Faithful Soul', who has actually and metaphorically 'died' the night before her wedding – perhaps to avoid committing herself to marriage.

'The Story of the Faithful Soul' may be a revision, conscious or not, of Dante Gabriel Rossetti's 'The Blessed Damozel' (published in *The Germ* in February 1850). The form, metre and rhyme of the poems are very similar.[4] In Rossetti's poem a damozel leans out 'From the gold bar of Heaven' and longs for reunion with her lover.[5] She is depicted as static, imprisoned by 'The golden barriers' of Heaven, and as heavy: 'her bosom's pressure must have made / The bar she leaned on warm'.[6] This image of entrapment is countered by Procter in 'The Story of the Faithful Soul' in that the protagonist is depicted as attempting to avoid the imprisonment of the 'faithful soul' or 'damozel' (or that of the male lover on earth who longs for her) by keeping on the move and remaining single or spare. She is depicted as spare in that she metaphorically frees herself from both the 'fleshliness' Robert Buchanan associated with Rossetti's damozel and from a relationship with a man.[7]

---

   4   *The Germ. The Literary Magazine of the Pre-Raphaelites*, Preface Andrea Rose, Oxford: Ashmolean Museum and Birmingham City Museums & Art Gallery, 1979, pp. 80–83. 'The Blessed Damozel' has six-line stanzas in 4 3 4 3 metre and an abcbdb rhyme scheme. 'The Story of the Faithful Soul' has six-line stanzas in 3 3 metre and an abcbdb rhyme scheme.

   5   ibid., p. 80.

   6   ibid., pp. 83, 81.

   7   Robert Buchanan, *The Fleshly School of Poetry and Other Phenomena of the Day*, London: Strahan & Co., 1872. 'The Fleshly School of Poetry' first appeared in the *Contemporary Review* in 1871. The Scottish critic Buchanan attacked *The Germ* as an 'unwholesome periodical' (p. 39) and accused Rossetti of exposing 'the

Her position, however, remains uncertain as she is depicted at the point of transition and as not having actually moved on. As in 'The Inner Chamber', the single woman existing on the threshold, or in an in-between space, is depicted as isolated and cut off from the full 'joy' or 'song' of her desires. Procter would almost certainly have read Elizabeth Barrett Browning's poem 'The Prisoner' (1844), which she may have been invoking when she wrote 'The Inner Chamber'. In this poem the prisoner of the title describes her or himself as cut off from the 'music' of 'Nature', which may be read as her own 'Nature':

> Nature's lute
> Sounds on, behind this door so closely shut,
> A strange wild music to the prisoner's ears,
> Dilated by the distance, till the brain
> Grows dim with fancies which it feels too fine . . .[8]

As well as cutting herself off from romantic love and desire, the singer in 'The Inner Chamber' may also be understood to be retreating from the father's 'Nature' and his 'music'. In Chapter 4 I discussed Procter's problematic relationship to her father's potency and weakness as a poet, and to the fear of entering into his world of often violent and deathly visions. In 'The Inner Chamber' Procter seems to be expressing a fear that her father's 'magical art' may transform her own music and throw it 'back on' her 'heart', perhaps to the detriment of her singing ('Yet I sing not the song of old').

She may fear his voice of 'soft despair' – the voice of someone who feels trapped by his own particular brand of 'magic'. Bryan Procter, in the poem

---

most secret mysteries of sexual connection' (p. 37) and of choosing to convey 'mere animal sensations, that we merely shudder at the shameless nakedness'. Buchanan is referring to Rossetti's sonnet 'Nuptial Sleep' in these comments.

It is interesting that Procter chose to exclude most of the details of the folk-tale upon which, according to F. Janku, 'The Story of the Faithful Soul' is based (op. cit., Janku, p. 59). In the Flemish folk-tale 'L'Ame du Purgatoire', a young woman, Beatrix, falls in love with her husband's nephew and when her husband finds out he has Beatrix murdered. Her lover, who does not know of the murder, thinks Beatrix has deceived and left him. When Beatrix returns to earth, by permission of the archangel, she arrives to find her lover, Paul, very drunk in his castle and carousing with a young woman ('sa tête reposait sur les genoux d'une jeune fille'). The rest of the story is the same as in the poem (*Legendes et Traditions Surnaturelles des Flandres*, S. Henry Berthoud, Paris: Garnier Frères, Libraires, 1862, pp. 415–422). Procter's poem is free from the more 'fleshly' details of the folk legend.

   8   Elizabeth Barrett Browning, *Poems*, Selected and Arranged by Robert Browning, London: John Murray, 1908, p. 349.

'An Interior', which Adelaide Procter may well be invoking, gives voice to and names the fear of the potency associated with 'the inner chamber' of his daughter's poem. He investigates the heart's interior: 'What's here? Belief? – impiety?' He also sees something which threatens the capacity for thought and feeling:

> A bubble, swollen to its best,
> Its largest shape; yet overmuch.
> 'Twill shrink, I fancy, at a touch:
> Yet I'll not touch it: – Let it rest,
> An egg within a viper's nest.
>
> Hatched into life, I see it swell,
> Burst, bare at once its poison fangs.
> Alas, sir, on how little hangs
> My life; your doing ill or well.
> Who'd think that *you* would ring my knell?

The speaker concludes, though, by unconvincingly reassuring himself that the secret 'unborn sins' once 'mixed and massed with other ground' will not be life-threatening.[9]

Adelaide Procter's fear of the viper's 'sting', expressed in her poem 'From "Phantastes"' (see Chapter 4), takes on an added significance when read in the light of her father's poem. It is a 'sting' at the heart of the creative process which her father so often avoids in his poetry by expelling pain through depictions of exile, madness and death.

Bryan Procter's repeated anticipations of his own demise or death 'knell' as a poet suggest that he had given up the struggle with his own potentialities as a poet and preferred to let things rest. In an undated, unpublished and untitled poem Bryan Procter writes:

> 1
> *You* are soaring to the sun;
>   *I* rest in shade:
> *Your* delights are never won;
>   *My* couch is made
> Underneath the evening hours,
> Amidst sweet (the sweetest) flowers.

---

9   Barry Cornwall, *Dramatic Scenes With Other Poems*, London: Chapman and Hall, 1857, pp. 316–318.

2
Your road is strewn with strife;
  Mine with perfume;
You burn the rose of Life:
  I nurse the bloom
In the sun the shade the showers,
Thorough all the circling hours.[10]

If this poem was written with his daughter in mind it would seem that Bryan Procter was passing on the 'strife' to a poet daughter who will achieve where he has failed. She is therefore burdened with the struggle for creativity he has relinquished as well as with her own. The temptation not to look any further at the 'meaning' of her song may have been strong if she felt weighed down by such responsibility. Procter may even have envied her father's capacity for resting in the 'shade'.

The poem 'Envy' in this light may be read as a daughter's anger at the enviable position of a father who *as* her father is 'first always' and perhaps wins the race by not having fully entered into it in the first place:

He was the first always: Fortune
  Shone bright in his face.
I fought for years; with no effort
  He conquered the place:
We ran; my feet were all bleeding,
  But he won the race.

(p. 166, ll. 1–6)

Procter's editorial father, Charles Dickens, may well have appeared to Procter as a father who exerted a stronger, more controlling and apparently less fraught authority. Crossing the threshold of Dickens's journals enabled Procter to become a recognised and acclaimed poet. She may have felt, though, that she was still to an extent like 'An infant crying in the night . . . And with no language but a cry'.[11] Dickens's placing and framing of her poetry in the Christmas numbers of *Household Words* and *All The Year Round* shows the extent to which Procter's poetry is both included and metaphorically excluded by Dickens.

Procter's poem 'The Child and the Bird', which appeared in *Household Words* in 1856 (but was not published in any collected works until 1905),

---

[10] MS P964, University of Iowa Libraries.
[11] Tennyson, 'In Memoriam', *Poems and Plays*, Ed. T. Herbert Warren, Oxford University Press, 1971, p. 243.

graphically and poignantly illustrates what the singer on Dickens's threshold may have been feeling. The poem takes the form of a dialogue between a child and a bird. The child asks the bird why she no longer sings and whether she would prefer a 'silken chain' to the 'coarse thread' which keeps her tethered. The child then ties the bird with 'a golden string' but as this still does not satisfy the 'Ungrateful bird' bids the bird 'fly!'. The bird replies:

> Ah! these chains are bright and fine,
> But for these I did not pine.
> Thou hast made me once more free,
> And I longed for liberty.
> Keep, oh! keep thy chains of gold,
> But never more a captive hold.
> What is silver to the sheen
> Of the dew-drops on the green?
> What is gold to beams of light
> That sparkle in the morning bright?
> Nought glads me like my own free will,
> And golden fetters are fetters still.[12]

By remaining on the threshold of 'the inner chamber' the speaker remains in thrall to whatever is behind the 'door of gold' which shuts her out but still exerts power over her. Like the bird in 'The Child and the Bird' she remains fettered by her 'golden' authorities. The fact that the bird escapes from a child suggests that the metaphor of the child which Procter often employs in her poetry may itself be imprisoning. By investing the figure of the child with unresolved emotions and with responsibility for those emotions the adult woman poet may be held back from pursuing her own 'free will' and authority.

'The Inner Chamber' powerfully suggests the presence of fear and acute anxiety that the poet will lose the words of her song by moving from her place and her childlike status on the threshold into the 'inner chamber' and a deeper knowledge of what it holds, as well as by moving away into unexplored territory.

By the close of Procter's poetic career she had boldly explored and critically responded to the religious, poetic, paternal and editorial voices

---

[12] *The Complete Works of Adelaide A. Procter*, Intro. Charles Dickens, London: George Bell & Sons, 1905, pp. 364–366.
  Adelaide Anne Procter, 'The Child and the Bird ("A Fable versified")', December 1862, MS P9638ch, University of Iowa Libraries. This manuscript postdates the appearance of the poem in *Household Words*.

which peopled the 'inner chamber' of her imagination and thought. If she had lived longer no doubt she would have continued to develop an already maturing poetic voice. The intelligence and lyrical intensity of her voice, however, continue to resonate. Thomas Carlyle wrote:

> all passionate language does of itself become musical, – with a finer music than mere accent; the speech of a man even in zealous anger becomes a chant, a song. All deep things are Song . . . See deep enough, and you see musically; the heart of Nature *being* everywhere music, if you can reach it.[13]

Adelaide Procter's poetry is both 'passionate' and 'musical', and it is unafraid of exploring emotional depths. Such an exploration enabled her to recognise that, with all the important and complex searching of and for 'meaning', there remains something 'unexpressed' – an 'undercurrent' which resists the specificity of words but is strong in the knowledge that:

> the music sounds just the same.
>
> ('The Inner Chamber', p. 263, l. 32)

13 Thomas Carlyle, 'The Hero as Poet: Dante, Shakespeare', in *On Heroes, Hero-Worship, and the Heroic in History*, 1840 (*The Victorian Poet: Poetics and Persona*, Ed. Joseph Bristow, London: Croom Helm Ltd., 1987, pp. 68-69).

Appendix

Poems and articles by Adelaide Procter published in *Household Words, All the Year Round, The English Woman's Journal, The Cornhill Magazine* and *Good Words*

The titles in parentheses are the titles which appear in Adelaide Anne Procter, *Legends and Lyrics Together with A Chaplet of Verses*, Oxford University Press, 1914.

Most of the poems appeared in the First Series (1858) and the Second Series (1861) of *Legends and Lyrics*. The poems printed only in *Household Words* and *All the Year Round* are 'Words Upon the Waters' (1854), 'Hidden Light' (1854) and 'Watch Cry: from a German Patois Song' (1856). 'A Fable Versified' was published under the title 'The Child and the Bird' in *The Complete Works of Adelaide A. Procter*, London: George Bell & Sons, 1905, pp. 364-366. The poem 'Moonrise' (26.8.1854) which is attributed to Procter in Lohrli (see below) is by Edmund Ollier.

The poems printed in the Christmas numbers of *Household Words* and *All the Year Round* were usually untitled. The titles given are the titles which appear in *Legends and Lyrics*.

Most of the poems were unattributed in the journals. The poems appearing in *Household Words* and *All the Year Round* are attributed in *Household Words. Table of Contents. List of Contributors*, Compiled by Anne Lohrli, University of Toronto Press, 1973.

Household Words

Vol. VI

5.2.1853	Old Echoes (The Voices of the Past)
5.3.1853	Friend Sorrow
14.5.1853	Hush!
21.5.1853	The Settlers
30.7.1853	Listening Angels

Vol. VIII

3.9.1853	Echoes
10.9.1853	Pictures in the Fire
15.10.1853	A Lament for the Summer
26.11.1853	Now
Christmas 1853	The Angel's Story

Vol. IX
11.3.1854	The Voice of the Wind
18.3.1854	Home-Sickness
6.5.1854	Words upon the Waters
13.5.1854	Treasures
20.5.1854	A True Knight (A Knight Errant)
8.7.1854	Illusion
15.7.1854	Recollections
22.7.1854	Shining Stars

Vol. X
26.8.1854	Hidden Light (co-written with Charles Dickens)
14.10.1854	Waiting
21.10.1854	My Picture
11.11.1854	A Vision
18.11.1854	Give
Christmas 1854	The Sailor Boy
	A Legend of Bregenz
13.1.1855	The Two Spirits
27.1.1855	The Cradle Song of the Poor

Vol. XI
3.2.1855	The Lesson of the War
10.3.1855	Passing Clouds (A Doubting Heart)
17.3.1855	One by One
7.4.1855	The Unknown Grave
14.4.1855	A False Genius
5.5.1855	God's Gifts
19.5.1855	A First Sorrow
2.6.1855	The Wind
9.6.1855	Strive, Wait, and Pray
30.6.1855	A Vision of Hours (Hours)
7.7.1855	The Angel (The Angel of Death)
14.7.1855	Time's Cure (Changes)

Vol. XII
11.8.1855	Judge Not
18.8.1855	Comfort
22.9.1855	Wishes
6.10.1855	A Dream
13.10.1855	The Present
17.11.1855	The Dark Side
15.12.1855	The Two Interpreters
Christmas 1855	The Wayside Inn
29.12.1855	A Tomb in Ghent

Vol. XIII
19.1.1856   Murmurs
2.2.1856   Lavater's Warning (Borrowed Thoughts, I. From 'Lavater')
22.3.1856   Watch Cry. From a German Patois Song
29.3.1856   A Fable Versified (The Child and the Bird)
12.4.1856   A Remembrance of Autumn
31.5.1856   Sowing and Reaping
14.6.1856   The Chain (A Chain)

Vol. XIV
6.9.1856   My Journal
6.12.1856   Patient and Faithful (Fidelis)
Christmas 1856 Homeward Bound

Vol. XVI
1.8.1857   A Dead Past

Vol. XVII
2.1.1858   Sixty New Years' Days Ago (True Honours)
6.2.1858   A Woman's Question
20.2.1858   Words
27.3.1858   Two Dark Days (Life in Death and Death in Life)
24.4.1858   Home and Rest (Home at Last)

Vol. XVIII
21.8.1858   Three Roses
28.8.1858   An Ideal
2.10.1858   Beyond
9.10.1858   Two Worlds

Vol. XIX
Christmas 1858 Three Evenings in a House (Three Evenings in a Life)
1.1.1859   A New Mother
8.1.1859   Hidden Chords (Unseen)
5.3.1859   A Warning
12.3.1859   Envy

All the Year Round

Vol. I
14.5.1859   A Thought From 'Phantastes' ('Borrowed Thoughts, II, From
                "Phantastes"')
27.8.1859   Over the Mountain
3.9.1859   Dream-Life

Vol. II
29.10.1859   Our Dead
Christmas 1859 A Legend of Provence

Vol. III
2.6.1860   Too Late

Vol. IV
13.10.1860   My Will

The English Woman's Journal

Poems

Vol. I
March 1858   Grief

Vol. II
September 1858   Maximus
February 1859   Optimus

Vol. IV
October 1859   Loss and Gain (Light and Shade)

Vol. V
March 1860   A Lost Chord
May 1860   Requital (The Requital)

Vol. VI
November 1860   A Comforter
January 1861   The Old Year's Blessing

Prose

Vol. IV
September and   Adventures of Your Own Correspondents in Search of Solitude
   October 1859
December 1859   Letter reporting on a visit to a watch-making factory in
                 Christchurch, Dorset

Vol. VI
December 1860,   Madame Récamier
   January and
   February 1861

The Cornhill Magazine

Vol. I
March 1860   A Changeling
May 1860   The Carver's Lesson

Vol. II
September 1860   Fate and a Heart (The Tyrant and the Captive)
November 1860   Sent to Heaven

Good Words

1862   True or False? (True or False) (Illus. A.B. Houghton)
1863   Golden Words

Bibliography

1. Manuscripts: poems by Adelaide Procter

Girton College Library (By Permission of the Mistress and Fellows of Girton College, Cambridge):

BRP X 79:   'For M.M.H', signed 'Adelaide', dated 23rd January, 1858. [Matilda Hays] This poem appeared in *Legends and Lyrics* under the title 'A Retrospect'.

BRP X 80/1:   Untitled poem beginning 'Thou hast done well to kneel and say', signed 'Adelaide A. Procter'. This poem appeared in *The English Woman's Journal* under the title 'Loss and Gain' (October 1859) and in *Legends and Lyrics* as 'Light and Shade'.

BRP X 81/1:   Printed copies of 'The Army of the Lord'.

BRP X 82:   Untitled poem beginning 'Oh, to have dwelt in Bethlehem'. This poem appeared in 'A Chaplet of Verses' under the title 'A Desire'.

University of Iowa Libraries (By Permission of the University of Iowa Libraries (Iowa City)):

'The Child & the Bird (A Fable Versified)' signed 'Adelaide Anne Procter', dated December 1862.

2. Manuscripts: poems by Bryan Procter (Barry Cornwall):

University of Iowa Libraries:

'To my Child', signed B.C., dated 30th October 1825.
Untitled and undated, 'You are soaring to the sun'.
Undated, 'To a Poet, abandoning his Art', signed B.C.

3. Manuscripts: letters

Two substantial holdings of letters in manuscript relating to the Procter family are held by Girton College Library and University of Iowa Libraries.
Girton College hold 56 letters, 54 of which constitute the holding BRP VIII: 1-58. The letters are to Bessie Rayner Parkes.
The University of Iowa hold approximately 157 letters, most of which are letters written by Bryan Procter. There are five written by Adelaide Procter.

The following are the letters quoted in this volume:

Abbreviations: AP   (Adelaide Procter)
                BRP   (Bessie Rayner Parkes)
                BP   (Bryan Procter)

Girton College Library:

23.6.1848	BRP to Mary Swainson, BRP III, 17.
17.2.1855	AP to BRP, BRP VIII, 3/1.
4.7.1862	Letter and note, AAP to BRP, BRP VIII, 24/1, 24/2.
30.7.1862	AP to BRP, BRP VIII, 25.
undated	AP to BRP, BRP VIII, 37/1.
undated	AP to BRP, BRP VIII, 38/2.
undated	AP to BRP, BRP VIII, 39.
undated	AP to BRP, BRP VIII, 58/1.

University of Iowa Libraries:

23.5.1851	BP to Robert Browning.
5.11.1851	BP to Robert Browning.
21.11.1856	BP to Robert Browning.
22.6.1857	James Leigh Hunt to BP.
7.9.1858	BP to Robert Browning and Elizabeth Barrett Browning.
23.7.1860	AP to John Pyke Hullah.

4. Adelaide Procter: poetry

The poems quoted in this volume, with page and line number, are from *Legends and Lyrics Together with A Chaplet of Verses*, Oxford University Press, 1914, unless otherwise stated.

[Procter, Adelaide Anne], 'Ministering Angels', *Heath's Book of Beauty*, Ed. The Countess of Blessington, London: Longman, Brown, Green and Longmans, 1843.

Procter, Adelaide Anne, *Legends and Lyrics. A Book of Verses*, 2 Vols, London: Bell and Daldy, 1858-1861.

Procter, Adelaide Anne, *A Chaplet of Verses*, With an Illustration by Richard Doyle, London: Longman, Green, Longman, & Roberts, 1862.

Procter, Adelaide Anne, *Legends and Lyrics*, Intro. Charles Dickens, Illustrated by W.T.C. Dobson, Samuel Palmer, J. Tenniel, George H. Thomas, Lorenz Frohlich, W.H. Millais, G. Du Maurier, W.P. Burton, J.D. Watson, Charles Keene, J.M. Carrick, M.E. Edwards, T. Morten, London: Bell and Daldy, 1866.

Procter, Adelheid Anna, *Ausgewahlte Gedichte*, Ed. C. Schluter & H. Brinckmann, Koln und Neuss, 1867.

Procter, Adelaide Anne, *Legends and Lyrics*, London: Bell and Daldy, 1868.

The Poems of Adelaide A. Procter, Boston: Fields, Osgood & Co., 1870.

Procter, Adelaide Anne, *Legends and Lyrics. A Book of Verses*, Intro. Charles Dickens, London: Bell and Daldy, 1871.

The Poems of Adelaide A. Procter, Boston: Houghton, Mifflin and Company, 1881.

Procter, Adelaide Anne, *The Angel's Story*, Illustrated by Charles O. Murray, London: George Bell and Sons, 1881.

Procter, Adelaide Anne, *Legends and Lyrics. A Book of Verses*, Intro. Charles Dickens, London: George Bell and Sons, 1882.

Procter, Adelaide Anne, *Legends and Lyrics. A Book of Verses*, Intro. Charles Dickens, Illustrations by Ida Lovering, London: George Bell and Sons, 1895.

Procter, Adelaide Anne, *Legends and Lyrics. A Book of Verses*, First Series, London: George Bell & Sons, 1903.

Procter, Adelaide Anne, *The Complete Works of Adelaide A. Procter*, Intro. Charles Dickens, London: George Bell & Sons, 1905.

Procter, Adelaide Anne, *Legends and Lyrics Together With A Chaplet of Verses*, Oxford University Press, 1914.

Prose

Adelaide Anne Procter, 'Adventures of Your Own Correspondents in Search of Solitude', *The English Woman's Journal*, IV, 1859, pp. 34-44, 100-114.

Letter to *The English Woman's Journal* (re: watchmakers), IV, 1859, pp. 278-279.

Adelaide Anne Procter, 'Madame Recamier', *The English Woman's Journal*, VI, 1860, pp. 225-236; 1861, pp. 297-305, 373-383.

5. Nineteenth-century poetry

Arnold, Edwin, 'Adelaide Anne Procter. "Ilicet."', *The Victoria Magazine*, II, 1864, pp. 385-386.

Arnold, Matthew, *Poems*, London: Longman, Brown, Green, and Longmans, 1853.

Arnold, Matthew, *Selected Poetry*, Ed. Keith Silver, Manchester: Carcanet Press Limited, 1994.

Barrett Barrett, Elizabeth, *Poems*, 2 Vols, London: Edward Moxon, 1844.

Barrett Browning, Elizabeth, *Poems*, 2 Vols, London: Chapman & Hall, 1850.

Barrett Browning, Elizabeth, *Aurora Leigh*, London: Chapman and Hall, 1857.

Barrett Browning, Elizabeth, *Poems*, Selected and Arranged by Robert Browning, London: John Murray, 1908.

Barrett Browning, Elizabeth, *Selected Poems*, Ed. Malcolm Hicks, Manchester: Carcanet Press Limited, 1988.

Blake, William, *Songs of Innocence and of Experience*, Intro. Sir Geoffrey Keynes, Oxford University Press, 1970.

Bowles [Southey], Caroline, *The Birth-Day; A Poem in Three Parts: to which are added Occasional Verses*, London: William Blackwood and Sons, 1836.

The Poetical Works of Caroline Bowles Southey, William Blackwood & Sons, 1867.

Breen, Jennifer (Ed.), *Women Romantic Poets. 1785-1832 An Anthology*, London: J.M. Dent & Sons Ltd., 1992.

Breen, Jennifer (Ed.), *Victorian Women Poets. 1830-1901. An Anthology*, London: Everyman, 1994.

Browning, Robert, 'The Boy and the Angel', *Hood's Magazine and Comic Miscellany*, II, 1844, pp. 140-142.

Browning, Robert, *Bells and Pomegranates*, London: Edward Moxon, 1844, 1845.

Browning, Robert, *Men and Women*, 2 Vols, London: Chapman and Hall, 1855.

The Poetical Works of Robert Browning, 3 Vols, London: Chapman and Hall, 1863.

Selections from the Poetical Works of Robert Browning, Ed. J. Forster and B.W. Procter, London: Chapman & Hall, 1863.

Robert Browning's Poetry, Ed. James F. Loucks, New York and London: W.W. Norton & Company, 1979.

Browning, Robert, *Selected Poetry*, Ed. Daniel Karlin, London: Penguin Books Ltd., 1989.

Cary, Alice, *Ballads, Lyrics, and Hymns*, New York: Hurd and Houghton, 1866.

Cornwall, Barry, *Dramatic Scenes and Other Poems*, London: Printed for C. and J. Ollier, 1819.

[Cornwall, Barry], 'Midsummer Madness', *The Literary Gazette and Journal of Belles Lettres, Arts, Sciences, etc. For the Year 1820*, 1820, p. 161.

Cornwall, Barry, *Marcian Colonna. An Italian Tale with Three Dramatic Scenes and Other Poems*, London: John Warren and C & J Ollier, 1820.

Cornwall, Barry, *The Flood of Thessaly, The Girl of Provence and Other Poems*, London: Printed for Henry Colburn and Co., 1823.

The Poetical Works of Milman, Bowles, Wilson and Barry Cornwall, Paris: A. and W. Galignani, 1829.

Cornwall, Barry, *English Songs and Other small Poems*, London: Edward Moxon, 1832.

Cornwall, Barry, 'An Apology in Verse', *Heath's Book of Beauty*, Ed. The Countess of Blessington, London: Longman, Brown, Green and Longmans, 1843.

Cornwall, Barry, 'A Song for Greybeards', 'Flax Spinners', 'The Last Stave', *Hood's Magazine and Comic Miscellany*, I, 1844, pp. 169, 395–396, 423.

Cornwall, Barry, *English Songs and Other small Poems*, London: Chapman and Hall, 1851.

Cornwall, Barry, 'Verdict – "Found Dead"', *The Keepsake*, Ed. Miss Power, 1850, pp. 37–39.

Cornwall, Barry, 'The Mother's Last Song', *The Keepsake*, Ed. Miss Power, 1851, p. 101.

Cornwall, Barry, *Dramatic Scenes With Other Poems*, London: Chapman and Hall, 1857.

Cornwall, Barry, 'Trade Songs', *All The Year Round*, I, 1859, pp. 20, 36, 61, 88–89, 109, 131–132, 156, 189.

'Ghent', *Fisher's Drawing Room Scrap-Book*, 1851, p. 49.

The Germ. The Literary Magazine of the Pre-Raphaelites, Preface. Andrea Rose, Oxford: Ashmolean Museum and Birmingham City Museums & Art Gallery, 1979.

Hays, Matilda M., 'In Memoriam. Adelaide Anne Procter', *The English Woman's Journal*, XIII, 1864, p. 109.

The Complete Works of Mrs Hemans, Edited by Her Sister, [Harriet Hughes], 2 Vols, New York: D. Appleton and Company, 1856.

Hood, Thomas, 'The Bridge of Sighs', *Hood's Magazine and Comic Miscellany*, I, 1844, pp. 414–417.

Howitt, Mary, *Hymns and Fire-Side Verses*, London: Darton & Clark, 1839.

Howitt, Mary, *Ballads & Other Poems*, London: Longman, Brown, Green, & Longmans, 1847.

Ingelow, Jean, *Poems*, London: Longman, Green, Longman, Roberts, & Green, 1863.

The Poetical Works of John Keats, London: Edward Moxon, 1846.

[Keble, John], *The Christian Year: Thoughts in Verse for the Sundays and Holydays Throughout the Year*, 2 Vols, Oxford: Printed by W. Baxter, for J. Parker; and C. and J. Rivington, London, 1827.

[Keble, John], *The Christian Year: Thoughts in Verse for the Sundays and Holydays Throughout the Year*, London: James Parker and Co., [1870].

[Keble, John], *Lyra Innocentium: Thoughts in Verse on Christian Children, Their Ways, and Their Privileges*, Oxford: John Henry Parker; F. and J. Rivington, London, 1846.

The Poetical Works of L.E.L., London: Longman, Rees, Orme, Brown & Green, 1830.

Leigh Hunt, James, *Rimini and Other Poems*, Boston: William Ticknor & Company, 1844.

Leighton, Angela & Margaret Reynolds (Eds),*Victorian Women Poets. An Anthology*, Oxford: Blackwell Publishers Ltd., 1995.

Longfellow, Henry Wadsworth, *The Belfry of Bruges and Other Poems*, Cambridge, Mass: John Owen, 1846.

Meredith, George, *Modern Love and Poems of the English Roadside, With Poems and Ballads*, London: Chapman & Hall, 1862.

Miles, Alfred H. (Ed.), *The Poets and the Poetry of the Century. Joanna Baillie to Mathilde Blind*, 10 Vols, London: Hutchinson & Co., 1891-1897, Vol. 7.

Neuberger, Julia (Ed.), *The Things That Matter. An Anthology of Women's Spiritual Poetry*, London: Kyle Cathie Limited, 1992.

Norris, Pamela (Ed.), *Sound the Deep Waters. Women's Romantic Poetry in the Victorian Age*, London: Little, Brown and Company (UK) Limited, 1991.

Parkes, Bessie Rayner, *Poems*, London: John Chapman, 1855.

Procter, Adelaide A. (Ed.), *The Victoria Regia: A Volume of Original Contributions in Poetry and Prose*, London: Printed and Published by Emily Faithfull and Co., Victoria Press, (for the Employment of Women,) Great Coram Street, W.C., 1861.

Procter, Bryan Waller, *A Sicilian Story and Mirandola*, Intro. Donald H. Reiman, New York and London: Garland Publishing, Inc., 1977.

Reilly, Catherine (Ed.), *Winged Words. Victorian Women's Poetry and Verse*, London: Enitharmon Press, 1994.

Ricks, Christopher (Ed.), *The New Oxford Book of Victorian Verse*, Oxford University Press, 1987.

The Collected Poems. Lyrical and Narrative of A. Mary F. Robinson (Madame Duclaux), London: T. Fisher Unwin, 1902 .

Rossetti, Christina G., *Time Flies. A Reading Diary*, London: Society for Promoting Christian Knowledge, 1885.

Rossetti, Christina G., *Poems*, London: Macmillan & Co., 1891.

A Choice of Christina Rossetti's Verse, Ed. Elizabeth Jennings, London: Faber and Faber Limited, 1970.

Rossetti, Christina, *Poems and Prose*, Ed. Jan Marsh, London: Everyman, 1994.

The Poetical Works of Dante Gabriel Rossetti, Ed. William M. Rossetti, London: Ellis and Elvey, 1891.

Sharp, Mrs William (Ed.) *Women's Voices. An Anthology of the Most Characteristic Poems by English, Scotch, and Irish Women*, London: Walter Scott, 1887.

Tennyson, *Poems and Plays*, Ed. T. Herbert Warren, Oxford University Press, 1971.

Tennyson, *A Selected Edition*, Ed. Christopher Ricks, Harlow: Longman Group UK Limited, 1989.

Webster, Augusta, *Mother and Daughter. An Uncompleted Sonnet Sequence*, Introductory Note, William Michael Rossetti, London: Macmillan & Co., 1895.

[Williams, Isaac], *The Cathedral, or the Catholic and Apostolic Church in England*, Oxford: John Henry Parker, F. and J. Rivington, London, 1848.

Wordsworth and Coleridge, *Lyrical Ballads. 1798*, Ed. W.J.B. Owen, Oxford University Press, 1969.

6. Nineteenth-century prose

[Belloc, Bessie Rayner (née Parkes)], 'The Poems of Adelaide Anne Procter', *The Month*, IV, 1866, pp. 79-88.

Belloc, Bessie Rayner (née Parkes), *In a Walled Garden*, London: Ward and Downey, 1895.

Belloc, Madame (née Parkes), *The Flowing Tide*, London: Sands & Co., 1900.

Berthoud, S. Henry, 'L'Ame du Purgatoire', *Legendes et Traditions Surnaturelles des Flandres*, Paris: Garnier Frères, Libraires, 1862, pp. 415-422.

Boucherett, Jessie, 'Adelaide Anne Procter', *The English Woman's Journal*, XIII, 1864, pp. 17-21.

Bristow, Joseph (Ed.), *The Victorian Poet: Poetics and Persona*, London: Croom Helm Ltd., 1987

Brodrick, G.C., 'A History of the University of Oxford', *Epochs of Church History*, Ed. Rev. Mandell Creighton, London: Longmans, Green & Co., 1886.

Brontë, Charlotte, *Jane Eyre*, Ed. Q.D. Leavis, London: Penguin Books Ltd., 1966.

Brontë, Charlotte, *Shirley*, Ed. Andrew and Judith Hook, London: Penguin Books Ltd., 1974.

Brontë, Emily, *Wuthering Heights*, Ed. David Daiches, London: Penguin Books Ltd., 1965.

New Letters of Robert Browning, Ed. William Clyde De Vane and Kenneth Leslie Knickerbocker, Yale University Press, 1950.

Robert Browning and Elizabeth Barrett. The Courtship Correspondence 1845-1846, Ed. Daniel Karlin, Oxford University Press, 1990.

Buchanan, Robert, *The Fleshly School of Poetry and Other Phenomena of the Day*, London: Strahan & Co., 1872.

Buckle, Henry Thomas, *History of Civilization in England* (1857), 3 Vols, London: Longmans, Green and Co., 1869.

Cornwall, Barry, 'A May Dream', *The London Magazine*, 1821, III, pp. 477-483.

Cornwall, Barry, *The Life of Edmund Kean*, 2 Vols, London: Edward Moxon, 1835.

Cornwall, Barry, *Essays and Tales in Prose*, 2 Vols, Boston: Ticknor, Reed and Fields, 1853.

Cornwall, Barry, *Charles Lamb. A Memoir*, London: Edward Moxon & Co., 1866.

[Costello, Dudley], 'Blank Babies in Paris', *Household Words*, VIII, 1853, pp. 379-382.

Darwin, Charles, *The Origin of Species By Means of Natural Selection or the Preservation of Favoured Races in the Struggle for Life* (1859), London: John Murray, 1911, pp. 207-208.

Darwin, Charles, *The Expression of the Emotions in Man and Animals* (1872), Ed. Francis Darwin, London: John Murray, 1892.

Dickens, Charles, *David Copperfield*, Ed. Trevor Blount, London: Penguin Books, 1966.

Dickens, Charles, *Bleak House*, Ed. Norman Page, Harmondsworth: Penguin Books Ltd., 1971.

Dickens, Charles, *Christmas Books*, London: Chapman and Hall, 1852.

[Dickens, Charles and W.H. Wills], 'Received, a Blank Child' , *Household Words*, VII, 1853, pp. 49-53.

Dickens, Charles, *Hard Times*, Ed. David Craig, Penguin Books, 1985.

Dickens, Charles and Wilkie Collins, *The Wreck of the Golden Mary*, Illus. John Dugan, London: Methuen & Co. Ltd., 1961.

Dickens, Charles, *Christmas Stories*, Intro. Margaret Lane, London: Oxford University Press, 1956.

The Ghost Stories of Charles Dickens, Ed. Peter Haining, 2 Vols, Sevenoaks: Coronet Books, Hodder and Stoughton, 1982.

The Letters of Charles Dickens, Ed. His Sister-in-Law and His Eldest Daughter [Georgina Hogarth and Mary Dickens], 2 Vols, London: Chapman and Hall, Limited, 1882.

The Letters of Charles Dickens, Ed. Walter Dexter, 3 Vols, Bloomsbury: The Nonesuch Press, 1938.

The Uncollected Writings of Charles Dickens. Household Words 1850–1859, Ed. Harry Stone, 2 Vols, London: Allen Lane, The Penguin Press, 1969.

'A Triad of Poetesses', *Dublin University Magazine. A Literary and Political Journal*, LIII, 1859, pp. 398–406.

Eliot, George, *Silas Marner: The Weaver of Raveloe*, Edinburgh and London: William Blackwood and Sons, 1861.

Eliot, George, *Middlemarch*, Ed. Rosemary Ashton, London: Penguin Books Ltd., 1994.

'Legends and Lyrics. A Book of Verses. By Adelaide Ann [sic] Procter. Bell and Daldy, London', *The English Woman's Journal*, I, pp. 341–344.

'Legends and Lyrics: A Book of Verses. By Adelaide Anne Procter. Second Volume. Bell and Daldy, Fleet Street', *The English Woman's Journal*, VI, pp. 354–356.

The Essays of Ralph Waldo Emerson, Intro. Edward F. O'Day, San Francisco: John Henry Nash, 1934.

Fields, James T., *Old Acquaintance. Barry Cornwall and Some of His Friends*, Boston: James R. Osgood and Company, 1876.

Fisher's Drawing Room Scrap-Book, London: The Caxton Press, 1851.

[Fothergill Chorley, Henry], 'Legends and Lyrics: a Book of Verses. By Adelaide Procter. (Bell & Daldy)', *The Athenaeum*, I, 1858, p. 712.

[Fothergill Chorley, Henry], 'Legends and Lyrics: A Book of Verses. By Adelaide Anne Procter. Second Volume (Bell & Daldy)', *The Athenaeum*, II, 1860, p. 907.

Froude, James Anthony (Ed.), *Reminiscences by Thomas Carlyle*, 2 Vols, London: Longmans, Green, and Co., 1881, I, pp. 223–229.

Gaskell, Elizabeth, *Mary Barton: A Tale of Manchester Life*, Ed. Stephen Gill, London: Penguin Books Ltd., 1970.

Gaskell, Elizabeth, *Sylvia's Lovers*, Intro: Arthur Pollard, London: J.M. Dent & Sons Ltd., 1964.

The Letters of Mrs Gaskell, Ed. J.A.V. Chapple and Arthur Pollard, Manchester University Press, 1966.

[Gibson, Mary W.A.], 'Lost Alice', *Household Words*, XVII, 1858, pp. 438–445.

Goethe, J.W. von, *Wilhelm Meister's Apprenticeship and Travels*. From the German of Goethe, Trans. Thomas Carlyle, 3 Vols, London: Chapman and Hall, 1842.

Greenwell, Dora, *Essays*, London: Alexander Strahan, 1866.

Hall, S.C., *A Book of Memories of Great Men and Women of the Age*, London: Virtue & Co., 1871, p. 416.

Hawthorne, Nathaniel, *The Scarlet Letter*, London: The Amalgamated Press Ltd., 1905.

Heisterbacensis, Caesarius, 'Item de Beatrice custode', *Dialogus Miraculorum*, Ed. Joseph Strange, 2 Vols, Cologne, Bonn & Brussels: J.M. Heberle (H. Lempertz & Comp.), 1851, II, pp. 42–43.

Jameson, Mrs, *Sisters of Charity and The Communion of Labour. Two Lectures on the Social Employments of Women. With a Prefatory Letter to The Right Hon. Lord John Russell, President of the National Association for the Promotion of Social Science. On the Present Condition and Requirements of the Women of England*, London: Longman, Brown, Green, Longmans, and Roberts, 1859.

Anna Jameson, *A Commonplace Book of Thoughts, Memories, and Fancies*, London: Longman, Brown, Green, and Longmans, 1855.

Anna Jameson. Letters and Friendships (1812–1860), Ed. Mrs Steuart Erskine, London: T. Fisher Unwin Ltd., 1915.

Jones, Edmund D. (Ed.), *English Critical Essays (Nineteenth Century)*, London: Oxford University Press, 1916.

Julian, John (Ed.) *A Dictionary of Hymnology. Setting Forth the Origin and History of Christian Hymns of all Ages and Nations With Special Reference to Those Contained in the Hymn Books of English Speaking Countries, and Now in Common Use*, London: John Murray, 1892, pp. 913, 975.

Keble, John, *National Apostasy Considered in a Sermon Preached in St Mary's, Oxford, Before His Majesty's Judges of Assize, On Sunday, July 14, 1833*, Oxford: S. Collingwood for J.H. Parker and J.G. and F. Rivington, London, 1833.

[Keble, John], 'Tract No. 89. On the Mysticism Attributed to the Early Fathers of the Church', *Tracts for the Times by Members of the University of Oxford*, 6 Vols (1833–41), London: J.G.F. and J. Rivington; and J.H. Parker, Oxford, 1840–41. V and VI for 1838–41.

Keble's Lectures on Poetry. 1832–41, Trans. Edward Kershaw Francis, 2 Vols, Oxford at the Clarendon Press, 1912.

Kemble, Frances Ann, *Record of a Girlhood*, 3 Vols, London: Richard Bentley and Son, 1879, p. 176.

Kinglake, A.W., 'Preface' to *Eothen*, Intro. Barbara Kreiger, Vermont: The Marlboro Press, 1992.

The Language of Flowers with Illustrative Poetry; To Which are now First Added The Calendar of Flowers and The Dial of Flowers, London: Saunders and Otley, 1835.

[Lockhart, J.G.], 'On the Cockney School of Poetry. No. I', *Blackwood's Edinburgh Magazine*, II, 1817, pp. 38–41.

[Lockhart, J.G.], 'On the Cockney School of Poetry. No. IV', *Blackwood's Edinburgh Magazine*, III, 1818, pp. 519–524.

[Lockhart, J.G.?], 'Dramatic Scenes, and Other Poems, by Barry Cornwall', *Blackwood's Edinburgh Magazine*, V, 1819, pp. 310–316.

[Lockhart, J.G.], 'Remarks on Mr Barry Cornwall's New Poems', *Blackwood's Edinburgh Magazine*, XIII, 1823, pp. 532–541.

'Review of *A Sicilian Story, with Diego de Montilla, and Other Poems*. Barry Cornwall', *The London Magazine*, I, 1820, pp. 84–86.

'The Flood of Thessaly, The Girl of Provence, and Other Poems. By Barry Cornwall', *The London Magazine*, VII, 1823, pp. 460–462.

[Loudon, Agnes], 'The Little Chorister', *Household Words*, XII, 1855, pp. 27–36.

Macdonald, George, *Phantastes. A Faerie Romance for Men and Women*, Ed. Greville MacDonald, London: Arthur C. Fifield, 1905.

The Diaries of William Charles Macready 1833–1851, Ed. William Toynbee, 2 Vols, London: Chapman and Hall, Ltd., 1912.

Maurice, F.D., *Inaugural Lecture: Queen's College: 1848*, London: The Saint George Series, Alexander Moring Limited, The De La More Press (no date).

Mayhew, Henry, *London Labour and the London Poor; A Cyclopaedia of the Condtions and Earnings of Those that Will Work, those that Cannot Work, and those that Will Not Work*, 3 Vols, London: George Woodfall and Son, 1851.

M***, [Madame M.E. Mohl], *Madame Recamier with A Sketch of the History of Society in France*, London: Chapman & Hall, 1862.

[Newman, John Henry], *Loss and Gain*, London: James Burns, 1848.

[Patmore, Coventry (Ed.)], *Bryan Waller Procter (Barry Cornwall). An Autobiographical Fragment and Biographical Notes With Personal Sketches of*

Contemporaries. Unpublished Lyrics, and Letters of Literary Friends, London: George Bell and Sons, 1877.

Pugin, A. Welby, *Contrasts: or, A Parallel Between the Noble Edifices of the Fourteenth and Fifteenth Centuries, and Similar Buildings of the Present Day; shewing the Present Decay of Taste*, London: Printed for the Author, and Published by Him, at St Marie's Grange, Near Salisbury, Wilts., 1836.

Richter, Jean Paul Friedrich, 'Life of Quintus Fixlein', *German Romance. Specimens of its Chief Authors; With Biographical and Critical Notices*, Trans. Thomas Carlyle, 4 Vols, Edinburgh: William Tait, 1827.

[Ritchie, Anne], (née Thackeray), 'Toilers and Spinsters', *The Cornhill Magazine*, III, 1861, pp. 318-331.

Robertson, Eric S., *English Poetesses: A Series of Critical Biographies With Illustrative Extracts*, London: Cassell & Company, Limited, 1883.

[Sala, George], 'Little Children', *Household Words*, VIII, pp. 289-293.

The Saturday Review of Politics, Literature, Science, and Art, 'The English Woman's Journal', V, 1858, pp. 369-370.

George Smith. A Memoir with Some Pages of Autobiography, For Private Circulation, Ed. Mrs E. Smith, London, [1902].

A Collection of Letters of W.M. Thackeray. 1847-1855, Intro. Jane Brookfield, London: Smith Elder & Co., 1887.

The Letters and Private Papers of William Makepeace Thackeray, Ed. Gordon N. Ray, 4 Vols, London: Oxford University Press, 1945, 1946.

Trilling, Lionel, and Harold Bloom, (Ed.), *Victorian Prose and Poetry*, New York: Oxford University Press, 1973.

Valentine, Laura L., *The Language and Sentiment of Flowers and the Classical Floral Legends*, London: Frederick Warne & Co., 1860.

von Ploennies, Maria, *Die Sagen Belgiens*, Koln: F.C. Gifen, 1846, pp. 93-99. (Translated for Gill Gregory by Philip Jenkins)

[Williams, Isaac], 'Tract No. 87', *Tracts for the Times. By Members of the University of Oxford*, 6 Vols. (1833-41), London: J.G.F. & J. Rivington, 1840, V for 1838-40.

[Wilson, John ?], 'A Sicilian Story, With Other Poems; by Barry Cornwall', *Blackwood's Edinburgh Magazine*, VI, 1820, pp. 643-650.

7. Twentieth-century and other sources

The Prometheus and Suppliants of Aeschylus; Construed Literally and Word for Word, The Rev. Dr. Giles, London: James Cornish, [1858].

Aeschylus, 'The Suppliants', *Prometheus Bound, The Suppliants, Seven Against Thebes, The Persians*, Trans. Philip Vellacott, London: Penguin Books Ltd., 1961.

Andrews, Malcolm, *Dickens and the Grown-up Child*, London: The Macmillan Press Ltd., 1994.

Apuleius, Lucius, *The Transformations of Lucius Otherwise Known as The Golden Ass*, Trans. Robert Graves, London: Penguin Books Ltd., 1990.

Armour, Richard Willard, *Barry Cornwall. A Biography of Bryan Waller Procter With a Selected Collection of Hitherto Unpublished Letters*, Boston: Meador Publishing Company, 1935.

Armstrong, Isobel (Ed.), *Writers and Their Background. Robert Browning*, London: G. Bell & Sons, 1974.

Armstrong, Isobel, *Language as Living Form in Nineteenth Century Poetry*, Brighton:

The Harvester Press Limited, 1982.

Armstrong, Isobel, *Victorian Poetry. Poetry, poetics and politics*, London and New York: Routledge, 1993.

Bates, Stephen, 'Arsene and an old case', *The Guardian*, 27.12.1995.

Battiscombe, Georgina, *John Keble. A Study in Limitations*, London: Constable and Company Ltd., 1963.

Best, Geoffrey, *Mid-Victorian Britain 1851–75*, London: Fontana Press, 1979.

Blackburn, Helen, *A Record of the Women's Suffrage Movement in the British Isles with Biographical Sketches of Miss Becker*, London: Williams & Norgate, 1902.

Blain, Virgina, Patricia Clements, Isobel Grundy (Ed.), *The Feminist Companion to Literature in English. Women Writers from the Middle Ages to the Present*, London: B.T. Batsford Ltd., 1990.

Bloom, Harold, *The Anxiety of Influence. A Theory of Poetry*, New York: Oxford University Press, 1973.

Blunden, Edmund, *Leigh Hunt. A Biography*, London: Cobden-Sanderson, 1930.

The Decameron of Boccaccio, London: Charles Daly, 1845 .

Bolitho, Hector (Ed.), *Further Letters of Queen Victoria*, London: Thornton Butterworth Ltd., 1938, p. 191.

Briggs, Asa, *Victorian People. A Reassessment of Persons and Themes 1851–67*, London: Penguin Books Ltd., 1990.

Brookfield, Charles and Frances, *Mrs Brookfield and Her Circle*, 2 Vols., London: Sir Isaac Pitman and Sons Ltd., 1905.

Brown, Penny, *The Captured World. The Child and Childhood in Nineteenth-Century Women's Writing in England*, Hemel Hempstead: Harvester Wheatsheaf, 1993.

Burke, Edmund, *A Philosophical Enquiry into the Origin of our Ideas of the Sublime and Beautiful*, Ed. Adam Phillips, Oxford University Press, 1990.

Burton, Hester, *Barbara Bodichon 1827–1891*, London: John Murray, 1949.

Cassidy, James F. *The Life of Father Faber*, London: Sands & Co. (Publishers) Ltd., 1946.

Cherry, Deborah, *Painting Women. Victorian women artists*, London and New York: Routledge, 1993.

Collins, Philip (Ed.), *Dickens. The Critical Heritage*, London: Routledge and Kegan Paul, 1971.

Coveney, Peter, *Poor Monkey. The Child in Literature*, London: Rockliff, 1957.

Cunningham, Hugh, *The Children of the Poor. Representations of Childhood since the Seventeenth Century*, Oxford, Basil Blackwell Ltd., 1991.

De Vane, William Clyde, *A Browning Handbook*, New York: Appleton-Century-Crofts, Inc., 1955.

Dhanens, Elisabeth, *Van Eyck: The Ghent Altarpiece*, Ed. John Fleming and Hugh Honour, London: Allen Lane, 1973.

Doughan, David, Denise Sanchez (Ed.), *Feminist Periodicals 1855–1984. An Annotated Critical Bibliography of British, Irish, Commonwealth and International Titles*, Brighton: The Harvester Press, 1987.

Doughty, Oswald, *A Victorian Romantic – Dante Gabriel Rossetti*, Oxford University Press, 1949.

Drain, Susan, 'Adelaide Anne Procter', *Dictionary of Literary Biography. Victorian Poets Before 1850*, Ed. William E. Fredeman and Ira B. Nadel, Detroit: Gale Research Company, 1984.

Eliot, T.S., *Selected Essays*, London: Faber and Faber Limited, 1932.

Ferguson, George, *Signs & Symbols in Christian Art*, Oxford University Press, 1954.

Fitzgerald, Percy, *Memories of Charles Dickens*, Bristol: J.W. Arrowsmith Ltd., 1913.

Flint, Kate, *Dickens*, The Harvester Press, 1986.

Freud, Sigmund, 'The Theme of the Three Caskets', *The Standard Edition of the Complete Psychological Works of Sigmund Freud*, Ed. James Strachey, 24 Vols, London: The Hogarth Press and the Institute of Psycho-analysis, 1958, XII (1911–1913), pp. 289–301.

Freud, Sigmund, 'Symbolism in Dreams', *The Standard Edition of the Complete Psychological Works of Sigmund Freud*, Ed. James Strachey, London: The Hogarth Press and the Institute of Psycho-analysis, 1963, XV (1915–16), pp. 149–169.

Findon, B.W., *Sir Arthur Sullivan. His Life and Music*, London: James Nisbet & Co., Limited, 1904, p. 211.

Gardner, Helen (Ed.), *The New Oxford Book of English Verse 1250–1950*, Oxford University Press, 1972.

Gilbert, Sandra M. and Susan Gubar, *The Madwoman in the Attic. The Woman Writer and the Nineteenth-Century Literary Imagination*, New Haven and London: Yale University Press, 1979.

Glynn Grylls, Rosalie, *Queen's College 1848–1948*, London: George Routledge & Sons, Ltd., 1948.

Hare, Augustus J.C., *The Story of My Life*, 6 Vols, London: George Allen, 1900, VI, pp. 462–463.

Harrison, J.F.C., *The Early Victorians 1832–1851*, London: Weidenfeld and Nicolson, 1971.

A Choice of George Herbert's Verse, Intro. R.S. Thomas, London: Faber and Faber Limited, 1967.

Hedrick, Joan D., *Harriet Beecher Stowe. A Life*, Oxford University Press, 1994.

Hickok, Kathleen, *Representations of Women. Nineteenth-Century British Women's Poetry*, Connecticut: Greenwood Press, 1984.

Irvine, William and Park Honan, *The Book, the Ring, and the Poet. A biography of Robert Browning*, London: The Bodley Head Ltd., 1975.

Jaduiga Swiatecka, M., *The Idea of the Symbol. Some Nineteenth Century Comparisons with Coleridge*, Cambridge University Press, 1980.

Janku, Ferdinand, *Adelaide Anne Procter. Ihr Leben Und Ihre Werke*, Wien und Liepzig: Wilhelm Braumuller, 1912.

Karlin, Daniel, *Browning's Hatreds*, Oxford: Clarendon Press, 1993.

Klein, Melanie, *Love, Guilt and Reparation and Other Works 1921–1945*, Intro. Hanna Segal, London: Virago Press Limited, 1988.

Lacey, Candida Ann (Ed.), *Barbara Leigh Smith Bodichon and the Langham Place Group*, New York and London: Routledge & Kegan Paul, 1987.

Lehmann, R.C. (Ed.), *Charles Dickens as Editor*, London: Smith, Elder & Co., 1912.

Leighton, Angela, *Elizabeth Barrett Browning*, Hemel Hempstead: Harvester Wheatsheaf, 1986.

Leighton, Angela, '"Because men made the laws": The Fallen Woman and the Woman Poet', *Victorian Poetry*, 27, 1989, pp. 109–127.

Leighton, Angela, *Victorian Women Poets. Writing Against the Heart*, Hemel Hempstead: Harvester Wheatsheaf, 1992.

Lerner, Laurence (Ed.), *The Victorians*, New York: Holmes & Meier Publishers, Inc., 1978.

Lohrli, Anne (Ed.), *Household Words. A Weekly Journal.1850–1859. Conducted by Charles Dickens*. Table of Contents. List of Contributors and Their Contributions based on the *Household Words* Office Book in the Morris L. Parrish Collection of Victorian Novelists, Princeton University Library. University of Toronto Press, 1973.

Maison, Margaret, 'Queen Victoria's favourite poet', *The Listener*, 73, 1965, pp. 636–637.

Marsh, Jan, *Christina Rossetti – a literary biography*, London: Jonathan Cape, 1994.

Mellor, Anne K., *Romanticism & Gender*, New York & London: Routledge, 1993.

Meynell, Alice, *Poems*, London: Burns & Oates, 1919.

Nead, Lynda, *Myths of Sexuality. Representations of Women in Victorian Britain*, Oxford: Basil Blackwell Ltd., 1988.

Nicholas, David, *The Metamorphosis of a Medieval City. Ghent in the Age of the Arteveldes. 1302– 1390*, University of Nebraska Press, 1987.

Ormond, Leonee, *Tennyson and Thomas Woolner*, Lincoln: The Tennyson Society, Tennyson Research Centre, 1981.

Ormond, Richard, *National Portrait Gallery. Early Victorian Portraits*, 2 Vols, London: HMSO, 1973. *The Metamorphoses of Ovid*, Trans. Mary M. Innes, Harmondsworth: Penguin Books Ltd., 1955.

Page, Norman, *A Dickens Companion*, London: The Macmillan Press Ltd., 1984.

Pontalis, J-B, 'Dream as an object', *The Dream Discourse Today*, Ed. Sara Flanders, London and New York: Routledge, 1993, pp. 108–121.

Poovey, Mary, *Uneven Developments. The Ideological Work of Gender in Mid-Victorian England*, London: Virago Press Limited, 1989.

Providence Row Annual Review 1993/1994, London: Lansdowne Press, 1994.

Ratcliffe, Eric, *The Caxton of her Age. The Career and Family Background of Emily Faithfull (1835–95)*, Upton-Upon-Severn: Images Publishing (Malvern) Ltd., 1993.

Ray, Gordon N., *Thackeray: The Uses of Adversity (1811–1846)*, London: Oxford University Press, 1955.

Rendall, Jane (Ed.), *Equal or Different. Women's Politics. 1800–1914*, Oxford: Basil Blackwell Ltd., 1987.

Richardson Gee, Karen, *'Kinswomen of the Shelf': Emily Dickinson's Reading of Women Writers*, PhD dissertation, The University of Tennessee, 1990 (Order No. 9121715).

Ricks, Christopher, *Keats and Embarrassment*, Oxford University Press, 1974.

'The unconscious phantasy of an inner world reflected in examples from literature (1952)', *The Inner World and Joan Riviere. Collected Papers: 1920–1958*, Ed. Athol Hughes, London: Karnac Books for The Melanie Klein Trust, 1991, pp. 302–330.

Rodger, N.A.M., *The Insatiable Earl. A Life of John Montagu, Fourth Earl of Sandwich 1718–1792*, London: Harper Collins, 1993.

Rosenblum, Robert, *The Romantic Child. From Runge to Sendak*, London: Thames and Hudson, 1988.

Rousseau, Jean-Jacques, *Emile or On Education* 1762 Trans. Allan Bloom, London: Penguin Books, 1991.

St George, E.A.W., *Browning and Conversation*, London: The Macmillan Press Ltd., 1993.

Shattock, Joanne (Ed.), *The Oxford Guide to British Women Writers*, Oxford University Press, 1993, 347–348.

Showalter, Elaine, *A Literature of Their Own. British Women Novelists from Bronte to Lessing*, London: Virago Press Limited, 1978.

Slater, Michael, *Dickens and Women*, London and Melbourne: J.M. Dent & Sons Ltd., 1983.

Sprengnether, Madelon, *The Spectral Mother. Freud, Feminism and Psychoanalysis*, Ithaca and London: Cornell University Press, 1990.

Steedman, Carolyn, *Strange Dislocations. Childhood and the Idea of Human Interiority. 1780–1930*, London: Virago Press Limited, 1995.

Steinmetz, Virginia V., 'Images of "Mother-Want" in Elizabeth Barrett Browning's *Aurora Leigh*', *Victorian Poetry*, 21, 1983, pp. 351–367.

Strachey, Ray, *The Cause. A Short History of the Women's Movement in Great Britain*, London: Virago Limited, 1978.

Tennyson, G.B., *Victorian Devotional Poetry. The Tractarian Mode*, Cambridge, Massachusetts: Harvard University Press, 1981.

Thomas, Deborah A., *Dickens and the Short Story*, Philadelphia: University of Pennsylvania Press, 1982.

Thomas, Leesther, *A Poetry of Deliverance With Tractarian Affinities. A Study of Adelaide A. Procter's Poetry*, PhD dissertation, The Florida State University, College of Arts and Sciences, 1994.

Thomson, David, *England in the Nineteenth Century 1815-1914*, London: Penguin Books Ltd., 1978.

Todd, Janet (Ed.), *Dictionary of British Women Writers*, London: Routledge, 1989, pp. 547-548.

Uglow, Jenny, *Elizabeth Gaskell. A Habit of Stories*, London: Faber and Faber Limited, 1993.

Virgil, *The Aeneid*, Trans. W.F. Jackson Knight, Harmondsworth: Penguin Books Ltd., 1958.

Von Arnim, Elizabeth, *The Pastor's Wife* (1912), Ed. Deborah Singmaster, London: Everyman, 1993.

Warner, Marina, *Alone of All Her Sex. The Myth and the Cult of the Virgin Mary*, London: Picador, 1985.

Weeks, Jeffrey, *Sex, Politics and Society. The regulation of sexuality since 1800*, London and New York: Longman Group UK Limited, 1981.

Winnicott, D.W., *The Child, The Family, and the Outside World* (1957) London: Penguin Books Ltd., 1991.

Winnicott, D.W., *Playing and Reality* (1971), London: Routledge, 1991.

Winnifrith, Tom, *Fallen Women in the Nineteenth Century Novel*, London: Macmillan Press, 1994.

Index